the Ivory
Adventure
Classics

A collection presented by
Wolfe Publishing Co., Inc.

Limited Edition of 1000

CHANTING HAWK AND MANY-BANDED SPARROW HAWK
(*Melierax musicus*) (*Accipiter polyzonoides*)
From Mosita and the Maritsani River, British Bechuanaland

See page 66

GUN AND CAMERA

IN

SOUTHERN AFRICA

*A YEAR OF WANDERINGS
IN BECHUANALAND, THE KALAHARI DESERT, AND THE
LAKE RIVER COUNTRY, NGAMILAND*

WITH

NOTES ON COLONISATION, NATIVES, NATURAL HISTORY AND SPORT

BY

H. ANDERSON BRYDEN

AUTHOR OF "KLOOF AND KARROO IN CAPE COLONY," ETC. ETC.

WITH NUMEROUS ILLUSTRATIONS AND A MAP

Wolfe Publishing Co., Inc.
6471 Airpark Drive
Prescott, Arizona 86301

Originally published in 1893 by Edward Stanford, London

Manufactured in the United States of America
Reprinted September 1988

ISBN: 0-935632-73-5

1988
Wolfe Publishing Co., Inc.
Prescott, Arizona

PREFACE

BETWEEN 1840 and 1850, when Livingstone began first to turn his thoughts towards exploration, all the vast territories beyond the Vaal River—north, east, and west—were termed by the frontier Boers "*onze veldt*" (our country); and so determined were these stubborn folk to close the door of the interior to all save those of their own blood, that they fined an unfortunate explorer, named Macabe, 500 rix-dollars for daring to write to the Cape papers recommending a certain route for the discovery of Lake Ngami—then unknown to the white man. These Transvaal Boers even went the length of imprisoning Mr. Macabe until the fine was paid.

Between 1840 and 1880 Britain, interested and occupied in other possessions, knew little of and cared less for South Africa. Even down to the year 1884 it seemed more than likely that the Transvaal Dutch were to be, as they had always threatened, masters of the interior. Happily at the eleventh hour a revulsion of feeling came; the British public suddenly awoke to the imminence of its prospective loss; Sir Charles Warren's expedition was sent out, and the "hinter-land" was saved.

Recent events, and especially the Transvaal gold
discoveries, the enterprise of the British South Africa
Company, and a more enlightened colonial policy at
home, have combined to assure finally the future of a
great British South Africa. The Afrikander Dutch,
thanks mainly to the wonderful developments of the
Witwatersrand gold industry, have become alive to
the fact that a fusion of ideas and even of nationality
is possible with the once-detested Britisher; and for
the future two vigorous and hardy races, who never
ought to have had bad blood between them, seem
likely to join hands in the making of an immense and
prosperous country. Nowhere is this more evident
than in the new colony of British Bechuanaland,
where at this moment Dutch Boers from the Transvaal and Orange Free State are constantly to be
found taking up farms under a British government.

The march of events in the countries between the
Vaal and Zambesi has within these last three years
been immense. The solitudes, where to-day the wild
Bushman burns off the winter grass to induce the
fresh vegetation and attract the game, resound to-
morrow with the echoing waggon-whips and the
cheery voices of the digger and the colonist. In
every corner of those lands, which the frontier Boer
of a generation since delighted to call "onze veldt,"
is now heard the Anglo-Saxon tongue.

In this book I have endeavoured to give a plain
account of life and conditions in some of the new
and promising regions thus opened up to the
European, to wit, Bechuanaland, the Kalahari, and

Ngamiland. I am hopeful that information useful to the colonist and the settler may be found within these pages. In the course of the various chapters there is a good deal of matter which may be of interest to the naturalist and the sportsman. I have devoted a chapter to the game-birds of Bechuanaland, and another to the present distribution of the large game of the countries of which I treat. This last is a melancholy subject enough for the lover of wild animal life. Even in the last ten years the fauna of the interior have been terribly reduced, their range is constantly becoming more circumscribed, and the day is not far distant when large game south of the Zambesi will be but a memory.

Finally, in the chapter on " Waggon Life and Camp Requisites," I have devoted space to those useful minutiæ of travel which are not always to be found readily in the pages of South African literature.

I cannot pretend that my pictures represent a high order of photographic art. But I will ask the reader to remember that the originals were taken and developed (where development was possible) usually under very trying conditions. Often the water available was so filthy as to render successful development an impossibility. In the waggon journey to the Lake River I was unable from various reasons to develop at all, and could merely take " shots," and pack away my plates for a more convenient season. Such as the illustrations are I offer them as faithful delineations of places, objects, and people hitherto not often accessible to the camera.

The views taken on the Lake (or Botletli) River, Ngamiland, are of interest as depicting—I believe for the first time with the camera—some of the scenes of Livingstone's first great discovery.

For the benefit of travellers, I have shown plainly in the accompanying map the few and scanty waters of the North Kalahari region (well called "Thirstland" by the Boers), separating the Lake Country from Bechuanaland proper. Several of these waters do not appear in published maps, and are apparently little known. For the westerly course of the Molopo River (hitherto imperfectly known) I have followed a recent map of my friend Mr. Edward Wilkinson, who has made two interesting expeditions in that part of the Kalahari.

Some portion of this book has appeared in the pages of the *Field*, *Longmans' Magazine*, and *Chambers's Journal*, and I have to thank the Editors of those publications for their kindness in allowing me to reprint here. I am indebted to Mr. Kemp of Mafeking for the originals of my pictures at pages 38 and 184, and to the "Gaseitsive's Concession Syndicate" for the one at page 226.

H. A. BRYDEN.

March 1893.

CONTENTS

xii CONTENTS

LIST OF ILLUSTRATIONS

GUN AND CAMERA IN SOUTHERN AFRICA

CHAPTER I.

FIRST DAYS IN BECHUANALAND

Arrival in Kimberley—Purchase of horses—Start up country—Drive through Griqualand West and South Bechuanaland—Arrival at Vryburg—Vryburg hospitality—The Stellalanders—Description of Vryburg—Past history—The orange-shouldered bunting and its habits—Tame crowned crane—Its evil ways—Cost of living—"Scotty Smith," a border character—His exploits—"Big Mick"—Leave Vryburg—Journey to Setlagoli—The Setlagoli district—Arrival at junction of Maritsani and Setlagoli rivers.

AT the beginning of 1890, business matters connected with a large tract of land in British Bechuanaland required that I should make some sojourn in that latest of England's Crown colonies. From one cause or another, the sojourn lengthened out into a stay of fifteen months, during which time many parts of the interior of Southern Africa—most of them remote, all of them interesting—were visited and explored.

After a delightful passage in the *Norham Castle*, Cape Town and Kimberley were reached in due course. It was some years since I had been in South Africa, and, although in time gone by I had seen much of Cape Colony, the territories north of the Orange River were as yet new and unknown to me. My companion,

A

Mr. W. Mackay, who had come out to have a look at the country, had determined to spend some months with me; and we were both agreed, my business being completed, to push northward, to the end that we might there indulge our mutual yearnings for sport and exploration.

Kimberley, at the end of January, was extremely hot and not extremely attractive; the shade temperature running up as high as 97°, with a sun heat (blackened bulb *in vacuo*) of 161·7°—hot enough for a salamander—and so, having seen the well-known sights of the place, and having despatched our heavy luggage by waggon, and no post cart running to Bechuanaland for some days, Mackay and I cast about for some other method of making the journey.

We were not long in finding a townsman—Mr. Reinegger—who possessed (*inter alia*) a strong Cape cart and four capital greys, and was willing to drive us over the 140 hot miles between Kimberley and Vryburg for the sum of £19—feeding his own horses. This was a good offer, and we at once closed with it. Next morning on the market we bought a stout pair of South African horses (ponies would be nearer the mark), greys, at £30 the pair, and a smart little chestnut at £13; and in the afternoon, all being ready, we spanned in Reinegger's four greys and our own pair, fastened up the chestnut alongside one of the middle pair—where he trotted gaily enough—and set off along the Barkly Road. We had expected preliminary difficulties with the mixed team of six, but rather to our surprise, after a few plunges, the greys all settled well together, and for the remainder of the journey we had no sort of trouble with them. I need not dwell on our interesting drive across the flat plains of Griqualand West, and through the pleasant grassy veldt and over the gentle undulations of Southern Bechuanaland. My first impressions of the Cape had been gained among the arid and peculiar vegetation of the Great Karroo, where Angora goats, sheep, and ostriches were the mainstays of the farming population, or amid the wild mountain interiors of the Eastern Province. Here in Griqualand West and Bechuanaland vast expanses of long grass everywhere met the eye—chequered occasionally by Vaal bush or acacia thorn—herds of cattle were to be seen grazing contentedly, and it was at once evident that we were passing into a great cattle country. It was a pleasant thing to learn, as we did at Thorn Grove—Mr. Muller's homestead—on our road, that game in Griqualand, thanks to preservation and a close season, is looking up again. Koodoo, hartebeest, springbok, vaal and rooi rhebok, duyker, and steinbok are all to be found on farms in this part of Cape Colony.

We left Kimberley in the afternoon of the 29th January. Moving steadily along, we passed Taungs —a large native town of the Batlapings under Mankoroane—on the 31st, and on the following day, shortly before noon, from a high undulation of the veldt, we beheld Vryburg, the capital of British Bechuanaland, lying not far below us. Vryburg is not an imposing place ; indeed, even now that the railway has reached it, it is a mere glorified village, and I am bound to confess that our first impression of it was a disappointing one. At the distance of three or four miles from where we stood, the tiny collection of white or corrugated iron houses, dotted upon a wave of the vast plain, looked for all the world like

a good-sized agricultural show at home. The railway
from Kimberley (which, begun in 1890, proceeded
at a phenomenal rate, and reached Vryburg in the
autumn of that year) had not at this time made
much impression upon the quiet and uneventful life
of this primitive up-country town. The post cart,
passing through once a week to the north, or the
advent of an occasional traveller, were all that
happened to break the drowsy monotony of the
place. At the end of 1890 all this had changed.
Creeping gradually like a snake over the smooth
plains, the railroad had arrived ; the early excitement
of it had passed away ; the natives, at first all amaze-
ment, now viewed the passage of trains with amused
indifference ; and, worst of all for Vryburg, a vile
collection of thieves, drunkards, gamblers, broken
men and desperadoes—most of them the scum of
the Transvaal—had drifted here from depressed
mining communities such as Johannesburg, Klerks-
dorp, and Barberton, in hopes of a temporary boom,
and the erst sleepy village had become, temporarily,
a hell upon the veldt. January and December of
1890 at Vryburg were indeed in sharp and unpleasant contrast.

Shortly after noon we drove into the little town
and outspanned at the Vryburg Hotel, a corrugated
iron building, not differing greatly in its scant
luxury and accommodation from other South African
hostelries. As I remember it, and as most travellers
will remember it in those days, the most conspicuous
object of the broad, sandy main street was the
white helmet (encircled by a blood-red puggaree, and
glaring painfully in the strong sunlight) of a well-
known advocate. The advocate, like his helmet, " a

burning and a shining light to all that place," was ever the first to welcome the toil-worn traveller—from His Excellency the High Commissioner downwards—and extend to him the hearty hospitality of the then sparse population. In those early days the same dazzling headpiece was the prime focus and rallying point of gossip and narrative. Its owner could be relied upon to decide authoritatively whether Vrouw A. had been brought to bed of her twelfth or thirteenth child, how it was that B. had fallen into C.'s well overnight on his way home, how much Jew X. had won from German Z. on Sunday morning at solo whist, when the Afrikander Bond was to open the campaign in the district, or upon whose farm the latest gold discovery had been made. The scandals, harangues, quips, cranks, and odd sayings of the white-helmeted advocate were in truth, in those days, very meat and drink to the Vryburgers.

Business matters detained me in Vryburg for some few days, during which time Mackay and I made the acquaintance of most of the inhabitants and received much hospitality. One of the funniest functions we assisted at during our stay was an extempore concert at the Vryburg Hotel, in which a famous Bechuanaland song, " The Stellaland Brigade," was a principal item. The song deals with events just prior to Warren's expedition, and is written from the loyal Stellalander's point of view. Stellaland, I should remind the reader, was the title of the Republic, or *soi-disant* Republic, erected by the filibusters prior to the advent of the British Government. Here is the chorus, which will sufficiently indicate its style :—

" Then shout, boys, shout, and don't you be afraid,
To-night we'll all be marching in the Stellaland brigade ;

So bundle up your haversacks and go it while you can,
To hell with the Lime Juice Parliament,[1] we'll fight for Mankoroane."[2]

The song has a catching swing and a rousing chorus, and is still sung with great éclat at festive meetings in Bechuanaland. It has now of course lost its old political significance, and the lame metre and rather questionable taste of some of the verses are pardoned for the sake of a hearty, roystering air.

At the impromptu concert I write of, not the least interesting fact to me was that some of the original Stellalanders—now loyal subjects of the Queen— sat in our midst and joined heartily in the function. One of them, a Transvaal Dutchman, now an official of the town, was first despatched by the filibusters, then gathered on the Transvaal border, to spy out the land and fix upon a site for the new Stellaland township. This was in 1882, and Mr. Barend Fourie—who will, I know, forgive my mentioning his name—at once drove across the veldt and selected the present site of the town, mainly on account of its ample water supply, and called it in Dutch Vrijburg, which has since become famous and anglicised as Vryburg.

Well! we had a merry evening; the white-helmeted advocate was in great form, and made us shriek with laughter by rendering various English music-hall songs in a unique way of his own (he was an Afrikander, but had made the grand tour); Mackay, who is a master of the instrument, had his banjo, and I assisted in a lesser degree.

South Africa in general and Stellaland in par-

---

[1] An opprobrious term for the Cape House of Assembly.
[2] The Chief of this part of the country, from whom the Stellalanders got their land titles.

ticular are countries where conviviality is carried to a rather inordinate degree, and I can testify that at Vryburg some of the performances with the whisky bottle rather opened the eyes of my comrade and myself. At a later period of the year, when the railway came up, I have been informed by experts that the drinking capacities of Vryburg surpassed even those of Kimberley and Johannesburg in their wildest days. Certain it is that drunkenness became horribly and unpleasantly rife. In spite of fines and imprisonments, the very salutary laws, prohibiting the sale of liquor to natives, were daily and hourly evaded, and natives were constantly to be found as drunk as their white brethren. While upon this topic, I am bound to say, however, that in Bechuanaland as a whole the native liquor laws are admirably kept and enforced, to the immense comfort and welfare of the Bechuana population. The splendid climate of this territory and the healthy open-air life tend greatly to mitigate the ill effects of over-indulgence in stimulants, and alcohol is undoubtedly taken with impunity in quantities that would quickly destroy the same man in the pent-up existence of an English city. None the less, at Vryburg, as in all other parts of South Africa, drink is a chief curse among a certain number of the inhabitants, and a very ill example is set before ignorant natives, who are yet expected to acknowledge the much vaunted superiority of the white man.

There is not much to see in Vryburg; one broad main street runs through the town—or village; around this, in parallels and at right angles, are a few other streets, sparsely set with houses. Below the main street, a few hundred yards away, lies the

spruit or watercourse—a respectable brook—which
issues from a strong fountain of excellent clear water
in a small stony kopje.   At the top of a gentle rise
above the main street are situated the Government
offices—very humble erections—and the Administrator's residence, an equally unpretentious villa,
quite unworthy of the high and responsible office
held by Sir Sidney Shippard.   The Border Police
camp is upon the same low hill; while on a small
kopje at another end of the town is the prison, a
well-built edifice of native stone—quite the most
imposing in Vryburg or, indeed, all Bechuanaland.
Many of the houses, such as the Administrator's, are
of brick, rough cast; the majority of brick, cased and
roofed with corrugated iron; a very few of stone,
which is procurable in any quantity, and of excellent
quality, from a quarry about a mile away.

The population in 1891 was, I think, all told, just
under 1200.   When I state that during 1890, almost
whenever I walked up the gentle hill (quite a central
part of the place) in the direction of the Administrator's house or the Government offices, I encountered a covey of partridges ; that in the main pool of
the water spruit wild duck were occasionally to be
shot; that we hunted small buck with foxhounds, and
shot partridges and hares within a half-mile of the
Post Office and Court House ; and that snakes were
not inconstant visitors in any quarter of the town,
it will be gathered that this metropolis of Bechuanaland is yet in its infancy, and its census a thing of
easy accomplishment.

Away to the south-east, towards the Transvaal
border, the long bold range of the Marokani Hills
heaves in a deep blue line from the vast expanse of

plain. Upon every other hand save to the north-west, where a single hill—Massouw's Kop—can be distinguished, broad rolling grassy plains stretch far as the eye can reach.

The new railway station lies to the eastward of the town, about three-quarters of a mile from the Court House, which, with the Post Office, stands in about the centre of the main street. At present Vryburg is bare, shadeless, and unlovely. There are a few blue gum-trees planted here and there, all of which are thriving, as they always thrive in South Africa, vigorously. And, thanks to the care and forethought of the resident magistrate, a piece of land by the watercourse has been set apart as a small public park or garden of the future. Here are planted a number of trees, shrubs, and flowers, a small lake has been dammed in, and all promises well. But hitherto private enterprise has done little towards breaking the bare monotony of this city of the plain. Some day, when trees, which are cheap enough, have been planted, a proper water-supply has been en-sured, and watercourses laid along the streets, some relief may be looked for, some mitigation of the present hopeless glare during the long dry months of African winter. Marico, not very far across the border, in the Transvaal (although a town planted and reared by *unprogressive* Boers), may be cited as an example of what a South African upcountry town should be, whether æsthetically or economically considered. Perhaps some day, when the people of Vryburg, and Mafeking also, can find time to turn their attention that way, these places may be found planted, beautified, and embowered in gardens. At present, as in most South African towns, the European inhabitants are in far too great a hurry to make their pile and get away from the country.

This regretable habit has gone far to retard all real progress in South Africa, and the bulk of voting and therefore of political strength remains, properly enough, with the Dutch, who stick to the soil and look upon this fair land as their home and abiding-place. Already the Dutch farmers are creeping into Bechuanaland, filling up the farms and preparing their future homes. Unless the British make up their minds to settle down and people this promising territory, the Boers will presently have here, as they have in the Cape Colony, the balance of power in their own hands.

I have neither space nor inclination in this book to refer to the recent history of Southern Bechuanaland, during those anxious and unsettled times when the freebooters were overrunning the country; when it seemed that England had relinquished all interest in the territories beyond the Vaal, and was prepared to see the trade route to the interior finally blocked by President Krüger.

Where, it may be asked, if the cold fit had been persevered in and the advice of certain politicians had been followed, would have been our present fair possessions in Bechuanaland, our illimitable prospective cattle lands in the Kalahari, our enormous interests in Khama's country, Mashonaland, Zambesia, Ngamiland, and the rest of them? Echo may well, with a blush, answer where?

Three men saved Bechuanaland for the British; the Rev. John Mackenzie, who came home and first stirred up public opinion in the critical months of 1884; the late Mr. W. E. Forster, who first recognised the vital importance of Mackenzie's views and at once set about bringing his great influence to bear upon Government and the House of Commons; and Sir Charles Warren, who most ably conducted the expedition to Bechuanaland, routed out the hornet's nest of freebooters and filibusters, settled the country, and brought it without a blow, and in a few short months, within the Queen's peace.

I assert unhesitatingly that, but for these three men, the Transvaal Government and not the British would at the present moment be masters of the interior of Southern Africa. Since Warren's expedition English influence has resumed its old position —all but ruined by the Boer war—and is becoming widened and deepened as the native races note our restored prestige, and the remote frontier Boers see what the English really can do towards governing and opening up a country. I am not an anti-Boer. I admire these sturdy farmers of the wilderness as much as any man; but I hold that British government and British progress are better things for South Africa as a whole than a Boer government and Boer ideas.[1]

I strolled one morning, among other rambles of discovery, down to a reedy pool near the head of the watercourse, just above the town. Here were many interesting birds to be seen, foremost among them being the remarkable orange-shouldered bunting or Kaffrarian grosbeak (*Vidua Phœnicoptera* of Swainson). This curious bird is found

---

[1] "Austral Africa; Losing it, or Ruling it," by John Mackenzie, is well worth the reader's attention. It deals largely with the history of Bechuanaland between 1880–85, and presents many curious pictures of life, policy, and events in those days.

abundantly in the Eastern Province of Cape Colony and in Kaffraria, but I have never seen mention of it in books dealing with the interior. Andersson's "Birds of Damaraland" makes no reference to it. I found it abundantly in many parts of British Bechuanaland, usually near water and mealie gardens, or water and long grass or reeds, where cover was to be found. The male bird in breeding plumage is of a deep glossy black, having large patches or shoulder-knots of the most brilliant red. He sports soft, broad, and enormously long tail-feathers, which hinder him to such an extent that he is utterly powerless to fly against the wind. It is most amusing to see these birds get up and wriggle against a fair breeze. They look in their struggles for all the world like huge feathered tadpoles, and finally, giving it up as a bad job, go down to cover again. In length they average from 20 to 22 inches, of which the tail occupies from 16 to 17 inches. Even in the absence of wind they are very helpless, and cannot fly far. They are easily shot, and form an interesting and extremely handsome trophy for the collector. The hen birds and young males are yellowish brown in colour, having black and brown-edged wings, while the shoulder patch is of a brilliant orange in place of crimson. These buntings are usually seen in some numbers when found. I saw them in 1890 as far north as Mafeking; probably they extend beyond, although I did not observe them further.

One of the most amusing creatures in the town was a semi-domesticated crowned crane, nominally supposed to belong to Mr. Tillard, the resident magistrate, but in reality enjoying a more complete independence than any burgher of Vryburg. This bird, with its bluish grey plumage, white and red wings, glossy black head—crowned with a curious erection of long, stiff, wiry bristles, alternately yellow and white, and tipped with black—and with the bare spaces around the eyes and beneath the chin painted a brilliant vermilion, is among the most striking and graceful of the feathered denizens of South Africa.

It is known to the colonists as the Kaffir crane, to naturalists as *Balearica Regulorum* or *Grus Balearica*. They are not unfrequently caught and tamed; and as a rule they display the most perfect composure—nay, even effrontery—before all persons and under all circumstances.

This particular crane wandered about Vryburg wherever it listed, fearing neither man, dog, nor devil. It knew many kitchen doors and most dinner-hours, and had no compunctions about turning up uninvited.

It did its best to spoil all the cricket matches and absolutely refused to be driven from the field, where it followed loose hits, impeded the fielders, bothered the bowlers, and generally caused vexation and evil language. I have remonstrated with this crane, and attempted to drive him away on such occasions, only to be charged, threatened, and hindered at the next opportunity. Still with all his faults the magistrate's crane, with his perfect deportment and brilliant colouring, was a great ornament to the place, and could have been ill spared by any one. Just at sunset the crane, wherever he was, sauntered up into the air, and made his way to the watercourse for the night, where no doubt, standing contemplatively on one leg, he plotted to himself fresh devilments for the coming morrow.

Each day, rain or shine—and it is mostly shine in Vryburg—*Grus Balearica* turned up again, fresh as paint, his radiating crest in perfect order, not a feather awry, his vermilion cheeks as brilliant and shining as if newly rouged, and his bold, wicked eye roving hither and thither in search of fresh conquests. Some few months later, when I was in Vryburg again with my camera, I announced my intention of photographing this crane. He was in the vicinity as I spoke, stalking daintily about with his usual air of easy "you be damnedness," and I believe he heard me. At all events next morning, when laden with my camera I sought him about the village, I could find him nowhere, high or low. After a heated search I gave him up, and put my implements away. Of course, towards evening, I found him by the tennis courts. He gave me a cunning look, as much as to say—or my fancy deceived me—"Yes, my friend, you've put your camera away, and here I am again." The crane, I hear, still survives, and when his end comes, it will be a distinct loss to the community. His latest exploit was to effect an entry by means of a chimney into the Standard Bank premises. It was out of banking hours, the place was locked up, and yet sounds were heard within. Presently the manager came along with a *posse* at his back, the door was cautiously opened, and the Kaffir crane was discovered making himself at home. The Bechuana and other natives up country rather prize the curious crest or crown of this crane, and use it in their hats or hair as an ornament. The bird has a wide distribution ; I found it as far north as the Botletli River, and I believe its range extends beyond the Zambesi.

There is a fair local trade in Vryburg, and there are several good stores and shops. But although the volume of business has been somewhat extended since the arrival of the railway, Vryburg can never hope to compete with the trade of Mafeking, which town must, in the future, command a very large business as a chief depot and emporium of interior trade. When the railway proceeds from Vryburg to Mafeking, Vryburg will occupy the position of a quiet country town, while Mafeking will tap and supply a great mass of trade to the north, and will flourish accordingly. Even in 1890 the Mafeking banking business of the Standard Bank was considerably ahead of the Vryburg branch. Then, again, Mafeking lies adjacent to the richest agricultural districts of the Transvaal—Marico and Rustenburg— which Vryburg does not.

Hitherto life in Vryburg has been rough and rather shiftless. There are few good houses, and ladies have to put up with a number of small discomforts and worries, which would drive an English housewife crazy. Native servants are scarce, dear, and as bad as can be. European servants are almost out of the question; they can do better for themselves in other ways. Consequently delicately nurtured ladies have in Vryburg and Mafeking to turn their hands to a variety of domestic work, and help themselves, if they wish their house and table to be at all presentable.

On the whole, living in Bechuanaland is dear, nearly half as dear again, all round, as in England. The cost of groceries and all other stores, and of liquors, beer and mineral waters, is largely added to by the long transport, roughly 800 miles, from the

seaboard.   Meat is fairly cheap, beef, which is good
and plentiful in Bechuanaland towns, especially so.
Vegetables, which might be largely grown in the
neighbourhood, are scarce.   Fruit is now supplied by
rail from the Cape.

Here are a few prices of commodities in the month
of August 1891.   The colonial "bag," I may premise,
contains 205 lbs. English—

VRYBURG MARKET.

Market quotations for Colonial produce for week ending
1st August :—

	£	s.	d.		£	s.	d.
Barley, green, per bundle .	0	0	5	to	0	0	6
Beans, Kaffir, per bag	0	8	0	,,	0	9	0
Bran, per bag .	0	10	0	,,	0	11	6
Chaff, per bale .	1	2	0	,,	1	3	0
Forage, per bundle .	0	0	7	,,	0	1	0
,, ,, 100 lbs. (Colonial) .	0	15	6	,,	0	16	0
Kaffir corn, per bag .	0	10	0	,,	0	11	0
Meal (Boer), unsifted	1	15	0	,,	1	16	6
,, ,, sifted .	2	1	0	,,	2	2	6
Mealies, yellow, per bag .	0	12	6	,,	0	14	0
Mealie meal, white, per bag	0	17	0	,,	0	0	0
,, ,, yellow, per bag .	0	16	0	,,	0	17	0
Oats, per bag .	0	15	9	,,	0	16	6
Onions, per bag	1	0	0	,,	1	5	0
Potatoes, per bag	1	2	6	,,	1	7	6
Tobacco, cut (Transvaal) .	0	0	6	,,	0	0	7
Butter, per lb. .	0	1	0	,,	0	2	6
Eggs, per doz. .	0	1	0	,,	0	1	2
Fowls, each	0	1	6	,,	0	2	0
Wood, per load .	1	0	0	,,	2	10	0

Remarks.—Good supplies of chaff and Kaffir corn.   Mealies
are rather scarce and in demand.   Forage is equal to demand.
Wood is plentiful and sells readily.   Eggs plentiful.   Butter of
good quality is scarce.   Poultry in great demand.

As a set-off against dear living, horseflesh is cheap;
and a good deal of pleasure can be got out of the

morning and evening scamper across the veldt. There are not many ways of wasting money on pleasures, with the sole exception of alcohol, if that form of gratification may be so included.

Bechuanaland a few years before must have greatly resembled the border marches of Scotland and England in the good old times so magnificently sung by Scott in the "Lay of the Last Minstrel." Cattle and horse-lifting were the recreations of all gentlemen (mostly broken gentlemen) of spirit, and Boers and Europeans alike became extraordinarily expert.

"Scotty Smith" is the nickname of a man perhaps better hated and feared a few years since by the Western Transvaal Boers than any Briton in Africa. His adventures and escapades would fill a volume. He has long since settled down, and owns property in the town, has dropped his *nom de guerre*, and is now known by his true name. No man knows the Kalahari Desert (to which he retreated when times were hot and Boers troublesome) as he does. As a "veldt" man he is unsurpassed. His career has been a diversified one. He fought in the Franco-German war on the side of the French ; afterwards in the Carlist war for the Carlists. Then he came to South Africa, where he has wandered, hunted, explored, fought, raided, and finally settled down. Latterly he has been much engaged in opening up the Kalahari country, and in aiding syndicates to obtain concessions from various chiefs in that waterless but interesting *terra incognita*.

Some of his escapes have been marvellous. Here is one of them. During the troubles—in '83, I think —he was surprised and captured by the marauding

Boers and taken to their headquarters at Rooi Grond, near Mafeking. He was condemned out of hand to be shot on the following day, and fastened up with ropes inside a hut at some distance from the camp fire. During the night " Scotty " slipped his bonds, crept to the place where the Boer horses were stabled, saddled and bridled two of the best of them, and got clean away right under the noses of the Dutchmen. A day or two after he met a Boer, who was personally unacquainted with him, who informed him that he was looking for " Scotty Smith." " Well ! " said Scotty in Dutch, " I'm looking for ' Scotty Smith ' too ; we'll go together." They rode together for some hours, and then " Scotty " found an opportunity, slipped his man, and betook himself to a safer locality. I doubt whether the more staid Mr. L—— of the present day would, even after these years, dare to venture his person on Transvaal soil. I had many conversations with Mr. L——, or "Scotty," as he is still called by his familiars. Here is a veldt wrinkle he once gave me. " Do you know the reason so many men cannot find their way, and lose themselves in the veldt ? Well ! the fact is this ; they look always in front of and never behind them. The man who occasionally casts his eye over the country behind him sees it in a different aspect altogether, and can therefore often recognise landmarks when he returns that way." I have tested this wrinkle, and it is worth remembering. But Mr. L—— himself has the true native eye or instinct for a country, and would find it hard to lose himself even in the worst stretches of the Kalahari.

" Big Mick," another genial freebooter of Stellaland

days, to whom I shall refer in the next chapter, I also met at this time. "Big Mick," a magnificent giant of Irish descent, distinguished himself greatly in the defence of Mankoroane's capital—Taungs— where he acted as a sort of captain-general against the Transvaal Boers.

At the time I met him he was engaged in the more peaceful occupation of house-building, in which also he was a shining light.

After a stay made very pleasant to us by the hospitality of many of the inhabitants, Mackay and I set out on the 6th February for Setlagoli, a district fifty miles further north, half-way between Mafeking and Vryburg.

There had been heavy summer rains for some days, during which Vryburg had become a quagmire, and the inhabitants waded forlornly about, as is their custom, in "field" boots, top boots, mackintoshes, and any other gear calculated to withstand the swamps, holes, and "sluits," that everywhere abounded. We waited till 3.30 P.M., and then set forth in a Cape cart under a lowering, stormy sky. Two hours and a half of heavy travelling brought us to Fincham's, a farm and accommodation house fifteen miles out, where we outspanned for half-an-hour. Our next stage was Monjana Mabeli (literally, "the two sisters," a name given to two rounded hills lying close together, which here stand out from the flat plain), nine miles further on. It now became suddenly dark, the rain poured in torrents, a terrific tempest of thunder and lightning fell upon us, and the four horses would scarcely trek. We toiled on, occasionally losing the road, till nearly at Monjana Mabeli, where the country resembled a lake, through which we ploughed dismally.

At length, after being within an ace of an upset, we hit upon a farm-house, where the horses were put up and we were offered such shelter as could be given us for the night. Mr Keeley, a well-known cattle-dealer, has the farm here, a very excellent one for stock ; but the house occupied by his foreman was small and poorly thatched, and the rain was pouring merrily through the roof. Some other travellers coming in shortly, we opened a tin of " bully-beef," had some whisky, and then the four of us camped on a mattress and some sacks upon the floor, warding off the rain with our rugs and mackintoshes. We slept soundly till dawn, by which time the storm had passed away, the sun was out, the air was crisp and clear, and the veldt looked everywhere freshened and rejuvenated.

The next water and outspan, Jackal's Pan, where also are the postcart stables, is fifteen miles on. The road between lies across a dead flat, unbroken by tree or bush, and is inexpressibly wearisome. The telegraph posts, which follow the road between Vryburg and Setlagoli, rather add to than detract from the monotony. This fifty mile stretch to Setlagoli, dull, flat, and uninteresting as it is, especially if you follow the post road and do not call at Fincham's, is to my mind one of the most trying in British Bechuanaland. I have ridden it several times alone, and I have noticed at such times, that the utter lack of relief over this deadly bit of veldt seemed to impress itself even upon one's horse. You canter along, wearily counting the telegraph-posts—seventeen to the mile—and wishing to heaven you could somehow cheat the never-ending series, that stand against the sky line, gaunt and unlovely

to the eye, in one interminable vista. Although a
lion was killed at Monjana Mabeli only eight years
before—a sure proof that game was then fairly
abundant—little of wild life is now left upon these
plains. A few springbok, the inevitable steinbok
and duyker, and of course the usual partridges, koorhaans, and an occasional paauw, are all that here
survive to remind the traveller of the once teeming
wilderness.

There is an alternative route, more to the eastward, *via* Maribogo, where the stages are shorter,
a farmstead or two are to be found, and spruits and
rivercourses are less troublesome during the rains.
However, on this occasion we followed the post road,
and in two hours and a half reached Jackal's Pan,
a bare, ugly spot, relieved by a decent pool of water.
The Bechuanaland Exploration Company, who have
the mail contract and run the post carts, sunk a well
here later in the year, and have now a good and
permanent supply of water during the dry season.
Another fifteen miles over more diversified and
improving country, brought us, after crossing the
dry sandy bed of the Setlagoli River, to Setlagoli
itself. There had been little rain up here, and the
river was not flowing. The Setlagoli is, however, a
sand river, water flows beneath the sand ; and even
in time of drought pools of water are to be found
here and there over its course. At Setlagoli, where
Lamb's Hotel and Store stand, there is a good
and permanent supply in the river-bed, and many
thousand head of cattle can be watered throughout
the year.

Here is a stony rise or kopje, upon the highest
point of which is perched a strong little fort, built

by Sir Charles Warren, and still garrisoned by a few
files of Bechuanaland Border Police.   From Setlagoli
there is a beautiful view of the surrounding country,
amid which the picturesque hills of Woodhouse
Kraal and Koodoo's Rand, eight or nine miles distant, and the bold blue range of Kunana farther
away, close upon the Transvaal border, are prominent
landmarks.

Setlagoli is a pleasant district; extensive forests
of camel-thorn trees (*Giraffe Acacia*) are spread
over the country, the views are soft, pleasant, and
picturesque, and relieved by hills here and there ;
and at Lamb's Store and Hotel, a large block of
well-built, well-found brick buildings—forming one
of the best establishments in all Bechuanaland—
excellent accommodation for man and beast is
provided by the Messrs. Lamb, two energetic and
enterprising brothers, Englishmen, who have here
established a successful business.

Having rested a day at this place, Mackay and I
rode over on a fine Sunday morning to the property
upon which we proposed to settle ourselves for some
months.   We had brought our nags up with us, and
traversing eighteen miles of a charming bit of country,
across pleasant hills and through groves of acacias,
now in the full dark green of their spreading leafage,
reached some huts on the Maritsani River, where Mr.
Raynar St. Stephens, a mining engineer, was con-
ducting some tentative mineral explorations.   The
day was beautiful, the air clear, soft and warm, the
veldt and trees in the perfection of their summer
prime, and the Maritsani River, where we crossed,
was, for a wonder, flowing briskly along, the result
of a heavy thunderstorm.   We spent half a day with

A POOL ON THE MARITSANI—BRITISH BECHUANALAND

Mr. St. Stephens, and then, towards sundown, cantered along the Maritsani to its junction with the Setlagoli, ten miles further, where, in some good-sized Bechuana huts, we proposed for a time to make our home and abiding-place.

CHAPTER II.

FOUR MONTHS IN BAROLONG HUTS

Setlagoli and Maritsani Rivers—Our huts and their interiors—Thatches and snakes—White ants and their Queen—Aspect of the "Junction" —Historical interest—Bad water—Native servants: their uselessness —Making beds—"April," a Matabele, and the picture of Moselikatse —Native love of clothing—Our day's proceedings—Journey to Mafeking—Interview with Chief Monsioa—A Sechuana letter—Chartered Company's camp—Recruits—Mr. F. C. Selous—Bechuanaland beef— Dear mealies—Weevils—Return to Junction—Our dress—Pleasant evenings—"Big Mick" again—"Old Thomas"—Our neighbours— Wildfowl shooting—Goose dinner—Moroka's Kraal—Poultry— Ravages of hawks—The ride to Setlagoli—Beautiful country—Vaal bush and eland's boenje—The Bechuanas and their characteristics— A good talking to—Our cameras—Developing difficulties—Cold nights —Our new chimney.

ALTHOUGH we had seen water running in the Maritsani, ten or twelve miles nearer the Transvaal border, the flow had ceased before reaching the "Junction," as we called the place where our huts stood, at the point where that river unites itself with the Setlagoli. Here and there were standing pools, some of them quite respectable sheets of water for South Africa; but the early rains of 1890 were light and capricious, and at the Junction during the whole of this season neither the Maritsani nor Setlagoli ran throughout their courses. The years 1889 and 1890 were, however, years of partial drought, following a real wet summer season in 1888. At the end of 1890 and beginning of 1891 again, when the rains returned, they were prodigious, and both the rivers ran strongly for weeks together, so strongly, indeed, that my successor at the Junction, Mr. P. Gethin, had occasionally to swim the torrent just below the huts in order to receive his mails from Setlagoli, which awaited him on the further bank.

The residences prepared for our reception were two in number; first, a good-sized hut containing two iron bedsteads, a table, a chair or two, a filter, and a quantity of whisky and beer cases; second, a still larger hut, unfinished as to the walls, the poles of which required to be filled up with mud. In addition we had a small hut which served as a store house, saddle room, and game larder, and beyond that again a long thatched shed without walls, which had been intended as a rather ambitious cottage, but which had never been completed, and did duty only as a sort of rude stable for our horses.

Mackay and I at once took up our quarters in the complete hut, which was surrounded by a circular " kotla," or screen of high poles and bushes, affording a welcome privacy. Close alongside this hut we erected a little tent which we had bought at Kimberley, and which Mackay forthwith furnished with a tiny folding bedstead and proclaimed his bedroom. Above the tent floated a small Union-Jack, a signal to all and sundry that upon this soil, once torn by faction and harried by filibusters, the *pax Britannica* now reigned. The interior of this our private hut was, upon our arrival, dark and unkempt. It had but one small square aperture, which served as a window, and no door; and, barring the few articles of furniture I have mentioned, and forlorn whisky cases, there was nothing to indicate even rudimentary comforts. Gradually, however, with the aid of a handy man and carpenter, Thomas by name, who afterwards appeared on the scene, we improved the aspect of affairs, putting in doors to the huts, opening out more apertures—they were not windows, for we had no glass —and making decent hinged and padlocked boxes of the whisky and beer cases bequeathed to us. By the time our kits and gunnery had reached us from Kimberley we had shaken down into fairly ship-shape fashion, and what with books, writing materials, guns, spurs, a banjo, coaching horn, cartridge belts, a looking-glass, camera and other odds and ends neatly bestowed in their proper places, a little table in front of the centre pole of the hut, covered with a gaudy blanket, on which usually reposed a bottle of lime-juice, some tumblers, a case of " Dog's Head " cigarettes and the rest of our smoking tackle, and a thorough cleansing of the whole establishment, we were not unjustly proud of the appearance of our Bechuana mansion.

Later on in the year, when the frosts of winter came, and the indescribably keen winds of early morning blew, we were glad to add rough wooden shutters to our glassless windows ; and even then, with shutters and door alike closed, there was an abundance of air to be found within the huts. The Bechuana hut is by no means a despicable house. It is circular, constructed so as to offer the least resistance to the fierce winds that at times sweep the plains, and has plenty of space and air. A good-sized hut will measure 18 or 20 feet in diameter, with a height at the centre of the roof of 14 or 15 feet. The roof, composed of strong acacia branches partly supported by and radiating from a stout upright central post—usually a straight acacia bole

—is well and thickly thatched with grass, strongly
and carefully fastened with strips of a certain tough
bark first steeped in water. The ends of the roof
poles rest upon and are fastened to the wall posts.
The walls and floor are composed of anthill clay
and cow-dung, which sets perfectly hard and clean,
and will last for years. The timbering of these huts
is usually done by the men kind, the thatching and
mudding by the women. The total cost of such a
hut—which is used extensively by Europeans up
country—is from £1, 10s. to £2. These residences
are exceedingly cool in summer and warm in winter,
and, if properly thatched, are fairly waterproof even
against the torrential downpours that arrive in the
hot season.

Just outside the hut, and within the kotla, stood
a small iron washstand wherein our ablutions were
performed, always in the open air. On either side
of the doorway hung a large, evaporating canvas
water-bag, having a tap to it. These simple and
excellent inventions ensure on the hottest day a
cool supply of water, which, with a touch of lime-
juice cordial, formed our principal thirst-quencher
between meals.

Above each of the bedsteads, which stood on either
side of the hut, was slung a blanket. This protected
the sleeper from the constant dropping of white
ants—which had unfortunately before our arrival
been suffered to effect lodgment, and which we could
never quite exterminate—as well as from a possible
snake now and again. The only objection that can
be urged against these cool thatched roofs is that
snakes, lizards, and white ants, if they are not carefully watched, all have a strong affection for them.

Sometimes, but not often, a snake will fall from the roof; it happened once among a party of sleepers in one of St. Stephens' huts at the other camp, and there was a pretty scramble in the dark, as may be imagined. We ourselves killed a long green tree-snake in the thatch of the horse-shed, and it is not pleasant to reflect that one of these creatures may drop down upon one during the night. The blanket above the bed at all events removed this source of terror. If I had to live in these huts again, I would line with cheap calico the interior of the thatch; snakes could then only approach from the floor.

The largest hut, which lay thirty paces beyond the "Kotla hut," as we called our headquarters, served as a dining saloon. Here also slept at night "Old Thomas," the carpenter who afterwards joined us, and Elliott, an English lad left to us by our predecessors, who helped generally about the place. In this hut, which before the advent of the cold season we had re-thatched, and walled and floored with mud, we stored our cases and portmanteaus, as well as lock-up boxes containing a good supply of provisions for daily use. These were arranged round but not touching the walls. Every article reposed on glass bottles, as the only known protection against the depredations of white ants.

These insects, interesting as they are to the scientist and observer of nature, are a perfect pest all over Bechuanaland, and indeed throughout Africa. They will eat large holes in a thick tweed coat in one night, and anything softer than metal left to their tender mercies for a night or two is irremediably ruined. There was no reason why we should have found them in the roofs of our huts if reasonable care had been exercised from the beginning. The white ant as he climbs upward builds his curious tunnel of hard, self-made mortar (composed of the red soil of the country and a viscous secretion of his own) over every inch of his journey, and although he is an industrious insect, and his engineering occupies no great time, if the huts are inspected every few days these tunnels can be swept away, and the depredator kept at all events to the flooring. Once in the thatch, as we found to our cost, it is a difficult task to dislodge him. While upon the subject of white ants, I may add that they are as troublesome in towns, such as Vryburg and Mafeking, as upon the open veldt. Most housewives have at least once during the year to institute a crusade against the marauders, dig up the flooring, and attempt to find the queen. If the queen-ant can be successfully located and dug up, the nuisance is ended ; the rest of the ants, bereft of their sovereign, at once quit the building, and for a season trouble no more. The puzzle is " to find the Queen." Her majesty is a most loathly body—a mere glorified white maggot of about three inches long, hideously fat and lifeless, and her horribly swollen aspect intensified by her tiny limbs and head, which are merely those of an ordinary ant and out of all proportion to her body. Her mission in life is solely to bring forth the prolific swarms that devastate the neighbourhood. In the forests to the north and west the mischief done by these insects is enormous. As the traveller or hunter rides through the country he will notice, in a day's journey, numbers of dead trees killed by the white ants. The tree is attacked, the tunnels are run up along the bole, the wood is pierced and riddled, and the work of destruction is soon completed. Many a tough giraffe-acacia tree, which has reared itself painfully and laboriously during hundreds of years (for the camel-thorn is a hard-timbered, slow-growing tree), has cast its shade over many a thousand head of noble game, and offered its dark green leafage to the long tongues of many a hundred graceful giraffes, has ended thus miserably. It is always saddening to see such instances of the untimely death of these tough and slow-growing trees.

White ants, especially in the winged stage, are a favourite prey of many of the smaller hawks— hobbies and kestrels in particular. I was witness, during the rains of 1890, of a most curious spectacle. An immense swarm of white ants filled the air ; preying upon these insects, literally in hundreds, were small hawks sweeping and darting hither and thither in all directions, and feeding voraciously upon the fat, succulent insects as they flew. It is a matter of wonder whence and how the hawks appear so suddenly and in such numbers. But although the white ant is sought after as food by innumerable birds and animals of Africa, little impression appears to be made upon his myriad swarms. He lives and thrives, and in his turn strikes and devours all that comes in his path, and, excepting only metal and glass, all is grist that comes within his terrible milling powers. After the first rains fall these insects may sometimes be observed swarming in the air in countless myriads. The flying period is not very prolonged ; when they alight again the white ants usually take off their wings, which they do by twisting up the tail over the back

and deftly unfastening their flying apparatus; they
leave their now useless gear upon the ground and
proceed vigorously to work upon fresh excavations.
The unwinging operation is exceedingly curious and
interesting.

When we first arrived at the Junction the country,
diversified as it is by spreading woodlands and gently
rising ground, looked very beautiful. The rains had
at once banished from the soil the garb of parched
yellow, with which everything is clothed during the
dry months. The veldt was green and lovely, the
trees were at their best, gay bulbous flowers of many
kinds starred amid the grasses. This verdant beauty
unhappily lasts but a little while, and in a couple
of months the grass has faded beneath the ardent
sun, and the dry yellow glare settles upon the veldt
again.

Our huts stood, as I say, upon a gentle slope a
hundred yards from the Maritsani, two hundred
from its junction with the Setlagoli. Looking south,
the land rose softly again upon the further bank of
the Maritsani, and was clothed for some miles with
a dense forest of camel-thorn (*Giraffe Acacia*). To
the right, across the Setlagoli, was a good deal of
forest and bush again, while behind us the terrain
sloped gradually upwards to a dry timbered plateau
which ran unbroken to the Molopo River, thirty or
forty miles away. On our right flank the sandy
bed of the Setlagoli, heavily bushed along its course,
meandered in a deepish valley with here and there
a scant pool of water, until it met the Molopo fifty
or sixty miles to the north-west. To the left of
us the Maritsani might be followed between its
attendant slopes westward almost to the Transvaal

border, where, forty miles away, at a spot called the Eye of Maritsani, it took its source. Scattered round about our huts were a fair number of camel-thorns, which afforded welcome relief to the eye, and among which we might always be certain of finding game—birds, and small antelopes, steinboks, and duykers.

Our "Junction" was not altogether lacking in historical interest. At the end of the first quarter of the century this very spot was the scene of a fierce encounter between the Matabele Zulus (who, under the redoubted chief Moselikatse, had recently occupied the present Marico district in the Trans-vaal) and a body of mounted Griquas. The Griquas were defeated with heavy slaughter, and an English traveller, Mr. Bain, who was in the vicinity, only saved his life by instant flight, and was plundered of his waggons and equipment. Burchell's old waggon road—in bygone years the main and only route from Kuruman to Pitsani and the north—ran by close at hand.

Everywhere around us flourished the long grass veldt, excellent for cattle and goats, and even—except during the fatal months of horse-sickness—for horses also. The veldt here is what is called warm veldt; that is, there is plenty of timber and bush, and shelter from sun and wind is readily to be found. From almost every point of view ours was as desirable a place of sojourn as any in broad Bechuanaland. Water was, however, scarce and not too good, and in a month or two later, when the rain-pools were disappearing, we not only found our supply falling rapidly in quantity, but deterio-rating with equal rapidity in quality. By April our

solitary pool was foul and muddy, and strongly
impregnated with animal matter, from the fouling
of cattle ; so much so that we had first to precipitate
it with alum, and then to filter it, before it was fit
even to make a decent cup of tea.   It is only fair
to say that this was an exceptional season, and we
were then at the end of nearly two years of drought.
In the month of May—to obtain our water supply—
we were sending the waggon every two days, loaded
up with empty barrels, to be filled from a hole in
the Setlagoli, six miles distant.   At the beginning
of 1891, when there were excessive rains, the cry was
all the other way ; there was too much water.   Conservation of water, and especially well-sinking and
dam-making, will greatly tend to adjust these matters
as the country becomes filled up.   All this Setlagoli
district in which we were living was, until 1885,
under the sway of Monsioa, Chief of the Barolong
tribe.   Monsioa and his tribesmen are now, however,
restricted to native locations, the ground of which
they are unable to alienate.   Even now, outside the
locations, the Barolong and Vaalpens tribesmen are
loyal to Monsioa and obey his orders, although much
of his power is gone.

The extent of ground over which I was entitled
to exercise sway was between 65,000 and 70,000
acres—more than 90 square miles.   I found on
my arrival a number of black servants of various
breeds—Zulu, Bechuana, Matabele, Mozambique, and
Vaalpens ; these in their turn again encouraged
hangers-on of many sorts and numbers.   Discipline
had been very slack, there had been scant super-
vision, and the new régime, under which I endeavoured to evolve some sort of order, cleanliness,

c

and method out of a happy-go-lucky chaos, was not approved of.

It was not long, therefore, before I made a clean sweep of most of the old gang, after which things settled down ; such of the younger boys as I kept on, together with the new hands, conformed to my ideas or did their feeble best to do so.

Although there are large numbers of natives in Bechuanaland who have little or nothing to do, and who pass their time idling in their native towns, while the women work in the fields, thatch and mud the huts, carry the water, and undertake most of the heavy labour, it is a most difficult matter to obtain servants.   Often when a boy has been hired, he will stay a month or two, draw his money, and depart to his kraal again, leaving his master stranded.   He has always an excuse ready ; either he is sick, or his friends are sick, or the " Baas " speaks too sharply to him, or he is misunderstood ; and so off he goes, having first secured some old clothes and the few pounds he required.   We suffered a good deal from this sort of thing, and were unfortunate in never being able to command a decent cook or house-boy. We had a number of incapables it is true, but, help and instruct them as we would, we succeeded in dinning very little efficiency into them.   They are poor whining creatures too, and can stand very little scolding or correction—by which I mean, not corporal, but verbal correction.   If we required a baking of decent bread, or the mealie meal porridge and the stew or roast up to time for breakfast and supper, we had to look sharp after it ourselves.   I have known breakfast, the preparation of which began at sunrise, not to appear for three hours afterwards, if left to the lagging hands of our so-called cooks—T'Choko and Tony. What on earth they were doing, heaven knows; they appeared to be preparing, and yet the breakfast tarried and tarried. One of these boys, T'Choko, or another, an amusing young rascal called Peetsi, I usually deputed to make the beds. We had some sheets in use, and I have, time after time, shown these boys how to make the beds so that the sheets might be in their proper places. My teachings were utterly in vain; day after day the sheets were to be found, either tucked hopelessly at the bottom of the blankets, or disposed in some other extraordinary fashion, in which it was quite impossible to get at them for sleeping purposes. After a time we gave it up in despair, and the water supply failing, and a large "wash" being therefore out of the question, the sheets were relegated to limbo, and blankets only used. Peetsi, whom I have mentioned above, was a young Vaalpens, with a fondness for horses, a quite unrealisable yearning for the cooking department, and a leaven of rather quaint humour. Peetsi is the Sechuana name for horse, and as the lad's proper designation was rather complicated, and he was attached to the horse department, we called him for short "Peetsi." He and the upper groom, "Dottie," a lame Barolong, who had had a leg broken by a Boer bullet in a fight at Mafeking some years before, were perhaps the most satisfactory servants we had. Dottie's right leg was as stiff as a poker, but he was by no means a bad boy on a horse for all that, and had plenty of pluck. And out of Peetsi, with his white teeth, brilliant red gums, rolling eyes, bare head—each woolly kink neatly shaved with a bit of broken glass—and quaint

angular ways (he was a thin, leggy creature, wore
ruined boots four sizes too large, and was all feet and
elbows), we extracted a good deal of amusement.
Dottie and he were both fond of horses, and did what
they could in the way of grooming, feeding, and
catching, when required. "April," our head waggon-
boy, was a Matabele, a fine, well-set-up savage, now
passionately attached to European clothing. "April"
was very fond of his donkey team, and managed
them extremely well on the whole, and when he had
work to do, was smart and active enough.

These Zulus—for the Matabele are of Zulu blood
—are finer men physically than the mild Bechuanas.
April had taken part in the last Matabele raid,
despatched by Lobengula against the Batauana—the
Lake Ngami tribe—in 1884. This "impi," after a
terrible journey across the desert, had been led into
ambush, and defeated with great slaughter, by the
Lake people. April, like most other Africans, had
a great gift of narrative. He used to describe the
scene most graphically. How the Batauana betook
themselves and their cattle to an island; how the
Matabele advanced into the water until they were
up to their chins or swimming, and were then shot
down in numbers, before they could get to work
with their stabbing assegais; and, finally, how they
broke and fled.

Very few of them—a mere handful—got back to
their own country to tell the tale, and the bones
of their comrades to this hour whiten the desolate
swamps of the Lake country. I had with me Cornwallis Harris's book on Southern Africa, in which
appears a coloured drawing, by the author, of Moselikatse, the founder of the Matabele nation, father of

the present King Lobengula. When I showed this to April and explained who it was, he became half frantic with delight. Afterwards he was perpetually requesting to see again the "great black one," "the elephant," "calf of the black cow," as he called the departed chief. Moselikatse, who wrought terrible havoc among the Bechuanas during his passage north, is equally remembered by them, if in a different manner.

Besides these boys, we had others, a shifting population, some staying a few weeks, some a few days only. It is amusing to watch the progress of these natives towards that acme of their ambition— European clothing. A boy will at first appear in his native garb of nothingness or next to it. He then begs or picks up an old sack, through the bottom end of which he thrusts his neck and arms, and assumes his first air of civilisation. From the sack he wheedles, begs, or buys his way to a waistcoat, trousers, and even a shirt, and then to crown all a coat. I have witnessed many of these courses of evolution, and from the naked or chrysalis stage by anxious degrees to the full-blown butterfly stage of brand new store outfit, they are each and all full of interest, instruction, and amusement.

At sunrise each morning—that is, from about 5.30 in February to 6.30 in May [1]—one of the boys set off with two empty bottles for a supply of fresh milk, which was most kindly furnished by our near neighbours, the Gethins, a mile away across the

---

[1] The longest day in Bechuanaland is the 21st December, when the sun rises at 4.47 and sets at 7.10. The shortest day occurs on the 21st June, when the sun rises at 7.6 and sets at 4.47—less than ten hours of daylight.

river.   We ourselves meanwhile had our early morning coffee brought to us in bed, and then prepared
for the day.   Very frequently we took a stroll with
the gun before breakfast, to pick up a few head of
partridge or koorhaan, and now and again a small
buck.   Meanwhile, if supplies permitted, a goat was
being slaughtered and the fry prepared for breakfast.
These early mornings were brimful of charm.   During
the summer season, while the rains are about, the
dews are heavy ; earth and air are alike delightfully
cool ; the veldt and the woodland are arrayed in
smiles ; there is a pleasant scent from bush, and
grass, and shrub ; the birds are at their merriest, all
nature ripples with good humour.   Before the dry
winter season has set in many of the birds have
trekked north—although many still remain—and, as
the long parched months slowly succeed one another,
the country is reft of much of its charm and beauty.

After breakfast we had various matters to occupy
ourselves with ; explorations of the estate, hut improvements, carpentering, interviewing petty chiefs
and natives, some of whom were allowed to run
stock upon the land, journeys to St. Stephens' camp,
journeys to Mafeking, Vryburg, or Setlagoli, mail-
day correspondence ; these and many other details
required our attention.   Even the more sordid cares
of housekeeping, baking, and cookery, with which
we had perforce to interest ourselves, occupied some
portion of our time.

We had not long been at the Junction before it
became necessary to ride up to Mafeking—fifty miles
north-east—and interview the chief, Monsioa, for
the purpose of obtaining more native labour for St.
Stephens' camp.   Monsioa happened to be away from

MOLOPO RIVER, NEAR MAFEKING—BRITISH BECHUANALAND

the town at this time, and we were therefore taken by
one of his sons to see him at his country seat, a collection of half-a-dozen huts six miles from Mafeking,
whither the old man had betaken himself to superin-
tend the completion of a large dam.   I had a letter
to the chief from the Rev. John Mackenzie, a very
old friend of his, and at once secured an audience.
Monsioa must have been even at that time (1890)
more than eighty years of age.   He told me he remembered sea-cows (hippopotami) in the Molopo, and
the Molopo of to-day, which, like other South African
rivers, has dwindled greatly, would find it a hard
matter to hold a single sea-cow.   The old chief,
whose locks were white as snow, was feeble and
infirm, and his eyes troubled him greatly.   He was
exceedingly civil, and sat up at the foot of his bed
wrapped in a blanket, with his favourite young wife
at his side.   He promised to send down some of his
young men to work for us.   He had then many
questions to ask about England, its Queen, and so on,
and several minor grievances to unfold.

   Monsioa has always been a firm and faithful friend
to the British.   Even in the dark days, when it
seemed that the Boers must overwhelm him and his
people, he stuck to his guns, defended Mafeking, and
still believed that the Queen of England would come
to his aid.   His long and most gallant defence of
Mafeking cannot be too highly praised.   Assisted by
Mr. Christopher Bethell, who organised the forces
and was himself treacherously slain by the Boers in
one of the fights at that time, Monsioa successfully
resisted all the assaults of the Transvaal freebooters,
until at last England came to the rescue and
Bechuanaland was saved.   He and his people, under

the new government of the country, are now settled on their own ample locations, while the old chief further draws a pension of £300 a year (not one whit too much for his services) from the British Government. As this pension is periodically drawn, it is banked until required in a very simple way—under the old man's pillow.

While the chief complained of his troubles and his ailments, I happened to remark that even the great Queen of England was not altogether exempt from the ills of mankind, and herself had had many and grievous sorrows and was believed to suffer from rheumatism. The knowledge that his ailments were shared by so great a personage seemed immensely to lighten the old man's load of woe; he expressed frequently by his curious Bechuana "Eh!" his great surprise and interest, and for the rest of the interview brightened up in a wonderful way. We were glad to have had a chat with this old chief, an interesting link with the days when white men were strangers to the Bechuanas; when arms of precision were unknown, and the wilderness was one vast, teeming game-preserve; when Moselikatse and his hordes had not yet broken from the Zulu power and whirled forth a hurricane of war and bloodshed on their career to the north; when even Sebituane —Livingstone's Sebituane—and his Mantatees (for they were known first as Mantatees before they were called Makololo) had not yet swept north-westward through the Bechuanas to the Lake Ngami country, and thence beyond the Zambesi to found the Makololo nation, a nation which has long since seen its day and vanished. Returning to Mafeking, we were shown Monsioa's house, a neat oblong building, an improvement on the circular huts, and much resembling an English cottage. The interior was neat and fairly furnished. On the wall hung, framed and glazed, one of the chief's most treasured possessions, an award of merit presented to him by the proprietors of *Ally Sloper* in recognition of his gallant defence of Mafeking. It was impossible to repress a smile on seeing this printed document, so little comprehended and yet so highly valued by the simple old chief. In a kotla near by stood another Barolong fetish, a solitary cannon, got up with immense trouble by Christopher Bethell, and used during the siege of the town.

Before leaving England I had obtained from Mr. John Mackenzie letters to Monsioa and other chiefs, asking them to introduce me to their best hunting veldt, and show me what sport they could. Monsioa's country, except to the westward in the Kalahari, has little heavy game left to it, and his assistance therefore was hardly of much avail. He offered to do what he could for me along the desert part of the Molopo, where koodoos, gemsbok, and blue wildebeest are still to be found. A letter in Sechuana may be thought of interest. Here then is a copy of a similar letter, introducing me to Sechele, the old chief of the Bakwena, further north in the protectorate :—

"PORTOBELLO, SCOTLAND,
"*December* 31, 1889.

"GO SECHELE MOCOASELE,
    "Kwa Molepolole, Isala ea me.
    "Ga Ke gu Kwalelemahoko ; Ke Kwala he la go gu itsise Isala ea Mr. Bryden. Ena a re, o rata go bona dipoloholo tse di Tona. Me Kana di sale gona mo hatshiñ ya Khosi go tla

itse wena Mokwena.   Ki tla i tumela ba u Ka mo shupetsa
dipholoholo mo hatshiñ ya gogo.   U dumele thata Mokwena,
le Baga enu ba dumele thata.—Re na, Isala Ea gogo,
                                          " JOHN MACKENZIE."

Lekoko, a son of Monsioa, who conducted us to his
father, and round the native town, speaks English
excellently and can read and write.   The Bechuanas
have plenty of brains, and when taught appear to be
able to acquire English with at least as much facility
as an Englishman can pick up Sechuana.

The English portion of Mafeking, a little beyond
the native town, was at this time a scene of immense
bustle and excitement.   Recruits for the Chartered
Company's police and pioneers were being enrolled
and drilled, a camp was formed just outside the
town, the market square was crammed with waggons
mustering for the northward trek, and the stores
and hotels were doing a roaring trade.   Johannesburg, which was then suffering from the effects
of a financial debauch, seems to have been the
happy hunting-ground for recruits at this time.
Armies of brokers (every one styled himself a
stockbroker in those days) were on their beam-
ends, and these men, strong, youthful, and still full
of faith, though penniless, came pouring into the
camp.   Kimberley, and even far-off Cape Town,
also supplied contingents.   Hunters, soldiers, sailors,
barristers, university men, solicitors, farmers, all
these came to swell the forces of the Chartered
Company.

I had the pleasure of renewing here the acquaintance of Mr. F. C. Selous, the well-known hunter and
explorer, who was going north to show the way into

the Promised Land, and to whose energy and forethought, and wonderful knowledge of the interior,
much of the success of the pioneers' subsequent
march into Mashonaland was due. Mr. Selous, on
hearing that my companions and I were thinking
of making a distant hunting trip later in the year,
strongly advised the Lake River country. This
advice we afterwards followed, and had no reason to
be dissatisfied with.

It was at dinner at Isaac's Hotel, Mafeking, that
I first discovered the virtues of Bechuanaland beef,
which is not to be excelled out of England. We had
an excellent *table-d'hôte*, and I am bound to say
that some of the roast beef sampled at this time
was equal to prime English beef—tender, juicy, and
well-flavoured. All the Bechuana territory, indeed,
seems to be peculiarly fitted for the production of
high-class cattle. Some day, I suppose, when ranching has been introduced, canning factories will
follow ; there is not the slightest reason why meat-
canning on a large scale should not be successfully
introduced. With the enormous demand all over
South Africa for " bully beef"—as the American
tinned article is called—and the low price of cattle,
I am convinced that the financial future of such
an industry would be assured. It was a pleasant
thing to note how the Boers from Marico and
neighbouring parts of the Transvaal come nowadays
into the Mafeking hotels, enjoy the *table-d'hôte*, and
mingle with English folk. The friendly greeting,
better fare, and good cooking of the enterprising
British, all have their effect, and these matters—
trifling though they are—distinctly tend to that
union of Boer and British so necessary to all South

African progress. It is undeniable that in the last two or three years immense strides have been made in this direction.

Mainly owing to the scant rainfall of this season, the native crops had failed, and with the increased demand caused by the Mashonaland expedition, mealies, of which we were running short, now stood at thirty-five shillings the bag (205 lbs.), instead of the normal price of ten shillings or less. At this ruinous figure I laid in a stock, and even these were of poor sample. Every bag, when it reached the Junction, was badly "weevilled," and our mealie meal breakfast porridge was in consequence strongly leavened with weevils, which were ground up in the mill together with the mealies. However, our appetites were usually healthy, and although chopped weevils are not an ornament to one's porridge, they are at least endurable, and one gets quickly used to them, if the milk be plentiful.

I believe, by the way, that mealies may be kept entirely free of weevils by the simple expedient of placing branches of dacca—a local plant well known in South Africa—between and under the various sacks. Thus protected, mealies may be kept sound for two or three years.

Business being completed at Mafeking, we returned to the Junction *via* Medebi Wells and Maritsani (Wright's Farm), a route of which we afterwards knew by heart every sandy yard.

We now set to work to put our huts in order. Thomas, our carpenter and handy-man, was great at shifts and contrivances of all sorts, and, with suggestions of our own, the huts soon emerged phœnix-like from their pristine nakedness. Among other tasks we started sinking for water, but the drought beat us here.

Our dress was that usual to the up-country sojourner in South Africa. A broad-brimmed felt hat, than which there can be no better headpiece; item, a flannel shirt, open at the neck and with the sleeves rolled up to the elbows; item, a pair of breeches or knickerbocker breeches; item, gaiters—pigskin for choice—and strong lace-up brown leather boots, or "field boots." The pleasures of a shirt-sleeve life cannot, I think, be too highly estimated. In Bechuanaland and the interior a coat is seldom indeed required. And when, after a spell of this sort of existence, one comes down country, the worry of braces, the struggles with a waistcoat, which at first seems all too tight, and the painful reminders of starched stand-up collars, are harsh and unpleasing evidences of the sorrows of civilisation. In the evening, when the day's work was over, the putting on of a pair of easy Boer velschoens in place of the heavier boots was a pleasant relief. After supper was over, Mackay and I used to sit in our chairs outside the hut and enjoy our pipes; not seldom the banjo was produced, and we had a song or two. At this time the summer lightning played nightly in the far horizon to the eastward over the Transvaal, and was a most beautiful spectacle. Yet, somehow, the rain never came our way, and the veldt was fast losing its mantle of green, and the pools were drying up again.

It was not long before "Big Mick," whom I have mentioned in the first chapter, paid us a visit. That genial ex-freebooter, having tired once more of town life, was on his way to Mosita, a place a little to the westward, where gold had been discovered, and where prospectors were getting to work. Mick turned up one day on a rough white pony, which under his gigantic form looked like a good-sized dog; an old Snider rifle was slung at his back, and a pipe was in his mouth. In South Africa, where one never knows when one may require it, hospitality is an instinct of self-preservation; besides, up country one is always glad to see a fresh face. Mick was heartily welcomed. Of course he off-saddled, and we had the pleasure of his company for a couple of days, before he struck again for the gold valleys of Mosita. I fancy our musical tastes had something to do with Mick's stay. His father had been a regimental bandmaster, and Mick himself was passionately fond of music. He played the piccolo, and wherever he went there went his little flute. With Mackay's banjo and Mick's piccolo, and every song and chorus we could think of, we knocked up two quite decent evenings of music; and, sitting out under the warm, starlit sky, thoroughly enjoyed ourselves. Lime-juice and the whisky bottle were at hand to wet the whistle at need.

"Old Thomas" often came round to our kotla to have a pipe and enjoy the music. He was a great conversationalist, with a somewhat roaming tendency, which more often than not bordered on the diffuse. He was a Welshman, and had a knack of putting his speech into doggerel rhyme, which, especially at meal-times, often was more than Mackay and I could well bear. We had then to put down our feet, sometimes with a show of heat, and the doggerel vanished perhaps for an hour or two. The old man's experience had been vast, gathered in all countries and under all conditions.

He was out and out the best hand at topping a
yarn or an anecdote I ever met with. If a state-
ment was made, however florid, or tall, or impossible,
Thomas would cap it with some astounding experience
in Peru, or Australia, or the States, or even in lonely
isles of the Pacific. And all delivered with the most
perfect solemnity and sobriety, without fuss or excitement. It was wonderful—too wonderful; our gorges
sometimes rose, and Mackay would express his dis-
belief in no measured terms; the old man would
manfully attempt to stop the torrent of opposition,
and then subside, only to lie in ambush and emerge
again armed with some new and mightier fable. But
withal old Thomas was a capital workman, and did
good service for us at the Junction.

For a remote up-country locality we were fortunate
in our neighbours. Just across the Maritsani, less
than a mile distant, lived the Gethins, two brothers
—one of them married—who were running cattle and
goats on their own farm of 6000 acres. We often shot
together, and it was a great treat, after a hot afternoon ramble in search of game, to call in and have
a cup of tea at Mrs. Gethin's. I am afraid the quantities of tea, or milk, that we drank at these " at
homes " would have rather appalled a hostess in
England. Then there was the baby—absolutely the
only white baby in the district, and a most well-
behaved, good-tempered baby, always ready to welcome us with a smile. He was a capital little chap,
perfectly happy whether lying in his cradle, crawling
on the floor, or carried in the arms of his little
Bechuana nurse. After a time Mrs. Gethin lost this
girl, and the post was filled by a succession of black
boys, who really performed their duties very well, and

were kind and good-tempered with the child. The
Gethins, like ourselves and other settlers in the
district, lived in Bechuana huts, and from the
proximity of the cattle kraal, and the abundance of
milk, flies were troublesome in the hot weather. It
struck me as a singular instance of the adaptability of
the human race, that this white child, recently born
in the country, should appear perfectly untroubled
by the plague of insects. Although half-a-dozen flies
might settle on its face at the same time, it took not
the least notice, nor attempted to knock them away ;
and when asleep in its cradle was equally undisturbed
by these irritating visitors. At home, I am certain,
an infant of a few months would be excessively
worried under similar circumstances.

Sometimes Mrs. Gethin mounted her pony and
rode with us shooting. More than once she was of
the greatest assistance in driving geese and ducks
towards us as we lay in ambush. A mile above
the Gethins' huts a watercourse, called the Mesemi
Spruit, joined the Maritsani ; when rain fell, a broad,
shallow vley of water attracted at this point numbers
of ducks and geese, widgeon and teal. After a heavy
local shower some great spur-winged geese paid us
a visit, and for a short time gave us pretty sport.
The first goose shot formed the *pièce de résistance*
at a banquet to which we were invited by the
Gethins, and so towards dusk, having put on our
coats and our best manners, we rode over. The
goose was excellent, and the evening a great success.
These little social amenities, which we interchanged
now and again, formed very pleasant breaks in our
rough up-country existence. Other neighbours we
had in Messrs. Knox and Fanshawe, farming fifteen

OUR NEAREST NEIGHBOURS—MARITSANI RIVER, BRITISH BECHUANALAND

miles further up the Maritsani, and the Cutlers, who were living five miles away on the Setlagoli, on a farm called Sherwood, in the midst of some of the most beautiful woodland scenery in all Bechuana-land. In fact, so thickly did the giraffe acacias grow in this locality, that unless one were actually on the road, it was a difficult matter to "spot" the neat wattle and daub cottage in which the Cutlers lived.

These were our only white neighbours. A few miles away, on the further slope of the Setlagoli, was a large kraal of Barolong living under a petty chief called Michael Moroka. Moroka is the son of the chief of a well-known Christianised branch of the Barolong, which had been settled for generations in the present Orange Free State territory, at a place called Thaba N'Chu, near the Caledon River, on the western border of Basutoland. The Free State Boers had long coveted and even threatened this Barolong territory, and at last, a few years since, it was arranged that Moroka should sell his location to the Free State Government. The tribe then came over to their ancient lands in the Bechuana country, and bought from the British Government two large tracts near Setlagoli, where they now live happily enough under Michael and his uncle Richard Moroka. Michael Moroka's lands marched with ours, and we were very good neighbours, and if we required labour for hut-building, we could usually get it from his kraal.

Michael himself was a smart, well-dressed man, who could speak and write English, owned waggons, and did a good deal of transport-riding—a paying business for natives ; but I fancy was rather too apt

D

to be bitten with the meretricious attractions of a temporary sojourn at Kimberley.

Our supply of poultry usually came from Moroka's kraal. These were brought over periodically by a bevy of women and girls, all looking forward, of course, to a delicious morning of palaver and bargaining. The inevitable haggle into which we were dragged usually resulted in the purchase of the fowls at the standard price of one shilling a head.

Poultry in this country have an extraordinary faculty of disappearance. The hawks and falcons, which are inordinately daring, account for a good many in the course of the season. The Gethins lost by these winged marauders alone forty fowls in a season. Raptorial birds are very numerous in Southern Africa; so numerous that shooting apparently has no sort of effect upon their constantly recruited legions. At certain seasons, when they are most numerous, their audacity is astonishing. A friend of mine, travelling not long since in the Kalahari, was sitting by the waggon preparing for supper. One of his boys was busily plucking some partridges for the pot. While he was in the act, a falcon stooped, seized one of the plucked birds, which was lying close to the fire, and sailed clean away with his booty. I have seen a large hawk stoop at a meer-cat, as it ran across the road less than ten yards in front of me, apparently not in the least abashed by my proximity.

I had frequently to send into Setlagoli for mails or telegrams. If the Bechuana boys are good for nothing else, they can certainly run post. I have despatched a young, lathy-looking lad for letters; and

in seven hours the same lad has returned to me with
his parcel, having compassed the thirty-six miles, over
a rough country and under a hot sun, without turning
a hair. I am an old athlete myself, and this struck
me as a highly creditable performance—remembering
that the boy had rested at least an hour at Setlagoli
before returning.

The ride to Setlagoli from our huts, following
pretty closely the Setlagoli River, was a pleasant
and a picturesque one, and I was always fond of it.
First the road led for some miles through the charming woodlands of Sherwood Farm; then, passing an
old prospector's hut and crossing the dry river-bed,
one ascended the high slope that rose above the
southern bank. For some miles again the road followed the brow of the uplands. Below ran the rivercourse, fringed heavily with brush and camel-thorn;
the forest lands stretched far and wide to the left
hand; in front, as one rode—far towards the horizon
—lay, blue in the distance, the hilly ranges of
Koodoo's Rand and Woodhouse Kraal; beyond these
again swelled in deeper blue the Kunana Hills, just
upon the Transvaal border. Presently, after crossing
a gentle vale or two, the stony kopje of Setlagoli,
crowned with its tiny fort, rose upon the view, and,
after an eighteen mile ride, usually compassed at a
hand canter in just over two hours, the store and
post office were reached, and news of the outer world
was to be had. The forest scenery about this country
reminded me strongly of the wilder bits of the Surrey
woodlands. If the reader knows the woody commons
of Ashstead or Bookham, or other portions of the wild
Surrey commonlands, and will exchange in fancy the
giraffe acacia of Africa for the oak of England, he

may picture to himself pretty faithfully much of the
country about Setlagoli.

In these regions, even after the brief greenery of
summer has gone, there is some repose although the
yellow mantle of winter has settled over all.   The
dark foliage of the acacias is a pleasant relief to the
eye wearied and tortured with the eternal glare of
the grass veldt.   But, when the woodlands are left
behind and the bare grass plains encountered, there
is no escape from the fierce pale blue of the hot
skies and the blinding dazzle of the sun-scorched
veldt.

There are two species of vegetation that resist,
even upon the shadeless plains, the almost irresistible
attack of the African sun.   The Vaal-bush, with its
grey-green leafage, still holds its own and flourishes,
and spreads in some localities very thickly over the
country.   And down among the long grasses there
thrives a graceful feathery plant having about its
fronds and leaves something of the fern, something
of the acacia.   Its root, far embedded in the soil,
somewhat resembles that of the horse-radish.   The
Boers call this graceful plant elands'-boenje (elands'
bean), probably from the reason that in the old days
the herds of eland fed upon the plant or its root.
There is little of the bean about it that I have been
able to discover ; but then the Boers have a knack
of miscalling things.   They call the giraffe "kameel"
—a camel ; the name eland itself means an elk, an
impossible comparison ; why not therefore call the
feathery plant, that spreads in tender green patches
here and there over the dry red soil, the elands'
bean ?   This plant, by the way, furnishes a most
excellent tanning material, which is well known to

the natives and ought to be of service to Europeans also.

During our sojourn at the Junction we had many opportunities of studying the Bechuanas and their ways; and we made this discovery, that as conversationalists and debaters, they can give the average Englishman any number of points. Every man, every woman is a born talker. They have good voices—many of the women and children very beautiful voices—they use plentiful and appropriate gesture, and their arguments are acute, weighty, and well reasoned out. In affairs requiring diplomatic management I don't think they have any strong regard for truth; but then few diplomatists have. In fact, argument, haggling, and the skill of bargaining are with them elevated to the fine arts; time is of no object; and there is nothing they love more than a downright good "jaw"—as a plain Englishman would call it—lasting half a day or longer. An Englishman has neither the time nor the inclination to waste a morning in argument as to the value of a goat, or the question whether the price of an article should be lessened or increased by a single shilling. As a rule he either gives way or loses his temper, and stalks off wishing the native at the devil—not seldom the latter, I fancy.

We had some Bechuana women to thatch and mud one of the huts. They were very amusing, especially their spokeswoman, a most voluble and finished speaker and actress. We could none of us comprehend the others, except through an interpreter, and somehow in the middle of the job a misunderstanding arose as to the price. Our lady friends slid off the roof forthwith, and the spokeswoman harangued us for nearly half-an-hour without allowing us to edge in a word.

She was only clothed in a ragged and extremely dirty old blue print gown, the usual loose white cotton blouse that Bechuanas affect when they take to European clothes (they make these blouses themselves, and they are, when clean, really rather pretty and effective), and an old native straw hat perched on her woolly pate. But her beautiful voice, her diction, running on in smooth Sechuana like the clear flow of a rivulet, and above all her gestures (she was not good-looking, but she had beautiful hands and arms), were things to remember. The woman was a born actress, and would have made her fortune on the stage. Although it was all against ourselves, I think we really enjoyed this lingual attack. In its way it was perfect. Ultimately we called in Dottie as interpreter ; the misunderstanding was settled, after much chaff and laughter, to the satisfaction of all parties ; and the ladies resumed their thatching again, mightily refreshed by the " talking to " they had given us.

Mackay and I had brought our cameras with us, and, in spite of difficulties with foul and muddy water, took and developed many fairly successful pictures, some of which may be seen among the illustrations. The wonderful sunlight of South Africa is at first rather troublesome to one accustomed to dull English skies. The allowance to be made is immense. Even after months of practice, I found that some of my pictures still had a tendency to over-exposure. Our great difficulty, of course, lay in the development. Our sleeping hut at night made a very good dark room, and, having previously been

at much pains to cleanse and filter the only water we
had available, we used to work usually from nine or
ten P.M. to twelve or one o'clock. Many pleasant
evenings were passed in this way. We sat scanning
anxiously and lovingly each picture as it slowly developed, and when our friend Dove (who joined us
at the end of March), who had meanwhile retired
to bed and enjoyed his first sweet snooze, woke up, as
he usually did towards the end of the performance,
we were ready for him with a batch of sun-pictures,
which he then proceeded to criticise by the light of
a candle. Considering that, filter and cleanse our
water as we might (and we struggled very hard to
evolve purity out of filth), the plates, on being taken
out of the bath next morning, invariably had a film
of mud and sand resting upon them, we were very
fairly successful within our limited resources. I
myself was a struggling novice, only just beginning
to acquire this supremely interesting art.

In April and May, when the frosts of winter had
set in, Mackay and I found this nightly employment
a cold one. We usually, therefore, by means of a
spirit lamp made ourselves a brew of hot cocoa and
ate a biscuit before turning in. As the frosts became
more intense, Thomas, during our short journey to
Morokweng, built a wonderful chimney on to the
hut, and we could then indulge in the luxury of a
fire. This chimney was a work of art. In default
of bricks, it was mainly composed of mud, stones,
and empty bottles—the necks of the bottles facing
outward, and bristling tier upon tier for all the world
like an immense battery of miniature cannon. Crown-
ing the edifice, and forming a hideous yet effective
cowl, were two or three large biscuit tins with the

bottoms knocked out, firmly plastered one above the other. Inside we had a large and cosy ingle nook, two flat stones serving as a hearth. Our chimney was the pride of ourselves, the wonder and admiration of the neighbourhood. Unfortunately, at a later period during the torrential rains at the end of 1890, the mud plaster became washed away, and the whole edifice fell at once into ruin.

CHAPTER III.

NATURAL HISTORY NOTES

Decadence of great game—Hartebeest, brindled gnu, steinbok, and
duyker—Leopards, hyænas, and jackals—The cheetah—African lynx
—Karosses—Vultures and their ways—Eagles, buzzards, and hawks—
The secretary-bird—Namaqua doves—Hornbills—The dwarf blossom-
pecker and its nest—Rollers—Shrikes—The social weaver-bird—
Swallows and swifts—Song-birds—Other Bechuanaland birds—The
green tree-snake—Puff-adder—Cobra—Ring-hals and other snakes—
The Python—Snake-bite remedies—Insects—The Hottentot god and
other *Phasmidæ*—Centipedes and spiders—Butterflies—List of those
captured in Bechuanaland and the Kalahari—Protective mimicry and
its wonders—How to pack butterflies—Bechuanaland flora—The bitter
water-melon : useful in the desert—Jack and Jenny, our tame baboons
—Their interesting traits and tragic ending.

In another chapter of this book I show how the wild
life of Bechuanaland has become of late years depleted and in many parts exterminated altogether.
The great game, which in Livingstone's early days
roamed so abundantly over all this country, have
been hunted, persecuted and destroyed, till the land
knows them no more.

A troop or two of hartebeests (*Alcelaphus Caama*)
still ranged about the Maritsani to remind us sadly
enough of the magnificent fauna that once thronged
these natural pastures. As a rule we left these hartebeests to graze in peace, desiring with our neighbours
to see them increase and multiply; and indeed they
had become so little accustomed to be shot at, that
they were not very shy of displaying themselves.
We indulged ourselves so far as to have one turn at

them (set forth in Chapter IX.) with our neighbours
Knox and Fanshawe, during the month of May ; but,
save on this occasion, they were unmolested by us.
So confident had they become, that Mr. and Mrs.
Gethin later in the year, when they took over our
dwelling, were for a short time accustomed to see the
big red antelopes pass within sight of the huts
nearly every day, at a certain hour, on their way
from one feeding ground to another.

The very last blue wildebeest (brindled gnu) on
the Maritsani, which had been accustomed—no doubt
for company's sake, poor beast—to consort with the
hartebeest, disappeared from the scene only a few
months before our arrival. Whether he was shot ;
whether he wandered off westward to the Kalahari
in search of more congenial scenes ; or whether, in
sheer despair at his forlorn state, he died of a broken
heart, somewhere in the dense bush near the Maritsani, heaven only knows.

The dainty steinbok (*Nanotragus Tragulus*) and
the stealthy duyker (*Cephalopus Mergens*) were of
course always with us. I know no part of South
Africa where they are not to be found. Alike independent, or all but independent of water, they seem
to live and thrive as happily in the driest pastures of
the Kalahari, as in more favoured spots.

In the worst recesses of the North Kalahari " thirst
land," at a later period, I met with these antelopes
in astonishing numbers—astonishing, I mean, when
it is remembered that they run in pairs or singly,
and not in herds like the springbok. Common though
it is, the tiny steinbok, with its perfect form, brilliant
ruddy colouring, slender legs and feet, delicate head
and dark melting eyes, is not easily to be surpassed.

The little beauty is very wary and wide-awake, and—unless, as sometimes happens, it gives way to an overpowering curiosity—is not easily to be surprised. Its speed is something wonderful, and it takes a very smart greyhound indeed to run up to a steinbok. Rapidly though South Africa is becoming shot out, these two small antelopes will long survive, and at the present time they may be looked for all through Bechuanaland as a certain addition to the day's bag, even when bird-shooting, if the guns are held straight enough.

We had a few leopards prowling about the run. A prospector, who met a brace of them on the veldt, was nearly frightened out of his skin, and beat a hasty retreat, and one of the Gethins came across another in the bed of the Maritsani. Occasionally the "tigers," as all South Africans call them, came round the kraals at night; later on they killed three of the Gethins' goats at a sitting, but as a rule nothing was seen or heard of these nocturnal marauders. I remember them in the mountains of Cape Colony as far fiercer and more troublesome neighbours.

Hyænas (*Hyæna Crocuta* and *Hyæna Brunnea*)—always called wolves locally—still existed, but were not plentiful. After our departure, however, the elder Gethin had a valuable horse destroyed by one or more of these brutes. A spring-gun was set, but the hyæna escaped with the loss of part of a jaw, which it may be hoped put an end to its rapacious career.

That curious creature the aard-wolf (*Proteles Cristatus*), not a true hyæna, although related to this hideous family, is still plentiful in Bechuanaland;

and its handsome striped skin is much sought after
by the natives.

Jackals, whose eerie cry imparts a distinct access
of melancholy to the lonely veldt, were of course to
be heard at night. These and the hyænas feasted
right royally in May, when the carcasses of five or
six of our horses, which died of horse-sickness, had
to be abandoned to the veldt scavengers.

The silver jackal (*Canis Mesomelas*) or "pukuye"
of the Bechuanas, and the Cape fennec (*Megalotis
Capensis*), "motluse" of the Bechuanas, are both in
high request among the natives for the sake of their
skins, from which very beautiful karosses are made.
A large silver jackal kaross, composed of from twelve
to fourteen skins, costs even up-country as much as
from £4 to £6, 10s., that of the motluse rather less.
The hunting of jackals, leopards, caracals, and other
fur-producing animals, and the manufacture of their
skins into karosses—most beautifully sewn with fine
sinew—is, and has always been, a chief industry of
the Bechuanas.

The African cheetah (*Felis Jubata*), called by the
Boers oddly enough "luipard," in contradistinction
to the leopard, which they perversely designate
"tiger" (there is of course no tiger in Africa), is still
found in British Bechuanaland. There is not much
in common between the cheetah and the leopard,
although there is a rough family likeness. The markings differ widely if closely inspected; the cheetah
is much taller on the leg and more dog-like, and this
dissimilarity is more readily apparent by comparison
of the foot of either animal—which can be done at
the Zoological Gardens. The cheetah's foot is dog-
like in the sense that the claws are non-retractile;

the leopard's foot is of the strongest feline type, and the claws are sheathed and unsheathed at will. The South African cheetah is of a shy and secretive disposition and is seldom seen ; but the fact that its skin is pretty often procured by the natives (usually by snaring or by hunting with dogs), and frequently sold in karosses, is proof positive that its occurrence is less rare than many people imagine.

Another of the felidæ found commonly all over Bechuanaland, and highly valued for its skin, is the red-cat or African lynx (Rooi kat of the Boers ; Tuane of the Bechuanas; *Felis Caracal* of naturalists). A good red-cat kaross is always worth in Bechuanaland from £4 to £5.

There is a general tradition that the skin of this handsome animal is a certain remedy against rheumatism. Many people in the country swear by them and use them as blankets. I am inclined to think from personal experience that there is some peculiar virtue in a red-cat kaross. It is certain that the fur has a high faculty of attracting electricity. I remember travelling down by post-cart from Khama's with a red-cat kaross in my possession. During one night in particular the kaross was absolutely charged with electricity ; if one stroked the fur a sheet of sparks appeared in the darkness, and the crisp crackling was very remarkable. Probably this electrical tendency or capacity has something to do with the high reputation which this skin undeniably possesses throughout South Africa.

The skin of the serval (*Felis Serval*), a handsome tiger-cat, and of some of the viverridæ—among which the civets, genets, and meerkats (South African ichneumons) are to be found—are also much sought after by the natives for kaross-making. One of the handsomest karosses is made from the skins of the blotched genet (*Genetta Tigrina*), a very handsome clouded tabby. A good kaross of this skin sells readily up-country for £5 or £6.

The kaross industry is a traditional and very ancient one among the Bechuanas. Their skin cloaks in the old days were sought far and wide by other tribes. No other people can so deftly shape and sew them, few indeed attempt it. In the course of the year, among the various Bechuana tribes from the Zambesi to the Vaal River, karosses to the value of some thousands of pounds are sold to the up-country traders. Hunting and snaring is systematically conducted ; the long grass of the desert is periodically set on fire, so that hunting with dogs may be more readily pursued ; and throughout the Kalahari, the Vaalpense and Bushmen, vassals of the various Bechuana tribes, are always at work collecting skins, which in turn are gathered together by a chief or headman from headquarters on his annual visitation.

It is impossible to deal fully in these pages with the avi-fauna of Bechuanaland. A book of serious dimensions would be required for such a purpose. I can but briefly indicate here some of the more common of the innumerable forms of bird life which at all times were to be seen about us.

First let me note a few of the raptorial birds in which Bechuanaland, and indeed all Africa, is so particularly rich.

Vultures, true lovers of all broad and open countries, are, of course, to be seen when game is shot, or an ox or horse lies dead ; not, as I have seen it stated, " as thick as leaves in autumn," but in great numbers.

The commonest kinds are the sociable or black vulture,[1] (*Otogyps Auricularis*), zwart aasvogel of the Boers ; the common fulvus vulture (*Gyps Vulgaris*), aasvogel of the colonists ; and the white-headed vulture (*Vultur Occipitalis*) ; the small Egyptian vulture (*Neophron Percnopterus*), witte kraai (white crow) of the Boers, is also fairly common.

I do not think that these repulsive but useful birds can be found in any place more numerous or more destructive than in the flat country along the Lake River, Ngamiland. My hunting friend, Dove, and I had many instances of this. I remember well Dove one day shot a springbok, and, riding to the waggons, at once sent out some boys to fetch in the meat. When the boys arrived, in less than half-an-hour, there was not an atom of flesh and very little skin to be found—the vultures had left little but the clean picked bones. On another occasion my after-rider, Joseph, and I had each shot two giraffe in the space of fifteen minutes. I returned quickly to the two larger animals, which had been shot first, in order to skin and save the heads. Alas ! before I could return I saw, half-a-mile off, the vultures descending in swarms. To my intense disgust, on getting up I found the eyes and the large soft lips of the dead giraffes, the softest portions of the body, picked clean ; the heads were utterly spoilt for setting up, and I had to content myself with the feet, tails, and slabs of the immensely thick skin.

I have seen two large elands, as big as cows, picked clean in a few hours. The numbers and the eating capacities of these birds in a wild desert country—where I suppose they are not in the habit

[1] The plumage of this vulture is not black, but brown.

of dining each day punctually—seem to be illimitable. That vultures usually find their prey by sight and not by scent is, I think, utterly beyond question. Far up in the heavens, out of sight of the human eye, the great birds range and quarter the sky, far apart from and yet within sight of one another. When a death happens below, the nearest vulture instantly perceives it and sails down. His nearest neighbour, distant though he is, observes the signal with that wonderful sight of his, and straightway follows. He is succeeded by others ; the signal of death flies instantly through space, and scores upon scores of the voracious birds come swooping down to earth. Scent can have no possible part in the case of a dead animal lying upon open plains with vultures so far away in the sky as to be beyond the vision of man. That vultures, however, have some power of scent, and can upon suitable occasion use it, I have no doubt. Darwin, in his " Voyage of the Beagle," has some interesting notes on the condor of South America, all going to prove that these birds trust entirely to sight and not to their powers of scent.

We shot one or two specimens of the great zwart aasvogel at the Junction (at the time they were feeding on our dead horses), for the sake of the wings, which are magnificent. The length of this, the largest of all South African vultures, is 4 feet or thereabouts, the wing measures 2 feet 8 or 10 inches, and the spread of both when extended looks enormous. There are, I think, few finer or more suggestive sights in the natural world than a band of vultures soaring and circling far up in the blue atmosphere, watching some prey beneath. The majesty of their flight, the

wonderful ease and grace of their aerial circles,
sweeps, and whirls, are the very triumph of motion,
the perfection of sustained force.

Of eagles, the commonest throughout Bechuanaland is undoubtedly the Bateleur eagle (*Helotarsus
Ecaudatus*), notable for its jet-black body-colouring,
rufous back and tail—the latter curiously short and
stumpy—crested head, orange cere (the bare skin near
the base of the bill), and crimson feet. This bold,
fierce, and striking bird is usually to be seen soaring
over the broad plains, and makes its nest at the top
of the highest and thorniest acacia tree it can discover. Riding one day on the flats between Woodhouse Kraal and Setlagoli, we startled a sitting eagle
of this genus off her nest—a rough bundle of dry
sticks—and Mackay jumped off and immediately got
up the tree. He found one egg only, a large creamy
white one, and got for his pains a most terrible
scratching, the tree being a mass of thorns.

The Senegal eagle (*Aquila Senegalla*), sometimes
called the tawny eagle (*Aquila Nævioides*), a fine
eagle well known in Cape Colony, is also fairly
abundant in Bechuanaland. A small, handsome eagle
known as the spotted-breasted hawk-eagle (*Spizaëtus
Spilogastòr*) is not uncommon. We shot a good
specimen close to our huts at the Junction, and at
once identified it. The general colouring is dark
brown, much variegated with white. The under
parts are white, blotched and marked with dark
brown. The tail is grey, barred with brown and
white-tipped. The legs and thighs are white and
heavily feathered. The cere, feet, and eye are
greenish yellow. This eagle rarely exceeds 24 inches
in length—an inch or two less is a fair average.

E

The specimen shot at the Junction was perched on a dead tree, a habit to which this species is rather attached.

These three eagles and the African fishing eagle (*Haliaëtus Vocifer*), which latter was very abundant on the Botletli River at a later period, were the only four eagles specifically identified by me during this sojourn in South Africa. We often saw eagles far up in the sky, but were unable to identify them; and these great raptorial birds are not always anxious to offer themselves for a closer inspection.

The jackal buzzard (*Buteo Jackal*) and desert buzzard (*Buteo Desertorum*) are found in Bechuanaland, the latter plentifully. Of kites, the black kite (*Milvus Ater*) and the yellow-billed kite (*Milvus Parasiticus*) are plentiful. These birds appear just before the rains.

Hawks and falcons are too numerous to dwell upon, fascinating as are their appearance and habits. I had determined if possible to make a complete collection of the skins of Bechuanaland hawks. I began fairly well, but from loss of arsenical soap, the ravages of a small skin-destroying beetle, and white ants, and much moving about, I was forced to relinquish my task. I brought a few skins home, two of which, the many-zoned sparrow-hawk (*Accipiter Polyzonoides*) and the chanting hawk (*Melierax Musicus*), blue hawk of the colonist, are given in the frontispiece. Of these two, the beautiful little sparrow-hawk is of a dainty pearl-grey, the back and wings rather darker; the stomach is whitish, strongly banded with thin brown bars. The tail is long and white-tipped, and barred with brown. The cere and legs are yellow. This charming little hawk, which measures just under a foot in length, was shot near to our huts on the Maritsani. The chanting hawk (so christened more than a hundred years ago by Le Vaillant the French naturalist), a much larger hawk, extending to two feet in length, is also of a pearl-grey colouring, white as to the stomach, which is marked by brownish lines. The shoulders are lighter coloured, the rump white. It is easily identified by the larger wing feathers, which are black. This splendid member of the great family of falconidæ, which is common all over South Africa, was shot by Dove in a big camel-thorn tree at Mosita, sixteen miles west of our huts at the Junction.

Here, briefly, are some of the many hawks and falcons to be found in and near Bechuanaland, most of which at some time or another fell to our guns : Rufous-necked falcon (*Falco ruficollis*), shot by me on the Botletli River in July ; South African peregrinoid falcon (*Falco Minor*), a small edition of the well-known peregrine ; South African lanneroid falcon (*Falco biarmicus*) ; the hobby (*Hypotriorchis subbuteo*) ; western red-footed hobby (*Erythropus Vespertinus*), very plentiful during the rains ; grey-winged kestrel (*Tinnunculus cenchris*) ; lesser South African kestrel (*Tinnunculus rupicolus*), very common ; greater South African kestrel (*Tinnunculus rupicoloides*), shot by me at T'Klakane waterpits, North Kalahari ; Gabar hawk (*Melierax gabar*), common north and south of the Orange River ; Tachiro sparrow-hawk (*Accipiter Tachiro*) ; minulle sparrow-hawk (*Accipiter minullus*), identified in North Bechuanaland and on the Botletli River ; and, to complete my list, Swainson's harrier (*Circus Swainsonii*) and Le Vaillant's harrier (*Circus ran-*

ivorus), both seen near the Limpopo and Botletli
Rivers.

It must not be understood that this catalogue exhausts, or anything like exhausts, the falconidæ of
Bechuanaland and its adjacent territories, by which
I include the Kalahari and Botletli River countries.
It would be matter of impossibility, in so vast a
country, for a score of the most ardent collectors to
arrive at even an approximate list in the course of
several seasons. The difficulties of the country ; the
fact that one far oftener carries the rifle than the
shot gun, when in the game country ; and the differ-
ences in migrations caused by very wet or very dry
seasons, all have to be remembered. But this family
of the falconidæ is so full of interest and of beauty,
that it would be well worth the while of a collector
to devote himself to it alone during a whole season.
I am convinced that the result would add considerably to our existing knowledge of African raptorial
birds.

The curious secretary bird (*Sagittarius secreta-
rius*), that strange blending of the vulture, the falcon,.
and the bustard, is plentiful all over Bechuanaland.
Indeed, north of the Vaal River one is never very
long without seeing it. On one occasion Mackay,
St. Stephens, and myself were riding from St.
Stephens' camp to the Junction, accompanied by
several dogs. A secretary bird chased by the dogs,
after running very swiftly, at last got up, flew a
couple of hundred yards or so, dropped again, ran,
and was again put up by the dogs. This performance,
which took place upon a huge flat, went on during
an exciting chase of two miles or more, and, although
we had a good view of the run, bird and dogs got

right away from us. At length the secretary appeared completely exhausted, was run into by the leading dog (Ponto), and quickly killed by the pack (which included, I am sorry to say, two South African pointers), all of which seemed more or less ashamed of themselves when we galloped up. For curiosity's sake we opened the secretary, and found its stomach to contain the following items : One small tortoise (not yet dead), one mouse, four lizards, and a large quantity of locusts. There were no snakes or remains of snakes, nor were there any indications that the great bird had been recently feeding on hares or game birds, as has been often asserted. By this I do not wish to imply that the secretary bird does not eat serpents or the young of game ; it is certain that he often destroys the former, and in my judgment he is exceedingly likely to devour the latter. As neither I nor my friends are wilful slayers of these interesting birds, I should mention that we were powerless to prevent our dogs killing the secretary on this occasion. This bird is a poor flyer, and seldom makes use of his wings if he can help it. Occasionally he will take a little journey into the air with a snake in his beak, and, as on this occasion, when pursued will make a series of short, shallow flights, with intervals of running. I have never seen one indulge in long or sustained flight, nor do I think they are capable of it. Indefatigable walkers these birds certainly are ; and the solemn, business-like way in which they stalk the veldt is unmistakable even at a long distance.

Besides raptorial birds and the various game birds —of which I treat in Chapter XXII.—we had an infinite variety of bird life about us. I can only here make brief mention of a few of the more noticeable.

When we stepped out of our huts in the morning and strolled in our pyjamas for a few paces to look round and inhale the fresh, cool air and bid good-morning to the tame baboons, the first birds almost certain to meet our eyes were half-a-dozen tiny Namaqua doves (*Æna Capensis;* La Tourterette of Le Vaillant), which, with an assured sense of trust and safety, were to be found walking swiftly hither and thither in the sand just outside our kotla, picking up crumbs, grain, grass seeds, or whatever else they could find. Often they were inside the kotla at our very door. In the long list of African doves and pigeons there is none more dainty or more beautiful than this friendly, diminutive creature. Imagine a tiny dove of nine or ten inches in length, at least five of which go for tail, of the most daintily perfect form and carriage; ash-coloured as to its upper colouring; rich red as to the wing feathers, which are darkly edged with brown; bluish with purple spots as to the secondaries; the breast, throat, chin, and cheeks of glossiest jet black;[1] the tail successively barred in white, black, and again black; with purplish pink legs and feet, and pink and orange-tipped bill, and you have before you this matchless bird. The Namaqua dove spends much of its time upon the ground; at other times it is to be seen or heard in bushes and low trees, and its deep, tender "coo" is a sweet and welcome sound. Common as it is all over South Africa (we met with it with the keenest pleasure even by the far-off, isolated pools of

[1] I am describing the male bird, the female has less black about her.

the North Kalahari), it is universally admired. These birds are easily tamed, and I much regretted that my subsequent wanderings prevented my bringing a pair home with me.

In the camel-thorn groves near us were always to be seen numbers of interesting birds. Prominent among these were queer, bizarre hornbills and brilliant plumaged rollers—the latter invariably miscalled blue jays by up-country colonists. The yellow-billed hornbill (*Tockus flavirostris*) is pretty generally distributed throughout Bechuanaland in suitably woody localities. Its curious yapping cry, Toc-toc-toc, often repeated and varied, is soon familiar. In the Protectorate, after passing into the Bangwaketse country, the red-billed hornbill (*Tockus erythrorhynchus*) is also seen. This species, known to the Bechuanas as the korwe, nests in holes of the camel-thorn or mopani. The curious imprisonment of the hen bird of this and other hornbills on these occasions was first noticed by Livingstone. When she enters the hole or hollow place for incubation, the male bird carefully plasters up the entrance with mud, so that just enough space is left for feeding purposes, to which he devotes himself until the young are ready to fly. The natives are well aware of this habit, and proceed to capture the unfortunate hen bird, which from lack of exercise becomes plump and attractive, and, imprisoned as she is, falls an easy prey.

There are other instances of a like tyranny—for surely it is a species of tyranny—to the hen bird during the period of incubation and nursing. A small bird which often nests along the river beds of Bechuanaland and other parts of South Africa

undergoes a somewhat similar captivity.   This is the
Paroides Capensis or dwarf blossom-pecker, a tiny,
greenish-yellow bird of the titmouse family.   The
nest of this diminutive creature is a triumph of art.
It consists of some fluffy, cotton-like vegetable fibre,
usually of a whitish colour, woven into the consistency of strong felt.   The nest is oval-shaped, and is
securely fastened to a branch or twig ; the aperture
is about the centre of the nest, and consists of a small
pipe or spout, which is, it is said, in case of danger
pulled inside and closed at will.   Underneath this
is a sort of hollow or pocket, where the male bird
sits on guard during the period of incubation.   These
beautiful nests, of which we brought some specimens
home, are well known, and are regarded as curiosities
all over South Africa.   Although the hen bird thus
undergoes a weary imprisonment, both in the case
of the ugly huge-billed yet striking hornbill, and of
the tiny three-inch titmouse, the male bird has no
very good time of it either.   What with feeding the
broody lady before incubation, and herself and her
progeny afterwards, her husband has quite enough of
it, and, as is well known in the case of the hornbill,
becomes himself worn to a feeble shadow.

The rollers (so-called blue jays of the colonists),
with their flashing and most brilliant plumage of
greens, violets, lilac, rufous, and pale and dark blues,
and the curious rocking flight[1] from which they
take their name, are always familiar and welcome
objects in woody parts of Bechuanaland.   The bird
is a swift, often a high flyer, and not always
easily to be shot.   The lilac-breasted roller (*Coracias*

---

[1] This rocking flight has been very well compared by C. J. Andersson
to the motion of a boy's kite when falling to the ground.

Caudata), Moselikatse's bird, as some call it, was common about the Junction, even during the dry season.

Further up-country we often encountered another member of this family, the handsome white-naped roller (*Coracias Nuchalis*). Coming down by train from Vryburg to Kimberley during the tremendous rains of February 1891, I saw vast numbers of these same rollers—easily distinguished by their rufous colouring—between Taungs and Kimberley. Many were sitting on the telegraph wires and posts, and they were to be seen right away down to Kimberley. On inquiry I found that this unwonted migration had been observed by Kimberley people, and that the bird had before been little if ever noticed in these parts. I presume the abnormal summer rains of 1890–91 had brought them so far south.

Many members of that interesting family the shrikes are to be found in Bechuanaland. The most striking is the crimson-breasted shrike (*Laniarius atrococcineus*; korokoba of the Bechuanas), which is widely distributed in bushy localities. I found this bird fairly plentiful in some dense bush fringing a dry watercourse near Woodhouse Kraal. The brilliant crimson feathering which extends over the whole of the under part, from the throat to the tail, affords, I think, one of the finest bits of colour to be seen in bird life. The upper portions, including the parts immediately beneath the wings, are wholly black, with the exception of a white stripe running from the shoulder to the end of the wing. This and other members of the family have a clear and pleasing note. One of the helmet shrikes (*Prionops taleacoma*), a black and white bird, which is to be seen in small flocks, is reputed to be much attached to the Burchell zebras found further up-country—perching on their backs and titillating their skins after the manner of starlings with sheep at home.

The shrikes pursue in Africa their slaughtering habits much as does our butcher-bird in England. Further down in the Cape Colony there is a well-known shrike (*Lanius Collaris*), which goes among the Dutch by the name of the " Fiskal "—the Fiskal, or Crown-Prosecutor, being in the old days of the Batavian Government an officer by whose exertions criminals were brought to justice and executed. The ancient Dutch name is by no means a bad one, and the "execution dock" of this bird, consisting usually of thorns, aloe-spikes, and other engines of terror, whereon may be seen displayed beetles, locusts, snakes, and even mice and lizards, is surely calculated to drive fear into the minds of evil-doers, or well-doers either. This shrike is replaced in Bechuanaland by a very near relative, the coroneted shrike (*Lanius subcoronatus*), a bird equally as fierce and daring as its Cape congener, and only to be distinguished from it by the white marking upon the forehead and over the eye. The general upper colouring is dark brown, almost black, with a white V-like marking ; the under parts are drabbish white ; the tail feathers black and white. I have many times come upon the larder of these birds among the thorns of acacia bushes—a ghastly but interesting garniture.

In the giraffe-acacia forests near the Setlagoli and Maritsani rivers the huge grassy dwellings in which the social weaver-birds, sometimes called the social grosbeaks (*Philæterus socius*), make their colonies

in common were, I think, more abundant than in any
other part of the interior.   These collections of nests
consist of dense masses of long dry grasses heaped
upon the branches in the shape of a huge hay-cock.
The pile is firmly compacted, umbrella-like in shape,
and often covers the greater portion of the tree.   At
the bottom of this mass, where it is dressed to a flat,
even surface, the little brown weaver-birds pierce
their nests, a whole flock settling in one establishment.   This habitation presents a most curious
and striking spectacle.   As a resting-place pure and
simple, it probably forms one of the cosiest dwellings
used by feathered fowl; rain and even wind having
no terrors for the occupants.

Swallows and swifts are of course visitants in
Bechuanaland.   I saw little of them after the rains
of the beginning of 1890 until the wet season again
appeared at the end of the year.   The common
chimney swallow of Europe (*Hirundo rustica*) is a
well-known visitant to the extremity of Southern
Africa.   I think an even more beautiful bird is the
Cape swallow (*Hirundo Capensis*), whose colouring
is perfect in its way.   The back is blue-black; the
wings and tail are green-black; the head, rump,
neck-collar, breast, and stomach, are all of a rich
rufous-brown; and as the bird flashes hither and
thither, or sits upon some vantage coign near at
hand, one cannot sufficiently admire its colouring.
It is even more attached to the dwellings of mankind than its European cousin, and is a welcome
resident inside the house of many a Dutch colonist
in South Africa, where it usually fastens its nest to
the reed roof and centre beam.   To such a point is
the little favourite tolerated that a board is usually

fixed immediately beneath the nest so as to prevent fouling upon the dining-table, which happens often to stand immediately below. This swallow performs contract on its part by ridding the Dutchman's house of vast numbers of the swarms of flies with which it is infested. This is, I think, one of the few instances in which the Boer of South Africa is known to bestow any sort of care upon wild animal life, and in this rare instance it is manifestly for his own comfort.

One cannot help but look upon the swallows, even in Africa, as old friends. One connects them instinctively with the old country. Some of them, at least the red-throated ones, have winged their flight over the hot face of Africa from the far-off northern lands ; some of them may have built their nests beneath the brown thatched eaves, or round the storm-worn chimneys of some quiet English hamlet, nay, even perchance the very village in Northamptonshire one remembers from childhood ; some of them may have flitted, hawked, and played about the lush grasses, and dipped among the cool, golden buttercups of English meads. It is pleasant at all events to picture these things to one's mind as one rides amid the dry vast plateaux-lands or the sun-scorched karroos of Southern Africa.

Riding up from Vryburg to Setlagoli in March 1890, I saw many thousands of these Cape swallows seated upon the telegraph wires or flocking in the air. They were evidently collecting for their return to some other part of Africa. It is a singular fact that this swallow passes through Bechuanaland and other parts of the interior on its passage to the Cape, where it arrives in September. In Bechuanaland it does not settle until another month or two later.

The swifts, of which several kinds are to be seen in South Africa, are, like the swallows, only periodical visitants; but there is a very pretty martin, the fawn-breasted martin (*Cotyle fuligula*), which remains in South Africa all the year round.

Upon the same ride from Vryburg my attention was much attracted by the odd ways of a handsome lark (*Megalophonus apiatus*), well known to the Dutch colonists as the "clapert leeuwerk." This bird, which is found commonly upon the vast flats of Bechuanaland, is of a greyish upper colouring, handsomely marked in red, dark brown, black and white, and has a brown speckled, pale-yellowish breast. Its habit is most singular. It rises close to the passer-by suddenly and without warning from the long grass, and, beating its wings so violently that quite a loud clapping is heard, flies upward straight as a line for twenty or thirty feet, then gives one long whistle and falls to earth as quickly as it rose. This seems to the traveller rather an idiotic performance, yet the lark probably has good reason for it. I can come to no other conclusion than that this habit is purely one of defiance. Larks are notoriously pugnacious birds, and the "clapert leeuwerk's" noisy little flight may be nothing more than an intimation of displeasure at intrusion upon the wastes it loves to frequent, or a challenge to mortal combat.

"God's poets," as some one (Mortimer Collins, I think) has well called the singing birds, are not proportionately anything like so numerous in Africa, or of such beautiful voices, as are our songsters at home. Radiancy of colouring here, as in other hot countries, too often goes with a voiceless or harsh-throated bird. Yet now and again, especially about

the season of the rains, one hears a beautiful song
or an exquisite note. . When the melody is heard,
it may be attributed pretty safely to one of the
warblers or reed-warblers, perchance even the European warbler, which is found thus far south; or to
the wheatears, larks, thrushes, or Berg canaries; or
perhaps it belongs to a drongo or white-browed
widow-bird.

Among the many varieties of birds to be found in
Bechuanaland at various seasons and places, besides
those I have mentioned, there are owls, night-jars,
kingfishers, sun birds, woodpeckers, honey guides,
cuckoos (among which appears the European cuckoo,
Cuculus canorus), crows (chiefly black and white),
herons, storks, cranes, plovers, many of the snipe
family (*Scolopacidæ*), wagtails, bulbuls, orioles, fly-
catchers, weaver birds, finches, sparrows, grosbeaks,
and many others.

More than twenty-five years ago, when the countries north of the Orange River were comparatively
little known, Mr. E. L. Layard had catalogued and
described, in his excellent " Birds of South Africa," no
less than 702 species occurring south of the twenty-
eighth parallel of south latitude.   If his labours could
have been continued to the present day and extended
as far as the Zambesi, the list would possibly be
nearly doubled.

Andersson's " Birds of Damaraland " (which includes other adjacent countries of South-west Africa),
published in 1872, shows a list of 428 birds, many of
which are, of course, included in Layard's catalogue.
Before I conclude these notes on avi-fauna, let me
say that no wayfarer in South Africa, who takes an
interest in bird life, should be without these two

books as references. They will be found most useful, and will often settle to his satisfaction a perplexing point in identity.

Although South Africa is fairly supplied with snakes, they appear in nothing like the abundance of India, nor do people trouble themselves very much about them. Towards the beginning of winter, *i.e.*, about the month of May, when nightly frosts appear, they seem to vanish from the scene almost entirely. From the end of May to the end of September, when traversing the vast stretch of country between Mafeking and the Botletli River, I saw positively only one snake—and that a small one, encountered on the flats bordering the Lake River. On the other hand, in February, March, and April, round about our huts at the Junction, serpents of various kinds had been pretty numerous.

We had an old kraal fence of thorn-bush near to us, which, I think, harboured, as these fences always will do, a good many of these undesirable neighbours. One morning we killed a large green tree-snake in the thatch of our stable. Curiously enough—as bearing out the familiar Afrikander theory that a dead snake will always attract its fellow—on the very next day a scuffle was heard among our dogs in a piece of bush a few yards away from our living hut, and, on running out, there was a magnificent tree-snake, in all the radiance of its wonderful grass-green colouring, standing up fiercely and showing fight. Quickly arming ourselves with sticks, we put an end to its career.

These green tree-climbers, which extend to seven or eight feet in length, and taper off greatly towards the tail, are, I think, the most active among African snakes. Their movements are lightning-like. I once saw a dog pick one up and run with it. The movements of that snake were astounding; it seemed to flash every way, and when it freed itself temporarily (it was killed with a waggon whip afterwards), its pace was positively terrific. This snake (*Bucephalus viridis*) is usually called a mamba in Bechuanaland, and is looked upon as highly poisonous. In reality it is no mamba at all, I believe, and from the conformation of its head, I doubt very much if it is poisonous. At the same time, I would not care to test the question in a practical manner upon myself. But the fact that the dog I speak of ran at least a hundred yards with one of these snakes in its mouth, the said snake striking all the time at its captor, and the dog afterwards taking no hurt whatever, offers strong presumption of the harmlessness of this brilliant reptile. Another species of tree-snake (*Bucephalus Capensis*) of a less brilliant colouring is occasionally met with.

The puff-adder (*Vipera arietans*) is common in Bechuanaland, as elsewhere in South Africa. Fortunately this deadly snake is excessively sluggish in its habits, and can be easily avoided, and as easily killed. On the other hand, its colour is strongly protective, and it is very fond of lying about on roads and paths, partially buried in the sand, and at night especially is liable to be trodden upon with dire results.

It is very amusing to see a swarm of small birds fluttering and chattering around their common enemy with a strange blending of anger and fear. Our attention was called in this way to a puff-adder close to our huts; and the snake was quickly put an end to and bottled in Boer brandy. The hideous, broad, flattened head, and vile, wicked eye of this loathsome reptile convey instantly to the beholder the patent warning of its deadly poisoning powers.

The African cobra (*Naja Haje*), which varies in colour from yellowish to a dark brown—almost black at times—is tolerably common. After rain, we occasionally found them indulging in tepid baths in the shallow pools and vleis near the river-bed. These are active, and at times rather aggressive snakes, and they too are deadly poisonous. The darker varieties of this cobra are usually called black mambas. I believe this to be a mistake. I have had no experience of the dreaded mambas of Natal (green or black), but I am inclined to think they are not identical with the so-called mambas of Bechuanaland, which are, in fact, the green tree-snake and the dark-brown cobra.

The ring-hals (*Sepedon hœmachatis*); the schaap-sticker (sheep sticker) (*coluber Rhombeatus*); the horned viper, " hornjesmann " of the Boers (*Vipera cornuta*); and the Berg adder or Cape adder (*Vipera atropos*), are also met with. A pretty and very slender riband snake is sometimes to be seen crawling about the branches of bush and shrubbery. Once, while out bird-shooting, I all but ran into one as I went to pick up a winged partridge. I had the pleasure—for I believe in destroying snakes whenever and wherever met with—of blowing the reptile to atoms a moment afterwards; although I am not at all certain that this is a poisonous species. The protective colouring of this slim serpent, its greenish-yellow and black riband markings, harmonising as they do very wonderfully with the foliage among

F

which it creeps, renders it often a hard matter to pick out.[1]

Huge pythons—called by the natives tāri—which are possessed of a certain amount of constrictive power and are dangerous to small antelopes and such-like animals on which they prey, are occasionally met with. We had them about the Maritsani, but in spite of their bulk and length—they attain as much as twenty feet—they have a strange faculty of concealment, and are seldom seen. Two were shot upon our land during two years. One of these was found with a partially digested steinbok in its interior. Another, shot by Mr. P. Gethin near the huts after our departure, measured over sixteen feet in length.

When, I wonder, is a reliable antidote against the terrors of snake-poisoning to be given to the world? I noticed not long since that Dr. Calmettes, residing at Saigon in Cochin China, had, as it was stated, proved to demonstration that subcutaneous injection of chloride of gold, applied before apoplectic symptoms supervene, is an infallible remedy. One would like to hear more about this. On the other hand, one cannot always carry about, or even procure, chloride of gold and an injector when far away up-country in the African veldt. In the case of the bite of a healthy puff-adder, I fear the apoplectic symptoms would supervene long before one's camp or waggon could be reached; probably ten minutes or a quarter of an hour would suffice in an extreme case against all the remedies in the world.

---

[1] I am by no means certain that this slender riband-snake may not turn out to be merely the young of a tree-snake. A plate in Smith's "Zoology of South Africa" gives me this impression.

As a matter of fact, I may mention for the comfort of intending colonists or settlers that the yearly butcher's bill from snake-bite in South Africa is an absurdly small one, and stout boots and pigskin gaiters are perhaps the very best all-round safeguards that can be suggested. Croft's Tincture, an old and tried South African remedy, is really, I believe, efficacious if used in time, and a bottle can always be kept at hand in the hut or waggon. A bottle or two of neat brandy or whisky, administered as rapidly as may be, is one of the soundest remedies against snake poison, and is the antidote usually resorted to by the Dutch farmers.

Of insects we had naturally many kinds about us. Saving, however, the house-fly, which during the hot season—and especially just before the rains fall— is somewhat of a trial, insects are not a supreme source of trouble in Bechuanaland. Many of them, indeed, are of great interest, and well repay a little observation. The curious praying mantis, or Hot-tentot god, as it is often called, perched upon the dining-table for the benefit of the company, fre-quently afforded us immense amusement. This insect belongs to the *Phasmidæ*, in which are in-cluded the leaf, spectre, and walking-stick insects, a numerous family in Africa. Some of these insects, nearly allied to the praying mantis, so exactly resemble a blade of grass that until one touches them it is impossible to say which is grass or which insect. The reverential way in which the praying mantis elevates his fore-limbs as if in the very attitude of prayer, is excessively comic. Spiders, trap-door spiders, and the lightning-like scorpion-spiders; the scavenger-beetle, perpetually collecting and pushing

away with her hind legs the round ball of dry dung
in which she deposits her eggs; ant-lion flies; the
noisy cicada, with its ceaseless, irritating, hurdy-
gurdy-like refrain; locusts and occasional bees, wasps,
and hornets—these of course we had with us.

Beetles are a very numerous and very interesting
order. An unpleasant-looking creeping thing clad
in a shiny black, shell-like skin, and provided with
an immense number of legs, is the *Spirostreptus
gigas*, a sort of smooth, enormous caterpillar which
is very common in Bechuanaland. The poor thing
is perfectly harmless, uncanny-looking though it is.
Poisonous centipedes are occasionally heard of, but
are not very common. A certain large hairy spider
is also commonly reported to be poisonous and is
much dreaded, whether with reason I know not.

Compared with tropical America, the hotter portions of Asia, and the Malay Archipelago, Africa is
at very considerable disadvantage in its display of
butterfly life. And especially in beauty of form and
gorgeousness of colouring is this the case. However,
as Mr. Roland Trimen in his great work on South
African butterflies has shown that the Ethiopian
region produces something over one thousand known
species, the average collector is pretty sure to find
here and there brilliant specimens of rhopalocera,
and a sufficient number and variety to interest and
amuse him in almost every part of Austral Africa.
But south of the Zambesi no very rare prizes are to
be expected. The area of distribution is very wide,
and a butterfly captured in some remote region,
reached with infinite toil and danger, is pretty sure
to be found, on the traveller's return to civilisation,
to be referable also to some easily accessible part of

the country. No doubt as the Zambesi and other river systems of South Central Africa are opened up, some new and valuable forms will be discovered. But hitherto the remoter districts have not yielded the rich stores of butterfly-life that might perhaps have been anticipated.

In Bechuanaland in the early part of 1890 we were unfortunate in having short summer rains and a prolonged drought, and butterflies were therefore rather scarcer than usual; we collected, however, in British Bechuanaland, at odd times, and in a very desultory fashion, a good many specimens of the following seventeen species, as well as a few moths :—

1. *Danais Chrysippus* (Linnæus)—
   A large, handsome, reddish-brown butterfly, with black margined wings and white spots towards the tips of the fore wings. Common all over Africa.

2. *Acræa Neobule* (E. Doubleday)—
   A curious reddish butterfly, variegated with black spots; the fore wings nearly transparent and with little colouring.

*3. *Pyrameis Cardui* (Linnæus)—
   The well-known "Painted Lady" of England; found all over the world.

4. *Junonia Cebrene* (Trimen)—
   A very handsome, but very common butterfly. Colours, black and ochreous yellow; a fine circular patch of metallic violaceous blue on the black of each hind wing.

*5. *Hypanis Ilythia* (Drury)—
   Rich yellowish brown, with very handsome black markings.

6. *Lycæna Mahallokoœna* (Wallengren)—
   A small, pretty, bluish-violet butterfly; the fore wings mainly yellowish-buff. Female dark brown.

7. *Lycæna Trochilus* (Freyer)—
   A tiny brown butterfly, carrying a patch of yellow on the hind wings.

*8. *Terias Zoë* (Hopffer)—
>   Bright yellow ; deep black border markings. Medium size. Female paler.

9. *Pieris Mesentina* (Cramer)—
>   White, with slight black border markings. Female yellowish.

*10. *Herpœnia Eriphia* (Godart)—
>   White, with strong black markings. Female yellowish. A striking butterfly, resembles the "marbled white" of England.

*11. *Teracolus Eris* (Klug)—
>   White, with yellowish and violet tips. Female yellowish and without the violet.

*12. *Teracolus Evenina* (Wallengren)—
>   White, with strong orange tips ; a dark longitudinal stripe in both wings ; a beautiful butterfly. Female, orange tips duller, black markings stronger.

*13. *Teracolus Antigone* (Boisduval)—
>   White, with orange-pinkish tips, black markings. Female yellowish, the orange tips paler.

*14. *Callidryas Florella* (Fabricius)—
>   All greenish white. Size about that of the English "Sulphur." A very swift flyer.

15. *Papilio Demaleus* (Linnæus)—
>   A large, handsome butterfly. Colour black, strongly variegated with pale sulphur. Two "eyes" of red, black and blue upon each hind wing.

16. *Papilio Constantinus* (Ward)—
>   A still larger brownish-black butterfly, strongly marked with pale sulphur stripes and spots. Hind wings tailed. Somewhat resembles the swallow-tail of Europe. A striking butterfly ; not common. A Bechuanaland specimen in my possession measures more than $3\frac{1}{4}$ inches across the wings.

17. *Hesperia Forestan* (Cramer)—
>   One of the well-known "Skippers." A dull brownish butterfly ; the hind wing darker and with a tinge of yellow.

In addition to the above butterflies, Dove and I captured in June 1890 at the pits of T'Klakane in the North Kalahari, between the Zambesi road and the Botletli River, several good specimens of

Acræa Aglaonice (Westwood)—
> A handsome species, bright brick-red and slightly tawny in colour, lightly margined and spotted with black, and having towards the apex of each fore wing a curious small transparent patch.

This is a scarce butterfly, and we esteemed ourselves lucky to have captured specimens in so dry and remote a part of the country and in mid-winter. These were almost the only butterflies seen by us during the whole of our shooting trip to the Botletli River during the months of June, July, August, and September. At present this handsome *Acræa* seems only to have been obtained from Lydenburg, Transvaal, by Mr. T. Ayres; from the Marico and Limpopo Rivers by Mr. Selous; and from Tati, Matabeleland, by the late Mr. Frank Oates, who first discovered it. I have two excellent specimens, both males, in my possession, and my friend has one or two also, all taken at T'Klakane.

The three moths captured were as follows :—

1. *Acherontia Atropos*—
> The well-known Death's-Head Moth. A specimen taken at Vryburg seemed to resemble precisely that of Europe.

*2. *Sphingomorpha Sipyla* (Variety A. of Guenee)—
> One of the great division of *Noctuæ*, family *Ophinoidæ*.

3. *Deiopeia Pulchella*—
> Fore wings white, minutely speckled with crimson and black; hind wings white, with irregular brownish-black outer borders. This pretty moth is identical with the "Crimson-speckled Footman" of England. Taken at the Junction Maritsani River.

Of the above twenty-one species of butterflies and moths, those marked with an asterisk were captured in the true Kalahari region between Mosita and Morokweng, in the western portion of what is now called British Bechuanaland, and were handed to Mr. Roland Trimen of the South African Museum, Cape Town. Most of these species were taken also on the Maritsani River, and in other parts of Bechuanaland. *Danais Chrysippus* and *Junonia cebrene* were seen plentifully in the same country between Mosita and Morokweng. I should perhaps remark that these were not all the butterflies we *saw*, but all we *caught*; very often we had no net with us.

Of these butterflies, the *Danais* and the *Acræa* are remarkable as being protected members of the much-persecuted *Lepidoptera*, an order cruelly preyed upon by many birds and insects and some reptiles—as lizards. These insects, owing to a certain disagreeable odour and flavour of their own, are left severely alone, and, indeed, are plainly avoided as uneatable.

Their remarkable immunity is intensified in another way; and here that wonderful faculty of protective mimicry (now so clearly established, thanks chiefly to the labours of Bates, Wallace, Darwin, Trimen, and others) steps in.

Recognising the immunity of these distasteful and so protected butterflies, other butterflies, which of themselves in their normal state have no protection, cunningly, and with the mysterious aid of Nature, shelter themselves from pursuit by assuming or mimicking the colours of the protected forms. The late Mr. H. W. Bates discovered many instances—thirty-six in all, I think—of this protective mimicry among tropical American butterflies. Mr. Roland

Trimen has done much the same among the butterflies of South Africa.   His recent magnificent monograph of course deals very fully and very ably with
these extraordinary phenomena.   Thus he shows in
his interesting table of cases that the common *Danais
Chrysippus* is mimicked for protective purposes by
the female of *Diadema Misippus* (Linn.), as well as
by a papilio (*Papilio Cenea*), also a female.   Further,
that one of the *Acreinæ* (*Acræa Acara*) is mimicked in
a similar manner by a butterfly of another genus, now
known as *Pseudacræa Trimenii*.   In this case both
male and female of the mimicked butterfly are copied
by the male and female of the mimicker.   In another
instance the male and female of *Planema Aganice*—
also one of the *Acreinæ*—is mimicked by two butterflies, *Pseudacræa Imitator*, and *Pseudacræa Tarquinia;* but, curiously enough, although in the case
of the *Imitator* both male and female mimic, in the
case of the *Tarquinia* the male only assumes the
protective garb.

The case of the *Papilio Cenea* is certainly most
wonderful.   She is not content with mimicking one
protected form, but imitates, and most closely, three,
viz.: *Amauris Echeria, Amauris Dominicanus*, and
Danais Chrysippus.   And to do this, besides assuming utterly different colours from the normal, she
actually discards the long, broad, notable tail with
which her male is provided.   Mr. Trimen considers
this, and I think with justice, the most remarkable
instance of mimicry yet recorded among butterflies.

The case is rendered yet more notable by the fact
that at Lake Tsana, in Abyssinia, the male and female
of *Papilio Merope* (of which our mimicking friend
Papilio Cenea is the South African representative)

are garbed alike. In Abyssinia it would thus appear, as Mr. Trimen points out, that the instinct of protective mimicry is not required or exerted. All this is very wonderful, and minutely illustrates the extraordinary methods by which Nature performs her work.

Geographical distribution seems among butterflies to be just as capricious as with mammals. During the whole fifteen months I was in Bechuanaland I never once set eyes on a handsome, speckled, brownish-grey butterfly known as *Hamanumida Dædalus*—the guinea-fowl butterfly, I may call it; and yet on a trip into the Marico country, only some thirty-five miles from Mafeking across the Transvaal border, we found them plentifully near Zeerust. We only had our hats, but managed to capture a few specimens as they settled on the road in some charming park-like country beyond Zeerust. Widely distributed though these butterflies are in other parts of Africa, they are not common south of the Zambesi.

We had many very beautiful *Palpares* in the long grass about our huts on the Maritsani. The delicate pinks and greens, variegated with black markings, of the transparent wings of these flies, which are similar in size to a large dragon-fly at home, are very remarkable. Unfortunately, after death these lovely colours usually fade completely away, much to the chagrin of the collector.

Let me add here, for the benefit of the uninitiated, that by far the best and simplest way to pack and preserve butterflies is to enclose them, with the wings folded together above the body, in little three-cornered envelopes, which can be made of any odd

pieces of clean paper cut rather oblong. As these
envelopes are filled and collected they should be
placed on edge in a tin tobacco or biscuit box until
they are fairly tightly packed. Then put in some
camphor, or sprinkle lightly with weak carbolic acid,
and send home. Butterflies posted by me in this way
travelled excellently, and were in good condition on
their arrival in England. Beetles are best packed in
sawdust sprinkled with spirit and carbolic acid, and
enclosed also in a well-fitting tin box.

We were a good deal disappointed in the Bechuanaland flora. No doubt the dry country and the exceptionally rainless season had something to account
for. But the wealth of flowers so noticeable at
certain seasons in Cape Colony was here lacking.
True, after rain there were fine crops of pink and
white lilies in the vleis and marshy places. At the
junction of the Mesemi spruit with the Maritsani this
was especially noticeable, and, during the tremendous rains of 1890–91, I noticed vast spaces in the
alluvial·valley of the Harts River made brilliant by
these handsome lilies. We had also some huge and
handsome bulbous flowers—*Amaryllis toxicaria* and
Amaryllis Brunsvigia multiflora—scattered about
the veldt.

But of smaller and humbler flowers there was little
display. A pretty, creeping, scarlet-coloured verbena
was to be seen in April, and there were a few tiny
lobelias and pansies, some asters, and a handsome
violet marguerite with a yellow centre. The blossom
of the various acacias (usually called mimosas in
South Africa, but true acacias in reality), and especially of *Acacia horrida*, *Acacia Giraffæ*, and *Acacia
Detinens* (the common acacia, the camel-thorn, and

the wait-a-bit), are, just before the rains fall, very
beautiful in colour and scent.   In the forest country
at this season vast tracts are perfumed with the
strong, sweet scent of these acacias.   The Vaal-bush
blossom, too, has a sweet and powerful scent.   But
there was little else to be seen, save the dwarf aloes,
which in the driest soil flourished and put forth their
red flowers.

Ixias, stapelias, convolvuli, cucurbits, commelynas,
bean-flowers, wild indigo, clematis, hybiscus, helio-
phila, squills, and many others are to be found ; but
I was not fortunate enough to observe them in bloom.
In the mountains of the Protectorate no doubt there
is a greater wealth of flora ; but here again I travelled,
unluckily, only in the parched season of winter.

Bulbous plants certainly hold their own in the dry
uplands of Bechuanaland, as in other parts of Africa.
Some of these, especially the magnificent *Amaryllis
Brunsvigia*, are enormous, and may be seen half-
protruding from the veldt as big as a man's head
and bigger.   In so vast a country, flowers, however
numerous, can make but a comparatively scant show.
We English people are too apt to measure the floral
capacity of a country by picked specimens crammed
into a hot-house, or by the blaze of colour contained
on the confined space of lawn-beds and parterres.   To
such the illimitable wilds of a sunburnt country, re-
splendent only for a brief season during and after the
rains, are disappointing indeed.   Again, the vegetation of Bechuanaland is essentially different from the
growths peculiar to the Karroo systems of Cape
Colony ; and the spectacle of miles upon miles of
plains carpeted with glowing masses of flowers (for
the most part flame-coloured or purple), sometimes

to be seen for a brief space after heavy rain on the
Great Karroo and in the wilds of Little Namaqualand,
are in Bechuanaland not to be looked for. The soils
of the Karroo and of Bechuanaland are widely different; the one being usually hard, sun-baked, and
impervious; the other friable, sandy, and pervious
to water.

A sharp and very penetrating kind of spear grass
is often very troublesome to the ankles and legs of
the pedestrian, unless clad in boots and gaiters; and
the well-known burr-weed (*Xanthium Spinosum*) has
proved so great a pest to stock farmers that special
regulations are enacted for its destroyal.

The wild bitter water-melon is often seen trailing
about the veldt. In the dry wastes of the Kalahari
this plant has many a time and oft saved the lives of
men and cattle when no water was to be found, and
by its aid many otherwise inaccessible portions of the
desert are hunted and passed through, especially in
good years, when the melon is plentiful. The fruit
is bitter as gall, but full of juice, and a variety of it is
systematically cultivated by the Bechuanas in their
mealie and corn gardens. The sight of these gardens
after the corn harvest, when the huge melons cumber
the earth in hundreds, is a remarkable one. Even of
these semi-cultivated melons only a small proportion
are sweet; the bulk being bitter and unpalatable
to Europeans.

Dr. Burchell, who travelled in South Bechuanaland
so far back as 1812, is one of the few people who
have attempted any classification of the flora of this
country; and his labours were necessarily incomplete
and scanty. A perusal of his travels is, however,
well worth attempting, if only for the sake of the

curious old coloured plates and woodcuts scattered about the book.

Before concluding these rough notes on natural history, I must add a few lines in which to describe our only pets, two tame baboons, named respectively Jack and Jenny.   Jack and Jenny were usually fastened by long riems of hide to a couple of stout posts close to the huts.   They were vastly comical and diverting, and afforded us not a little amusement.   Jack, with his harsh, grunting voice, was always ready to answer us if we called to him; and at sunrise he and Jenny, perched on the top of their posts, surveying the country, and basking in the warm rays, were among the first to greet us.   There is no better watch-dog in the world than a baboon. Nothing escapes his quick eye and ear.   Jack, from his perch, especially watched the road from Setlagoli to our camp, and, long before we had any idea of an arrival, his grunts and barks and excited gestures told us of the approach of messengers or visitors.

Baboons are pretty omnivorous, and these two were no exception to this rule.   We usually fed them on mealies, boiled or unboiled; occasionally porridge was given them; sometimes a piece of meat, or a bone or two, as a treat; but their greatest luxury consisted of slices of water-melon, which they devoured with characteristic greed and rapidity. With tit-bits of this sort Jack always got, if he could, the lion's share; and Jenny at these times, unless Jack was closely watched, invariably suffered.   In the same way Jack was always to be found on winter mornings with Jenny's piece of sacking spread over his shoulders as well as his own, until we put them further apart.   In simian life it is to be feared that the weaker sex suffer as much in these ways as too often do their sisters of the human race. And yet poor Jenny was greatly attached to Jack, and, with all his faults, loved him well.

Although tame enough with us, Jack was rather a rough playmate, with whom few liberties could be allowed. He had a trick of suddenly springing on to one's head from his lofty perch, and if any symptoms of fear were shown, especially by strangers, as likely as not he (and Jenny too) would inflict a severe nip. The teeth and jaws of these creatures are tremendous, and much to be dreaded. Fortunately, Jack and Jenny had a wholesome respect for white men much more than for black, curiously enough—and, if treated firmly and without any show of shrinking, could always be handled and petted. Of petting, stroking, and scratching they were extremely fond, and on such occasions would chatter and grunt with unconcealed pleasure. It is worthy of note that they were both beautifully clean and sweet, and their thick coats were always in magnificent condition.

Sometimes we unhitched their riems and led them for a walk on the veldt. At these times they always dragged us towards the Vaal-bushes, where a plentiful feast of sweet berries awaited them. Other berries, seeds, and bulbs, were eagerly picked up and devoured on these rambles. The seed-vessel of the trailing grapple-plant (*Uncaria procumbens*) was always spotted, dexterously ripped open with the teeth, and, the contents being extracted, the pod was cast carelessly aside. In these laughable yet instructive lessons in botany our baboons played the part of Aristotle, we humans following behind humbly

seeking to qualify ourselves as Peripatetics.   In the
science of what to eat and what to avoid, Jack and
Jenny were true philosophers.

Our dogs never could make friends with the
baboons, both of which manifested an intense jealousy
of them, and rushed savagely at them if they ever
approached their limited domains.   Jack and Jenny
were always secretly scheming and labouring to un-
fasten their hide riems.   On the rare occasions on
which they succeeded they straightway made for the
store hut, which they knew intimately well, and
played havoc with flour, sugar, and other luxuries.
Once, after an unusually destructive raid, our predecessors were so enraged that they sentenced the
marauders to banishment to their natural veldt.
The baboons were accordingly put on the waggon
and driven some twelve or fifteen miles away to a
bushy part of the country, where they were cast
loose.   But the rôle of "babes in the wood" little
suited the ideas of these clever apes.   They scorned
the wild veldt and its privations, and remembered
the good dinners and the never-failing flesh-pots of
civilisation.   Next morning, to the horror of the
camp, Jack and Jenny were found to have returned,
and, worst of all, to have passed most of the night
in rifling the sugar and flour sacks.

After this escapade they were perforce forgiven
—their captors were loth to shoot them—and their
bonds were made more secure.   When we left the
Junction, Jack and Jenny were taken over by the
Gethins as dependants of the estate.   Unhappily
Jack's behaviour grew rapidly worse.   Gethin had
often to be away from the huts ; Jack would take advantage of these absences, free himself, and proceed

to besiege Mrs. Gethin in her hut. He would climb the chimney, and from there threaten and terrify her. He seemed to comprehend his power ; and Mrs. Gethin's baby was, naturally enough, a constant source of anxiety to her on these occasions.

At last matters came to a climax. Gethin came home after an unusually threatening state of siege, and Jack was incontinently shot. Within a week Jenny, who was comparatively inoffensive and never aided Jack in his attacks, pined away, refused to eat, and died also. It was a singular and touching end, and illustrated aptly enough the theory that brutes upon occasion can and do feel acutely.

Alas! for our clever and amusing baboon friends ; they were pleasant in their lives, and in death they were not divided.

CHAPTER IV.

A DAY WITH THE SHOT GUNS

Difficulties of commissariat—Scarcity of sheep and goats—Trip to St. Stephens' camp—Orange River francolins—Black and white bustards —South African pointers—Sport along the Maritsani—Concerning hares—Bag a "legovaan" or monitor—Curious incident—Its habits —Midday rest — Birds around us — Afternoon sport — Among the koorhaans—Our bag.

ALTHOUGH one may live in Bechuanaland in close proximity to native kraals and cattle posts, where goats and cattle are run in considerable numbers, it is often a matter of extreme difficulty to procure butcher's meat. In a scattered community and under a hot sun beef is usually out of the question, for an ox is worth from £4, 10s. to £7 ; and among a small party it would be gross extravagance to sacrifice an animal, the meat of which must of necessity be more than half wasted. The Bechuana hates breaking into his flocks ; his wealth lies in their numbers, and if he is induced to sell a goat or two, or a native sheep now and again, he drives an uncommonly hard bargain. I have paid (through the nose, of course) as much as 15s. and £1 for a miserable goat or sheep worth at the outside from 5s. to 7s. While sojourning temporarily in our huts at the junction of the Setlagoli and Maritsani rivers, I and my companions were often driven to our wits' end to procure meat. The few months of our stay at this place rendered the acquisition of flocks and herds of

our own undesirable, and although now and again
we succeeded in collecting a few goats about us, as
a rule our "scatter guns" had to be constantly
carried, to keep the pot filled for the evening and the
morning meals. The native or fat-tailed sheep are
found in Bechuanaland in but small numbers, while
merino sheep are at present few and far between.
Bechuanaland is a new country, and the latter breed
is hardly yet acclimatised, although here and there
upon a few farms, after heavy losses for a year or
two, the corner has been turned, the flocks from
down country have overcome the trials of a virgin
veldt, and their successors are now doing well.

Early in April, Dove having recently arrived from
the Cape, he, Mackay, and myself settled to pay St.
Stephens a visit, and have a turn at the partridges
and koorhaan, which on that portion of the Maritsani
were extremely plentiful. We rode off early on the
morning of March 31, with our shot guns and a
brace of pointers, and, here and there pausing for a
shot on the way, reached Hutton Farm with a leash
of partridge, a brace of koorhaan, and one hare.
Taking a short turn round St. Stephens' camp just
before sundown, we added to the bag by two brace
of partridge, one koorhaan, and one hare before
supper. Here let me remark that the so-called
"partridge" are not true partridges, but the Orange
River francolin (*Francolinus gariepensis*), a very
handsome partridge-like game bird, found in abundance all over Bechuanaland and part of the Kalahari Desert. I have found them as far north as
the Botletli River, Ngamiland; and the late C. J.
Andersson has recorded them in Great Namaqualand
and Damaraland. These Orange River francolins

bear a strong resemblance to the redwing partridge
of the Cape Colony (*Francolinus Levaillantii*)—so
much so, that they are usually termed "redwing"
even in Bechuanaland—but the species are distinct,
the colouring of the Cape bird is darker and redder,
while in size the Orange River francolin has a slight
advantage. These striking game birds love grassy
slopes, low stony kopjes, and the light bush and
shrubbery fringing the banks of dry rivercourses.
They are excellent eating, fleshy, and well tasted, if
slightly dry, as with most African game; but after
an hour's simmering in the stew-pot they are all
that can be desired, and help to eke out the scanty
menu of many an up-country traveller. Their call, a
sharper and shriller rendering of that of the English
partridge, to which, however, it bears a distinct
family likeness, is one of the most familiar of up-
country sounds at sunrise and sundown, and once
heard can never be quite forgotten. The coqui francolin, another "partridge," we found more plentiful
further north and west.

The koorhaan I have referred to is the black and
white bustard (*Eupodotis afroides*), and is a very
near relative of the black koorhaan of the Cape
Colony. Indeed, save that one lives south, the other
north of the Orange River, and the quill feathers of
the northern bird have a large and noticeable splash
of white upon them instead of being all black, as
in the Cape Colony species, there is scarcely a point
of difference between them. Both are insufferably
noisy, both are to the gunner exasperating in the last
degree, and will, time after time, disturb the veldt
for the space of a square mile or more with their
harsh scolding cackle, which is delivered incessantly

as they rise to a great height over the veldt, and then drop, still scolding, a few hundred yards further away. Yet with all his faults the black and white koorhaan is a fine sporting bird, requiring much circumvention; he is, in addition, not by any means despicable eating, and the gunner could ill afford to be without him. The huts at St. Stephens' camp, which lay on a little slope above the Maritsani (now,

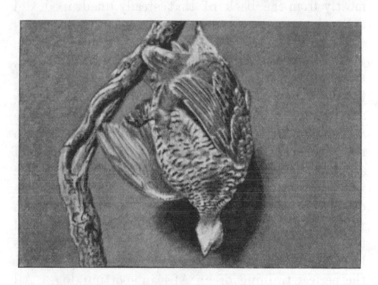

COQUI FRANCOLIN.
Drawn by G. E. Lodge, from a Photograph by the Author.

after nearly two years of drought, a mere dry and sandy watercourse, save for a scant pool of water here and there), were small and poorly built, and as there were but two bedsteads pertaining to the establishment, my friends and I lay in our blankets upon the mud floor, and slept soundly enough till morning. The 1st of April broke gloriously clear and bright, and after breakfast we took our guns and made for the banks of the river, where, during the heat of day, the partridges were usually to be found.   Behind us, at a respectful distance, followed a couple of native boys leading our horses, upon the saddles of which were fastened water bottles containing a refreshing mixture of lime-juice and water, and saddle-bags to carry the game we shot.   Dove, who had been out of health, rode his hunting pony Dunboy, and, shooting mostly from the back of that steady quadruped, did as much execution as any of us.

We had two pointers with us, St. Stephens' Lassie, a capital and steady worker, and my Don, a big, liver-coloured young dog, possessed of a rare nose, but not very well broken, and a little too headstrong and impetuous at times.   Few dogs at the Cape are as completely broken as at home.   There are so many things against them.   The running habits of so many of the game birds, the catchy nature of the scent in a parched and burning climate, and the exhausting character of their labour over a terrain more often than not cruelly rough, broken, and thorny, under a strong sun, and with little water to be encountered—all these points tell hardly against the perfect training of an African sporting dog.   All things considered, Cape dogs do their work extremely well, and come up to time day after day, after work that would ensure collapse to their English brethren fresh from cooler skies, a softer soil, and less vexatious quarry.   It is beyond question that the pointer is better adapted for South African shooting than any other sporting dog.   Its short, smooth coat gives it a wonderful advantage amid the thorny and hindering tangle of so much of the South African bush and undergrowth, in which the handsome coats of the retriever, setter, and spaniel are hopelessly handicapped.

Arrived at the river bed we divided forces; Mackay and I taking the further bank with my pointer; St. Stephens and Dove remaining on the hither side with Lassie; and we then proceeded to work steadily down.   As a rule we were pretty sure of finding a fair number of birds gathered among the bush fringing the rivercourse during the hot hours—between ten and three—and this morning was no exception.   Mackay began the scoring, first one partridge, then immediately another falling to his gun; then a little way further, the rest of the covey, four in number, getting up just beyond shot, crossed a bend of the river and settled in thickish bush in front of St. Stephens and Dove, who shortly after cut down their numbers by another brace.   It is seldom that these francolins get up in a covey with the noisy whirr so familiar to the gunner at home. They lie much closer, or run from shelter to shelter until actually forced into flight by the too imminent approach of the sportsman or his dog.   Not seldom when scent fails they are passed by, and rise behind the gun.   We trudged steadily along, every now and again adding to the bag, until at the end of two hours five brace had been obtained, as well as a hare and one koorhaan.   These hares are smaller than their English cousins, but in colouring and habit are not very dissimilar.   They run very stoutly before dogs, but usually have rather the best of the course from their trick of going to ground in some of the innumerable holes with which the African veldt is studded.   The native cry on sighting a hare or a small buck is " Sa! sa!" and it is very amusing, as the waggon moves slowly over the plains, to see every available dog of the mixed contingent that usually accompanies a trek issue forth, with ears cocked and head in air, all eager and agog for the exciting and most ludicrous scramble that follows the signal.

On the vast plains fringing the lower course of the Botletli River hares were very numerous, and Dove and I, at a later period, often enjoyed from our waggon boxes a view of some most prolonged and laughable courses, in which our solitary grey-hound and Ponto, a speedy mongrel, usually played leading parts.

Presently, having joined forces temporarily on the right bank of the river, to complete the extermina-tion of a strong covey which had dispersed in some thick and tall shrubbery, out of which, after some pretty work on the part of the dogs, we secure two brace and a half, we are puzzled by the baying of Don at some unknown game hidden in a dense bit of thorny covert. The thing refuses to bolt, and, after a good deal of stirring up, Don at last, having made up his mind that it is not a snake, goes for his quarry, and shakes, or attempts to shake it. Then we see that it is a huge lizard—"legovaan," as the Boers call it all over South Africa—about $3\frac{1}{4}$ feet in length. The legovaan is now roused in turn, and shows fight, slaps with its tail, and makes use of its sharp teeth, and still holds his position, making the angered noise peculiar to these reptiles, which can best be compared to the blowing of a pair of small blacksmith's bellows. At length the ugly creature is forced to bolt, and, after a good deal of worrying and some heavy blows from our sticks, is despatched and

slung by its tail to a dee of Dove's saddle. Dead
as mutton it was pronounced by all, and yet five
hours afterwards, at sundown, just as we were nearing
camp, the tough saurian was alive and hearty again.
Dove's pony had stopped several times, twisting his
head round and gazing steadfastly towards his tail.
Looking round also, Dove was rather horrified to see
the great legovaan, apparently in rude health, sitting
comfortably upon Dunboy's rump, just behind the
saddle. The creature had evidently revived with the
cool of evening, and, scrambling up *en croupe*, had
thus disturbed the pony's equanimity. The poor
battered reptile was then suffered to depart in peace,
and no doubt made a complete recovery.

By some curious mistake this lizard is called an
iguana by most English-speaking colonists in South
Africa. In reality no true iguana is to be found in
the old world—except, I think, one solitary species in
Madagascar. This reptile—legovaan I will call it,
in deference to its familiar Boer name—is in truth
a monitor (*Varanis albogularis*), a member of a
well-known group of great lizards found in Africa,
Asia, and Australia. This particular monitor, which
attains 4 feet or more in length, is of a dark olive and
grey-brown colour, strongly variegated—of a lighter
colour underneath—and is plentiful all over Bechuanaland. Its Sechuana name is Kopani or Gopani,
pronounced gutturally; "April," our Matabele-Zulu,
called it T'Klaam. It is never, I fancy, to be met with
very far from water, and in pools where fish are to
be found it loves to exercise its expertness as an
angler. Although I have seen it lying by the water,
I have never actually been witness of this interesting
performance; but I am told that the marvellous

dexterity with which the great lizard will seize its finny prey, after watching immovable as a piece of marble, is a revelation in silence and rapidity of movement. The legovaan loves the water also for its own sake, and its laterally flattened tail is well adapted as an aid and guide in swimming. It is pretty carnivorous, I fancy, and, like the secretary bird, probably devours a good many of the eggs and young of game birds during the course of the year.

This monitor is an uncanny and rather formidable-looking beast when first encountered, but, unless attacked by dogs, is perfectly harmless; and, unless we required them for their skins, we usually let them go their ways. There is a dim old legend that this lizard gave warning of the approach of the crocodile by means of its loud hissing faculty. The hissing, or rather bellows-like blowing, is accurate enough, and no doubt gave rise to the fable. Curiously enough, scientific naturalists seem to have fastened upon the old story, and the name monitor survives to perpetuate an idle legend. These Bechuanaland monitors may be styled good all-round sportsmen; besides being at home in water, they are great tree-climbers, and I remember once being horribly startled with Mackay at the sight of the head of one of them regarding us from behind the trunk of a giraffe-acacia tree. There are large pythons to be met with occasionally in this district, and at first sight we mistook the legovaan for one of these formidable-looking serpents.

By this time it was near two o'clock, and the dogs were fagged and in need of water and a rest, both of which we gave them. Then we rested ourselves in the dry sandy bed of the river, under a deep bank overhung with bush and low trees. The dogs having drunk their fill and wallowed in the scant pool, now scraped away the hot upper sand and lay cooling their feet and bellies. The ponies had meanwhile come up, and we ourselves partook of grateful draughts of lime-juice and water, which had been steadily cooling in those excellent felt-covered evaporating water-bottles of Silver's—articles we were never without.

As we rested, numbers of glossy starlings, the metallic blues and greens and violets of their shining plumage flashing in the sunlight, might be seen and heard—for they are noisy, garrulous creatures— in the bush around us. The best known members of this handsome family to be found in Bechuanaland are the Kaffir glossy starling (*Amydrus caffer;* Le nabouroup of Le Vaillant); the green spreo (*Juida phœnicoptera*), almost everywhere to be found in bushy or semi-bushy localities; and that large and magnificent species, Burchell's glossy starling (*Lamprotornis Burchellii*), less frequently met with.

Two South African (or lesser) hoopoes (*Upupa minor*) were to be seen darting with quick, nervous flight round and about an acacia tree beyond us, their ruddy colouring, prominent crests, and white-barred tails easily marking them out. These handsome birds are not by any means easy to secure as specimens; they seem to have an instinctive knowledge of the collector's gun, and give much trouble when one is actually in search of them. When one is after game, however, as on this occasion, they always appear less wary.

All along the banks of this, and indeed of every other river in Bechuanaland, overhanging the waterway, depend, often from a single long slender branch, the shapely, elegant, and most beautifully fashioned nests of the various weaver birds. Common as are their grass-woven nests, they are always worthy of admiration. What specimen of the basketmaker's craft can compare with the dainty and perfect handiwork of these clever birds ?

There is little noise around us at this hour of hot African afternoon; the scolding call of a koorhaan who has heard our guns, the chatter of the glossy starlings yonder, the shrill, hurdy-gurdy-like refrain of a cicada in the bush hard by, and the hurried panting of our pointers—these are the only sounds that break upon the hot and drowsy silence of the quiet veldt.

Twenty minutes and a well-earned pipe and we are up and off again. Following the river for another half-mile, we pick up a few more partridges, and then turn off right-handed from the Maritsani, and strike across to higher, more open and more grassy veldt, here and there thinly bushed, which rolls in smooth undulating slopes to a higher and wilder tableland, which in turn spreads northward to the Molopo many a mile away. It is hot, precious hot, although as usual we are shooting in our flannel shirts, with the sleeves well rolled up ; but the air is clear and sparkling, and we feel in excellent walking fettle as we step out on our homeward sweep towards the camp. The afternoon wears on, and presently the shooting changes somewhat. We are now well on the ground of the koorhaans, which are extraordinarily plentiful upon these grassy slopes. What dodging, running, squatting, exasperating wretches they are, with their harsh chiding " kraak,"

" kraak " as one approaches. And yet patience, care, and a watchful eye on the dog usually results in the downfall of these wily birds. Sometimes they stealthily run, hidden in the long grass, and the pointer, drawing on and on and yet on, seems, poor brute, as if he never will bring them to book ; until, suddenly, up gets the great black and white cackling bustard—in that clumsy way of his—a magnificent target against the pale blue sky and the yellow of the grass veldt ; " bang !" and down he falls, with a resounding thud, to my first barrel.

A flutter behind us, and the silent hen bird is on the wing. We have walked right over or past her. Mackay, over knee-deep in the yellow grass, slews round sharply ; " bang !" she is forty yards and more away, but the gun is held straight, and she, too, hits the dust. A pretty shot, and a pretty sporting scene, enacted as it is on the shoulder of the upland ; the alert gunner and the falling game bird both outlined against the clear sky ; close by the eager pointer thrusting his head up through the grass, and wondering where the deuce that bird got up from.

It is noticeable that the hen birds of this bustard —the black and white koorhaan—are far less noisy than their mates, and usually get up very silently, and with little notice to the gunner. As we pick up our game we can hear St. Stephens' and Dove's guns pretty frequently half-a-mile away on our left flank.

This sort of thing, with variations of course—for the choke barrel and No. 2 shot are often needed to account for these heavy bustards at long range— with the addition of an occasional partridge or dikkop plover (*Œdicnemus maculosus*)—goes on for the rest of the afternoon ; the bag is mounting up now.

Mackay and I, working round by a patch of native mealies roughly planted in a gentle hollow among the slopes, and now, although little aided by the short rains of January and February 1890, looking splendidly, rejoined our comrades towards four o'clock on the last low hill before home. Here we rested five minutes, and turned out the bag. We had had a very fair day's sport, our united bag comprising the following items : 10½ brace partridges (Orange River francolin), 7 brace koorhaan (black and white bustard), 3 hares, 3 dikkop plovers, 1 legovaan (lizard) ; total, 42 head. Here was game enough to supply all our wants for a couple of days at least ; and, well satisfied with our modest shoot, we were ready enough for the game stew awaiting us at the huts.

This day of rough and varied shooting is a fair sample of many and many a day of much the same class of sport enjoyed upon the health-giving uplands of British Bechuanaland during the first half of 1890. Sometimes our bag was larger, sometimes a little less. But at all times we had fair unclouded skies, a bright sun, a sparkling atmosphere, cool evenings, and often in April and May sharp, cold nights. The healthfulness and vigour of the atmosphere upon these lofty plateaux lands (from 3000 to 4000 feet above sea level) were not the least important factors of many a day of keen enjoyment.

> " Fair are the plains—to memory fair—
> The wide horizon clear and large,
> The breezy space, the ample air."

These are telling things, whether considered poetically

or otherwise, and with pleasant, keen, and hearty
comrades, add greatly to the charms and pleasures
of an otherwise rather rough existence.

In different localities—often a very little way
apart — we found different game birds ; but the
Bechuanaland partridge (Orange River francolin)
and the black and white bustard (koorhaan) were
always with us, at all places and all times. I do
not assert that the quiet pleasures of such a form of
shooting are quite equal to the fiercer joys of big
game hunting farther up-country. I have tested
both, and both are in their way super-excellent.
But it is comforting to reflect that for the Englishman—to whom it can never appeal in vain—this
soberer form of sport will be at hand long after
the great game have completely disappeared from
Africa south of the Zambesi, or, indeed, from Africa
altogether.

CHAPTER V.

BRITISH BECHUANALAND AND ITS FUTURE

Position, in 1885—Rapid growth of the colony—Aspect of the country—
Forests and their spoliation—Rainfall and water supply—Crops—
Farmers—Fruit and irrigation—Climate—Flocks and herds—Ranching prospects—Employment for settlers—Population ; recent Census
—Numbers of stock—Administration, Education, and Revenue—Re-
forms needed—Native tribes—Their aversion to labour—Origin and
development of Bechuanas—Their future—Drink traffic and its
dangers—Present comfort of natives—Doubtful effects of civilisation—Native occupations—A native letter—Recent enlargement of
colony—Paucity of police—General prospects.

FEW of our possessions can show more hopeful symptoms of a prosperous future than this youngest of
England's Crown colonies—a colony having a record
of but seven years of existence.

To those who remember the turbulent and distracted territory, mainly known to the outer world
up to 1885 as Stellaland and the Land of Goshen—
pseudo Boer republics—the change must seem more
than remarkable. The filibusters and freebooters
of those days have either retired into Transvaal
obscurity, or may now be found peaceful and law-
abiding subjects of the Queen at Vryburg, Mafeking,
and other parts of the colony. The natives, then
harassed and hunted to death, now sit quietly in
their reserves, increasing both in population and in
cattle (their own peculiar material wealth) with a
rapidity even startling.

In these seven years Vryburg, the capital, has

grown to a considerable town, possessing railway communication with the sea at Cape Town ; Mafeking is rapidly ousting Kimberley as the emporium of interior trade ; while Taungs, Kuruman, and other villages all show a steady and promising advance. At this day in British Bechuanaland life and property are at least as safe as in any part of the British Islands.

Hitherto no considerable mineral wealth has been discovered in this colony, and the chief impulses have arisen from the advance of the railway in 1890, the natural opening up of the country, and the extraordinary traffic created by the northward movement of the British South Africa Company's forces.

After the dreary railway journey from Cape Town to Kimberley, for the greater part over the most barren and forbidding portion of the Great Karroo, and after leaving behind the perfectly flat grass lands of Griqualand West, the entrance into South Bechuanaland comes as a welcome relief. It is true that, with few exceptions, there are not many mountain ranges to be seen until Mafeking is passed and the Protectorate reached ; but if the stranger should enter the country in January or February, after the summer rains have fallen, he will see stretched before him one of the fairest prairie countries in the world —a fine rolling veldt covered with an abundance of long, rich grasses, amid which the cattle graze middle deep, veritable pictures of contentment and well-being. True, the green summer grass pales and yellows as the season advances, until the country resembles in midwinter one vast, over-ripe hayfield ; but the nutriment is yet there, and cattle retain their condition easily until the rains fall again. Much

of the timber has disappeared from British Bechuanaland south of Vryburg, in the more immediate
vicinity of the Transvaal border, to supply insa-
tiable Kimberley with firewood; but to the westward and northward, as Setlagoli is approached, very
extensive forests are to be met with, and the graceful
giraffe acacia adds a wonderful charm to the landscape. Forests of bastard yellow-wood and other
trees are also encountered, and the northern and
western part of the colony may be considered as,
on the whole, extremely well timbered. Not far to
the westward and north-westward, in the Kalahari
region, dense forests of giraffe acacia are met with.

It is a matter of great regret that the well-timbered
lands to the north and west of Vryburg are at the
present time being despoiled and disafforested exactly
in the wasteful and shameless way in which much of
Cape Colony, Griqualand West, and South Bechuanaland have been already despoiled. Wandering Boers
and natives go with their waggons into these localities,
cut down as much timber as they can load up and
trek to Kimberley, or Vryburg, or Mafeking, and
sell at a good price. Now Bechuanaland is a dry
country—much dryer than it was of old, if empty
river-beds and shrunken fountains are any criterion
—and cannot afford to undergo further dessication
by the theft of its forests in this way. The ground
from which the timber-thieves lift their spoil is either
Government ground or belongs to private owners.
For the sake of the future of the colony, for the sake
of its own pocket, which must surely suffer in the
long run, and for the sake of private owners (who,
even if they are at present absentees, pay heavy
quit-rents and deserve protection), the Government

ought to devise some system of checking this most reprehensible practice before it is too late.

And, while upon this point, I do not wish it to be thought that Bechuanaland is a waterless desert—far from it. Anciently, before some great upheavals and changes in the land took place (changes that were probably most acute in the immense water systems of the Zambesi and Ngami countries, before the Zambesi was torn from its ancient southerly course and diverted to its present channel), Bechuanaland and the Kalahari must have been exceedingly well watered. Many an old river-bed, long since dry and useless, testifies to this fact.

Even now the rainfall is ample, and averages over 25 inches per annum. During the summer of 1890–91 the rains were enormous, and gave a total of not less than 50 inches. This was of course an abnormal season, the natives stating that such rains had not happened within their memory. At Vryburg, from October 1891 to April 1892 the rainfall was 27.24 inches, which means a fair average season. But at the present time much of this excellent rainfall goes to waste, not, as in Cape Colony, by pouring off a series of sloping terraces by means of rivercourses into the sea, but simply by absorption into the thirsty friable soil of the country. Underground, consequently, and probably at no great depth, there must be immense reserves of water only waiting to be tapped and made use of. This underground supply, and a system of conservation by dams and other methods will beyond all question, as a population spreads into the territory, do much to alter and improve many a now waterless and useless tract of land.

For instance, as I have seen upon the Karroo of
Cape Colony, by sinking a well and putting up a
windmill pump, a supply of water sufficing for thousands of stock throughout the year may be obtained
in places where at present, owing to the absence of
surface water, cattle, sheep, and goats cannot be supported. A system of Government loans to farmers
for purposes of irrigation and water supply would
work well in this territory, and is highly desirable.
Such a system has obtained in Cape Colony for years
past, and with good results. A Government boring
apparatus for finding water has long been talked
of, but unhappily has not yet appeared. Such an
apparatus, whether in the hands of Government or
of a private firm, would undoubtedly pay very handsomely. Unfortunately no capitalists (save a land
company or two) have up to the present time made
their appearance in British Bechuanaland, although
the territory offers many inducements to exploration.
It is unquestionable, I think, that in time much of
the subterraneous basin of the Kalahari country will
be tapped in this way, and vast herds of cattle
thereafter depastured in what is beyond all doubt
one of the finest natural ranching countries in the
world.

In Algeria extraordinary success has attended the
introduction of artesian wells. The French Government has set an excellent example in this matter,
and Algeria in consequence is fast becoming a great
wine and tobacco producing country. The British
authorities might well emulate the irrigation operations of the French in North Africa ; a moderate
expenditure in British Bechuanaland would bear
ample fruit, and that speedily.

All over the country plenty of bush—principally Vaal-bush and mimosa—is to be met with, and cattle, sheep, and goats find almost everywhere that desideratum of the South African farmer, a warm veldt. The Bechuanas are large producers of mealies (maize), Kaffir corn, melons and pumpkins, and in good years like 1891, after bountiful rains, the mealie fields are pictures of beauty and abundance. All down the Harts River valley, in the Batlaping location, under the chief Mankoroane, the railway passenger travels through miles of rich corn lands, in which tall mealies are growing in wonderful luxuriance, and giving promise in February 1891, as the writer came down country, of the superabundant harvest which was afterwards gathered in. All the principal Bechuana tribes, as far as and including Khama's country, now use light American ploughs, supplied to them by the local storekeeper at the exchange rate of an ox per plough, and their tilling operations are, in seasons like the present, plenteously rewarded. On the other hand, it must be admitted that years of drought prevail, when but little corn can be grown, and prices rise proportionately. In 1890, after two years of drought, mealies rose from 10s. to 36s. per bag of 205 lbs., and long-headed people, who bought up stocks in time, realised small fortunes. Hitherto no irrigation has been seriously attempted, although in many places the country offers opportunity for its introduction. With the influx of a farming population and capital, great advances will doubtless be made in this respect in the near future. Up to the present but few British or even colonial farmers have made their homes in the country; but recently colonists are beginning to come in from the Orange Free

State and Cape Colony in some numbers; indeed, owing to the enforcement of a new Fencing Act in the Free State, quite an influx of Boers from that State is setting in. No more striking proof of the growing Boer belief in the advantages of British government and British justice can be adduced, than the fact of these farmers quitting their own republic and taking land under British rule. In the few instances where homes have been made, water furrows opened out, and fruit gardens and corn lands planted, success has invariably attended the colonists' efforts, and within two hours of Vryburg there may be found some notable examples of what can be done in these respects in the space of three or four short years. Apples, pears, peaches, apricots, grapes, oranges, citrons, shaddocks, and other fruit, all do exceptionally well. Much of the soil is of a good, rich, deep red character, containing iron, and, being virgin, is capable of producing almost anything. Tobacco is being attempted, and attempted successfully, in suitable localities.

The climate is, in the opinion of most people who have tested it, the finest in all South Africa. I do not know that a healthier country can be found upon the face of the globe. With an elevation of nearly 4000 feet above sea level, the air even in the height of summer is clear and bracing, and the noon-day heat is never too great to prevent ordinary outdoor occupations being followed. For consumptives and those suffering from pulmonary delicacy, the dry, clear, exhilarating air of Bechuanaland is of quite extraordinary efficacy. Nights are always cool; in winter even cold. During the beginning of the winter of 1890 (in May) the night temperature at

Vryburg sank on several occasions to ten degrees
below the freezing point.   Every winter day, however, is blessed with a bright, warm sunshine, and
there are few days indeed throughout the year when
the sun is obscured or overcast.   As in many other
parts of South Africa, wind storms are now and then
experienced, but these, as a rule, may be looked for
mainly in the months of September and October;
and, except on the road, and in new and dusty towns
like Vryburg, they are not of a very troublesome
nature.   During these hot wind storms there is an
immense amount of electricity in the atmosphere.
If the hand is passed lightly over a fur kaross, a
brisk crackling is instantly produced, and if in the
dark, a sheet of flaming sparks is seen.   At present
cattle, goats, and the fat-tailed African sheep are the
main pastoral productions of the country.   Horses
and merino sheep are not yet acclimatised, or, rather,
the veldt is not at present in a fit condition for their
use.   The horse-sickness, which to this hour remains
in South Africa a completely incurable disease, is
greatly to be dreaded ; a very large percentage of
animals perish each year, and have to be renewed from
the Cape Colony and Orange Free State, and a dead
loss of many thousands of pounds is thus annually
entailed.   But, as has happened in the Cape Colony
in the past, this disease will at no distant period
recede further north.   At present pasturage is too rich
for merino sheep ; but already, on a few farms where
the veldt has been eaten off, sheep have got through
their troubles and are doing well.   Goats flourish
in abundance and everywhere.   Ostriches run wild
in the western parts of the colony, edging on the
Kalahari, and tame ostriches, so soon as the price

of feathers shall again become remunerative, will no
doubt be farmed extensively.

Throughout the colony there is to be found a
good sprinkling of Boers, who, to their credit be it
said, now remain loyal and contented subjects of
the Queen. Many of these farmers gained their
holdings under award of the Land Commission which
sat after the settlement of the country by Sir Charles
Warren. Others have come in and bought land
within the last few years, and all are thriving.
Many other Dutchmen from the Free State and
Transvaal may be expected to settle in Bechuanaland
within the next few years; and it behoves British
settlers to purchase land at the moderate prices still
obtaining, before the best of the farms are picked up
and larger sums are demanded. At present the usual
South African farm of 3000 morgen (about 6000
acres) can be purchased at from £500 to £1500,
without improvements; prices varying according to
locality, water supply, and pasturage. In several
instances large blocks of land are held by the richer
transport riders, who are thus enabled to keep up
the necessary head of trek oxen to replenish their
teams upon the road, and to recruit wearied spans
on their return from the long trek to the interior.
Preparations are already being made for ranching
operations on a considerable scale in several parts
of the colony; and with the drain on ox-flesh consequent upon the ever-increasing trade with the
interior, and with the markets of Kimberley, Pre-
toria, Johannesburg, and other towns adjacent, and
the new railway communication with Cape Colony,
cattle-farming on a large scale may be expected to
pay handsomely. Store cattle of excellent quality

are periodically brought across the Kalahari from Damaraland, and sold to farmers at wonderfully low values. Even during the dry winter season, when the tall grass has been sun-parched for months, oxen keep their condition in a wonderful manner. I watched closely the trek oxen of a neighbour of mine on the Maritsani River during 1890, and was astonished to find, even after a peculiarly trying season, how well they had retained their flesh. At the end of the drought they were still actually fat and well nourished, although they had slight waggon work every week.

The British South Africa Company, in consideration of building the line from Kimberley to Vryburg, is entitled to 12,000 square miles of land in this colony. A commission of farming experts has lately been sent up by the Cape Government to survey and demarcate this land, and it is hinted that a considerable scheme of settlement is shortly to be promulgated. Under the controlling hand of Mr. Rhodes, it is pretty certain that such a scheme is likely to be complete and successful.

Among white men, farmers possessed of a thousand pounds or two of capital and some experience of African soil, are sure to do well. But it is not a small farmer's country, except here and there in favoured spots where water is plentiful and lands can be easily irrigated. A poor man with a capital of only a hundred or two is likely to be eaten up during the first two or three unproductive years.

A pastoral farm is usually reckoned at 3000 morgen, or rather more than 6000 acres. To run cattle, sheep, or goats in South Africa, experience has long since shown that less veldt can hardly

suffice. It is probable that the tendency will be to
fence in and stock much larger areas. Ranching on
a large scale is no doubt to be the future of much
of this country.

Farm hands can always do well in this colony,
and there is a pretty constant demand for black-
smiths, farriers, bricklayers, masons, carpenters,
saddlers, bootmakers, and grooms ; a gunsmith would
do excellently well, and gardeners would unquestionably get on. Among servants, cooks, nurses, and
general servants may be sure of employment at good
wages. Laundresses command highly extravagant
prices in all the towns. " Out of town," as often as
not, one wrings out one's garments for oneself and
dries in the sun ; the whole operation being a simple,
speedy, and economical one. Few other workers,
and least of all clerks, are likely to find employment
at the present day in Bechuanaland.

As to population, there is room enough and to
spare for many a year to come in this territory.
The first Census ever known in British Bechuanaland
was taken in 1891, with the following results :—

Europeans (including Boers)	5211
Hottentots, Kaffirs, Malays, and other natives not belonging to the native Reserves . .	7525
Bechuana Native Reserves—	
Taungs	19,800
Kuruman	11,770
Mafeking	10,015
Vryburg	6065
Total . .	60,386

Considering that the towns of Vryburg, Mafeking,
Taungs, and Kuruman may probably claim at least
3000 of the European population, it cannot be con-

tended that the rural white population of a territory nearly as large as England is at present inordinate.

Of the 5211 Europeans, it is interesting to note that there are 3113 males to 2098 females. The 47,650 Bechuanas settled in native locations hardly represent the aboriginal native population of the colony. The Kalahari country holds a good many hundreds of scattered natives—Bakalahari, Bushmen, Vaalpense, and others ; and the " werfts " or villages, such as Virlander's and others, help to swell the very scanty sprinkling of mankind to the square mile. I do not anticipate that British Bechuanaland will ever hold a very crowded population ; but that some day, when it has become better known and appreciated, and its water supplies have been enlarged and discovered, it will support a fair population, I have no doubt. It is worthy of note that there are no paupers and no persons living on charity within the territory.

Not including the stock run in the Kalahari, there are in the colony at present no more than 48,686 head of cattle ; 4714 horses, mules, and donkeys ; and 314,407 goats and sheep (including 24,798 woolled sheep, 153,002 native sheep, 15,048 Angora and 121,559 common goats)—an absurdly small number for so vast a country.

Hitherto this colony has been, as it were, merely struggling to exist, and to justify existence ; its system of government and the administration of justice have been conducted at great disadvantage, and with a most rigid and freezing parsimony. The court houses—one at least of them a relic of Stellaland days—poor and insufficient as they are, have, as in the case of Vryburg, been allowed to fall into disreputable ruin. There has been, till quite lately, absolutely no sort of provision for education, even of the most elementary nature; and busy parents are at their wits' end to know what to do with their rising offspring.

These things are not as they should be, and require mending. At Vryburg, it is true, a school has recently been opened, but the Government grant in aid for the whole colony amounts to no more than £300, and that for the education of a territory as large as Ireland. The revenue, small though it is, is steadily increasing, and, with the completion of the railway to Mafeking, is likely to progress much more rapidly. In 1890–91 the revenue totalled £45,313;[1] the British Parliamentary grant being £115,992, and the expenditure of the colony £159,545. The colony is not yet self-supporting, it is clear; but after a few more years of judicious and not too parsimonious aid from the parent country it may be made so, and the steadily increasing population is a satisfactory feature. A readjustment of the expenses of the Border Police, now—although the force is mainly employed in the Protectorate—charged to this colony, is needed, and the establishment of a Court or Courts of Record, and trial by jury, are urgently demanded. By a reorganisation of the present system of justice, the Administrator would be enabled to devote his whole time and attention to the actual duties of Government. Probably Sir Sidney Shippard would be the first to welcome such a change. As it is, the Administrator is frequently called away to distant territories, and upon long and fatiguing expeditions. Now he is at

[1] The estimate for 1892 was £55,230.

Buluwayo, interviewing Lobengula in Matabeleland;
now pacifying or admonishing unruly chiefs (such as
Lintshwe or Sebele) in the Protectorate; now holding
commission with the Transvaal authorities—as in
Grobelaar's affair—on the far Limpopo River. During
these enforced absences prisoners accused of the more
serious crimes cannot be tried, and justice is practically at a standstill.

The three principal tribes in British Bechuanaland
are the Batlaping, under the chief Mankoroane,[1]
at Taungs; the Barolong, under the old and loyal
chief Monsioa, at Mafeking; and the Batlaro, under
Chief Toto, round and beyond Kuruman. In addition,
there are various branches of these two latter tribes
to the west, at Honing Vlei, Langeberg, Morokweng,
and other places. The Batlaping number some
24,000, the Barolong 14,000, and the Batlaro 9000.
These people have all large areas of land allotted
to them as reserves, which, happily for themselves,
they are unable to alienate. The chiefs now realise
that much of their sway has departed, and, forgetting
that but for English intervention they would now
own probably not one single rood of land, are disposed to grumble and lament their vanished power.
The locations were but a few years since amply
sufficient for the tribes occupying them; but five
years of peace and order, and a complete immunity
from fighting and freebooting, have wrought great
changes for the better among these people, who now
complain that their lands are all too small for them.
But the remedy lies with themselves.

Of all South African tribes, these Southern

---

[1] Mankoroane died December 1892, and was succeeded by his son
Malala.

Bechuanas are least inclined to work or to take
service with the white man.   They prefer to remain
upon their old acres, leading a comparatively idle
and useless, if idyllic, life (in which, however, the
women do all the hard work), until a natural increase
of population begins to make them uncomfortable
and to bring the pinch to their doors.   They even
encourage or permit strangers from other tribes—
from the Transvaal and elsewhere—to squat on their
reserves, build to themselves huts, and form units of
their social system.   These people have been fairly
dealt with by the British Government under extremely difficult circumstances, and their cry for
more land cannot now be considered, unless, indeed,
they choose to pay for it.   Labour is scarce, and
wages are absurdly high, and natives can everywhere
obtain employment at rates that would make many
a starving Englishman stare.   The Bechuana is a born
cattle-man, and loves oxen more than he loves wife
and child, and some day, when he wakes up and finds
that he must bestir himself, will do good service—it
may be hoped—on the cattle ranches of the future.

Whence came the Bechuanas, and what was their
origin ?   They have a curious mingling of the commercial and pastoral, and, of all the Bantu tribes,
theirs is the nimblest intellect.   For fighting they
have little stomach, although upon occasion they
can and have fought pluckily.   But natural-born
warriors like the Zulus and Kaffirs they are not and
probably never were.   Their skill lies rather in the
pastoral, hunting, argumentative and oratorical directions.   Strong commercial instincts they have, but
hitherto these have lain fallow, or have been exercised in the way of barter and exchange of cattle,

ivory, and other spoils of the chase. They have always in modern times been the best clothed, the best housed, and upon the whole the most civilised of African natives. When the earliest English travellers penetrated to Bechuanaland in the first decade of this century, it was quickly reported that here had been found a far more advanced race than the Hottentots—a people dwelling simply, pastorally, yet in comfort and under settled government.

Have the Bechuanas always been as they are now, a race of herdsmen and hunters, a people loving passionately their troops of cattle, their flocks of goats, and the chase of game? Have they wandered with their flocks and herds down from North-East Africa—nay, from Asia itself—from pasture to pasture, settling here and there perhaps for a century or a score of years and planting crops, for they are agriculturists also? Are they sprung from some Semitic race far back in the womb of time? Their close bartering ways, their strong commercial leanings, their custom of circumcision and other traits, point to such an origin. Are they akin to the Egyptians, whose type many of them strongly recall, or to the Abyssinians, whose huts theirs almost exactly resemble?

These are unanswerable questions, unfortunately, and yet with almost each there lies a strong element of plausibility. Probably, as their traditions indicate, they did come from North-East Africa ; probably theirs was before the dawn of history a Semitic origin; and still more probably they were very anciently allied to the Egyptians and Abyssinians. I speak of the tribes north of the Batlaping, who from their proximity to the Griquas and Hottentots are of less

pure descent than other Bechuana races. Two things
are at least certain. In the long centuries they have
passed slowly, painfully through dim old savage
Africa, and at one time, to have made their way at
all, they must have been bolder fighting men than
they are at present. There is a strong resemblance
in much of the dialects of the Bechuanas, Zulus, and
Kaffirs (many words are identical); and it would be
interesting to know when in the migration southward they broke asunder, and how, and why their
habits became changed.

Just now the Bechuanas stand upon the threshold
of a new era. The white men are swarming into
their country; British Bechuanaland is a Crown
colony; the Protectorate, which at present is neither
native nor British (and hangs, like Mahomet's coffin,
in a state of suspension), must shortly follow suit.
Is the white man's influence to be for good or evil
among this quick-witted race? It is a tough question. The drink traffic, which, thanks to Dutch
influence, has ruined the Hottentots, and now bids
fair to ruin the magnificent Cape Kaffir, is the main
arbiter of life and death, of happiness and misery in
this case. If the Bechuanas are absolutely restrained
from strong drink, as they now are by the wise and
well-administered laws of the Crown colony and
Protectorate, they have before them, I firmly believe,
a good and prosperous future. If, on the other hand,
Bechuanaland is handed over to the uncontrolled
mercies of the Cape Colony, and the old Dutch wine-
farming, brandy-selling party (and it is a strong—
almost a supreme—party in the Cape Parliament) is
suffered to work its will, the country will be flooded
with vile, cheap liquor, and the natives ruined irre-

deemably. It is a momentous, a terribly momentous question, and one to be well weighed by the Colonial Office, and still more by the British people, before the future of Bechuanaland is settled once and for ever.

There is no objection to the Cape as a Government having the control of the Bechuanas if—and it is a tremendous if in this case—the drink question is settled without fear of relapse or change. The Cape could and would administer the country as well probably as it is now administered; but there must be no loophole for the entry of the death-dealing Boer brandy, and this ought to be absolutely secured before Bechuanaland is handed over—if it is to be handed over—to the Cape Government, which even now has upon its hands a country huge and scattered enough in all conscience. These are not the views of rabid temperance advocates, but of every sensible and thinking man in South Africa, who is not a brandy-grower or an advocate of the old Boer idea of no quarter to the black man.

I have visited nearly every native town of consequence in Bechuanaland, including Taungs, Mafeking, Takwaning, Morokweng, Kanya, Ramoutsa, Pilans, Molepolole, Mochudi, and Palachwe, with populations varying from 2000 or 3000 to 20,000; and I say unhesitatingly that these people are at this moment physically and morally far better off than many thousands of the population of our great cities in Britain. The Bechuanas are not all Christians— admitted; but, by any stretch of imagination, can the bulk of the squalid, toiling, seething masses of our "submerged tenth" be classed as Christians. I trow not. In every other respect—in housing, food, clothing, fire, and comfort—the native has an enormous advantage. Throughout Bechuanaland at this day the people live on the whole in peace and contentment. They have no great sins ; crime is almost unknown ; they grow their crops, look after their cattle and goats, and live, within a perfect climate, happier and healthier lives by far than seven-tenths of English poor folk at home. Here and there in the remote districts they may lack English clothing ; but those of them who cannot afford that longed-for luxury are decently clad in their picturesque skin cloaks and blankets, and have all they need. There are grumblers, of course—there are in all countries and communities.

The Bechuana complains that under the British settlement he has not enough grazing ground, and that his folk are becoming too numerous for their tribal lands. The white colonist on his part cries out not only that the Bechuana has by far too much the best of it—the best waters, the fertile valleys, the fattest corn lands—but that he won't come out of his locations and work for a good wage when it is offered him. These are matters which will right themselves. The land settlement cannot be disturbed. The Bechuanas, on giving up their country to the Queen of England, were placed in their present locations by solemn treaty, and it would be an act of gross perfidy to attempt now to displace them. These Barolongs and Batlapings and Batlaros (who after all have had but six years of British rule) will no doubt begin to seek work in time, as their numbers increase and their spaces become overstocked.

Civilisation is now creeping apace far up into these

territories. Trade is being rapidly and very successfully pushed into the Protectorate, where large
numbers of the Border Police are now quartered, and
a hut tax is being spoken of ; and it is unquestionable that out of the Bechuanas and their country
large profits and other increments will not long hence
be drawn throughout the whole territory.

Will civilisation bring a blessing or a curse to this
people ?   It is a moot point.   I am induced to think
that these quiet pastoralists are happier and better
off now than they will be fifty years hence, when,
perchance, unless a sharp look-out has been kept,
they may have become levelled down to the de-
praved, bastard Hottentots of Cape Colony, ruined
and besotted by drink.   On the other hand, if
drink is kept from them, these Bechuanas, with
their quick minds, strong reasoning powers, and
ready adaptability, are quite capable of rising to
a far higher and more refined life than they enjoy
at present.

But that they will be truly happier—even for
such a change—than they now are in their pleasant Arcadian simplicity, and their free communal
equality, I declare I greatly doubt.   After all, civilisation, with its frightful wear and tear, its waste,
its hideous aggregation of life within the great cities,
its awful squalor, crime, and misery in the lower
strata, is a serious thing to contemplate, when with
the mind's other eye one looks at the Bechuanas,
peaceful, unworried, and with their simple wants
easily supplied to them.

In addition to their future as pastoralists on their
own account, and as shepherds, herdsmen, and servants to the white man, the Bechuanas are gradually

acquiring a large proportion of the transport-riding (or carrying) business of the country.   They possess large numbers of waggons and are rapidly becoming possessed of more, and have any amount of cattle ; they have been found to be reliable and trustworthy ; and it is the opinion of many white transport-riders that in a few years the bulk of the carrying trade will be in native hands.   A pleasing trait in the Bechuana life is the love of children.   The mothers have, poor creatures, a hard time of it, what with carrying water and working in the fields.   But the piccaninnies are well cared for.   It is a perfect sight to see the tiny brown rascals, so fat that they can hardly waddle, staggering about the native villages stark naked.   Their fat is mainly attributable to a diet of thick soured milk called " maasi," which is kept in skin bags (*Lekuka*) much resembling Highland bagpipes, having a wooden plug at top and bottom, and is curdled by hanging in the sun.   This coagulated milk, from which the whey is drained off, eaten either alone or mixed with meal, forms the main dietary of all the better class Bechuanas, and is a most wholesome and nutritious food.

The Bechuanas have received more advantages from missionary teaching than any other South African race.   In Khama's country, where the influence of that great native chief has been strongly exercised for good, this is most noticeable.   Here and there you will even find a native who can read and write in English.   But that a little learning is often as absurd as it is dangerous is evident from the following epistle (recently published in the *Independent*), written by a half-educated Kaffir in the De Beer's Diamond Mining Compound to his sweetheart outside :—

"DEAR MISS JUDEA MOSES,—My dear, I am take this lettle time of write you this few lines hoping that it will find you in a good state of helth as it leaves me here in the compound. My dear girl I am very sorry that you did not write my ansert back. My dear Judea Moses, be so kind and let me know how it is with you my dear girl. I mean to say that you must cry out and shout thou in the habitant of Zion, for great is the holy one of israel My dear Miss Judea i glided by lawns and grassy plats. My dear friend please anxer me as soon as you get this lettor. My dear oft in sadness and in illness I have watched they current glide till the beauty of its stillness overflowed me like a tide. I steal my lawns and grassy plats I slide by hazel covers, i move the sweet forget me-nots that grow for happy lovers my dear darling Miss J. Moses. Here I shall drup writting with Best loves, geod By 2222 kises to youe."

It is manifest from this ludicrous concoction that the " Christian gentleman " who wrote it either " conveyed " passages direct from some book or books (Tennyson among them), or interpolated lines which he had learnt by heart. In either case there is a lamentable want of fitness, sequency, and artistic treatment, not to speak of grammar and punctuation, about this precious production.

Quite recently some disturbance had arisen upon the extreme western border of the colony, in the territory of David Virlander, chief of a tribe of Bastards long settled in the Kalahari. Virlander's country, situated though it is in the so-called desert, contains capital grazing land, and large numbers of stock are depastured there. Dutch farmers from the north of the Cape colony had been pushing their way into this region, and something very like armed conflict had nearly occurred on more than one occasion. The position was further complicated by the fact that various rights over Virlander's country had been granted to concessionaries or syndicates. It became desirable that this portion of the Kalahari, so far as the German border—that is, up to parallel 20 of west longitude—should be added to the colony of British Bechuanaland, which would then comprise a symmetrical and compact area, and this has been happily carried into effect. It may here be noted that the Kalahari is fast losing its old denomination of desert, and, its value as a cattle country having been proved, is largely being taken up by syndicates, who are acquiring concessions and leases from the various petty chiefs inhabiting the territory. This has happened already as far as Lehutitung, lying in the centre of the desert, on the tropic of Capricorn. Probably by this time enterprising concession hunters have extended their operations yet further north.

During the last year or two, the Border Police Force—a most excellent body of irregular horse— has been withdrawn almost entirely from the Crown colony and employed in the Protectorate and beyond. In the opinion of many this depletion of force has been premature. British Bechuanaland is a huge territory, and law and order, and a due respect for the established government, are not and cannot be sufficiently maintained without police in large and distant native towns such as Morokweng, Honing Vlei, Motito, Maneering, and others. The Bechuanas are easily governed, but a display of authority is at times necessary to remind chiefs that they are not now independent, as some of them still appear to think.

On the whole, British Bechuanaland has, in an unobtrusive way, already amply justified its existence, and, with its magnificent and salubrious climate, its excellent geographical position, and its vast potentialities of pastoral wealth, will in a few years be well able to hold its own with older dependencies. I am not convinced that Bechuanaland can ever become a great corn-producing country, but I am absolutely convinced that it will prove itself one of the finest cattle countries in the world.

But among farmers there, as in other places, capital is, above all things, necessary, and the means of existence during the first two or three years of colonial life require to be provided for.

CHAPTER VI.

THE KALAHARI AND ITS SERFS

UNTIL very recent years the immense stretch of
country lying between the Orange River and Lake
Ngami, bounded on the west by the lands of the
great Namaquas and Damaras, and on the east
by Bechuanaland, was to be found a mere blank
upon the maps, bearing across it the idle legend,
"Kalahari Desert." But South Africa, since 1885,
has been so rapidly developed, and the rush of explorers, concession hunters, and prospectors has been
so keen, that even the desert itself has begun
slowly to yield up its secrets ; and it has now come
to be known that here is a country of rich grasses
and ample forests, healthy in the highest degree,
and offering, so soon as its subterraneous water
supply shall be tapped and made use of (for it carries
almost no surface water), perhaps the most magnificent field for ranching that the world can show.

It may be convenient here to indicate briefly the
divisions, tribes, and chiefs of this great and interesting region, as they are at present known.

West and north-west of Kuruman, then, lies the

CHILDREN OF THE DESERT: MASARWA BUSH-PEOPLE—NAQUA POOL, NORTH KALAHARI

territory of Toto, chief of the Batlaro, a Bechuana tribe whose headquarters lie at Phuduhuchwe, and of Bareki, chief of another branch of the Batlaro, who is settled at Honing Vlei. At Morokweng, a large native town, and in the country adjacent, Monchus, a Barolong chief, holds sway. Beyond him, to the north-west, in the country on either side of the sharp southerly bend of the Molopo River, come the hunting grounds of the Western Barolong, who own the chieftainship of Letlogile, whose principal town is Ganesa.

Along the Molopo, on either bank, for a long way westward from Mafeking, are the hunting grounds subject to Monsioa, the aged Barolong chief at Mafeking. It seems to be a moot point as to who is the paramount Barolong chief. Monsioa and Letlogile both claim the honour, and both have independent followings ; while Monchus, at Morokweng, who also is quasi-independent, is yet a third claimant. It is probable that Letlogile (who represents the elder branch of the royal house) has the best title, while Monsioa's age, experience, and valour against the Boers strengthen his hands in the eyes of many.

West of Toto and his Batlaro comes the territory of David Virlander and his Bastards, a mixed people who have been long settled at and around Hogskin Vlei, just north of the 26th parallel of south latitude. Their present station is known as Riet Fontein, or Naas, some nine miles west of the Vlei, whither they removed from Mier on the waters of that station becoming brack and salt. Virlander is reputed to have under his orders some 400 fighting men, mostly good shots, and his territory runs down south to the district now called Gordonia, just upon the Orange

River.   To the westward Virlander's country (now
a part of British Bechuanaland) abuts on the great
Namaquas (German sphere of influence); while to
the north it extends nearly to Lehutitung on the
tropic of Capricorn, where a Vaalpense or Bakalahari
chief named Maparo has managed, by some force of
character, to gather about him a following and assume
lands of his own.   Maparo's power has latterly been
augmented by fugitive Barolong and Bakalahari who
have sought his protection.

Although Maparo claims to be, and probably is in
fact, independent (for he is in the very heart of the
Kalahari, and is not easily approached), Ramalulu,
a minor Barolong chief, settled at Seledimolong, on
the Molopo River, claims to be his lord.   Ramalulu,
however, has under him only a small clan, and is
himself (as Monsioa has assured me) really a tributary
of Monsioa, and his power over Lehutitung and its
chief may be put down as *nil.*   Far north of Lehutitung, at a place called Oliphant's Kloof, at some
distance to the south-west of Lake Ngami, is a turbulent and restless settlement of Namaqua Hottentots,
Bastards, and others, gathered under a Namaqua
chief, known by some as Andries Lambert, or Lamert,
by others as Vliermuis (literally Flittermouse, or the
Bat).   The Oliphant's Kloof gang have a shady
reputation, and have been known to plunder traders'
waggons; they are cattle-stealers, and raiders on the
Damaras; they possess horses, and are good hunters
and shots, and not long since were even threatening
to attack Moremi, the Lake Ngami chief.   The Lake
tribe (the Batauana or Western Bamangwato) have
vast hunting grounds, running far south into the
desert, in which, besides troops of elands, gemsbok,

hartebeest, koodoo, ostrich, and other game, a troop or two of elephants and innumerable giraffes wander undisturbed.

Returning to the south-eastern portion of the Kalahari, we find that north of Monsioa's lands lie the hunting grounds of Batoen and his Bangwaketse people, whose territories run far westward into the desert until they impinge upon the Lehutitung chief. North again of the Bangwaketse, and again far westward into the desert, stretch the grounds of the Bakwèna under the aged chief Sechele—Livingstone's Sechele—or rather his son and regent Sebele. Here, too, great game, such as eland, gemsbok, and giraffe, are to be found.

The whole of the north-east corner of the Kalahari, touching south upon the Bakwèna, and west on the hunting grounds of the Batauana (the Lake tribe), forms part of the vast hunting veldt of Khama, chief of the Bamangwato. Owing, however, to its waterless character and inaccessibility little of this part of the desert is explored or even hunted, save in the vicinity of the waggon road running to Lake Ngami, and for a day or two's journey south of the Botletli River.

In such a territory as the Kalahari, little explored by natives, and even less known to white men, to allocate boundaries to these various tribal hunting grounds is a matter of absolute impossibility. They are vague and undefined, and even the tribesmen themselves and their chiefs have very misty ideas concerning them. The Vaalpense, or Bakalahari, the vassals, or rather slaves to the Bechuana tribes, squat here and there wherever a pit of permanent water is to be found, and tend the scant flocks and herds of their chiefs, and hunt for skins and ostrich feathers,

which periodically are collected by their over-lords.
The wild, untameable Bushman hunters still wander
after the game with their poisoned arrows and
assegais, and find sustenance and moisture, where
water is lacking, from the bulbs and melons in places
where no other living beings—native or European—
could exist. These are not the people to concern
themselves greatly about boundaries. It is recognised that from time immemorial certain waterpits
have belonged to certain tribes ; that and a vague
expanse of wild hunting veldt is sufficient.

Although in the last few years a sprinkling of
travellers and hunters have crossed and recrossed the
Kalahari, and wandered hither and thither among
the petty chiefs for the purpose of picking up concessions of land, very little is known of the country
even in adjacent South Africa. The spaces are so
immense, the surface waters so scant, and the
danger from death by thirst and starvation (for it
is a terrible country to get lost in) so imminent,
that extreme caution has to be exercised in opening
up the region. Let no man, unless he wishes to
leave his bones in some drear, grassy waste or lone
forest, attempt to exploit the Kalahari without the
best of guides and the advice and good offices of
local chiefs—who, by the way, are extremely jealous
and secret about the whole territory—else will he
surely come to grief. The flat, monotonous expanses
of grassy plain, the dense bush and forest, the rolling
sand dunes, are so perplexingly alike ; the sands so
heavy ; the utter silence and desolation and vast-
ness so oppressive, as to create doubt even in the
strongest minds. Even the very denizens of the
desert themselves at times lose their bearings and

are forsaken by their wonderful instinct of locality.
At present, whatever may be its future, the Kalahari
is assuredly not to be trifled with.

There are many indications that long ages since
this country was a well-watered one. Old rivercourses and "laagtes," or shallow valleys, here and
there score its surface. The Mokopo, along which
Livingstone found his way to Lake Ngami, and
which cuts the lake road near T'Klakane pits, is
one of them. But now they are always dry. The
Molopo, although figuring boldly upon the maps
as an important river system connecting with the
Orange, is nothing but a desiccated channel, a mere
mockery of a river. Nowadays no water flows in
the Molopo, even in time of rain, for more than
thirty miles beyond Mafeking. So also with the
Nosop, Oup, and Hygap, a channel or dry system
running north and south, which is another snare
and delusion of the cartographers. Rivers there are
none in the Kalahari, and surface water is practically an unknown quantity.

And yet during the brief weeks of rainfall no land
can assume a fairer or more tempting aspect. The
long grasses shoot up green, succulent, and elbow-
deep; flowers spangle the veldt in every direction;
the giraffe acacia forests, robed in a fresh dark green,
remind one of nothing so much as an English deer-
park; the bushes blossom and flourish; the air is full
of fragrance, and pans of water lie upon every hand.

Another month and all is drought; the pans are
dry again, the grasses are turning to their winter
yellow, and travel is full of difficulty. Only the
introduction of capital and well-sinking operations
on a large scale can cure this difficulty of water.

Water is there beneath the surface, and at no great distance ; and, once secured, ranching operations upon a large scale are, in such a country, certain of great and lasting success.   Hitherto hunters and traders have moved about the desert mostly in the season of rain; at other times they have been dependent on the wild bitter water-melons, which in certain years are very abundant.   The whole of the Kalahari may be classed as fine cattle country, carrying in every direction abundance of sweet grasses, capable of supporting stock even through the dry months of winter.   Part of the south and much of the northern portion of this so-called desert is clothed with immense stretches of excellent timber (mainly the slow-growing giraffe acacia, varied occasionally by the bastard yellow-wood, and, in the northern portion, by the mopani—a species of Bauhinia), and the whole region needs only permanent water stations—which can without doubt be provided—to transform it into the ideal ranching country of the world.

The Crown colony of British Bechuanaland is now, under recent proclamation, master of most of the Kalahari country claimed by the Batlaro, the Barolong, and Virlander's people.   Northward the remainder of the territory is included in the Protectorate and sphere of influence.   The next few years will inevitably witness great developments in this vast and interesting region.

But there is a sad and a dark side to this picture. Out in the Kalahari, and along the whole of its Bechuanaland border, there exist at this hour, in a state of absolute slavery and of hopeless degradation, a race of people known to their Bechuana lords as Bakalahari, and to Europeans by the Boer name

IN THE THIRSTLAND

(Between T'Kiakane and Inkonane, North Kalahari)

Vaalpense—literally "grey bellies"—a term of low
scorn which pretty accurately describes their miserable
condition. The Vaalpense have few traditions and
know little of their own history beyond the fact
that for long years—so long that the memories of
themselves and their fathers and fathers' fathers
run not to the contrary—they have squatted here
and there at waterpits throughout the desert.
Although more often than not depressed, half-
starved-looking people, they partake of the true
Bechuana type, and are specifically distinct from
the Masarwa Bushmen (a race of pure and simple
hunters to be found in the North Kalahari, and
thence so far as the Zambesi); and there seems no
reason to doubt that they are descendants of broken
septs or clans of Bechuana origin, who, having fled
or been driven into the desert, have subsisted there,
in a state of hardship and degradation, deteriorating
generation after generation, and owning allegiance to
the nearest tribe of Bechuanas who use the Kalahari
as a hunting ground and as pasture land for store
cattle. Thus the Barolong, Batlaro, Bangwaketse,
Bakwèna, and even lesser tribes, all own Vaalpense,
or Bakalahari, whom they keep in a state of perennial
slavery, employing them as hunters and collectors
of ostrich feathers, skins, and the like, and as shepherds of their surplus flocks and herds. It is note-
worthy that among the Bamangwato, under Khama's
wise and kindly rule, the Vaalpens system has been
nearly abolished, or greatly ameliorated. The Vaalpens has no status or rights whatever in the tribal
system, he is a serf who may have about him no
cattle, or sheep, or goats, save as caretaker for his
lord. Whatever spoil of the chase he may collect is

to be strictly accounted for, and, periodically, when some headman, or the paramount chief himself, comes round to collect his tribute, the poor wretch has to deliver up all that he has gathered with infinite toil and skill, and to account for every head of stock entrusted to his keeping. Woe betide him if the hunting season has been bad, or if the wild beasts have made havoc with flock and herd. He and his family must answer for it, in such a case, with heavy stripes; not seldom, indeed, a brutal death is the penalty. Even his children and women-folk are not his own, but may be and are seized and carried away into domestic servitude or concubinage.

In a word, the unfortunate Vaalpens exists at this day, and that within the boundaries of the Crown colony of British Bechuanaland and of the Bechuanaland Protectorate, in a state of cruel and abject slavery, the ill-used property of some insolent and overbearing chief, who himself dwells in contentment and plenty under the shadow of Queen Victoria's peace. The poor wretch has, in truth, nothing he may call his own, save perhaps his assegai and skin cloak and an ostrich shell or two, or a rude earthen pitcher in which his women-folk collect the scanty water supply. It is impossible to estimate even approximately the numbers of these poor people, but there are some thousands of them scattered about the Kalahari and in the Bechuana country. These things are not as they should be, and it is certain that if the Administrator of British Bechuanaland had his way, and could employ a few Border Police in carrying out his wishes and commands, the system of slavery would be soon abolished. When, however, it is remembered that at the great native towns of

Morokweng and Honing Vlei, and at Takoon, Motito Pitsani, Maribogo, Mosita, Takwaning, and other places, all adjacent to or in the Kalahari, and all in British Bechuanaland, there is not a single representative of law and order, it can scarcely be surprising that the detestable system of Bakalahari slavery remains rampant and unchecked. There have been one or two cases in recent years in which an unfortunate Vaalpens has attempted (knowing in a dim fashion that the British are morally upon his side) to withstand the oppressor and retain a miserable goat or two for his own use. In one instance at least death has been the penalty, and in others all sorts of cruelties have been perpetrated upon the offenders when the annual tribute visits have taken place.

Physically considered, the Kalahari can scarcely be called a desert. It abounds everywhere in long rich grasses, upon which cattle thrive to perfection. In the northern portion, as I have shown, great game is yet plentiful. If the poor Bakalahari could but be freed from the grinding yoke of their present task-masters, theirs would be a pleasant life enough. So soon as capital is introduced, and well-sinking comes into operation, and ranching is established on a large scale, the Kalahari is certain to prove itself one of the richest and most profitable cattle countries in South Africa. Already in the south-east farms are being demarcated and surveyed. With the advent of ranching operations and of British settlers, the good time of the Bakalahari will have come; but this must of necessity be a gradual process, and meanwhile, unless something is done for them by the Colonial Office at home, it is to be feared that they will continue to fare as ill as they have done these

K

generations past. British Bechuanaland has been hitherto somewhat starved by the Colonial Office. It is a promising colony, but it cannot in fairness be expected to emerge from its swaddling-clothes without help. The expense of the Border Police Force of the Protectorate and beyond is charged wholly to the debit of this Crown colony, which is itself all but denuded of police, and has year after year to witness, from sheer inability to help them, the miserable Vaalpense robbed and maltreated within its boundaries. Let these matters be fairly adjusted, and a great wrong can speedily be set right. We English boast that we have abolished slavery. Is it honest that slavery should yet be suffered to exist within our borders?

CHAPTER VII.

A TREK TO MOROKWENG, SOUTH KALAHARI

The start—Dogs—Early sport—Mosita—Recipe for game-stew—Shooting
at Mosita—Guinea-fowl—Reach Matlaping—Fine crops—Shoot a cobra
—A case of snake-bite—Matlaping valley—Display of butterflies—Trek
to Kudunque—Good shooting—Brack pan and spoor—Violet-winged
courser—A row with " April"—Bechuana servants—Kudunque Pool
—Salt licks and game—Bush quail—Cold night—Reach Morokweng
—Mr. Smith's hospitality—Native trading—Another shoot—Stilt
plovers—Native dance—Sights of Morokweng—Chief Monchus—Sea-
cow birds—Belles and bangles—Logolong Laagte—Night shooting—
Back to Mosita—Fine country—Large game—Lions.

ON April 5, having sent on the waggons previously
from our huts at the junction of the Setlagoli and
Maritsani rivers, we breakfasted at sunrise and rode
off towards Mosita in a westerly direction. Our
party of five consisted of Mackay, Dove, H. Gethin,
St. Stephens, and myself. With the waggon were
a driver ("April," our Matabele "boy"), leader, and
two boys to help with the horses, cook, and "boss up"
generally. We were all mounted on steady shooting
ponies, carried shot-guns, and were accompanied
by three pointers and a mongrel, the last of which
Mackay and I had picked up starving in Kimberley.
This dog followed my fortunes subsequently to
Ngamiland and back, thence being sent up to
Mashonaland in hopes of finding again his old half-
master Mackay—for we each claimed an undivided
moiety of him. Poor old Ponto, he was as faithful
a friend as ever man had ; but he could not be

moulded by coercion, coaxing, entreaty, or ensample, into a sporting dog. He was at least half pointer bred, and had a capital nose, but at the critical moment the evil portion of his nature came in and invariably drove from his brain all remembrance of previous lessons. He never could be induced to stand steadily to game ; and the amount of bad language that his misdeeds involved was sufficient to have blighted all the wide stretch of country from Mosita to Morokweng.

We set off in capital spirits—who, indeed, on the clear bracing uplands of this region can feel otherwise ?—and, crossing the dry bed of the Setlagoli, presently emerged upon a high flat tableland, much of it handsomely timbered with giraffe acacia. Here we spread out a little to provide our evening meal. St. Stephens was the first to score, his pointer Lassie finding him a brace of those beautiful little "partridges," as they are always called in South Africa, the Coqui francolin (*Francolinus subtorquatus*). Shortly after we put up five guinea-fowl, which flew towards Dove and myself. Of these Dove quickly bagged a brace—one as it flew from a tree, the other rising from the grass—while I secured a third. Then Mac legged the fourth, which was soon picked up, and, after a prolonged search, the fifth, and last, was found by my pointer Don, and instantly grassed by Dove, our crack shot. All these guinea-fowl were young birds in grand condition, and helped to furnish us that night with a supper fit for princes. I shot another partridge before sinking the hill to Mosita ; this time an Orange River francolin, the most common species in Bechuanaland. We trekked steadily on, passing the waggon towards afternoon, and reaching Mosita before sundown. The country in this neighbourhood is extremely picturesque and varied, carrying plenty of timber and bush, and broken here and there by fertile valleys, in which large crops of mealies and Kaffir corn are raised by the natives — hereabouts mostly of the Barolong tribe. There is a native location at Mosita, and, as it was Sunday afternoon, service was being held under a big camel-thorn tree. The people were all dressed in their best, and the gaily-coloured frocks and blankets of the women gave just the required touch of colour to a very charming scene.

Crossing the spruit, and passing some large water-pits, we made our way to the house of Mr. Reader (a large cattledealer having stock running here), near which we settled to outspan for the night.

Mosita had, a few months before our arrival, acquired the reputation of a promising gold area. A few prospectors were at work in places here and there, and some traces of gold had undoubtedly been found.

St. Stephens carefully inspected the formation in the course of this and the following day, with not very cheerful conclusions. The formation, it seems, is porphyritic granite of an extremely hard nature. What little gold there is is thin and patchy, and the hard, refractory nature of the rock renders it very unlikely that gold mining can ever be made to pay in this locality. This opinion seems to have been borne out by subsequent events, and the few prospectors have finally abandoned Mosita as impracticable. As soon as the waggon arrived we pitched the tent (in which Mackay and I slept), and made all snug for the night. Our supper consisted of the following ingredients : Five guinea-fowl, three partridges, water, sliced onions, potatoes, two dessert-spoonfuls Worcester sauce, two wineglasses Pontac (a rough, red Cape wine), pepper and salt, and half a teacupful of flour and water mixed into a paste. This stew I can, after a long and varied experience, strongly recommend. The liquor provides a delicious soup, and the meat a capital after-course. I will warrant that the most fastidious *gourmet* of the Amphitryon would not turn up his nose at such a repast, which, indeed, is calculated to appeal to the most delicate of appetites, much more to hungry men after a day on the veldt. We had a pleasant chat and smoke with Mr. Reader's foreman, an old interior man, and then turned in. The night was wet and thundery, which, however, did not prevent us from sleeping soundly.

On April 6 we were up early drying out after the stormy, wet night. We interviewed a Bakalahari after breakfast, who informed us that there were hartebeest, koodoo, gemsbok, springbok, and ostrich a little way ahead ; but that two Transvaal Boers had been standing for some time with their waggons at Kudunque, and had hunted the game about in all directions. This we found to be literally correct, and these miserable skin-hunters had greatly dis-counted our chances of large game for the time being. We found tobacco growing excellently well on a small patch just below the house, and mealies, pumpkins, and other crops were thriving. Mosita, with its rich valley, picturesque out-cropping rocks, and fine rolling grassy hills, looked beautiful towards afternoon, when the sun came out. It is, I think, one of the choicest situations in British Bechuanaland ;

and the next "laagte," or valley, at Matlaping, a
few miles further on, is equally attractive, whether
from an agricultural or artistic point of view. Towards afternoon, having explored the gold formation,
we strolled up the spruit (watercourse) with our guns,
but only succeeded in bagging two and a half brace
of partridge, koorhaan (black and white bustards),
and guinea-fowl. We wrote mails this morning, and
despatched a runner to Setlagoli, about twenty-five
miles distant. The horses had escaped from the
kraal during the night, and were not recovered till
late in the afternoon.

April 7. We were up early, as usual, and, the
morning being fine, three of us went for an hour's
shoot before breakfast, securing a few koorhaan,
guinea-fowl, and partridge. Birds were scarce and
wild in the neighbourhood, having, I suppose, been
a good deal shot at. We made bread—ingredients:
Boer meal, baking powder, and water—this morning,
and in the afternoon, having completed our inspection of Mosita, trekked away west up a beautiful
valley. In a couple of hours we reached a large
dense forest of bastard yellow-wood, a short, stunted
tree averaging about 20 or 25 feet in height. Just
before sundown Dove wounded a steinbok, but lost
him. About the same time, in another direction,
Gethin and I came upon some forty guinea-fowl preparing to roost, and, as usual, calling to one another
in a noisy manner with harsh metallic voices, making
the woods resound again. They were too sharp for
us, and we only secured a brace at long range, and
they afterwards ran in so rapid and persistent
a manner that we had to give them up, and find
our way back to the road. We outspanned on the

hillside, just above Matlaping, at 8 P.M.   The stew-
pot was, as usual, in requisition again, and, after a
hearty supper of game, and a smoke, we turned in
to the tent and waggon respectively.

Next morning, after a night's heavy rain, the torrent still steadily descended.   We all squeezed into
the little tent, and made shift for breakfast, with
the help of a case or two as tables.   At two o'clock
the rain cleared, and we sallied out for an hour's
sport.   There is a native village at Matlaping, and
in the valley on either side of the spruit, running
north to the Molopo River, were splendid crops of
mealies and Kaffir corn growing in rich, fertile soil.
Water is abundant and good ; besides the watercourse there are some deep, rocky pools, which should
last well on through the dry season.

We rode in various directions back to the forest
for a bird or two, but only secured among us a brace
of koorhaan, a brace and a half of partridge, and a
guinea-fowl.   The 9th of April still found us at
Matlaping.   In a short walk before breakfast I came
upon a large black or dark brown cobra (*Naia haje*)
which I shot as he darted swiftly away.   He measured
4½ feet long, and was a nasty-looking customer.
Just about this period, before the rains cease and
the sharp frosts of winter set in, snakes are very
plentiful in Bechuanaland.   But, as a rule, a good
stick will always account for them, and people trouble
themselves very little about them.   Shortly before
our arrival at Mosita, however, a Dutchman, as
he woke in the morning, was bitten on the arm
by a puff-adder, which had crept to him for warmth.
The puff-adder is deadly poisonous, and the man's
friends naturally feared exceedingly.   However, they

administered the usual up-country remedy—the contents of nearly two bottles of neat whisky—walked him about well, and, by great good fortune, pulled him through. The bitten arm, however, remained terribly swollen and inflamed for a long time. The wound was so offensive, and the stench from the virus and matter so dreadful, that strong men became sick and unable to stand near. The Boer subsequently recovered, after much suffering, and may well congratulate himself as one of the few people who have survived the poison of the terrible puffadder.

We had a chat with the headman of the kraal this morning. He was far too well-to-do and independent, asking 14s. for a goat (usual price 6s. or 7s.) and 1s. for a little milk. We bought eleven eggs for 1s. and left him.

At ten o'clock we set off in two parties for a food supply, Dove and I riding northward up the spruit. After a couple of miles we passed a huge mealie-field of some 100 acres. The crop was nearly ripe, and the corn was full of naked children, singing and shouting to keep off the swarms of doves and pigeons that came for food. They had a kind of monotonous chant; all Bechuana women and children have most beautiful voices, and the sound, as it fell upon the bright, clear, sunny air of this peaceful valley, had a very charming effect. As I rode past I exchanged calls with these merry black children, to their intense amusement. Peals of laughter ran around, and we kept up the exchange till I had ridden long past them. Presently we entered more forest land on the west of the spruit, and, although we were disappointed in getting a duiker or steinbok, we stumbled instead upon a most beautiful spectacle. We had come suddenly upon a large round clearing in the woodland, about 300 yards across, and covered with a thick rich carpet of many flowers. Among these flowers were thousands of brilliant butterflies sunning themselves, flashing hither and thither, feeding rapaciously at the sweet dainties, and making gay the veldt. The butterflies were nearly all newly-hatched and in the perfection of their wonderful sheen. I imagine the hot sun, after a night or two of rain, had brought forth thousands of newly-hatched butterflies, all in the very prime of their plumage. Most unfortunately, we had left the butterfly nets at the waggon, and, although we off-saddled and made strong play with our broad-brimmed hats, we were not so successful as we might otherwise have been. There were many kinds of butterfly, and during a year's sojourn in Bechuanaland I never saw them so numerous or so perfect as in this little forest glade. Among the species captured were *Pyrameis cardui, Hypanis ilythia, Teracolus eris, Teracolus evenina, Teracolus antigone, Herpænia eriphia, Terias zoë, Callidryas florella, Junonia cebrene, and Danais chrysippus.*[1] Many other rare and beautiful specimens escaped us.

Returning home I shot, as a contribution towards supper, a brace of koorhaan and an Orange River francolin ; and the rest of the party accounted for three and a half brace of partridges (Orange River and Coqui francolins) and a brace and a half of koorhaan. We had, as usual, a merry supper, and turned in early.

On the 10th we trekked away steadily, having

[1] Most of these were kindly identified for me by Mr. Trimen, curator of the museum at Cape Town.

crossed the Matlaping spruit, and, riding on, spread out through the dense forest and bush which surrounded the sandy waggon-track. Just as we left Matlaping, Dove shot two and a half brace of Coqui francolin on the stony hillside in excellent style, my pointer Don standing and working steadily. Shortly after, St. Stephens and I, who were together, bagged a leash of the same little game birds, and a bush koorhaan (*Eupodotis ruficristata*), a very handsome bustard, common to bush and forest country throughout Bechuanaland. This bustard has a swift, wavering flight, dodges a good deal among trees, and is excellent eating.

Presently we came across Mackay again, and as he carried my butterfly net slung to his saddle, and there were open glades about, we stopped and captured butterflies for half-an-hour or so. Towards noon we emerged upon open, undulating plains, covered with long yellow grass, where we continued our daily shoot for the evening pot. At three o'clock we found the waggon outspanned by a small vley of water, and, after "rowing" April, the driver, for his laziness, made him trek on until 8.30, when we outspanned at Kudunque Laagte. We, however, rode on, and off-saddled and kindled a good fire; but the donkeys (we had sixteen donkeys in our span) trekked very slowly through the sand. The stew took a good hour and a half to prepare, and we were desperately hungry by the time the savoury mess was ready. It was worth waiting for, though!

Before reaching Kudunque we had observed, at a small brack near the road, the spoor of gemsbok, which had evidently been to lick at the salt limestone. Our bag for the day was five and a half brace of francolin or "partridge," one variegated sandgrouse, one and a half brace bush koorhaan, one brace black and white koorhaan, and one very handsome plover, or rather courser—the violet-winged courser (*Cursorius chalcopterus*). These most beautiful birds, which we had not met with before, are rather local, and can nowhere be cited as very common. They arrive, I fancy, with the rains, and spread out in pairs over open grassy veldt. They average just under a foot in length ; the throat, rump, and under parts of the body are white, the back is pale-brown, the breast of the same colour banded in black. The wings are black, and are remarkable for the beautiful shining metallic violet of their tips. They lie very close, and are extremely difficult to flush.

During supper we wanted more wood for the fire, and as April had been shirking all day, and was now grumbling to the other boys, and vapouring in true Matabele style that he was one of the great Matabele Zulus, and his chief was Lobengula, and he wasn't going to do this, that, and the other, we thought it high time to call him to his senses. I therefore ordered him to cease, and go and get some wood. To this he very pointedly demurred, growling that he was not a dog, and wouldn't do it. He was a strong, athletic savage, but, there being no other course open, I jumped up, seized a sjambok, and went for him. Mackay sprang up at the same moment to assist in the operation. April, seeing we really meant business, got up like a lamb and went off for the wood, presently returning with a plentiful supply. We had no further trouble with him during the rest of the trek, and the timely display of firmness had its effect upon the other boys, none of whom were very keen about the journey. If these South Bechuanas can hang about one's huts, do odd jobs in their own way and at their own time, and have the run of the flesh-pots, they are not averse to serving the white man in a feeble, half-hearted sort of way. Directly, however, they are required to perform a little real work, they cry off and return to their kraals. The Batlaping, Barolong, and other tribes of the Crown Colony, are indeed miserable servants, utterly unreliable, and too often without an atom of pluck or self-respect in their composition. The labour difficulty, as all farmers and employers of labour rightly complain, is one of the main drawbacks to life in British Bechuanaland. Good wages are paid, good food is provided, and yet one cannot obtain decent servants. One of Khama's Bamangwato boys is worth, in working capacity, cheerfulness, and pluck, half a dozen of the miserable, whining, sneaking servants, who call themselves Batlaping, Barolong, or Batlaro. In justice to our Matabele boy, April, I am bound to say that, as a rule, he was a good willing servant, and managed his donkey team (of which he was inordinately fond and proud) extremely well.

In the morning we had a minute inspection of Kudunque and its surroundings. Here running at right angles to the waggon road is a shallow depression or "laagte" which extends northward as far as the Molopo River, and which holds during the rains a good deal of water. There is a fine deep limestone basin or pool, which we found to contain splendid clear water. So quickly do these desert waters fail, however, that on our return within a week the pool had shrunk to very small dimensions. We had a capital bathe, and after breakfast washed our socks, handkerchiefs, and flannel shirts, which soon dried in the sun and wind. From the northward, well-defined game paths led to the pool ; these were made by hartebeest, and were quite recent. On the left or southward of the road are two large bracks, or "licks," in the same limestone formation. Game here in bygone days must have been in extraordinary abundance, great hollows having been worn in the hard limestone by the tongues of myriads of animals during countless years. These bracks were and still are favourite places for night shooting. There were one or two scherms or screens near the edges of the pan, and on a moonlight night, upon the white expanse of the brack, game can easily be seen and shot. Our friends the Boers had evidently had a good innings here. We found fresh spoor of gemsbok, hartebeest, and ostrich, as well as of hyænas, jackals, and small bucks, but, as time was short, we were unable to stay for a night's shooting on this occasion.

It is a curious fact that many of the larger antelopes, such as gemsbok and hartebeest, will come and lick at these limestone bracks, and yet will pass by the water. In the dry season, of course, they have to do without water altogether. The preference for salt or brackish limestone over pure water is certainly a remarkable one.

We took some photographs of our camp, breakfast, &c., at this place, and then wandered about quietly exploring. Before the waggon trekked again I shot another violet-winged courser, and Dove a brace of tiny bush-quail (*Turnix lepurana*), dainty creatures, scarcely bigger than sparrows, which fly very fast, and lie more closely, I think, than any of the close-lying African game birds. Mackay also made a good shot off his pony, and knocked over a partridge at more than thirty yards. As a rule, we got off our horses when the dogs stood to game. The nags—all except St. Stephens' mount, which had occasionally a nasty habit of trotting away—stood admirably, and gave us no trouble. The reins were, of course, always thrown over the head, and hung in front of the forelegs in the usual South African fashion.

We trekked steadily all the afternoon and until nine o'clock at night. It was bitterly cold after sundown, so much so, that we horsemen were glad to lead our nags most of the evening and keep ourselves warm with the exercise. At length we came to a huge friendly vaal bush sticking up on the bare flats, and made a roaring fire long before the waggon turned up. The vaal bush, or mohatla (*Tarchonanthus*), common all over much of South Bechuanaland, is a true friend to the traveller; its branches, although covered with grey-green leafage, are highly inflammable and soon produce a cheery blaze. This night intense frost prevailed; Mackay and I, under our thin canvas tent, were nearly frozen, although we had each three blankets over us, as well as a dog or two at our feet. In the morning a bitter cold wind blew harshly over the veldt, and we were glad of our coats until long after sun-up. During the winter months in Bechuanaland this keen, cold wind is a noticeable and unpleasant feature of early morning. It usually rises about break of day, and continues for a couple of hours or more, until the sun has got the better of night. We were now in the midst of a huge expanse of grassy plains which extended in flat monotony until checked by the horizon. Long, pale sun-dried grass stood up to one's middle—the new growth not having yet arisen—and small buck could steal away unperceived without much difficulty. We rode steadily until four o'clock, passing a small native station at Masabaquane, and shooting a few birds by the way, when we outspanned just beyond two small pans of water in a charming bit of forest scenery under a big camel-thorn tree. On the 14th we pushed on steadily, and, after a trek of twenty-two miles—a good trek for the donkeys—the waggon reached Morokweng early next morning, we on horseback having ridden in during the afternoon of this day. We were now fairly in the true Kalahari country; boundless expanses of pale yellow grassy plains extending in all directions, broken only here and there by dark belts of timber, until they merged in the far blue of the horizon. We found quite fresh spoor of a large troop of hartebeest, but, having no spoorers with us, it was useless to follow. Unless one can tell to within an hour when game has passed —which no white man, unless he has lived great part of his life in the veldt, can do—it is useless following game spoor in the Kalahari. As a rule, only good native hunters can track game properly; and an Englishman might just as well search for a needle in a bundle of hay as track game, unaided by native hunters, in the vast solitudes of the Kalahari, where water is scarce, and losing oneself is a very simple and often dangerous operation. Of course I refer to those parts where game has become scarce and wild. At Logolong (pronounced Loholong) Laagte, another brack-pan, about ten miles from Morokweng, we found spoor of gemsbok, hartebeest, ostrich, spring-bok, and plenty of small antelopes. The country dips from this point towards Morokweng. We off-saddled at a small round pan of water further on, and then, cantering along through heavy sand, at length beheld from a bluff the large native town of Morokweng, the circular grass-thatched huts looking for all the world like a huge collection of bee-hives. Beyond, showing up in green patches from the pale grassy veldt, lay great fields of mealies and Kaffir corn, just now springing into strength. Passing a large salt-pan (all the shallow limestone pans of this country, which are dry in winter and hold a few inches of water in the rainy season, are dignified by the name of salt-pan) on the left hand, in another half-hour we rode into the town and off-saddled at the house and store of Mr. C. Smith—known everywhere as Charlie Smith—the principal trader. We had some fair shooting in the morning, and brought in five brace of partridge (Orange River francolin) and two brace of koorhaan. We also put up a rooikat (African lynx) which the dogs lost, and peppered a huge black eagle very hard, who, however, absolutely declined to fall to either No. 2 or No. 5 shot.

Mr. Smith, with his usual hospitality, insisted on putting us all up, and, after a capital supper of hartebeest venison, made up blankets for us, some on the floor, some on the counter of his store. Morokweng is, on the whole, a picturesque place. The native town is planted on the rise of a gentle hill, which slopes down to a huge limestone pan, just at this season covered with a few inches of water, and presenting to the uninitiated eye the appearance of a most beautiful lake. When, however, one sees, as we did, the boy herds driving their cattle home to kraal across this huge expanse of water, which barely covered their ankles, the illusion somewhat vanishes. None the less the dying sunset, lending a wonderful sheen to the mirror-like water, the cattle daintily reflected as they paused to drink, the warm red walls of the native huts upon the hill above, and the still atmosphere suffused with the rich glow of African evening, all united to form a picture of unique beauty.

At Morokweng, on the 15th of April, we prowled about over the store, and purchased some further supplies for the waggon, as well as curios, lion claws, odds and ends, and some capital karosses of the "motluse" and silver jackal. Mackay, who has a weakness for store clothes, insisted on arraying himself in a suit of bright canary-coloured moleskin, and, although we all jeered at his Boer-like figure, appeared highly pleased with himself for the rest of the day. Soon after breakfast—indeed, some of them before—natives came dropping in for small purchases. All trade here is done by barter. A native brings in an ox, or a goat, or a skin, or some ostrich feathers, or a kaross, and is paid its value in trade stores ; clothes—fustian and moleskin—hats, blankets, cotton prints, shawls, coloured handkerchiefs, knives, powder, lead, caps, cartridges, and guns, being among the most appreciated articles. Beads have not the vogue they used to have, but are still sold. Curiously enough the fashions change very rapidly in beads, and after one season a trader may have on hand a large stock perfectly unsaleable. This year a large dark blue bead, with white bird's eyes, was the thing in many localities.

Stuck up on the wall, just at the entrance, was a

large inscription plainly written in Sechuana. It ran thus : " Ga-ke-nee-Molato," which, being interpreted, means *I give no Credit*. Rather an unexpected legend this to meet out here ; commercial morality is, I suppose, at a discount even in these wilds. It is a notable fact that the Bechuana has very pronounced trading instincts ; he is an exceedingly hard man at a bargain—very bad to beat indeed ; knows the price of commodities in a wonderful way, even as far down country as Kimberley ; and, as he sets no sort of value upon time, he will spend a day, or many days, in haggling, until he obtains his object. In Bechuanaland, as in most places, things are now " cut very fine " compared with a few years back, and the enormous profits of the good old days are departed. Of course in the far interior, in Mashonaland, Ngamiland, and the Zambesi country, where severe competition has not yet set in, trading still pays very handsomely.

We traded some magnificent specimens of gemsbok heads this morning, and, having taken photographs here and there, and pottered about generally, rode out for a shoot in the afternoon. We were not lucky in finding guinea-fowl—hereabouts extraordinarily plentiful—and only shot a few hares, koorhaan, and partridges ; but, riding across a shallow pool of water, I came on a pair of black-winged stilt plovers (*Himantopus melanopterus* of Temminck ; *Charadrius himantopus* of Linnæus), which are not common even in this remote region. They were standing pensively, mirrored in the glassy water, at the far end of the pool, and got up as I approached ; but, my pony jerking his head as I fired from his back, I missed securing a specimen. No one can possibly mistake the extraordinary length and slenderness and brilliant red colouring of the legs of these interesting fowls. The body colour is snowy white, the wings are black, there is a spot of brown about the shoulders, and the tail is touched with the same colour. I afterwards found these birds on the Botletli River further north, but only sparingly even there. The average length of these beautiful waders is fifteen or sixteen inches. They are known to Europe and Asia as well as Africa, and in my opinion are one of the most remarkable of the great family of *Scolopacidæ*, or snipes, in which they are classed.

We saw a good many small buck during the afternoon, but, having no beaters, and the terribly thorny haak-doorn bush being very dense, could do no good with them. This haak-doorn or hook-thorn bush extends for twenty miles out into the desert to the westward ; in which direction a bold chain of hills— a continuation of the Langeberg—confronted the eye in the far distance, running nearly north and south. We noticed on our way out that the native gardens of mealies and Kaffir corn were showing promise of a grand harvest. As usual, women were hard at work hoeing and keeping off birds, while the men were in town sewing karosses, gossiping, or idling at home.

There is a good supply of water at Morokweng, contained in deep limestone wells all the year round, so that the people are not compelled to trek in the dry season.

In the evening, hearing a native dance in the town, we walked up and were considerably amused. Numbers of Barolong—young men and women mostly—were footing it together in measured time to the slow cadences of a monotonous chant, which never varied, and continued throughout the night until early morning. Wrapped in karosses and blankets, the elders were squatting or lounging about here and there by large fires, which served to impart a picturesque wildness to a curious scene. There was a good deal of dust floating in the air, and, as our arrival on the scene was the signal for renewed Terpsichorean vigour, the sand, turmoil, and *bouquet de l'Africaine* were all sufficiently pronounced. The chant itself is not unmusical, and the voices of these young Bechuanas were melodious and well-drilled, but when the same cadences are repeated for eight or ten hours at a stretch—often night after night at this season of the year—they become desperately monotonous, and the thing palls upon over-wearied ears. Next day a deputation from the dancers waited upon us at our waggon, and we rewarded them with a quantity of tobacco —in their eyes no doubt a sufficient tribute of admiration.

We were not long in exhausting the sights of Morokweng. We looked in at the tiny mud-walled church, in which were no chairs—the congregation all squatting in the usual Bechuana fashion—and the altar being represented by a small deal table. Then we visited the other trading store and over-hauled curios there, and afterwards had a good look round the town. The chief Monchus or Monsois we did not see. He is very ill-disposed to the English, and not at all inclined to be civil. Some months after our visit he fell foul of a Border policeman, obstructed him in the execution of duty, and actually induced his people to take away a stolen horse or horses from his custody by a display of armed force. This was going a little too far, however, even for the ill-supported powers of British Bechuanaland; the chief was taken, brought before the resident magistrate at Vryburg, and fined.   It would have done no harm if he had been imprisoned.   From laudable but mistaken motives of economy, the Government of the new colony is starved by the Home Government, and is not strong enough; the chiefs both there and in the Protectorate (with the exception, of course, of Khama), now that the fear of the Boer is for ever removed from their borders, are disaffected and impudent, and do all in their power to thwart and belittle the representatives of the Government that saved them at the very last stroke of the eleventh hour from utter extermination at the hands of the Transvaal freebooters, who would assuredly have made an end of them and their country.

It is high time that the additional police force required in Bechuanaland was granted, so that this huge territory might make some show of resolute government, which at present it cannot do.   Large native towns, such as Morokweng, require detachments of police to keep order and prevent Bakalahari slavery, the perpetration of cruelties on these poor unprotected serfs, and other abuses.   Only a year or two back a Vaalpens or Bakalahari slave (for they are nothing else but slaves) was murdered in the territory of this very chief Monchus, for daring to keep two or three goats of his own to himself, and not rendering them up to his Barolong lord and master.   The traders at Morokweng are too isolated and too much under the thumb of the chief, and a

OUR TREK AT MOROKWENG—SOUTH KALAHARI

(From Photo. by W. Mackay)

file or two of Border police would be much appreciated by them also. Monchus, as I have already mentioned, although nominally included by Monsioa, the old chief of the Barolong, among his vassals, himself sets up as a sovereign, and exercises independent sway. He is a gentleman who requires looking after. Mackay and I took photographs of the pan and of the expedition preparing to leave the town—waggon, donkeys, servants, horses, riders and all—just at sunset. Before lunch I walked down to the pan with Dove, and while there he shot, as specimens, a pair of that tiny plover known up-country as the sea-cow bird, from its habit of constantly attending the hippopotamus. Many kinds of African game have some special attendant feathered friends, who free them of parasites, gently titillate their skins, and warn them of danger.

On the Botletli, where sea-cows are found, I again saw these pretty plovers, which only average from six to seven inches in length. This, the treble-collared plover (*Charadrius tricollaris*), is in general colouring brown and white, the forehead is white, the throat is dusky, and is followed by a neat black collar, then by a white one, and then again by a broader black one. The stomach is spotless white. These charming little birds were busily scuttling about in the mud and water at the edge of the lagoon, picking up food here and there; they move very rapidly, but are tame enough and easily shot. Just at close of day the waggon moved off, St. Stephens accompanying it. We others remained for another night at Mr. Smith's, having arranged with him to ride on next day and try a night's shooting at Logolong Laagte.

There was a wonderful display of colour as the sun vanished; pale blues and greens, red and gold and pink vying with one another in gorgeous array. The thatched town behind us, the red walls blushing to the kiss of evening, the still lake beneath, and the distant desert fading into mystery in front, all tended to impress and kindle the imagination.

Next morning we were up betimes, and had rather an amusing scene trading bangles from native belles outside the store. We bought some very good copper, brass, and bead bangles and necklets, and then—I blush to say it—our fair friends had recourse to their legs and ankles, pulling off their cherished ornaments with immense alacrity the bargain once struck, after a good deal of haggling, and no end of laughter on both sides.

Presently we saddled up and rode on to catch the waggon. At one short halt Dove and I made a lucky shot from our ponies, each grassing a sandgrouse as a brace got up near at hand. Our morning bag as we went along totalled five brace of feathered game. At three o'clock we reached our camping ground, and rode on to the laagte, where we proposed to lie out for the night. Having seen what spoor was about and fixed up the shooting holes, we returned to the waggon, which had halted under a big tree a mile away. This tree must have seen many a good head of game skinned and cut up a few years back, for we found the horns of several wildebeest, hartebeest, and other buck, trophies of Mr. Smith's night shooting, still littering the ground. Having dined, we waited till sundown, and soon after, each carrying blankets and a rifle, we set off for the laagte. It was a dark night, with no moon, and somehow we lost our direction, and it was a good long hour, after floundering about the uneven veldt and the expenditure of some strong language, before we struck the brack pan. The shooting scherms lay about 300 yards apart down the length of the pan, and, having settled beforehand the choice of positions, Mackay and Dove took the top hole, Smith and St. Stephens the middle one, while Gethin and I lay at the further end. By 7.45 we had snugly ensconced ourselves in our shallow holes, well wrapped in blankets, and hidden by a screen of low bush from the brack in front of us. The night, as I have said, was dark; and, although the stars shone brightly overhead, we had no aid from the moon, and it was hard to see anything twenty yards away, even upon the white surface of the brack. Strain one's eyes as one would, it was impossible to pierce the dim pall of night that enveloped all things. A moonlight night is a necessity for the full enjoyment of this kind of shooting; but, as no moon could by any possibility appear, we had to strain our eyes and trust to our ears.

Properly to appreciate the weird solemnity of the veldt, one has but to lie out in such a fashion as I write of. By degrees the eyes become more accustomed to the uncertain darkness, the hearing is extraordinarily quickened, and the footsteps even of a small buck not far away can be heard very distinctly. The very stillness of the night is now and again broken by the wailing cry of a jackal, as he gets our wind, and proceeds to inform his friends of the fact. The howl of a distant hyæna, the mournful cry of a night plover, the occasional snort of some small antelope testing the air for danger, are the only sounds that break upon the ineffable solemnity for a long hour or so. Looking upward, the brilliant canopy of stars, burning as only they burn in Africa, fairly dazzles the eyes as they seek again the dim uncertainty of earth. The soft breeze, getting chillier as the hours creep on, sweeps almost straight down the brack.

At 9.45 my comrade and I hear the strong blowing of a hartebeest as he comes down to the pan. We gaze our hardest, but can see nothing, and the sound passes away. Soon after the loud crack of a rifle rings out upon the night. It is from the upper scherm, and we congratulate ourselves that at all events some sport is going on.

The night wears slowly on. Towards the small hours Gethin and I take it in turns to have forty winks. I am afraid my companion thought me a hard master when my watch had ended; he was so desperately sleepy. We neither saw nor heard any more large game during the night. The Southern Cross turned on its side in the heavens, the slothful dawn came round, and at length we rose stiff and benumbed, lit a well-earned pipe, and joined our companions. To our great dismay, we found no game had been killed.

What had happened was this. Dove had dozed off for half-an-hour while Mackay watched. He was wakened, and heard the whisper, "There's a great big devil of a buck over here." Straining his eyes, he presently got the loom of a big antelope against the white pan, about thirty paces distant. He whispered to Mackay to fire, but the latter thought the game eighty yards away, and waited. The antelope (its spoor next morning proved it to have been a large bull gemsbok) scented danger, and began to move away, and Dove, firing one shot from his Express, missed in the darkness.

It was a thousand pities to have lost so fine a buck, but in the darkness it was excusable, and these things will happen, as every hunter knows. Two nights later we lay out again at Kudunque Laagte, but at ten o'clock a violent thunderstorm came up, drenched us all to the skin, and sent us back to the waggon mere huddles of wet blankets, coats, rifles, and miserable men. We shall not readily forget the four-mile walk, loaded up as we were, in that thunderstorm.

The next night, of course, after a wonderful sunset, a sharp, silvery new moon came floating up in the pale blue sky, a rose glow below it, and beneath that again a blaze of orange and yellow. We had no time to wait for the moon to grow, however, on this trip, much as we wished to have fairly tried the splendid brack at Kudunque. We reached the Setlagoli and Maritsani Junction again on April 21, after a very interesting if rather hurried trek of 152 miles—seventy-six miles each way by waggon road. We sighted by the way a good troop of hartebeest as we rode in from Mosita. They were but a hundred yards off, but we had only shot-guns at the time.

The journey had been more in the nature of an exploration than a shooting party; we had had no time to pursue large game properly, and such feathered game as we shot by no means represented a fair sporting bag, but merely the humble, if necessary, everyday shoot for the pot. We had seen enough of the country, however, to convince us that much of it is a promising farming district. In the valleys of Mosita, Matlaping, Masabaquane, Marabani, and others, fine crops are and can be grown. Much of the veldt is well fitted for ranching on a large scale, although water will have to be sunk for and found to support any considerable head of stock far from existing waters. A few years hence will doubtless work great changes in this respect, when one remembers what well-sinking and water conservation have done in many parts of Cape Colony. Grass is good, and superabundant everywhere; and Bechuanaland cattle, whether as beef-producers or trek-oxen, cannot be beaten in any part of South Africa. During the last few months much of the land about Mosita, Matlaping, and Kudunque has, under the Government Survey, been surveyed and beaconed off for farms.

There is far more game in this part of the country than most people are at all aware of. Gemsbok, hartebeest, koodoo, springbok, ostrich, and of course duykers and steinbok, are all fairly plentiful. Unfortunately, no sort of protection is afforded; the natives of the various locations are permitted to slaughter at their pleasure; Dutchmen trek in and scour the country, and in a few years there will, I fear, be little of the *feræ naturæ* left. During the following season (1891) the natives from Ganesa location slew some twenty-seven gemsbok, and about the same number of hartebeest in a few weeks' hunting in the Mosita and Kudunque districts; and these noble antelopes are not likely to survive very long such indiscriminating onslaughts. Calves, cows, and bulls are alike slaughtered in these native hunts.

Lions have not yet quite departed from this region.

We heard of two having been spoored up the Setlagoli River as far as Marabani (near Mosita), just
about the time I write of. Another pair were shot
near Ganesa—four or five hours from Vryburg, the
capital of British Bechuanaland—only some four
years since.

CHAPTER VIII.

A TRIP TO MARICO, NORTH-WEST TRANSVAAL

Ravaged by horse-sickness—Vulture banquets—Visit to Knox and Fanshawe—A long shot—Superior cuisine—Show huts—Large game in
1836—Hartebeest hunting—Seven mile chase—Fleetness of the
hartebeest—Reach Mafeking—A crowded town—Start for Zeerust
—Malmani and its gold—Splendid scenery—Boers and their farm-
steads—Orange groves—Mynheer Botha's—Reach Zeerust—A charming town—Festive days—In search of horseflesh—Some of our
purchases—Lobengula's nag—Ride to Klaarstrom—The "schiet paard"
—Butterflies—Puff-adder—Lovely country—Water Kloof—More Boer
homesteads—A Boer deal—Back to Zeerust—Another purchase—Boer
rifle practice—Return to Junction.

Just at the beginning of May, when the first frosts
had set in, and we had flattered ourselves into the
belief that our nags were safe for the season, the
deadly horse-sickness fell upon us. First one good
pony, then another, then others, were snatched from
us; until, within a week, we found our united stud
reduced to a meagre remnant indeed. There was, as
usual in this disease, very little warning. A boy
would come in and report that one of the nags was
sick. We would then proceed to inspect the sufferer,
whose swollen eyes, fiercely beating flanks, running
and dilated nostrils, occasional cough, and dejected
appearance, told at once the miserable tale. A little
later the yellowish foam would begin to appear, the
breathing become yet more laboured, and then death
would ensue. In some instances the disease ran for
a day, or even a little more, before the end came;

in others it was a matter of but few hours; in one case the horse died within two hours of the early symptoms being noticed. We did what we could, tried the best known remedies, strong mustard and vinegar blisters, drenches of carbolic and oil (forty drops of carbolic in a pint of warm oil), hot fomentations, plenty of clothing, but all of little avail. Out of eleven horses five died, two recovered and became "salted," but much enfeebled for some months to come, while four escaped altogether.[1] It is a pitiable disease, this South African horse-sickness. One sees so much of one's nag in the long days together on the veldt; and a kindly companionship, often lacking at home, is speedily established, when, as usually happens, the master tenders the morning and evening feed of mealies with his own hands. In these circumstances the loss of an old and trusted equine friend and comrade becomes doubly embittered, and, as no remedy has yet been discovered for this sickness, it all seems a hopeless struggle when the favourite falls sick. Then, too, in this disease the poor beasts seem as if they must come to man, or man's habitations, for their closing hours; they will hang about your huts in a sort of mute appeal, which is sadly trying. Even in up-country towns this may be seen, and the poor dying wretch yields up its latest breath in the public street, as I have more than once seen. The horse-sickness season of 1890 was one of the most disastrous on record throughout Bechuanaland, the Transvaal, Griqualand West, and the Orange Free State. Even in Cape Colony, in

---

[1] The actual cause of death seems to be an intensely acute and sudden inflammation of the lungs and other parts, and suffocation ends the struggle.

localities where it had apparently died out, it re-
appeared again. The vultures round our huts at the
junction of the Maritsani and Setlagoli rivers gorged
themselves to their hearts' content during the week
of death. So soon as a pony died, we spanned in a
couple of oxen, and by aid of the trek-chain dragged
the carcase to a sufficient distance from our habitations, after which the aasvogels (vultures) and jackals
soon accomplished their foul task.

As we had business at Mafeking, and it was
necessary to procure remounts for present use and
our contemplated expedition to Ngamiland, my
companions—Mackay and Dove—and I rode off on
the afternoon of May 2 for the farm of Mr. H. H.
Knox, who, with Captain Fanshawe, was living on the
Maritsani River, some fifteen miles to the eastward.
We had been invited to stay a night or two with
these gentlemen, and our nearest neighbour, Mr. P.
Gethin, rode with us.

We carried our guns of course, and had the dogs
with us, and shot a few head of feathered game as
we went along. Just before reaching Knox and
Fanshawe's huts I made a remarkable, if lucky, shot
at a koorhaan (black and white bustard) as he flew
across our left flank, cackling noisily, as these game
birds always do. He seemed all but out of range,
but I pulled up my pony, fired from the saddle,
aiming well in front, and next instant, to the general
astonishment, the koorhaan fell dead as mutton—
" moors dood," as a Boer would say. I used the left
choked barrel and No. 2 shot, a combination that
in my opinion cannot be beaten for the larger game
birds so often met with in South Africa. It was a
long shot, the distance paced out being just under

"APEL," MY FIRST SHOOTING PONY

seventy yards, and these birds take much killing, and I am afraid my comrades extracted a good deal of chaff from the incident. Just at sundown we reached our destination, and were warmly welcomed. The waggon, which we had sent on with our rifles, blankets, and other articles, was outspanned, and very shortly we were doing justice to a most excellent dinner, the main honours of which rested, I think, with that excellent *chef* Captain Fanshawe. Delicious " cookies " of sifted Boer meal, roast partridges, a leg of goat done to a turn, and some wonderful onion sauce, helped out with jam, butter, whisky, and coffee, soon put us in trim for the soothing pipe of Transvaal tobacco (which is universally smoked up-country, and is excellent) and a tune from the banjo of that accomplished minstrel Mackay.

Knox and Fanshawe had built some capital huts on a plan of their own, thatched and roofed, of course, in the usual Bechuana style. These they had white-washed with a solution of soft kaolin found near the river bed, which, with tasteful green doors, imparted quite the appearance of neat English cottages. Tiny glass windows, artfully contrived from a number of spoiled photographic half-plates, completed the air of refinement, and rendered these huts quite the show-places of the country side—over an area of, say, two or three English counties. After a pleasant evening we turned into our blankets, and were soon asleep.

The larger game has, as I have said, now become very scarce in the less remote parts of British Bechu-analand, but a troop or two of hartebeest still roamed north of the Maritsani in this neighbourhood ; and, for the reason that our hosts carefully preserved

M

them as much as possible, these handsome antelopes, perhaps the most characteristic of all the Bechuanaland fauna, were generally to be found among the camel-thorn forests upon Knox's 6000 acre run, which, like all Bechuanaland farms, is at present unfenced. It had been settled, therefore, for some time that we should have a hunt on this favourite ground, and next morning at dawn we were up and in the saddle. Just fifty-four years before—in 1836—Captain Cornwallis Harris, the first of the great Nimrods who afterwards exploited this wonderful game country, passed through this very region. In those days this locality must have been a perfect paradise, teeming with countless herds of game—wildebeest, eland, buffalo, rhinoceros, lions, zebra, tsesseby, hartebeest, gemsbok, and the rest. Now, alas, all have vanished from these erst glorious hunting grounds, excepting a troop or two of hartebeest, a few springbok, and the inevitable duyker and steinbok.

The forests through which we rode to-day have altered little since Harris's time, but the game has gone. One of the best-remembered pictures in Harris's excellent work, "Wild Sports of Southern Africa," depicts a scene, "Hunting at Maritsani," in which crowds of game are being chased upon this very ground. I remembered the picture so well; it was a sad thing to find these pleasant forests and great plains now so depleted. There were the giraffe acacias, often built up with the rick-like grass nests of the social weaver-birds, just as Harris painted them in his clever sketches; but the fat elands and dumpy rhinoceroses resting in the shade, the crowds of game thronging the broad pastures, where, alas! were they? These thoughts ran through my head as we rode along on this warm, pleasant morning in search of our hartebeest.

In the first instance, we proceeded through flat, open forest-land to a part of the veldt where a pan of water stands during the rainy season. This was now dry, and although we found plenty of spoor about, no hartebeests were to be seen. Spreading out in line, we rode in another direction for an hour or two, and then off-saddled for half-an-hour to rest the nags and have a pull at our water-bottles. Having resumed our search, we spread out yet further apart, at intervals of five or six hundred yards. At about half-past one I, who was on the extreme right, suddenly noticed in front of me a troop of large, reddish-coloured buck. I had never seen hartebeest in the wild state before, but I knew them instantly by their long, old-fashioned faces, high withers, sloping quarters, and bright bay colouring. There was a good troop of them, about eighteen in all ; some were standing in low bush, others lying down, and they formed a beautiful picture, surrounded as they were by typical sylvan scenery. They saw me at the instant I set eyes on them, and springing up and away, loped off at a steady canter. Galloping hard, I got within 200 yards, jumped off, fired, and missed. The troop, now fairly alarmed, stretched themselves out, and were soon lost to sight among bush and acacia trees. I followed on at a good pace, and, presently emerging on some open rising ground, saw them galloping far away on a distant undulation of the veldt. I rode on their spoor some mile or two further, and then, turning, retraced my steps to the forest flats. Looking through an open glade, I presently noticed some way off a bay figure, which

I took to be Dove's pony, and so, taking off my hat,
I waved it, shouting lustily at the same time. To
my surprise the red figure turned and bolted swiftly
to the right hand. I at once guessed that I had
mistaken a hartebeest for a horse, and, ramming in
spurs, dashed off in the direction of the fugitive.
Very quickly I saw, cantering leisurely through the
open forest, another good troop of twenty hartebeest,
sailing away as if to cross my front. I set my horse
at his best gallop to cut them off, and although
they now increased their pace, I had too good a
start, and severed the troop right in half as they
tried to pass, part flying away beyond me, the other
half standing at less than 200 yards, evidently perplexed for the moment. So close were they, that
their black faces, rugged horns, and full black tails
were all plainly visible. I jumped off, took aim at
the nearest, a good bull some hundred and fifty yards
distant, and had the satisfaction of striking him
through the ribs, but, I fancy, rather high up, and
too far back to be immediately fatal. I was a little
unsteady from the gallop, or should have secured
him. The band, now startled into action, suddenly
swerved off and tore away at a great pace. I fired
again, but missed, and then turned to my horse for
more cartridges. I was as usual riding in a flannel
shirt — coatless — I had no bandolier on, and my
cartridge bag was fastened to the saddle. To my
intense disgust, my horse, for some fatuous reason,
had trotted away, and, as fast as I followed him,
he moved on. Despite my fierce wrath, there was
nothing for it but patience, and after ten minutes'
manœuvring I secured my errant steed. By this
time the hartebeest had gone heaven knows where,

and although I followed them for some way, I could never get within hail again.

Much disgusted, I rode off for home, where at about four o'clock I found the rest of my comrades. Strangely enough, not one of them had heard my shots or come across the spoor of my quarry. It is indeed astonishing at how short a distance, in African forest, the sound of rifle shots can be lost. Fired by the news I brought in, my friends determined to stop another day, and try again for the hartebeest.

Next morning, therefore, taking a Bakalahari to spoor, we made for the point where I had last seen the game. The native soon found the blood spoor of my wounded antelope, but although he and Mackay followed it up for some miles, they never got up with the buck. On the following day the Bakalahari, with another native, again went on the spoor, but whether he ever secured the wounded hartebeest I never learned, as we had then left. Meanwhile, Dove, Gethin, Knox, and myself had been looking in another direction. Dove, who was ahead, soon sighted a troop of eighteen or twenty hartebeest, and, calling to us, dashed after them. The buck had a long start and went at great speed, and, with Dove behind them forcing the pace, were soon a mile or more away, before we others had realised that there was game afoot. At length the crack of a rifle gave us the direction. We galloped for two or three miles, and at last, getting through the trees, caught sight of Dove riding about four hundred yards behind the game, which were flying down a long, shallow, open valley. It was a beautiful sight, a perfect picture of sport. The fleeing game ran in a compact troop, apparently going lazily at that heavy slow gallop which they assume till pressed. Every now and again Dove, on his little bay mare, would spurt up to within two hundred and fifty yards or so, dismount, and fire, when the hartebeest would stretch themselves out and sail away in wonderful fashion. In their slow paces they look awkward and somewhat mule-like, and the gallop appears high, but when pressed the action is magnificent—free, low, sweeping, and machine-like. For speed and staying powers there is only one antelope in all Africa, the tsesseby, a near cousin of the hartebeest, that can approach this game, as we found to our cost on this and other occasions. It is a hopeless task trying to run down hartebeest, even on good horses. Now Knox and I joined in obliquely, pressing distantly upon the near flank of the troop of red-coloured game. The chase swept on, mile after mile was compassed, and our horses were well-nigh spent. Dove and I had distanced our friends, and he was still leading, when suddenly, after another shot from his rifle, one antelope turned out from the troop and galloped off right-handed. It looked like a hit. I turned and pushed across up a rise to try and cut off the buck. My nag could hardly raise a canter now, but I got within two hundred yards of the line, jumped off, and fired shakily as the beast swept past. Naturally I missed. The sport was now over. Dove's plucky pony was run to a standstill, the rest of the troop had made good their escape, and Knox presently rejoined us. We had run these antelopes at top speed for seven miles on end, on fairly even veldt, and had made no sort of impression on them. We had to own ourselves well beaten, as we slowly rode back to the farm-huts. Nevertheless, it was a glorious gallop, and one of the prettiest phases of South African sport I have ever witnessed, and at heart none of us, I think, grudged the gallant game their escape. Dove's bay mare, a wonderfully good galloper, never, I think, recovered the day's chase. She died in her stable a few days after at Mafeking, though whether actually from her exertions of this run we never learned, as we happened to be away in Marico at the time. After a cup of tea at the huts, we sallied out again on foot with our shot-guns, Mackay and Fanshawe being already home, and before sundown secured four brace of partridges (Orange river francolin), a brace of bush koorhaan, and one steinbok, the latter of which fell to Dove's gun. The silly little antelope had escaped through our lines, but turned sharp back, ran the gauntlet, and fell to a charge of No. 5 shot.

Next morning, after inspecting Knox's crop of mealies, and the cattle and goats, all of which were doing excellently, we rode off for Mafeking, thirty miles distant, and arrived there by easy stages before sundown. Mafeking, as you enter it from the south-west, by the usual road, presents a very charming appearance. I know no other "stadt" in all South Bechuanaland that can vie with it in this respect. The native town, with its circular, grass-thatched huts and warm red walls, nestling among a mass of shrub and greenery and great boulders of rock, especially if viewed under the glow of sunset, looks beautiful. The little Molopo River flows beneath the gentle slope on which the town is planted.

At this time the English part of the town, which lies upon the plateau, about half-a-mile beyond the native location, presented a widely different aspect to that of a few months previous. The pioneers and

Chartered Company's police were still being enrolled;
and, passing through to the north, long strings of
waggons rolled through day after day; the market
place and main street looked like a miniature
Kimberley; both the hotels were crammed to reple-
tion, and we had the greatest trouble to get stabling
for our horses.   Isaac's Hotel being hopeless, we tried
Bradley's, where we were kindly provided with shake-
downs for the night, on the floor of the proprietor's
parlour.   Having seen the nags stabled and fed, we
entered the *table-d'hôte* room.   Here all sorts and
conditions of mankind were to be found—Jews,
Gentiles, Boers, transport riders, police, pioneers,
diggers, prospectors, general loafers; all the hetero-
geneous elements of South African life were well
represented.   One gentleman, with a broad Scotch
accent, who had evidently been some while " on the
burst," monopolised most of the conversation.   He
had one principal idea in his rather addled brain this
evening, which he insisted in enlarging upon to the
exclusion of all other topics.   His idea was that there
were no accidents in this world; all was carelessness.
Harking back to the loss of the *Sultan*, he exclaimed,
" Na, na, it was nae accident, but just millions and
drillions (he pronounced it ' mullions and drullions ')
o' neglact."   This phrase stuck in our memories
for some weeks, and was retailed upon appropriate
occasions if any mishap occurred.   As the Scotsman
rattled on from one subject to another, he was
funny for a time, but the thing presently began to
jar upon one.

   At Mafeking we found it impossible to pick up
horseflesh suitable for our expedition, and we therefore settled to leave our ponies behind and drive over

THE "WONDER-GAT," NEAR MAFEKING

(See page 462)

the border into the Transvaal, and see what we could
do among the Marico Boers. Thanks to the kindness
of Mr. Alfred Musson, we were equipped next day
with a Cape cart and four horses, looked after by
Moses, a capital coloured servant; and on May 7 we
drove merrily off for Malmani, our first outspan on
the way to Zeerust. Malmani lies fifteen miles from
Mafeking, to the north-east, in Transvaal territory,
amid some rather pretty scenery. The Boers certainly chose the pick of the country. Almost directly
one leaves the dry plains of Bechuanaland and enters
the Transvaal in this direction, running water is
everywhere to be found, pleasant streams are met
with, and at Malmani a full, deep river (a branch of
the Klein Marico) of most pellucid clearness, has to
be driven through, even at this the dry season of
South African winter.

The morning was bitterly cold as we started off,
and we were glad of the rugs and wrappers kindly
provided by our Mafeking friends. Malmani a year
before, during the "boom," was looked upon as one
of the most promising gold-fields of the Transvaal.
All was now changed. The one long street seemed
desolate, canteens and stores were closed, the bank
had shut up shop and taken its departure, and
Malmani sat, figuratively speaking, crooning over
the grey ashes of her vanished past. There was one
good hotel and store, however—that of the Messrs.
Weil—still open. Here we outspanned for an hour,
had a capital lunch, and, thereafter, pushed on again.
There is a good deal of expensive machinery lying
waste here. The notorious Crystal Reef Company
carried on operations at this place, as well as other
companies. Gold in considerable quantities has un-

doubtedly been found in the quartz formation, but
the general impression seems to be that, although
very rich deposits, or "pockets," are here and there
found, the gold is patchy and inconstant. There are
knowing people who affirm vigorously that Malmani
has not yet had a fair trial, and that, given honest
and capable management, fair play, and companies
not overloaded by vendors and promoters, the fields
here will some day turn up trumps. For the present,
however, Malmani, pleasant spot though it is, is very
much out in the cold, and almost deserted by its
erst bustling population.

Soon after leaving Malmani, the beautiful hills surrounding Zeerust began to open out in the distance,
the country became richer and more fruitful-looking
at every mile traversed, and after passing the little
village of Jacobsdal, we entered upon the fairest and
richest bit of country, from an agricultural point of
view, that I have seen from the Cape to Khama's
Country. Well may Marico be called the garden of
the Transvaal. Its fat corn lands, plenteous water
supply, smiling well-to-do homesteads, and fair
orange groves, all set among noble hills, amply
justify that title. The farms passed this afternoon
between Jacobsdal and Zeerust are equal to the best
parts of Devonshire. The soil is a rich deep loam,
red for the most part, water is unlimited, and is laid
out in sluits or courses to every part, and the crops
are magnificent.

Marico was and still is well known as the stronghold of the old stubborn anti-English Boers, sons of
the sturdy "Voer-Trekkers" who first occupied the
district some forty or fifty years since. The famous
old elephant hunter, Jan Viljoen, now a very old

man, one of the early trekkers, and his family live here. When Jan first picked his farm up here he called it, aptly enough, "Vär Genoog" (far enough), Marico, then lately wrested from the Matabele, being the extreme northward limit of the white men. In those days elephants wandered by hundreds over this part of the Transvaal, rhinoceroses were as plentiful as pigs, and all other game was equally abundant. It is not many years since such men as Viljoen led two widely different lives. In the winter they went elephant hunting far up into the Mashona, Matabele, and Lake Ngami countries; while in the summer they looked after their farms in Marico. Much of this is changed, however. Elephant hunting south of the Zambesi is nearly a thing of the past, and as the game is hardly worth the candle, the hunters stay more at home or have trekked to the wilds of Ovampoland and beyond. I am not certain that even in the good days those wilder spirits had all the best of it, and am inclined to think that the men who sat quietly at home on their land the year through have done better for themselves in the long run.

We were greatly surprised to find such capital homesteads in this region. Some of the farmhouses were excellently well built, and, with their deep thatches, white walls, and green doors and shutters, looked extremely picturesque. They were mostly embowered in groves of orange trees, just now positively aflame with luscious-looking fruit. Some of them, such as the house of Mr. Botha, where we next halted, are equal to most of the best homesteads at the Cape, and to many a good farmhouse at home. Here let me note that the Marico oranges are the

best in all South Africa; indeed, now that disease
has carried off most of the old plantations round the
Cape, they have no rival.   Of course, the difference
between a ripe orange plucked from the tree, and an
orange that has been plucked unripe to enable it to
be eaten in England (and which, therefore, never can
be said to truly ripen) is incomparable.

There had been very heavy rain recently, the
roads traversed this day were sticky, and before
reaching Mr. Botha's two of our team (which was
rather a scratch one improvised for the occasion)
showed signs of giving in.   We therefore outspanned
and left the two feeble nags behind, while the others
rested.   Mr. Botha, who came out and kindly undertook their charge until our return, is well known in
these parts as Danje Botha, or " Rich Botha " as many
call him.   A dark, stiff-built, well-to-do-looking man
of middle height, perhaps fifty-five or sixty years
of age—one would hardly imagine that the quiet,
taciturn, self-possessed individual clad in dark grey
tweed clothes, who now assisted us (not perhaps
altogether too gladly or gracefully), was one of the
moving spirits in the Boer war, and a commandant
at Laing's Nek and other places.   People may say
what they please, throw dirt at the Boers, vilify them
in every possible way ; but they were *men*—men of
strong wills, determined courage, and a sublime faith
who could boldly face the whole British nation, and
win the victories they did.

Well, Mr. Botha did not invite us into his house,
although the young ladies were at home, and, curiously enough, English music from a piano began
to issue through the open window.   Even as we
outspanned just below the road which passes close to

the house, the oranges were being plucked, piles of golden fruit littered the earth, and a waggon was being loaded up. It was a beautiful sight.

The fruit sells well, and is a highly profitable crop to the Marico farmers, and the rising town of Mafeking promises to be, as indeed it is already, a capital market for the produce of this rich district. Below the orange grove stretched the fertile farm lands, from part of which a magnificent crop of mealies had been recently harvested. Hearing that the house of Mr. Kersteyn, a son-in-law of Mr. Botha, to whom we had been directed for horses, lay but a few hundred yards distant, we walked over the brow of the hill, and came to a plainer but sufficiently comfortable habitation. We did not find Mr. Kersteyn at home, but we had a look at some of his nags, and agreed to drive over next day. Getting into the cart again, we drove on through a magnificent valley, and just after nightfall reached Zeerust, after crossing the Klein Marico River just outside the town. We drove up to the quiet little Marico Hotel, and, after supper and a smoke, retired to rest in a comfortable room, not unlike that of an old-fashioned village inn. It was very cold and very quiet, and we were not sorry to turn in at 8.30. Next day, May 8, we were up betimes, and before and after breakfast strolled round the town. Zeerust is a charming little place nestling under fine bold hills, and with a good river at its feet. The blue gum trees, here of immense height and in great plenty, are a feature of the place ; but everywhere there are good gardens, and abundance of trees, fruit, shrubbery, and flowers. In this last respect, indeed, Zeerust is quite the most English-like of up-country African towns. The flowers are everywhere profuse and charming. Grapes, oranges, peaches, apricots, strawberries, pears, apples, and other fruits abound here in season; the houses are good, and there are some capital stores and shops— run, of course, by English or Germans. Charming as is this Marico town, it is, under Boer sway, somewhat of a Sleepy Hollow, and during the last ten years has not improved and increased at the pace one might have expected. In some respects it has receded. In the old days, when elephant hunting was a profitable business, Zeerust was the Ultima Thule of civilisation. Before entering the wilderness, the hunters and traders fitted out and obtained supplies here; and, after long months and years of the wandering, solitary life of the veldt, returned hither to indulge in those wild "sprees" in which most interior men seem bound to celebrate their return to their fellows.

Those were festive times in quiet Zeerust, when the champagne flowed like water for days together, and the place was painted red, to the perturbation of the quiet Dutch folk. Now all this is changed.

Mafeking and the Bechuanaland route divert most of the trade and traffic, and Zeerust has suffered accordingly. After breakfast we saw one or two people to whom we had introductions, and inspected several horses. Later on we rode out to Mr. Kersteyn's, but, as he was away at a shooting match at Mr. Viljoen's, we were unable to do business. This day we met Mr. George Martin, an old Matabele trader, and Cigar, the well-known Hottentot hunter, who first initiated Mr. Selous into the mysteries of elephant hunting. Cigar, who was doing well at one time, seemed to have fallen upon evil days. He wished very much to accompany us on our hunting trip to Ngamiland, but, from the advice we received, we judged it wiser to decline his offer.

Next day we rode out to some Boer homesteads, about half a day's journey in the direction of Rustenburg. Mackay and Dove were mounted respectively on a white and a grey horse, belonging to Mr. Spranger, an Englishman in business at Zeerust, to whom we were greatly indebted for help and advice. These horses, after their trial trip of to-day, were purchased by Dove for £43 the pair, and turned out good useful animals on our trip up-country. They were finally sold at Khama's Town on our return at £22 and £23 each, thus realising a slight profit on their original price, after several months' knocking about. Upon the white pony, Witbooi as we called him, Dove secured his first giraffe, and our after-rider Joseph also killed eland with him; but Witbooi, hardy nag though he was, never took quite kindly to giraffe hunting, and needed a good deal of steering and driving to get him up to such gigantic game. The grey went through plenty of hard work, but was never much required for hunting heavy game, except during our last day at eland on recrossing the Kalahari. The pick of Dove's stud for running all kinds of game was a little dun pony with black points, barely fourteen hands in height, which he picked up at Kimberley for £16. Dunboy, as we christened him, was a willing, hardy, handy little nag, full of fire and courage, and a perfect wonder at game. Dove did some excellent shooting with him at giraffe, wildebeest, springbok, and lechwe. I used him while Dove was laid up, and, thanks to his speed and perfect behaviour, killed two giraffe off his back in

one afternoon, besides zebra and other game on different occasions.   He was an ideal shooting pony, had
evidently been in the veldt before (he was understood
to have been up in Matabeleland), and directly he
saw game, chased them like a dog, taking his rider
close up to giraffe, and thus affording an easy shot
from his back.   It was with great regret that Dunboy
was sold to one of Khama's headmen on our return.
He realised £35 as a "salted" pony, but unfortunately dying of horse-sickness in Bamangwato
within the year of guarantee, the purchase-money
had to be returned, under the usual South African
practice.   In Dunboy died one of the best ponies
that ever entered the hunting veldt.   He was a
perfect little mount, easy in his paces, a good galloper over the roughest veldt, had a capital mouth,
and turned and twisted in bushy forest country
in a marvellous way.   He had, further, a tough,
hardy constitution, and retained condition on much
work and often scanty fare, better than most of his
comrades.

I myself was mounted for the day on a knowing
old stager, named Charlie, lent me by Mr. George
Martin.   Charlie was something of a character.   He
was a "salted" schimmel (roan), and had been sold
years before by Martin, at a high figure, to Lobengula,
King of the Matabele, who had him for many seasons.
Recently Lobengula had lent him to Martin to come
down country with.   Charlie's best days were over,
it is true ; but he had been a good shooting horse,
and even in his old age—on the day I rode him—
was no despicable mount ; the spirit indeed was all
there, if that off fore-leg was a trifle groggy.   Riding
east from Zeerust, we traversed some most charming

country, passing among mountain scenes of romantic beauty, through which the river ran for a long way. It was a perfect South African winter day; the air was crisp, sparkling, and champagne-like, and full of that intense exhilaration which to my mind is to be found nowhere out of the high plateaux lands of Southern Africa. Everywhere were rich corn lands, lusty crops of oranges near the homesteads, and pleasant streams.

After one or two inquiries at farmhouses, our first halt was at the village of Klaarstroom, where a horse or two were shown to us, but without result. A very busy Dutch lady here, who gave us some milk, insisted that we should stop on the way back, when her son or son-in-law should show us something very superior in the way of horseflesh—"een sterk rij paard—ja een goed schiet paard" (a strong riding horse—yes, a good shooting horse) as she assured us. Alas! on our return, the "sterk paard" proved but a sorry three-cornered screw, for which the Boer had the temerity to ask £18. Needless to say we left him sorrowing with the "schiet paard" still unsold upon his hands. Most of the Boers we interviewed to-day had formed the impression that we were buying horses for Government, or at any rate for the Chartered Company's expedition (which they classed as the same thing), and we had some difficulty to disabuse their minds.

Leaving Klaarstroom, we presently entered some pleasant flats, timbered with thorns and other low trees, and still girdled by hills. We noticed a good many butterflies at this time, and especially a very handsome grey variety (*Hamanumida Dœdalus*), which we had not hitherto seen in Bechuanaland.

N

After no little trouble, for these butterflies were extremely active, and flashed and flirted hither and thither in a most heartbreaking manner, we managed to secure two or three good specimens by the help of our broad-brimmed hats. A little further we espied a puff-adder basking in the sun in the sandy road, as these dangerous reptiles will do. He had a magnificently marked new skin, and, after we had put an end to him with a stick, nothing would serve Dove but he must take him home for preservation. A party of Boers passed us, and seeing the snake being carefully disposed of, evidently took us for more of "those mad Englishmen." About one o'clock we halted at a little corrugated iron "winkel" (store), which had been lately erected in this solitary spot. Here we off-saddled for half-an-hour, procured some lunch, and obtained further directions as to the next farms we were to call at.

These farmhouses lay to the right hand, up a most beautiful fertile valley (Water Kloof I think it was called), lying among the hills. In another hour we reached Mynheer Beuke's, where we inspected two or three fairly good nags, but without coming to terms. Horse-sickness had been extremely rife in Marico this year, the Boers had suffered heavily, and horseflesh had gone up proportionately in value. Another twenty minutes' ride brought us to the comfortable "plaats" of another farmer, Mynheer Basson. Him we found at home, and were at once invited into the house, where coffee and tobacco were set before us in the good old Dutch fashion. We were then shown the horseflesh, among which was an extremely handsome chestnut, a big upstanding nag, much bigger and better than the average Afrikander

horse. Mackay took a fancy to this animal at once,
and a saddle and bridle being forthcoming, we tried
its paces. Its action and manners were as good as its
looks; but the owner asked too high a price, £40,
and after a long discussion we gave it up as a bad
job, shook hands with the friendly Dutchman and
his vrouw and olive branches, and rode away. Just
as we were crossing a stream a mile on our way
home, the Boer rejoined us riding the chestnut. We
moved on in almost perfect silence for a little way;
at length Mynheer Basson spoke, and said he would
take £37 ("ponds") for the horse, and it was his last
offer. Mackay was not to be tempted, and shook his
head. At last, just as the Dutchman turned to leave
us, Mackay jumped off his horse, took out a bag of
money, and counted out thirty-five golden sovereigns.
The sight of the "gelt" was too much; the oracle
was worked, the Dutchman handed over the big
chestnut, took the money, and, amid much friendly
laughter, we finally shook hands and parted. £35
is a long price for an unsalted horse in these regions,
but the nag was an exceptionally good one, and
Mackay sold him in Khama's Town later on for more
than he gave for him. It was very amusing to see
the Dutchman showing off the paces of his favourite.
As a rule, trotting is very little practised in South
Africa; the canter, or "tripple," being found more
easy for man and beast on long and fatiguing journeys.
But Mynheer Basson desired to call our attention
to the trotting powers of the chestnut, and stretching forward in the saddle, grasped his horse with
vigorous fingers about the middle of the neck, when
immediately it fell from a canter into a smart,
slinging trot. This is a common practice among

Dutch farmers, but when first seen it is certainly amusing.

Halting, as I have said before, at Klaarstroom to look at another horse on the way home, we reached Zeerust a little after dark, after a journey of some forty miles. We had not certainly transacted a great deal of business, but we had ridden through a most beautiful country, and thoroughly enjoyed a delightful and interesting day. On the whole, we found the farmers friendly and hospitable ; true, the fact of our being purchasers of horses may have had something to do with it, but not, I think, altogether. Next morning early, Dove having concluded the purchase of the white and grey ponies, we inspanned them in the cart with the pair with which we had arrived, and set off for Mafeking, calling on our way at Mynheer Kersteyn's. Here I bought a strong, useful, good-looking chestnut pony, upon which I had previously had my eye on our former visit. The price I paid was £18. I used the pony for some months on our expedition across the Kalahari to Ngamiland ; Giltboy, as I christened him, turned out a capital shooting horse, and on returning to Khama's I sold him in low condition, and after a deal of hard work, for £19 ; so that, on the whole, we did more than reasonably well with all our Marico purchases.

Mr. Kersteyn had one or two friends, neighbouring Dutch farmers, over at his place, with whom, as we drove up, he was engaged in rifle practice.

Now that the good old days have departed, and the game has been all but exterminated in the Transvaal, the Boers are perforce compelled to betake themselves to target-shooting, which they do to a considerable extent. The Government of the South

African Republic supplies good Martini rifles (made in Germany), to each burgher at the low price—so far up-country—of £4, 1s. 9d. per rifle, and all those farmers who had old or inferior weapons are availing themselves of this offer. President Kruger has on more than one occasion in recent years urged upon his Transvaalers to "keep up their shooting," and, from what one hears and sees, they are not very loth to take his advice. But practice at targets is, after all, a very different matter from that best of all practice at game, which every Boer until these last ten or fifteen years had his fill of. The new generation of young Dutchmen now rising to manhood are not what their fathers were—some hardly touch a gun at all—and it is not too much to say that another dozen years will see the Transvaal burghers very different shots (far less formidable in time of war) to their forefathers. On this occasion Mr. Kersteyn and his friends were shooting with a rest, the said rest consisting of the hide-laced seat of a wooden chair. The chair was laid upon the ground in front of the shooter as he lay prone, the muzzle of the rifle was poked through the thonged seat, and aim was taken at a square board placed 150 and 200 yards away. The practice, of course, was good under such conditions ; but this sort of practice must be vastly inferior to the old shooting at herds of flying game, when distances had to be judged, and the hunter hastily took his shot—having jumped off his horse—after a breathless gallop.

Taking the chestnut bought from Mr. Kersteyn, we picked up the other two horses left at Mynheer Botha's—having paid the forage bill there—and pushed on to Malmani. Here we inspanned all four

of our new purchases and drove into Mafeking soon
after nightfall, the team behaving extremely well.
Moses, riding one of his master's four horses, drove
the rest before him, and although he managed to lose
one on the way in (which was not recovered for more
than a month after), got in soon after us.

At Mafeking we picked up our old horses (except
Dove's bay mare, which had died meanwhile), and
next day, riding and leading, made our way down to
our huts at the Junction.

CHAPTER IX.

OUR STEEPLECHASES

So soon as we had reached the Junction again, after our horse-buying expedition, we set about trying the new purchases, and especially to see how they stood fire. On the morning of the 14th May we had each nag out in turn, and, mounting them, proceeded to fire from their backs, pointing the guns in various directions. English horses would strongly resent such practice ; but up-country in South Africa most ponies are well accustomed to the sound of firearms, and there is no difficulty in teaching them to stand steadily when a gun or rifle is fired from the saddle. And, even if the ponies be a trifle skittish to begin with, a week or so in the hunting veldt, where the work is hard and food other than veldt grass none too plentiful, has a marvellous effect, and the timid nags become quickly transformed into steady shooting ponies. This we soon discovered on our expedition to Morokweng, from which every horse returned warranted steady under fire. My chestnut, Giltboy, and Dove's two greys we found to be the least amenable ; but Giltboy quickly overcame his fears, and the other pair were not long in following his example. Mackay's big chestnut, Rooibok, was as steady as old time, and minded the gun no more than the low of an ox.

After an hour's practice, Mackay rode into Setlagoli, to fetch out the mails. I got out my camera and proceeded to photograph a green tree-snake, killed the day before close to the huts, and some Coqui francolins. Then nothing would suit Dove but we must set up the dead snake and a spotted-breasted eagle (*Spizaëtus Spilogaster*)—also killed the day before—facing one another as if in mortal combat. After no little trouble, and much propping up with sticks, the bit of still life was prepared and photographed.

We then had some practice with a Marlin carbine at 100 yards, at a target 1¼ feet square with a 6-inch bull's-eye, and made some pretty fair practice.

By this time P. Gethin, whom I had been expecting, had ridden over. I had arranged to hand over to him the charge of the farms from the 1st of June, at which time I was leaving the Junction for the shooting trip with Mackay and Dove, and we had many things to talk over. After lunch we all three rode over to Moroka's Kraal, in order that I might explain to Michael Moroka that Gethin was to succeed me as master, and arrange for obtaining a water supply at Michael's pits in the Setlagoli, our own holes in the Maritsani and Setlagoli being now all but dry.

Taking as usual our guns and dogs, we cantered across and satisfactorily interviewed Moroka. On leaving his place we passed some strong thorn kraal fences, and it was here that the idea of our steeple-

chases first took root in the sporting brain of Dove.
" Come on, you fellows !" he called out ; " I'll give you
a lead over these fences." We set our nags at the
thorny obstacles, and they were negotiated with ease
and despatch. We repeated the performances and
then turned for home, picking up a head or two of
game, including a steinbok shot by Dove, as we
came.

On the 15th we were busied in various ways ;
fencing in with thorns our precious last remaining
waterpit in the Setlagoli, to preserve it from stray
cattle ; interviewing Tatenyani, a local petty chief,
as to a constant milk supply for the Gethins, who
were sending their cattle further away for water ;
and arranging other matters. On the 16th, Dove,
who had been inspecting our own kraal fences,
announced that there was excellent material for a
steeplechase course, and all hands were called out
to assist in demarcating boundaries and strengthen-
ing jumps. Dove, let me premise, had been long
since accustomed to Irish steeplechasing, and, despite
many a bad fall and numberless broken bones, his
soul, even in sun-parched Bechuanaland, yearned to
tempt the fates once more and test the racing powers
of African shooting ponies. Mackay and I were
nothing loth, and, eager for new sensations in the
routine of our quiet existence, we laboured hither
and thither, and soon produced a sufficiently formidable course. Now we saddled our horses, and
taking them out in pairs, tried them one against
another in a series of off-hand matches. Despite a
fall sustained by Mackay, in which, however, no
harm was taken, the results were most encouraging.
It is a signal proof of the all-round adaptability of

the South African horse that here, upon the first onset, not one of our nags (there were eight in all tried) refused or attempted to refuse their fences. They jumped freely, willingly, and well, and seemed thoroughly to enjoy the game.

Suddenly another brilliant idea struck Dove. Our neighbours Knox and Fanshawe were arriving in the evening for a day or two's visit ; why not invite the Gethins, and have a private steeplechase meeting of our own? The proposition was put and carried unanimously and upon the instant. A note was despatched to the Gethins requesting their attendance, and begging the favour of Mrs. Gethin's and the baby's presence on this festive occasion, and presently a reply came back cordially accepting our hurried invitation.

We now proceeded to improve the course as far as possible, leaving a few items only until the morning. Knox and Fanshawe arrived just at sunset. After a merry supper, we drew up a programme of events. This business finished, with the aid of a strong consumption of Transvaal tobacco and Dog's Head cigarettes, after a little banjo playing we all turned in.

The morning of Saturday the 17th May dawned, as usual at this season of the year, in perfect splendour. The atmosphere, despite the strong, bright sunshine, was inexpressibly nimble and exhilarating, and before breakfast we set to work to complete our preparations. In the horse-kraal Dottie and Peetsi were busy providing the horses with their morning mealies; while, in view of the special nature of the occasion, an extra grooming was being bestowed, so that all the nags should stand before the starting flag in the pink of preparation—as understood in the wilds of Bechuanaland. In rear of the huts, at some distance from the first kraal fence, we set to work to dig our gallery jump. We had unfortunately no water, but we made a good broad trench, eleven feet in width, fronted by a moderate bank, the top of which we bushed thickly with brushwood. This "brook," as we called it, when completed represented a good, fair hunting jump, and we were mightily pleased with it. Our course ran thus. The start was 200 yards above the brook ; thence another 200 yards to the first kraal fence, composed of stiff, dry thorns thickly bushed to the height of a good hurdle jump at home, so that, horrid as it was with cruel thorns, no horse could gallop or slur through it ; thence across the kraal to another and similar fence. From there the course trended slightly downhill over two more fences, then bore to the right along the flat, thence turning up hill again, and then bearing right-handed along the level brow until the starting point was reached. This course had to be twice compassed, and the winning post, whereon fluttered our Union Jack, stood at a point some 200 yards behind and beyond the starting place. In all the distance to be run was about a mile and a quarter, and twelve fences (including twice over the brook) had to be negotiated.

We marked out the course here and there with tall poles upon which were fastened our gaudy blankets, which, offering their gay greens, yellows, and reds to the sun and breeze, imparted quite a gala aspect to the veldt.

These labours over, we turned heartily to breakfast, and in the meantime Knox's Scotch cart and four oxen were sent over the river to fetch Mrs. Gethin and her infant to the scene of the struggle. At ten o'clock the Gethins had arrived, and at eleven, having conducted our visitors over the course, we began the first race, Elliott, our English lad, assisting as starter. An unusually impartial judge was at hand in the person of old Thomas, who discharged his duties with becoming gravity and decorum, and appeared to prefer the " prospect " of this festive meeting to that of neighbouring " gold areas " where he had been recently at work.

It had become known among our attendants on the previous night that upon the morrow the "Baases" were going to indulge in some extraordinary festivities. These tidings had been bruited from kraal to kraal of the Barolongs and Vaalpense adjacent, and we had quite a small standful (if only we had had a stand) of dark and interested spectators, all on the tiptoe of excitement and anticipation—for steeple-chases were hitherto unknown in the district. The Scotch cart drawn up between the winning post and starting point, and, comfortably furnished with a chair, cushions, and rugs, served our sole lady visitor as a grand stand. Beneath the shade of a large umbrella she and the baby watched the various events. It was at first proposed to fit up a stand on the top of the horse-shed, but this was negatived as too arduous a climb, and too risky an altitude for the infant. The only other spectators were a few vultures and black and white crows, seated pensively on some mimosa trees near the skeleton of the last deceased horse. These creatures viewed the affair with an air of gorged and absolute indifference. As our assembled neighbours had suffered like ourselves from horse-sickness, and their studs were just now much impaired, we divided the mounts in as impartial a manner as possible, so that all should have a share in the fun. In all we mustered only some dozen horses, of which our Marico purchases were the pick ; and it fell therefore that most of the nags had to be pulled out more than once for the various events.

Our costumes were not of a high order of merit —considered from a racing point of view. No silk jackets flashed in the sunlight or fluttered to the breeze ; no snowy breeches or well-ordered boots were ours. But we had sharp spurs, persuasive sjamboks of giraffe hide, and good saddlery. We and our nags were all in sound, hard condition, and one and all braced to our level best performances.

Flannel shirts, open at the neck, and rolled up at the sleeves, displaying bare brown arms ; stout breeches and field boots or gaiters, and any cloth cap that would stick on ; these equipments would not fit the ideas of an English race meeting, but they were good enough for our purpose. Dove had a decent pair of brown boots—the envy of the camp —and he displayed also a bit of colour in the shape of a red silk nightcap, which glittered in the van of several of the races. Mackay rode bareheaded, for there is no fear of sunstroke in South African winter.

Our programme ran as follows :—

SETLAGOLI AND MARITSANI IMPROMPTU STEEPLECHASES.

Stewards—Captain Fanshawe, Messrs. H. H. Knox, P. A. H. Gethin, H. R. Gethin, W. Mackay, W. Dove, and H. A. Bryden.
Starter—Mr. Elliott.   Judge—Mr. Thomas.

1. *Match* (1 *mile and a quarter*).

Mr. W. Mackay's Buggins .   .   .   Owner   1.
Mr. W. Dove's Called Back   .   .   Owner   2.

Called Back, as his name may seem to imply, had only lately recovered from a severe attack of horse-sickness, and was barely at his best.   Buggins, a capital stamp of shooting horse, had manifestly the foot of his opponent, led all the way, and won in a canter.

2. *The Junction Steeplechase* (1 *mile and a quarter*).

Mr. W. Mackay's Rooibok . . .	Owner	1.
Mr. H. H. Knox's Captain . . .	Owner	2.
Mr. H. A. Bryden's Giltboy. . .	Owner	3.
Mr. W. Dove's Bluebuck . . .	Owner	4.

This was the principal event of the meeting, all the nags being of good class, and the winner in particular a grand stamp of galloping hunter.   All cleared the water jump in fine form.   Captain, closely pressed by Giltboy, cut out the running until the last fence, when Rooibok came to the front, and, being much the speediest in the straight run in, won, hard held, by half-a-dozen lengths.   Two lengths between second and third.

3. *The Maritsani Plate* (1 *mile and a quarter*).

Mr. H. A. Bryden's Wacht-een-bitje .	Owner	1.
Captain Fanshawe's Schelm. . .	Owner	2.
Mr. P. Gethin's No Name . . .	Owner	3.
Mr. W. Dove's Witbooi . . . Mr. Knox		4.

In this race the bay mare Wacht-een-bitje (Wait-a-bit) jumped away with a strong lead, was never headed, and won easily by ten lengths.   A good race for places.

4. *Match* (1 *mile and a quarter*).

Mr. W. Dove's Dunboy . . .	Owner	1.
Mr. H. A. Bryden's Giltboy. . .	Owner	2.

This promised to be a good race ; but Giltboy, who

ran unkindly at the turns, bolted before coming into
the straight for the last time, and, almost running
headlong into a high thorn kraal, threw his rider
(who escaped with a severe scratching), leaving Dunboy to canter home alone.

5. *The Setlagoli Scurry (three-quarters of a mile).*

Mr. W. Mackay's Buggins . . .	Mr. Dove	1.
Captain Fanshawe's Schelm. . .	Owner	2.
Mr. P. Gethin's No Name . . .	Owner	3.

Buggins, judiciously ridden by Dove, forced the
running from start to finish, and won, with a trifle
to spare, by two lengths.

6. *Match (1 mile and a quarter).*

Mr. W. Dove's Dunboy . . .	Owner	1.
Mr. W. Dove's Witbooi . .	Mr. Mackay	2.

This was quite the race of the day, and arose out of
an old discussion as to the merits of the two ponies.
From start to finish the affair was a ding-dong one.
Witbooi led off at a strong pace; in the second
round Dunboy shot to the fore and held possession
till the last fence but one, when Witbooi went away
again and appeared to be winning easily. Here
Dove's old steeplechasing experiences served him in
good stead; sitting down to his work, he brought
up Dunboy, who answered gallantly to whip and
spur, foot by foot, and, with an Archer rush at the
finish, won a magnificent race by a neck. It was a
rattling set to, and elicited loud plaudits from the
company—black and white.

7. *Match (1 mile and a quarter).*

Mr. W. Mackay's Rooibok . . .	Owner	1.
Mr. Knox's Captain . . .	Mr. Bryden	2.

Captain made running at a strong pace, with the idea of outstaying his opponent. Rooibok, however, always held him safe, and, coming away at the last fence, won easily by three or four lengths.

The festivities were wound up with a race among our boys, whom we mounted on various nags. This was a piece of screaming fun, and while it was enacting we could scarcely hold our sides for laughter. The prize to the winner was five shillings, an extensive sum to a Bechuana; and one and all, whether they were used to horseback or no, rode to desperation. At it they went, hammer and tongs, sjamboks and naked heels being freely plied. The water-jump was by a miracle safely passed, though the seats of more than one shifted uncomfortably. Down the hill they tear, over the kraal fences, Dottie and Peetsi making the running. One falls, one or two bolt out of the course, Elliott among the number; and presently Sam, our latest importation, who had evidently been on a horse before, comes flying first to the winning post on the white pony; his rags fluttering to the wind, his big toes grasping the stirrup in true native fashion, and his black face and white teeth set to a broad grin of exultation and delight. Sam, the despised Sam, has won on Witbooi; Peetsi, the light weight, is second on Wacht-een-bitje; Dottie third on Giltboy. The rest straggle in from the veldt at intervals. The races over, we turn our attention to luncheon. At such short notice the Junction establishment could not be expected to attain very great heights of gastronomic excellence, but we did our best. We had luckily a good English ham at hand; this and some chickens helped us out of our culinary *impasse.* Here is the menu of our cold collation :—

GAME SOUP.

TINNED SALMON.   DIGBY CHICKS.   SARDINES.

COLD (ENGLISH) HAM.   COLD CHICKENS.

CORNED BEEF.

JAMS (VARIOUS).   MARMALADE.

BISCUITS.   PRESERVED GINGER.

BOTTLED STOUT.   PONTAC (RED WINE).

TEA AND COFFEE.

Mrs. Gethin was good enough to declare herself delighted with the morning's sport; the baby was laid peacefully to slumber in a cot extemporised from an empty case and some pillows and cushions; and we all sat down to our modest banquet with excellent spirits and appetites. In the afternoon we sallied out with our shot-guns, and, forming line across the veldt, took a sweep up the Maritsani and home again by the further bank. Game now was less plentiful and wilder than it had been hitherto, and the grassy cover was becoming thin and scanty under the combined influence of sun and drought. None the less we had a pleasant afternoon, halting to take tea at Sligo Farm, whither Mrs. Gethin had returned; and at sundown we reached home with a bag of eight brace of bustard, partridge, and guinea-fowl.

By the time we reached the huts again the ponies had been got in from the veldt, where they usually fed until wanted, had had their feed of mealies out of nose-bags which we kept for the purpose, and were fastened up for the night.

During the season of horse-sickness it is an invariable rule that horses shall not be allowed to touch the veldt grass until the sun has been up for an hour or

o

two, and the grass is thoroughly dry and the veldt aired. In the same way horses must be got in before sundown, so that no risk from dews or dewy grass may be incurred.

Even these and many other precautions are often unavailing; and we ourselves, although taking every care, had, as I have shown, suffered heavily from the mysterious and perplexing murrain. As a rule, the first frosts are a signal for the disappearance of horse-sickness; but this year frosts had prevailed for some nights before our horses began to be attacked.

The suddenness and extraordinary vicissitudes characteristic of this disease are well illustrated by the case of a chestnut pony of Mackay's, which was at this time just recovering from the sickness, and took no part in the steeplechases. I rode on my bay pony one afternoon to Setlagoli to receive and post mails. Next day I left for the Junction, riding Mackay's chestnut (which had been left for a day or two) and leading the bay. Both ponies, as I left Lamb's Hotel, seemed fit and well. After I had cantered along four or five miles I noticed that the chestnut—usually a lively, excitable nag—was dull and heavy, and required frequent jogs of the spur. I changed saddles and mounted the bay. In another mile or two the chestnut laboured yet more, presently could hardly trot, and yellow matter and foam began to run from the nostrils. Its flanks were now heaving with ominous rapidity, and I saw that horse-sickness had got hold of it. With the greatest difficulty I dragged the poor brute to the Cutlers' cottage, and there turned him into a kraal, as I thought, to die.

Next morning Mackay and Dove rode over to ascertain the pony's fate. Mackay was mounted on a very handsome black pony (one of the lot brought up by Dove from Kimberley, and quite his favourite mount), which appeared as fit and well as possible. Before getting to the Cutlers' place, five miles off, the black was suddenly seized with the sickness, and had to be off-saddled and left behind. On reaching the Cutlers', to their utter astonishment the chestnut, left by me for dead on the preceding day, now appeared fairly well; it recovered in a few days, and not long after was getting strong and brisk again. The black pony, on the other hand, died shortly after. These are but common examples of the mysteries of this fatal and extraordinary sickness.

On the day following the steeplechases Knox, Fanshawe, Dove, Mackay, and H. Gethin set off for a day's shoot along the high veldt bordering the Setlagoli on its course to the Molopo. They had a fair day, getting eleven brace of koorhaan, partridges, hares, and guinea-fowl. I was very sore after my fall of the preceding day, and my right knee, which was sprained, troubled me with a limp for some time to come; I therefore stayed at home, writing up correspondence, putting the huts in order, and preparing the evening meal against the gunners' return.

Giltboy, by bolting in the match with the dun pony and putting me headlong into the kraal fence from which he swerved, gave me a nasty fall. I emerged from the thorns in very much the guise of the fretful porcupine. The whole of my left side bristled with long mimosa thorns—and they are no joke—my face was streaming with blood, and it took myself and Mackay no inconsiderable time to extract the thorns from my leg, side, and arm. One ran into the elbow joint and stuck there, and troubled me for months after. Beyond this and the sprain, however, I escaped easily, and have to thank the kraal fence, no doubt, for saving me from a broken arm ; a fact I may congratulate myself upon, as my left arm had been broken twice previously.

We had again a very merry evening with our visitors, who left us on the following day—after assisting in a series of photographs—for their own farms.

Our impromptu steeplechases had gone off capitally ; they had been a source of keen enjoyment and hearty fun to all of us ; and among many recollections of our Junction days, not the least pleasant will be that rough fragment of English sport, translated so successfully from the green pastures and grey skies of home to the embrowned veldt and sunny atmosphere of British Bechuanaland.

CHAPTER X.

A WAGGON JOURNEY THROUGH THE PROTECTORATE

IN preparation for our departure to the hunting grounds of the far interior—the time for which had now arrived—we had despatched the waggon, loaded up with saddlery, guns, rifles, and the rest of our kit and baggage, to Mafeking, there to await our arrival. Before sending the waggon we overhauled her as far as possible, strengthened the staves of the half-tent, which we covered with new canvas, and gave her a fresh coating of paint. She was a very old waggon, and the felloes of her wheels in particular were, from age, hard trekking, and the excessive dryness of the climate, so shrunk from the tyres as to make us seriously doubt whether she would safely compass the 360 miles from our huts to Khama's. Rickety waggons, however, like threatened folk, live long, especially in a sandy country such as Bechuanaland. We had not intended to take this

waggon beyond Khama's, but changed our minds
on reaching Palachwe, and the old vehicle eventually
travelled to the Lake River and back, serving Dove
as a comfortable residence during the months of that
expedition.   Old as she was before we started, her
aspect when we trekked into Khama's Town once
more on our return was a hundredfold more battered.
The after axle broke early in the journey, and a false
axle, cut from the hard wood of the giraffe acacia,
had several times to be improvised, and was a constant source of anxiety to us.   The fore axle smashed
in some rocky country, luckily only a day or two
before we got back into Palachwe, and was spliced
together with raw hide sufficiently to allow the poor
old wanderer to crawl home.   As for the felloes, we
were perpetually driving in wedges between the
woodwork and tyres to keep things together, and
copious libations of water were poured over the
wheels whenever water was handy, in order to swell
the woodwork as much as possible, or rather to decrease the shrinkage which in the dry air and heated
sands of the desert was incessantly going on.   It was
a risk taking the old lame duck upon so long and
anxious a trek, and we might easily have procured
a better but heavier waggon.   She was so light,
however, compared with a full-tent hunting waggon,
which we obtained at Palachwe, that we were glad to
make use of her; and no doubt her comparatively
light weight was a great saving to the second span
of oxen, and helped to avert what was nearly proving
to be a catastrophe on our return journey across the
"Thirst Land."

Leaving Mackay and Dove to place P. Gethin
in possession of the huts, and make their way to

Mafeking with the ponies and a Cape cart, I left
the Junction on the 23rd of May and rode down to
Vryburg by post cart to wind up certain business
matters there.   On the 24th—Queen's Birthday—
Vryburg races were held, which, although on a
bigger scale, compared as I thought not too favour-
ably with our sporting little meeting at the Junction
a few days before.   Early on the 27th, having completed my business matters, I embarked again on
the post cart for Mafeking.   Just at this time the
ravages of horse-sickness had completely disorganised
the postal service from Kimberley to Khama's Town
—which was then conducted by the Bechuanaland Exploration Company.   Nearly all the horses
were dead, and the post carts were for a time drawn
by a ragged and deplorable contingent of mules,
donkeys, and even oxen.

The passengers had had an upset during the previous night, and the cart was consequently very late.
After a weary journey to Setlagoli, we had a still
more miserable trek to Mafeking.   The unfortunate
mules, overworked as they were, after the usual
wild spurt from Lamb's Hotel (it is the thing in
South Africa always to begin a stage with a mad
gallop), subsided into a trot, and thence degenerated
to a walk.   All through a bitterly cold night, therefore, we toiled along at a snail's crawl, which, despite change of teams at Wrights' (Lower Maritsani), and Medebi Wells, had improved very little
ere we completed the 100 miles to Mafeking next
afternoon.

Happily I found in the crowded cart two pleasant
fellow-travellers in the Hon. Maurice Gifford and
the Master of Elphinstone, with whom I walked

ahead of the lagging post cart much of the next morning. The former of these gentlemen was on his way to assume control of the Bechuanaland Exploration Company's affairs at Palachwe; the latter to take up a commission in the Bechuanaland Border Police at Macloutsi.

To Mr. Gifford I was afterwards indebted for many acts of kindness and courtesy at Palachwe while preparing for and returning from our hunting expedition. The subsequent untimely death of the Master of Elphinstone, which happened under peculiarly sad circumstances, is well known. Not long after reaching Macloutsi he had been attacked by dysentery, and from a too great devotion to duty, and some neglect of that dangerous malady, added to the heat and lack of comforts, had suffered one relapse after another. In November Lord Elphinstone joined Sir Henry Loch in his progress through the Protectorate, and underwent the long and fatiguing trek to Khama's country in order to meet his son. He reached Macloutsi only in time to find the Master in a state of extreme weakness and exhaustion. The only hope seemed to lie in bringing the sufferer down country for change of air and better attendance. It was too late, however; Mr. Elphinstone died in his father's arms at Pallah Camp on the Limpopo River, and was there buried, adding one more name to the long roll of Britain's sons who have yielded up their lives in Africa.

It was a sad ending to a promising career, and aroused deep sympathy among all who had had the pleasure of knowing a kindly and most courteous gentleman. I told the Master what little I could of the fauna of the country, and the prospects of sport up north ; and he was evidently looking forward keenly to many a good day among the game of the Protectorate. Little did he or I think then how sadly it was all to end.

At Mafeking I found that Mackay and Dove had all but completed preparations for the start. As usual during this year of the Mashonaland Expedition, the town was very busy and full of life. We met, among others, Mr. John Strombom, the Lake Ngami trader, who was trekking to the lake shortly after ourselves, and from whom we picked up some useful information. All our stores, ammunition, and heavy gear had been sent forward, and was timed to arrive at Palachwe some week or two before ourselves. We were fitted out by Messrs. Whiteley, Walker & Co., whose experience of the interior was of the greatest service to us, and from whose excellent stores we were supplied at a most reasonable rate with everything that a hunting party could require. I don't think that people going into the hunting veldt can do better than fit out at Mafeking. The cost and trouble of transporting stores from Kimberley is materially lessened, much time is saved, and Messrs. Whiteley & Walker, as well as other traders, can supply all necessary outfit that can be required. Similarly, waggons and oxen can be procured here either for hire or purchase ; and the traveller can run up quickly from Cape Town by rail and post cart, and so start at no great distance from the hunting veldt. Messrs. Musson Brothers, the well-known transport agents, can be depended upon to procure all that is wanted in the shape of waggons and oxen. A short notice is of course necessary.

As Dove was somewhat pressed for time, we had

arranged to trek with the light waggon—now all but empty—by forced marches, so as to accomplish the 320 miles to Khama's Town (Palachwe) if possible in record time. As a matter of fact, although we had but scratch teams of oxen and servants (we were procuring both at Palachwe for the hunting expedition) and lost part of a day at Mochudi and another at Sofala, we accomplished the 320 miles in sixteen days —a performance of which we were reasonably proud.

Dove, who is a determined man, had fully made up his mind that our resolve to trek by night as well as by day should be lived up to. He therefore purchased a huge American alarum clock—having a face diameter of the best part of a foot—which was fixed up above the kartel. How we used to curse that awful clock when, after a hard day's travel and a late supper, we had sunk into well-earned slumber. The vile thing usually rang out its devilish summons at 2 or 3 o'clock A.M. or thereabouts. The nights were bitterly cold, the boys and oxen alike tired. But it had to be done. The boys were roused from their blankets, and, after shivering awhile and warming their velschoens over the dying fire, they proceeded to inspan and trek. The horses were unfastened and driven forward in the darkness, and we who remained in the waggon either smoked a pipe and waited for the chilly dawn, or snatched uneasy slumber amid the joltings of the rough and uneven roads. Ugh ! it was unpleasant, that forced trek, and we none of us much relished it. Mac and I seriously thought of slaying the clock, and when, towards the end of the journey, the rough mountain roads had done their work, and the sleep-disturber had succumbed, we rejoiced openly and without shame. Two of us shared the kartel ; the

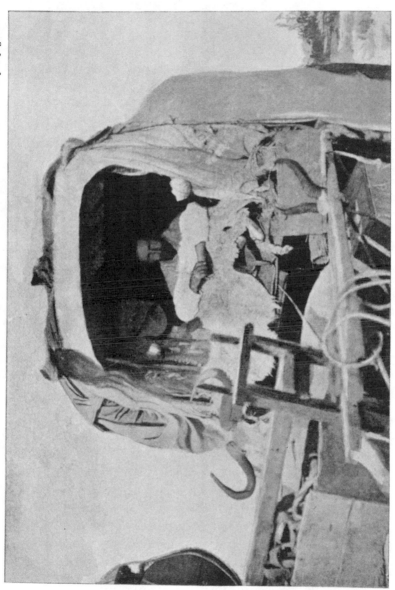

"SUN-UP"—DOVE IN HIS KARTEL

other fixed up his blanket underneath, and slept on a mattress on the floor of the waggon. It was a tight squeeze, but as it was for a short journey we put up with it.

Besides ourselves, the waggon carried our saddles and bridles, a gun and rifle or two, a vatje and water cask, pots, a kettle and a frying pan, and a few stores, such as " bully beef," sardines, jam, meal, tinned milk, coffee, tea, sugar, and tobacco, sufficing to carry us to Palachwe. We carried, of course, mealies for our good nags ; which latter, to save as much as possible, we rode very little. Day or night one of the horses was saddled, mounted by one of the boys or ourselves, and the rest were driven in front. At night this was cold and irksome work, especially in bushy or forest country, where the steeds easily strayed.

We sold off the donkeys before the start and hired ten oxen, which were to be changed at Mochudi. This was a scratch and rather a short span, even for our light, empty half-tent waggon, but the oxen behaved excellently, and were well handled by Jonas, our Basuto driver. For leader and horseboy we had two rather indifferent servants, who afterwards left us in the lurch. The cooking we undertook ourselves, as we had no room for a cook until we got to Khama's, and had another waggon at our disposal.

Having completed all business here and said good-bye to a host of friends, we rode out on the 30th of May at 12 o'clock, and after fifteen miles picked up the waggon at Ramathlabama, where the oxen had been outspanned. Here were some score or so of Chartered Company waggons on their way to Mash-onaland ; and what with recruits, natives, oxen, and a quantity of horses, the place looked lively enough, and the little store (at that time the last from Mafeking to Ramoutsa) was doing a good trade. At 6 P.M. we inspanned again and trekked till 10.20, from which time we rested till 4 A.M., when we pushed on till 7.30—breakfast.

This evening we passed the telegraph expedition on its way to the north. The chain of telegraphic communication has long since been extended to Palachwe and thence to Mashonaland—a great and important undertaking. On the morning of May 31, we moved across some big flats on which were a few springbok, the poor remnant of former crowds of game. We had for amusement a few long shots from the waggon at 700 or 800 yards, but did no execution. In the evening we trekked from 6 till 11, when we outspanned for a supper of "bully beef," sardines, and coffee. From 3.30 A.M. till 7 A.M. we again pushed on, and did a good trek.

On Sunday the 1st of June we found ourselves outspanned in semi-bushy country, near some water-pits which lie amid a collection of large, rounded boulders, and are now well known as "Boulder Pits" on the up-country trek. At breakfast we were surrounded by a number of women and girls, who came laden with the large wooden Bechuana pitchers containing fresh milk, as well as pumpkins and melons.

These people, who were of the Bangwaketse tribe, owing allegiance to Batoen, a powerful chief settled at Kanya to the westward, were extremely merry, and we had great fun with them over our purchases of milk, vegetables, and bangles. They pressed us much to stay, offering to undertake our washing, and were excessively curious over our outfits and clothes. A pair of well-cut breeches of Tautz's build,

worn by Mackay, seemed to especially attract their
notice ; they closely examined the texture, sewing,
and cut, and vented their surprise and pleasure in
expressive " Ous !" and exclamations. Indeed, their
attentions were rather embarrassing to Mackay,
although he is not naturally of a shy nature.

These people were tall, well set-up, and well fed—
in fact, pictures of health—and, as with all Bechuana
women, who are used to carry their great water-
vessels and other heavy weights balanced upon
their heads, their firm and erect bearing was very
admirable. Unlike many of the women of British
Bechuanaland, they wore no European clothes, but
walked about in blankets or their own native karosses
and skin petticoats. Having extracted all they could
from us, they sat down to watch our proceedings,
and amused themselves by singing various Sechuana
hymns to Moody and Sankey airs, which they did
very prettily. The Bechuanas, indeed, have a
natural aptitude for singing ; the only fault I have
to find with them is that their delivery is apt to be
slow and monotonous. At a later period some of
our Bamangwato boys were singing some hymn or
other to the air of " Drink to me only with thine
eyes." The music was taken at so slow a time as
to make me feel inclined to hurry them up. I afterwards explained that the air really belonged to a
secular song, and sang them a verse or two of it.
They were intensely amused, but I fancy, after all,
were inclined to think I was poking fun at them.
Dove meanwhile, seated on his waggon, was roaring
with laughter at my efforts in musical education.
All these hymns and airs are, of course, in the first
instance taught by the English missionaries ; the

natives soon pick up the tune, and learn without difficulty to sing in parts.

We had bought from a Marico Boer at Ramathlabama a quantity of splendid oranges at five shillings a hundred (a rather high price, by the way). Some of these we presented to our Bangwaketse lady friends, by whom they were greatly appreciated.

Having rested at Boulder Pits, we pushed on for a couple of hours through some very beautiful mountain scenery ; indeed, this portion of the Protectorate can boast of some of the finest landscapes in all South Africa, and, after the monotonous rolling prairies of the Crown colony, the rugged mountains, frowning cliffs, and bushy, timbered slopes and valleys are a wonderful relief to the eye.   Here, indeed, with the blaze of sunshine over all, the softer beauties of English scenery are wanting ; the tender dalliance betwixt earth and sky only appears at early morn and sunset for a brief period, when the hills and vales are in shadow here and there.   None the less this part of the Protectorate, with its bold mountains, its charming valleys, and woody expanses of park-like scenery, is full of a wild, romantic beauty of its own. The sunsets were magnificent.   Often there lay

> " A slumberous stretch of mountain land, far seen,
>   Where the low westering day, with gold and green,
>   Purple and amber, softly blended, fills
>   The wooded vales, and melts among the hills."

In this and the neighbouring Bakwèna country Livingstone passed much of his early years, and Gordon Cumming rioted in the chase of the wonderful fauna which forty-five years ago abounded here. Writing of this very locality after his first week of successful shooting among rhinoceros — white and black—giraffe, eland, buffalo, koodoo, zebra, gnu, pallah, tsesseby, and lions, he says in his enthusiastic way : " Throughout all this country and vast tracts beyond it, I had the satisfaction to reflect that a never-ending succession of herds of every species of noble game which the hunter could desire pastured there in undisturbed security ; and as I gazed, I felt that it was all my own, and that I at length possessed the undisputed sway over a forest, in comparison with which the most extensive moor and mountain tracts of the wealthiest European sportsman sink into utter insignificance."

Alas ! alas ! vanished are these glories ; gone now are all those magnificent forms ; and there remains to this fair land of the Protectorate, until Khama's country is reached, only a few koodoos and pallahs here and there, small duykers and steinboks, and upon the mountains rheboks and klipspringers, to remind one of the most glorious and abundant fauna that the world has ever seen.

Out in the Kalahari, however, in the western and north-western part of Sechele's country, are yet to be found eland, gemsbok, and hartebeest in some plenty, as well as occasional giraffe.

After the publication of Gordon Cumming's book, by the way, it became the fashion to set down his adventures and bags as mostly mythical. Here the great hunter was assuredly wronged. I do not defend all his shooting, which too often amounted to butchery pure and simple ; but that he did encounter and shoot an incredible quantity and variety of game is undoubted. There are still old men alive among the Bechuanas, who accompanied him, and can vouch for his courage and powers ; notably the aged Khosilintse,

a well-known headman still living among the Bakwèna ; Mollyee and Mollyeon among Khama's people ;
the great chief Khama himself, and others. These
men still remember the mighty Nimrod and his feats,
and swear by his undaunted courage and his wonderful
strength and endurance, just as the Matabele and
Mashona, and even Boer hunters, swear by Selous
at this day. It must be remembered, too, that in
Cumming's time all this country was well-nigh virgin
to the hunter ; guns were almost unknown, and game
were often as tame and approachable as cattle. All
this is sadly changed, and the remaining fauna is shy,
suspicious, and only now to be secured by extremely
hard work.

Kolobeng, a little to the north-west, between Ramoutsa and Molepolole, though long since deserted,
is famous as one of the early stations of Livingstone.
There it was that the marauding Transvaal Boers,
during one of the missionary's absences, made an
attack in force upon the Bakwèna, and in sheer spite
and devilment looted the great traveller's stores and
furniture—which were afterwards sold by auction—
destroyed his books, and smashed his precious stock
of medicines. In this attack, which was utterly
unprovoked, the Boers, who numbered 400, and
had with them 88 waggons and a cannon, slew
60 Bakwèna, captured a number of women and
children, and swept off a quantity of cattle, besides
plundering the goods of some English hunters then
up-country. They themselves lost, however, in the
fight 28 men.

Prominent among the mountains of this district,
between Boulder Pits and Ramoutsa, is Aasvogel Kop,
a headland celebrated from time immemorial as the

resting-place of vultures, and noticeable at great distances in the surrounding country.

At luncheon, as we were outspanned, we strolled with our guns about the surrounding rocky hills. I made a good shot with the little Marlin carbine, and dropped a pretty grey hawk (*Melierax Gabar*) with the bullet at fifty paces, as it sat on a branch. Along the frowning cliffs and ledges of the further side of a magnificent kloof, ran and chattered a troop of baboons. We had a shot or two at long range, but only succeeded in frightening the noisy rascals.

Towards sundown we inspanned and trekked again till ten o'clock, when we outspanned in a beautiful natural park, near good water and not far from Aasvogel Kop.

In the afternoon we all shot specimens of a bird which we saw to-day for the first time, a kind of touracou, known to the natives as the moochooey or mukuey, and to naturalists as *Schizorhis Concolor*—the whole-coloured plantain-eater. This bird, which is noticeable by its unrelieved, dull, drab colouring, its long tail, elevated cockatoo-like crest, and harsh screaming cry, is common in North Bechuanaland, and especially so among the great trees on the banks of the Crocodile River. In length it averages some eighteen or nineteen inches. Its startling, human-like cry is very remarkable.

Roused by that terrible alarum, we trekked again from 2.30 to 7.30 A.M., by which time, after a night of incessant jolting through the mountains, we were not sorry to be up and preparing for breakfast. Dove's Cape cart, which we were towing behind the waggon, came loose once or twice, and we had to get up and fasten it again with fresh riems. We were now

approaching Ramoutsa, the stadt or town of the
Bamaluti chief, Ikaneng. Mounting our nags, therefore, we presently rode on into the town, leaving the
waggon to follow.

We were now following the eastern or Notwani
road through the Protectorate. Ramoutsa, a large
native town of some seven thousand inhabitants, is
situate on the Notwani River, which here separates
Bechuanaland from Transvaal soil. Ikaneng and his
people are not true Bechuanas, but refugees from the
Transvaal, who were allowed by Batoen's father,
Gasetsive, to settle on his eastern border. By and
by, as often happens in these cases, the vassals became too strong for their lords, refused to pay tribute,
and finally defeated the Bangwaketse in pitched
battles ; since which time they may be reckoned as
an independent tribe. They are well armed, and
quite capable of taking care of themselves, and their
chief seems on the whole better disposed towards
British influence than Batoen, Sebele (son and regent
of Sechele, the aged Bakwèna chief), and Lentswe, chief
of the Bakatla, all of whom are a source of some trouble
to the Administrator of British Bechuanaland.

It may be convenient here to glance briefly at the
tribes and chiefs of the Protectorate. After quitting
British Bechuanaland, first come Chief Batoen and
the Bangwaketse, whose broad lands stretch far out
into the Kalahari to the westward. In the corner
eastward of the Bangwaketse, Ikaneng and his Bamaluti have, as I have shown, latterly established themselves ; but their domains are necessarily somewhat
circumscribed. North of Ramoutsa, on the Notwani,
at a few hours' distance only, are squatted in Bakwèna territory a small clan of Makatese or Transvaal

BECHUANA DRESS, ANCIENT AND MODERN: BANGWAKETSE PEOPLE—BRITISH PROTECTORATE

natives, also refugees, under their chief Gaberone. This is a small and poor sept only, and has very little ground.

North of the Bangwaketse, again, are the Bakwèna —formerly the most powerful Bechuana tribe—under the famous old chief Sechele, with their head town at Molepolole, where is a population of seven thousand or eight thousand souls. Sechele, once quite the king-maker of the Bechuana tribes, and, of old, Livingstone's principal convert, is now very aged and infirm, and his power is mainly directed by his son Sebele, chief-regent. The Bakwèna, like the Bangwaketse, are lords of a vast tract of Kalahari country to the westward of Molepolole, where their Vaalpense and Bakalahari slaves herd cattle and collect skins and feathers for them.

Some forty miles north-east of the Bakwèna are the Bakatla under the chief Lentswe, formerly a weak, but now, thanks to a strong and determined ruler, a powerful, united, and well-armed people. Like the Bamaluti, the Bakatla not many years back merely squatted on the Bakwèna lands as vassals. Lentswe has managed to so strengthen and augment his tribe, however, that they are now independent and possessed of a large extent of country, having defeated the Bakwèna in several attacks. Mochudi, the capital of these people, is an important town of five thousand or six thousand inhabitants, strongly planted among rocky hills on the Notwani. Northward of the Bakwèna and the Bakatla comes the vast territory of Khama, chief of the Bamangwato, whose lands run northward to the Zambesi, eastward to the Matabele border, and westward across the Kalahari as far as Sebituane's Drift, half way up the Botletli

River, near Lake Ngami. By some inscrutable reasoning of the Colonial Office, which Khama, who is ever ready to welcome the British, never could comprehend, the Protectorate proper ends at parallel 22 of south latitude, and therefore embraces only the southern portion of Khama's country. The "sphere of influence," however, extends far beyond this to the Zambesi.

At present no one quite understands what "the Protectorate" means, or what the English do there. No hut taxes are collected, and the chiefs exercise all their old powers—powers which have become naturally strengthened under the fostering ægis of British might. Since Warren's expedition these tribes have waxed fat, and they occasionally even show signs of kicking. On several occasions—as upon the entry of the telegraph system and police force into their country—Lentswe and Sebele, and even Batoen, have shown symptoms of opposing force to British demands, and their demeanour has been personally aggressive and even insolent.

It is high time that they were made to understand that, as the British have preserved them for ever from the fear of Dutch incursion, they owe something in return. Here the lame and miserably halting policy, so frequently displayed in South Africa, has had its usual results. If the country had been at once taken over in 1885, as Sir Charles Warren advised, the whole territory might have been settled without ado, and with the willing consent of most of the tribes-people. It is true that towards the end of 1890 an Assistant-Commissioner and Resident, Mr. W. H. Surmon, was appointed to the Protectorate, but his powers and duties are very ill defined, and his authority is, to say the least, looked very doubt-fully upon by the tribes-people. In 1891–92 further movements have been made, and a court is now held in the Protectorate, and trading, liquor, and other licenses are issued. These steps have been taken tentatively, almost furtively I had said.

As a whole, the more settled portion of the Pro-tectorate is diversified, well-watered, and capable of producing (as indeed it already does) large crops of corn ; it is, further, excellent for cattle, goats, and native sheep, and is quite one of the most beautiful parts of Southern Africa. Large areas of ground are at this day all but uninhabited, and there is room and to spare for years to come both for natives and white settlers, so soon as the territory, which at present is practically sealed to white enterprise, is thrown open. In the mountains of the Protectorate indications of minerals have already been found ; hitherto, however, little real prospecting work has been done. It is probable that in the future valuable mineral wealth will be discovered in this territory.

There are one or two stores in Ramoutsa, at which we bought a few of the native curios usually to be found at up-country trading stations. We strolled about the town, and then ascended a low hill from which we had a complete view of the crowded aggregation of huts beneath. It was a wonderful sight, and, as at Morokweng, resembled nothing so much as a mass of gigantic bee-hives planted thickly together.

The waggon, having come in and passed on to the drift outside the town later in the afternoon, we joined it on our horses towards 9 o'clock. At 2 A.M. we inspanned, and trekked steadily over terribly rough mountain roads until 9 A.M., when breakfast was the word. After the incessant jolting and flinging to and fro in the kartel of last night, we felt rather upset this morning; however, breakfast and a pipe made things look better, and towards noon we proceeded to Gaberone's kraal, where we rested till evening. In the forest passed through this morning we shot a few rollers and hornbills, but saw scarcely any game birds, oddly enough; as for other game, we were so set upon a rapid trek to Khama's that we found no time to wander far from the road in search of it; and unless one gets well away from native kraals and roads, there is small prospect nowadays of picking up four-footed quarry until within a few days of Palachwe.

We had a long haggle with Gaberone (pronounced Haberone) over a miserable goat which we required for slaughter. Eventually we gave him ten shillings for a consumptive-looking specimen. All morning as we sat outspanned here the women folk were passing and returning to the bed of the Notwani, hereabouts very dry, carrying their huge clay water jars upon their heads. The watering place was an immense hole deep down in the sandy bed of the stream, overhung by shady trees; and as the water only trickled slowly through the sand, it had to be "skepped" up with gourd spoons—a long process. The women sat about laughing and chatting far down in this shady hollow, waiting for their turns; and as the bright sun gleamed through the foliage, here and there checkering the soil and touching the bronze red skins and coloured kerchiefs of these Makatese, there lay before the eye one of the most beautiful effects of light and shade I have ever seen.

A few months after we were at Gaberone's it was deemed advisable to move some more Border Police into this part of the Protectorate, chiefly with the idea, I fancy, of keeping Lentswe and Sebele in order. A camp has been formed, and 100 troopers and a gun or two are now permanently stationed there.

On we went again at 4.30, trekking till 9 P.M. and again during the night from 3 A.M. till 7.30. Christian and Jacob, the forelouper and horseboy, now informed us that they were sick. We therefore administered to each a teaspoonful of Pain-killer, which had an excellent effect. The natives think nothing of medicine unless it is strong and "bites" well; a single drop of this Pain-killer, neat, is sufficient to choke a white man. These boys swallowed their spoonful of this fiery compound with evident relish. They first tucked down their heads, as they squatted for a minute or two, and then got up, vowing themselves hugely better. The black man's palate and stomach are truly wonderful. Six miles from Mochudi we watered the oxen, and then mounted and rode into the stadt, passing most of the way through fine stretches of mealie and Kaffir corn lands.

Here began a series of small disasters. In the first place, we found that no relay of oxen had arrived to replace our already jaded span, as had been arranged. Late in the afternoon, when we were thinking about trekking again, Jonas came to inform us that the two "boys" had bolted. It seems that some of Lentswe's people had maliciously told them that there was war up-country, and that they would all have their throats cut by the Matabele. Owing to Lentswe's strict and unfriendly instructions (he was away from the town just then), we found it impossible to hire fresh servants here. Indeed, throughout our passage through this chief's country we found nothing but scowling faces and unfriendly, even truculent, manners. On several occasions this year the Bakatla had attempted to prevent up-country travellers, as well as members of the Bechuanaland Border Police, from watering cattle at various places in their country, and had even threatened force. The subsequent posting of 100 police troopers in a fortified camp at Gaberone's, within easy reach of Mochudi, was decidedly a wise move on the part of the Administrator and Sir Frederick Carrington—the latter of whom, the Commandant of the B. B. P., appearing to be one of the few people of whom Lentswe stands in awe. It is a significant fact, too, that the Bakatla are better armed and carry their guns and ammunition more habitually than any tribe I have seen in South Africa.

Lentswe is a very "arbitrary gent," and occasionally takes curious freaks into his head. Not long before our arrival he had somehow taken offence at the cocks and hens in his stadt, and at once gave orders that all should be destroyed. Probably the cock-crowing annoyed him, as it does town residents in other parts of the world. There was said, at the time we passed through, to be one solitary cock alive, under some special exemption of this black-skinned Czar.

While we were hanging about at Lentswe's, towards sundown, a procession of young girls all but in a state of nudity, carrying reeds and branches, and surrounded by an escort of women, marched through

the town towards the river, where certain mysterious
rites, forming part of the ancient Bechuana ceremony
known as the Boyale, were to be celebrated. The
Boyale rites are considered necessary to induct girls
to the state of womanhood, and, as they consist
mainly of cruel and heathenish practices, are strongly
discountenanced by the missionaries. Except, however, in Khama's country, where they have been
effectually suppressed, these rites still obtain among
the natives of the Protectorate. The old hags who
conduct the parties of maidens guard them jealously,
and no man is allowed to approach them upon any
pretext.

As we could procure neither fresh cattle nor
servants at this inhospitable place, we made up our
minds to trek out at once, and, with the help of
Jonas, manage the waggon, cattle, and horses for ourselves. Two police troopers, Messrs. Meisegaes and
Whichelow, who wanted a lift to Pallah Camp, on the
Crocodile, kindly volunteered their help, so that late
on the same night (5th June) we trekked out. For
the next two days, until we struck the Marico River,
we had a toilsome and uncomfortable journey. What
with forelouping and driving the oxen, "bossing
up" the horses, cooking, and other odds and ends of
work, we had our hands pretty full. This part of
the road lies among much bush, and is waterless,
sandy, monotonous, and uninhabited. Usually we
made our principal meal at night, when a big pot of
porridge was also boiled for our pack of dogs. At
night and morning, also, the horses each had a good
feed of mealies from nose-bags, which we carried on
the waggon. Driving the oxen and looking after the
horses at night was cold, miserable work ; however,

we had to endure only three days of this sort of thing, as we picked up a Griqua boy at a post-cart station on the Marico, and another Bechuana lad further on, after striking the Crocodile River. Our first view of the Marico, in this part of the world, was delightful. We found it running in a clear full stream, in a deep bed overhung by umbrageous trees. How we revelled in a bathe after several days of dirty and comfortless toil. We had now plenty of game birds to vary the monotony of tinned beef, herrings, and sardines, of which we were becoming sufficiently weary.

Pushing on, we at length found ourselves on the Crocodile or Limpopo River, some way past its junction with the Marico. Of all South African streams the Crocodile is, I think, the most striking, and upon the whole the most beautiful. Set as it is along its course among noble forest trees, and quantities of bush and greenery, and flowing in a full and rapid current, with here and there, in the dry season, spits and stretches of yellow sand showing at angles and corners, it offers, after the dry wastes of Bechuanaland, one of the finest and most imposing sights that man can behold. No wonder Gordon Cumming and other travellers have written in such ecstatic terms of its beauties. Even at the present day the game has not quite departed from the neighbourhood of this river. Koodoos and pallahs in the bush not far away ; leopards, bushbuck, and smaller antelopes in the coverts fringing the river, are yet found ; as well as immense numbers of Francolin (partridges and pheasants), which were always to be met with in the shrubbery along the banks, and at early morning and near sundown were to be seen running in troops along the road in front of the waggons. Among these birds we made some good bags, and so added variety to our flesh-pots again.

Many other beautiful and interesting birds are to be found near the river, and our drab, Quaker-like friends the moochooeys (quah-quahs we called them, from their strange cry) were to be seen, as well as numbers of the pretty green, yellow, and blue Rüppell parrots.

On the 8th we had a midday outspan of several hours, and having lately picked up another goat, we roasted an excellent leg in our largest Kaffir pot, boiled some potatoes, stewed some game birds, baked a quantity of "cookies" (Boer-meal rolls) upon a griddle on the embers of the fire, and fell to on a good square meal, which we had not enjoyed for some days.

On the morning of the 9th June, Mackay, Meisegaes, and I rode forward to Pallah Camp, just above the junction of the Notwani and Crocodile, twenty miles ahead. Here we were hospitably received by four or five members of the B. B. P. at a comfortable camp on rising ground a little way from the river. The valley of the Crocodile is notoriously feverish, and, even in this the dry season, cases were not infrequently occurring, especially on the Transvaal side. These B. B. P. troopers and their corporal had, I fancy, rather a dull existence here ; their official duties were light, and there was little to be done to kill time ; and not a soul to speak to except at a passing waggon, or over on Transvaal soil at a store some way off.

Before reaching Pallah Camp we crossed the river, hereabouts as wide as the Thames at Hampton Court, and even now, in the middle of the dry season, taking our horses up to their necks and flowing swiftly, and crossed into the Transvaal. In summer the drift here is unfordable for waggons, and a boat takes passengers across. A mile or so further on we came to Francis's Store, where we required to purchase a few things and replenish supplies.

At this store, which is, or was, notorious for its prohibitive tariff (it was then the only "winkel" to be found in the district), we paid the highest prices that I have encountered in any part of South Africa. For the reader's information, here is our list :—

		s. d.			s. d.
3 lbs. tea .	. . .	9 0	4 pots of jam . . .		10 0
4 lbs. coffee	. . .	8 0	3 cotton Kaffir handker-		
6 lbs. common sugar .	.	4 0	chiefs		3 0
4 tins condensed milk	.	8 0	1 small kettle .	.	7 6
3 tins corned beef	. .	12 0	1 tin-opener .	. .	4 6
1 bottle Worcester sauce	.	2 0	1 tinned tongue .	.	10 0
3 lbs. of dates .	. .	6 0	2 tins Danish butter .	.	10 0

At these rates Mackay and I considered ourselves sufficiently "salted," and rode away grumbling and using language which may have been strong, but which under the circumstances was pardonable. I am afraid at such a tariff the unfortunate police troopers at Pallah Camp, who had no other available store at which they could purchase little luxuries, had rather a bad time of it.

At "September's Post," a cattle station just below the camp, we were able to arrange with "September," Messrs. Musson's head boy here, for a fresh span of oxen—a very welcome relief. Next afternoon, the 10th, after we had passed a quiet morning at the camp, our waggon came in, the oxen were changed, a new forelouper was engaged, and so with renewed

spirits we were enabled to trek again at night, now
certain of making Palachwe in fair time. We
travelled from 1.30 A.M. till 7.30—a capital trek—
and outspanned near a beautiful bend of the Crocodile. After breakfast we had some rifle practice
down the river, and afterwards Dove and Mackay
each shot a Kiewitje plover at fifty and fifty-five
yards respectively, with single bullets from the
Marlin carbine—excellent shooting. This plover
(*Hoplopterus Coronatus*), with its noisy, chiding
voice, is well known all over South Africa. At
night, when it is particularly lively, its shrill melancholy cry is one of the typical sounds of the African
veldt. Common though it is, this handsome plover,
by reason of its bright eye and red bill, its metallic
grey-brown upper plumage, beautifully tinted with
purple, its striking snow-white black-barred stomach,
and the curious white wreath or crown which en-
circles its head, is yet very remarkable. It may be
found in flocks varying from ten to thirty, in the
driest and most dreary spots, and I have remarked
time after time that a particular flock will haunt
with unswerving devotion the sites of old huts and
cattle kraals, which have been long since deserted.

We shot some pheasants in the evening, and Dove
secured also a most beautiful bee-eater (*Merops
Bullockoides*), whose brilliant crimson throat, green
back, buff head, bright blue rump, and deep electric-
blue stomach, separated from the ruby throat by
a handsome patch of buff-chestnut, presented a
glorious bit of colouring.

On the 12th, after a good early morning trek from
3.15 to 7.45, we outspanned for the last time near
the great river, and breakfasted.

Not far from here we met the well-known Dutch hunter, Mr. Van Rooyen, who, with his family, waggon, flocks and herds, was trekking out of Matabeleland, fearing war troubles. We found Mr. Van Rooyen, who, next to Mr. Selous (of whom, by the way, he is an enthusiastic admirer), is perhaps the greatest hunter now left to South Africa, a pleasant, well-informed man, and, strange to say, speaking good English. We had coffee and a long chat at his camp close by.

In these days of railway travelling, a Boer trek and its quaint and singularly picturesque surroundings can hardly be realised, unless one has crossed the Equator and journeyed in the interior of South Africa. The long train of huge white-tented waggons, the toiling spans of eighteen oxen to each waggon, the pistol-like cracking of the long whips, and the shrill volleys of shrieks and curses levelled by native drivers at the straining teams; the vrouw and her children huddled in the waggon, all mingled with furniture, pots, kettles, pans, poultry, and other necessary impedimenta; the rifles always carefully slung ready to hand on the inner side of the waggon-tent; and the throngs of cattle, sheep, and goats raising clouds of dust as they accompany the march of the trekkers—all these are things well fitted to strike upon the imagination. In this way, from small beginnings, and amid the inconceivable difficulties offered by a rude country, fierce savages, and fiercer wild beasts, have these rough farmers of the wilderness toiled, and fought, and struggled, and carved out their homes. Small wonder, then, that they are so tenacious of the land thus hardly won !

Van Rooyen's trek was on a small scale only, yet

was it sufficiently picturesque. He laughingly said to us as we sat at coffee, " Yes, I brought away everything, even the pigs. The vrouw could not leave the pigs behind, and so they are under the kartel (waggon-bed) : " and so indeed they were, and some cocks and hens as well.

Van Rooyen accompanied us a little way towards our waggon, which meanwhile was moving on. He rode his well-known shooting horse " Pony," the best trained and most sagacious horse in the South African hunting veldt. At fourteen this Dutch Nimrod began his campaign against big game, and during that season he slew eight elephants—a great record for a boy. Van Rooyen's admiration for Mr. Selous, with whom he had at times hunted, was immense. It is seldom a Boer can be found to speak well of an Englishman's skill in venery, or even of the not uncommon attribute of courage. But Van Rooyen spoke of Selous as a man in a thousand. " Ah ! " he said, " we shall never see another like him in the veldt ; he is a man and three-quarters, with a heart of stone." It was refreshing, indeed, to hear one's countryman spoken of in this way—and by a Transvaal Dutchman.

The hunter was now suffering much from fever, contracted in the Tati district during the recent summer. We were able to give him a bottle of Eno's Fruit Salt and some oranges, the former of which he thought might afford some temporary relief till he could obtain quinine. All our medicines were in front of us at Palachwe, or we would gladly have provided him with other and better drugs.

We now pushed on through a flat, dry country, well bushed, and furnished with big trees here and there. Since entering Khama's country—near Pallah Camp—we found ourselves (in strong contrast to the offhand, unfriendly Bakatla of Lentswe's country) among the pleasant, well-behaved Bamangwato people, from whom we were always able to procure plenty of fresh milk. This evening we made a quantity of Boer-meal porridge for supper, which, with an unlimited supply of milk, was, as Mackay elegantly expressed it, "ripping."

Next day, the 13th of June, after another capital early morning trek, we outspanned near a good pan of water lying in the bush a little to the left of the road, to which we had been directed by Van Rooyen. We were now only five miles from a bold range of hills, known as Sofala—the first seen since we had quitted Lentswe's Town—which stretched across our front, and in the early light of morning looked magnificent. The rosy flush of sunrise crept over the crest, bathing it in a warm glow, and presently there lay before us a lovely mass of purplish-blue and brown hills, with the shadows of early morning for the present lying over on our side. We had trekked twenty-seven miles over heavy road, and with no water, in twenty-four hours, and we settled therefore to give the cattle a good rest.

Meanwhile, a Mangwato boy having come up with a great wooden pitcher holding about a gallon of new milk, for which he was contented to take six copper caps, we baked some "cookies," and then fell to breakfast.

After this performance we took our last remaining shot-cartridges—we had brought but a small quantity with us—our guns and the Marlin carbine, and hied us to the pool. Here we found a flight

or two of the large red-billed teal, out of which we
accounted, with the two shot-guns, for four couple,
all excessively plump and in high condition. Besides
the teal, we secured a single dabchick, specifically
identical with the little grebe of England (*Podiceps
Minor*), and a couple of very curious diving ducks
(furnished with singular cocked-up tails), which
proved to be *Erismatura Maccoa*. One of these
latter was shot by Dove with the little 44 Marlin
carbine, after performing some extraordinary diving
feats. These Marlins, by the way, although cheap
American weapons, costing only £3, 10s. or £4
apiece, gave us some extraordinary shooting ; their
accuracy being equal almost to the costliest rook
rifles. For small buck, paauw, and odd shooting,
they cannot be too highly commended. The magazine
carries thirteen cartridges if necessary, and the action
is simple and well secured from sand and dust. We
gave one of these handy little weapons to Khama,
who was very pleased with it.

The day was magnificent, clear, sunny, and bracing ;
and, after the hot valley of the Crocodile, we felt
pounds better men than for days past. As we had
to retrieve some of the quarry, we indulged in a very
welcome swim, during which we gathered some fine
water-lilies of a lovely heliotrope colour, with yellow
centres, the stamens being also tipped with heliotrope.
These great lilies had a peculiar and most delicious
scent of their own, reminding one strongly of Jockey
Club Bouquet. Flocks of sand-grouse every now and
again came to the pan to drink, offering, as they
swooped down in a band, a very charming spectacle.
At this pool we met with some young Mangwato
boys, pleasant-faced, nude rascals, pictures of lissom

activity, who were amusing themselves with a singular pastime. They each carried a supply of short, peeled wands, smooth and slender. Taking one of these in his hand and holding it at the end, a lad would make a short, quick run forward, and with great force cast it from him, as if throwing a cricket ball. The stick was hurled obliquely at the earth, which it struck some twenty or thirty paces off, thence ricochetting like an arrow far and swiftly away. The game was simple enough, but the shapely brown naked figures of these lads, the beautiful manner in which they discharged their missiles, and the swift flight of the wands after they struck the hard ground, were very remarkable. I never saw the pastime elsewhere ; on trying my hand, although I can throw a cricket ball well enough, I hopelessly failed to effect the desired ricochet (which the boys never missed), and, amid much laughter all round, resigned the game. Having thoroughly enjoyed ourselves for an hour or two, we returned to the waggon, meeting as we went a hunter laden with a big rooikat (African lynx) which he had snared somewhere in the bush.

Towards three o'clock, when we were thinking of inspanning again, Jonas informed us that the oxen had wandered and were lost, and might not be recovered till next day. This was vexatious, but could not be mended. The fact was, Jonas had had very little rest for ten days past, and was tired out. He had lain under a shady bush for a long sleep ; the forelouper, who had less excuse, had probably done likewise, and the cattle had moved away, evidently grazing towards some other water. It was settled, therefore, that Mackay and Dove should ride for-

ward to Palachwe early next morning, leaving me
to follow with the waggon. We had a sumptuous
supper of teal, excellently roasted in a Kaffir pot,
and turned in, after a smoke by the camp fire, for a
long night's sleep, free from the usual joltings of a
night trek, and by this time secure also against the
hideous screech of that agonising alarum, which had
succumbed to internal injuries.

At sun-up (6.45) on the 14th, therefore, my comrades set off, after an early breakfast, leaving me to
" boss up " and bring on the caravan. First I made
and baked bread, plucked and prepared some teal for
dinner, and roasted and ground coffee.

Our bread we always made very simply and effectually with coarse Boer meal, a little baking-powder,
and water—sour milk is a capital thing, if it can be
had, instead of all water. After kneading, the dough
is placed in a common Kaffir pot, or baking pot, over
a slow fire of hot embers, the top of the pot being
also covered with embers. With care and a little
practice, good bread of a yellowish brown colour
results. Coffee, which is always carried up-country
in the raw bean state, is easily and well roasted by
placing in small quantities in a clean frying-pan, in
which is a little water to prevent burning. Stir the
beans over an ember fire with a piece of stick, and
delicious, well-roasted coffee is soon ready. A coffee-
mill is fixed to the buck rail of the waggon, and the
grinding completed. Thus one has the daily luxury
of coffee in its virgin freshness and aroma, instead of
the stale ground and chicoried stuff in tins—perhaps
months or even years old.

During the morning a boy came up to the waggon
with a fine native sheep, which he wanted to trade

for a rifle-cartridge bandolier of mine, upon which
he had set his heart the evening before. He had a
rifle, now his ambition was to possess a cartridge-belt,
and so make his equipment complete. I was sorry
not to be able to accommodate the lad, but I really
wanted the bandolier myself, and he would trade
nothing else. These indigenous African sheep would
puzzle the eye of an English farmer. They are
covered not with wool but with hair; and, as a rule,
their colouring is brown and white, or black and
white. The average up-country specimens are not
remarkable as flesh producers; but then they are
not very well cared for, and all their fat seems to be
concentrated in the broad tail, which will sometimes
weigh as much as 12 lbs.—all pure fat. This provision of nature, which is peculiar to all native South
African sheep, is very extraordinary. If you take
the tail in your hand, it reminds you of nothing so
much as a skin bag full of soft jelly; and the thin
smooth skin underneath adds much to this resemblance. The fat of these tails is much sought after
for cooking purposes, and among the Boers often
takes the place of butter. Where they are well fed
and looked after, these sheep thrive rapidly, and
readily command a good price for slaughter purposes.
A friend of mine, formerly farming in Cape Colony,
made some interesting experiments with fat-tailed
sheep. Instead of allowing the tails to grow, he
cut them off when the lambs were quite young;
the results were interesting and valuable. As the
animals grew to maturity the lower parts of their
backs became clothed with fat—very much more so
than is usual with tailed sheep—and the flock as a
whole carried more flesh and sold for better prices

than average native sheep. Nature has apparently provided the indigenous African sheep with this curious supply of pure fat as a reserve of sustenance and strength in times of drought and scarcity. At such periods the fat steadily decreases, and it is evident that the waste going forward in other parts of the body is thence supplied.

It is remarkable that the two races of mankind, who, when Europeans discovered the Cape, were found to be dwelling on the parched karroos and deserts of South-West Africa, have been provided for by nature in much the same manner.

The Bushmen and Hottentots, who undoubtedly for long ages before the advent of the Dutch had been the sole inhabitants of this part of the continent, are peculiarly distinguished (and especially the Hottentot) by the enormous fatty development of the lower parts of the back. This unsightly prominence seems by their own admission to have served these people as a reserve force in seasons of want and hunger, in much the same way as does the tail in the case of the fat-tailed sheep. As hunger and scarcity increase, so does the abnormal development decrease.

An old friend of mine (the late Mr. J. B. Evans of Riet Fontein, near Graaff-Reinet), who farmed for many years in Cape Colony, and who was a close observer of nature, once particularly noticed this natural waste in the case of a Bushman who had endured great want and hunger during a long drought. He taxed the Bushman with his loss, and the little aboriginal admitted with a grin that the drought had robbed him of all his fat supply.

These are plain facts in anthropology ; whether they are singular instances among mankind in hot climates, as I am inclined to think, or whether they can be supported and explained by reference to other native tribes, I am uncertain. In cold climates, as among the Esquimaux of Arctic regions, the incessant waste of material is supplied by a corresponding diet of fat and blubber. Here arises an obvious question. If the Hottentots and Bushmen and fat-tailed sheep have been thus partially insured against a waste of power in a hot zone, why should not the Esquimaux much more have been provided naturally with a fatty reserve against the dreadful cold of the regions they inhabit? Probably the answer may be found in the fact that the Esquimaux can at all times provide themselves with supplies of fat and blubber, while the Bushmen and Hottentots, from the very occurrence of the devastating drought, could not.

The pure strain of Hottentot has, by constant intermingling with other races, almost disappeared from Cape Colony (the present Cape Hottentot being a gentleman of very mixed blood), although still to be found plentifully among the inhabitants of Great Namaqualand. The tiny aboriginal Bushman hunters are now very scarce ; they have been exterminated or driven by the ancient system of Boer commandos almost completely from the old colony ; and although here and there still to be found along the Orange River, or in the lower portions of the Kalahari, another hundred years will probably witness their final extinction.

The oxen having been found under the hills of Sofala, I dined sumptuously on a couple of teal, and we then inspanned at 3, and trekked steadily till 9 P.M. At Sofala, on the right hand of the road, a stream issues from a bright green marshy spot on the hillside, and spreads out into quite a bog on the flat beneath—an unusual sight in these dry regions. There were numbers of active little red meerkats to be seen near the road this afternoon, as well as a few hares, and the dogs were extremely busy. Before leaving the last outspan two Boer waggons came by, with which I was glad to find my pointer, Don, who had been missing for some days. The Boers, who were from Waterberg going up to Khama's with oranges and tobacco, hoping to obtain hides, handed the dog over without ado, and having had some coffee with me, passed on.

Next day, after passing a rather miserable post station lying under a quartz kopje, I picked the Boers up again by a pan of water, and we had a long afternoon together. Having smoked and chatted for some time, I produced the Marlin carbine, which they much admired. They appeared to be particularly struck by the convenience of the magazine, holding thirteen cartridges. We had a few shots each at a piece of paper stuck on a "stompje" seventy yards off, at which I was surprised and secretly delighted to find myself their superior. Fired by this display, and hearing that I and my friends were on a shooting trip towards Lake Ngami, the Dutchmen offered to buy all the skins we shot; "kameels" (giraffe) at £2, 10s. each, elands at 15s., and so on. I explained that we were shooting for sport and not for skins, at which they seemed disappointed. They were astounded when they heard that all the best heads we got we wanted to take home as trophies. A Boer is not yet educated to the idea of decorating his house in this way. He usually has a pile of horns rotting somewhere near his door, if there is game about—horns that an Englishman would often jump at. Up-country hunters are, however, beginning to find out that good horns have nowadays a value of their own, and are thus induced to bring them down with the skins.

We trekked together at 5 P.M., and so much were the Dutchmen in love with my company that they sat on my waggon, smoked my tobacco with great zest (I had some Transvaal tobacco which they highly approved of), and spat very freely all over the waggon floor. I am afraid Mackay's velschoens, which were unfortunately lying about, suffered in this process, though I did not discover it till afterwards. The Boer is an immense, but, unlike the Yankee, an inartistic expectorator, and the habit is not one that commends itself, especially when performed on a decently kept waggon.

However, barring this nasty habit, which I could hardly expect to eradicate during an afternoon call, the Boers were decent fellows enough, rough and uncouth it is true, but friendly and inclined for an exchange of ideas. They had discovered that I was married and had "kinder," and this, I think, rather won their hearts. The discovery brought with it, however, a long description of their own large and to me uninteresting families, with which I was duly inflicted—especially as my Dutch conversational powers are not of the best. These men had some excellent tobacco, grown on their farms in Waterberg, as good as any Transvaal tobacco (which is usually very good indeed) I have ever tasted.

The grand Chapong Hills, among which lies

Khama's Town, were now in front of us, and I was anxious to push on. I quitted the Dutchmen, therefore, at sundown, and making a long and steady evening trek through deep sand till 9.30, inspanned again early next morning, and drew up just outside Palachwe at 7 A.M. It was Sunday, and as I knew that Khama has an objection to waggon traffic in his town on that day, I left the waggon and rode forward to the Bechuanaland Trading Association Store,[1] where I found Dove and Mackay billeted. Mr. Gifford, who was in charge, was good enough to make me free of the mess also till our waggon came in, and gave me a shake-down in his own hut for the night.

[1] An offshoot of the Bechuanaland Exploration Company.

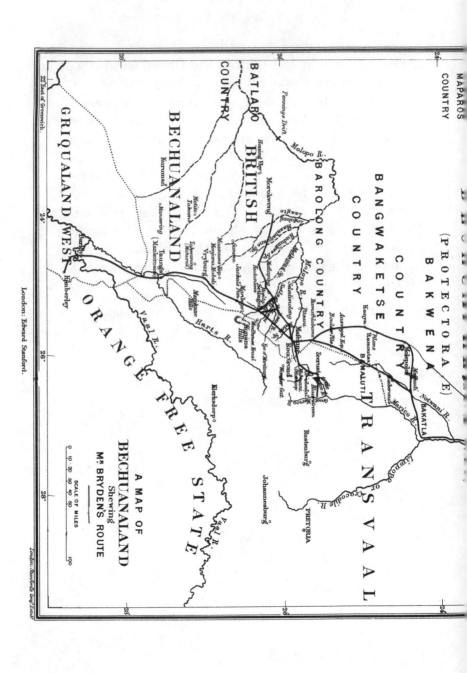

A MAP OF
BECHUANALAND
Shewing
Mr BRYDEN'S ROUTE

SCALE OF MILES
0 10 20 30 40 50   100

London: Edward Stanford.

London: Stanford's Geog. Estab.

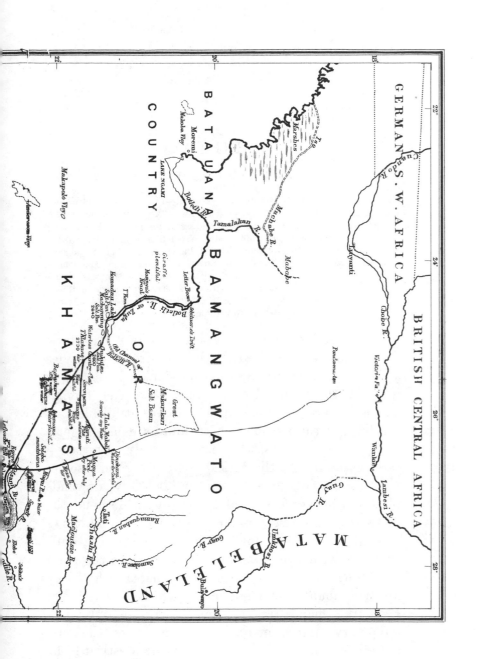

CHAPTER XI.

KHAMA AND HIS COUNTRY

SUNDAY the 16th June was a pleasant day at Palachwe. After lunch we went up the hill to afternoon service at Mr. Hepburn's, the resident missionary here. Then we had tea with Mrs. Hepburn and her family, and afterwards strolled up a most beautiful kloof at the back of the station, where, amid a dense vegetation of trees, shrubs, and ferns, a lovely waterfall— rare sight in South Africa—reminding one somewhat of the falls of Acharn near Loch Tay, descends plashing in ever cool and luxuriant shade amid the rocks, and, presently issuing on lower ground, flows through a romantic gorge, shut in by beetling cliffs and clad with every kind of greenery, into the plain and town beneath. From the plateau, half-way up the mountain-side, upon which is situated Mr. Hepburn's manse (at the time I write of only in a temporary stage), magnificent views over the surrounding country lie spread. To the westward the

hills of Seruë, Letloche, and others, billowing blue
and distant upon the horizon, shut off the dry
wastes of the Kalahari thirstland. Northward, beyond
the Serule Hills, we look right away to the Matabeleland border, seventy good miles distant. Beneath
us, spread out in a broad, flat valley, and thickly
embushed in trees and shrubbery, lies the great
native town of Palachwe itself. Behind and flanking
us tower, close at hand, the rocky masses of the
Chapong range.

There are few places in South Africa where a more
beautiful landscape can be seen.

> " But pleasures are like poppies spread,
> You seize the flower, its bloom is shed."

Peaceful as looks the scene, all is not peace beyond.
Even as one looks over the fair champaign and the
sweet blue hills northward and westward, one remembers that there in Matabeleland is the home of
the fiercest, most savage, and most bloodthirsty tribe
that ever desolated Africa ; while to the north-west,
before we can reach our happy hunting-grounds on
the Lake River and return safely, we have to cross
and recross one of the dreariest and most waterless
stretches of the Kalahari desert—that grim thirstland, in which the trek Boers suffered so terribly
thirteen years before. The presence at Mr. Hepburn's
of two Matabeleland missionaries, Messrs. Elliott and
Carnegie, with their families, waggons, and belong-
ings, reminded us forcibly of the critical aspect of
affairs at this juncture.

The expedition to Mashonaland was just preparing to start, every one predicted war, and nearly
every white man had cleared from the Matabele

country before the troubles should begin. The
Bamangwato themselves, as next-door neighbours
and old adversaries of the Matabele, were in a state
of preparation ; for, if Lobengula's men once got out
of hand and tasted blood, it seemed much more than
probable that they would attack Khama, the constant friend and ally of the British.

Early next morning we found the waggon outspanned by a big tree near Mr. Clarke's store, where
we had arranged to camp and complete our outfit.
We now set to work in earnest to finish our preparations. The tent was pitched for use during our
sojourn, and early in the morning Khama came to
pay us a visit and bid us welcome to his town. I
had for years heard so often and so much of this
great chief, that it seemed to be perfectly natural
to be shaking hands with the tall, slim gentleman
with the refined face, friendly smile, and shy yet
self-possessed manner, to whom Mr. Clarke now presented us. The chief, as he had promised our friend
Mr. Frank Whiteley, was finding us a waggon, a
span and a half of oxen, and servants ; and he now
informed us that the whole would be ready for us
in a day or two. He was sending us to his best
hunting veldt, and providing us with his most
trusted hunters, drivers, and servants, and in short
doing everything in the kindest and most generous
manner. We had expected, and were prepared, as
had been arranged for us by Mr. Whiteley, to pay
a considerable sum for the hire of a good hunting
waggon and twenty-eight oxen for three or four
months, and before we left we asked Khama what
we were to pay him. His reply fairly staggered
us. " No," he said, " I will take nothing for the

hire of these things. You are the friends of my friend, and I am pleased to do whatever I can to show you my country, and the game (poloholo), and oblige you ; I will only ask you to be good to the men I am finding for you, and to pay them fair wages."

We had a long argument with the chief about this matter ; but it was of no avail, and we could not move him. This was handsome treatment indeed, and the whole thing was done in so quiet and modest a way as to make Khama's generous kindness doubly magnificent. We were utter strangers to the man ; purely private individuals coming into his country for sport and travel ; and he had no ulterior motive or reason for going out of his way to render obligations to us. I don't think a more disinterested offer could be made by any person, black or white. No doubt we owed much to our introductions. Mr. Frank Whiteley is an old and trusted friend of Khama, and the name of John Mackenzie (whom I had known in England) is a potent one to conjure with, when dealing with his ancient pupil and lifelong friend, Khama of Bamangwato. But Khama's conduct to us is of a piece with his unceasing friendliness to the English throughout his career. Only a short time later Mr. Lochner, who had been detained for many months in the deadly Barutse valley, negotiating a treaty with the Trans-Zambesian chief Lewanika on behalf of the Chartered Company, came down from the Zambesi half dead with fever, and with his oxen in a sorry plight. Khama heard of his distress, and at once sent off fresh teams of oxen to bring him through the bad country between the Zambesi and Palachwe, and aided not a little in saving a precarious life.

Many a time and oft has Khama helped the white man in these and other ways. And while upon this topic let me say a few words here concerning Palachwe and its ruler. Palachwe itself, unlike every other native town in South Africa—where the huts lie huddled together (often upon some strong, inaccessible kopje) for defensive purposes—is scattered over a huge area of ground. The plain on which the "stadt" is set is thickly covered with trees ; graceful acacias, Kaffir orange, mopani, and others ; these have been wisely suffered to remain, and, even as you look from the hills above over the town below, it seems impossible— so hidden are the huts amid the vegetation—that a population of 20,000 people, representing the largest native town in South Africa, finds shelter here. Khama's old capital of Shoshong, some fifty or sixty miles away to the south-west, although a safer retreat from the Matabele, was but ill supplied with water. Palachwe, furnished as it is with pleasant streams, flowing from waterfalls that spring in kloofs of quite romantic beauty, now boasts an exceptional water supply. Each hut or small cluster of huts has around it a good space of land for garden ground, the whole being enclosed within a smooth clay wall or a neat fence or " scherm" of bush and thorns. The ant-clay walls, which are soon burnt by the sun into a kind of brick-work, are usually loop-holed and the exteriors variegated, mostly in black, in quaint arabesques and patterns.

The Bechuana huts are, as I have before remarked, quite the best in South Africa—probably in all Africa—and the interiors are in nearly every case kept scrupulously neat. Khama himself lives in a good-sized hut having two chambers or compart-

ments, and differing but little from those of the rest
of his people, save that it is furnished with a bedstead, chairs, table, and a few other European articles.

In the middle of the town is a large open com-
monage, where as a rule all incoming waggons stand,
unless, for convenience sake, the traveller outspans
near one of the three trading stores, where goods and
necessaries for the far interior may be more easily
loaded up. Probably, as I have shown, you will not
have been very long outspanned before Khama in his
ubiquitous way has ridden up to pay you a visit and
exchange friendly greeting. As you look at this
tall, lithe, thoughtful-looking man, with his keen yet
kindly eye, and pleasant smile, you realise that before
you stands the chief by whom all white men in the
South African interior (if they are not Transvaal
Boers) swear, a chief probably in his way quite as
powerful as that renowned savage Lobengula.

Khama has long worn European clothing, and held
close intercourse with refined and educated European
men, and he has acquired quite English manners.
As a rule, the black man cuts but a poor figure in
the white man's clothes ; Khama may be cited as a
remarkable instance to the contrary.

The chief stands about six feet in height, is of a
slim, wiry habit, and although now verging on sixty
years of age, might be taken for at least twelve or
fifteen years younger. And yet this man, so quiet,
so unobtrusive, yet withal so self-possessed, has seen
a life of much stress and many dangers. His activity
has been, as all men are agreed, phenomenal. He
never rests. In his younger days his father and
brothers, hating him for his ideas of reform and his
friendship to white men and missionaries, conspired

against him; he passed some years in a self-imposed exile (across the Kalahari in the Mababē and Botletli River country), and his life was often in danger. Since he became paramount chief of the Bamangwato

KHAMA, CHIEF OF BAMANGWATO, NORTH BECHUANALAND.

he has had much trouble on his hands and occasional warfare, and even the fierce Matabele warriors have been repulsed in attacks upon his strongholds. In one attack by the Matabele, indeed, Khama himself wounded his great rival Lobengula, who carries to this day the mark of the bullet at the back of his neck.

There is no braver man south of the Zambesi. Over and over again has Khama proved his mettle against the lion, the elephant, the buffalo, rhinoceros, and all that wonderful variety of game with which his country formerly swarmed, and still in parts abounds. The chief can as a youth remember Gordon Cumming in the old days when elephants roamed in undisturbed profusion about the Shoshong hills and valleys, when tusks were worthless and rotted upon the veldt, and when firearms were almost unknown among the Bamangwato. Times have changed since those glorious hunting days! The chief is a capital rider, dearly loves horseflesh, is a judge of a rifle, and took the greatest interest in our hunting studs and equipment as we sojourned at his town. We had many a friendly chat together (conducted through an interpreter), and the chief once or twice breakfasted at our camp. When I returned from our hunting expedition I told him as we sat at breakfast of our success with giraffes, at which he was highly delighted.

His keen eye lighted up as he said, in reply to a remark of mine, " Yes, it is good hunting. I hope to hunt ' tūtla ' (giraffe) again some day soon ; but for the last three years, what with fear of Matabele troubles, the moving of my town, and other matters, I have not had a moment's time."

Khama, as I have said, has had much intercourse with clever and enlightened white men. In the missionaries resident with him for many years past he has been singularly fortunate, and the names of Mackenzie and Hepburn will be long remembered

R

among the Bamangwato for the wonderful progress, peace, and enlightenment which have attended their efforts. On the other hand, few missionaries have been more blessed in their material. It is seldom indeed that such a man as Khama can be found to second missionary effort. The chief himself exercises complete toleration among his people. There is no forcing into religion, but at the same time the old barbarous customs and rites have been gradually put aside. It is an excellent trait in this man's character, and one very rare among native Christians, that he never obtrudes his piety upon you. Good man and pious though he is, he would be the last to make pharisaical display of it.

There is no busier man in the world than the Bamangwato chief. From earliest dawn he is up and riding about, here directing native labour in the cornfields outside the town, there selling grain and oxen to the passing expedition, helping the hunter, traveller, and explorer in every possible way, administering justice in his " kotla," holding prayers for a short space in the afternoon for such as like to attend, buying and inspecting ploughs and other implements for his people, or seeing that they are fairly dealt by in their negotiations with the up-country traders. We ourselves owed much of the success of our expedition to his efforts. Khama busied himself in the most unwearying manner in procuring servants, hunters, grain, and cattle for us, not with any hope of reward, which he would be the last to expect, but for the plain reason that for an Englishman he will do anything in his power.

From time immemorial native chiefs have looked upon the white man as a calf to be bled, a cow to be

milked, and the first question asked on the arrival
at a powerful chief's kraal is, "What presents has
the white man brought?" Khama has changed all
this. He discourages and usually declines presents,
having very good reason to know that the old-time
trader too often took out his change in the shape of
a roaring liquor traffic among the tribes-people.

There is only one thing the chief will not tolerate
from the white man. Liquor traffic, or the running
of liquor into his country, he will not permit; and
the offender in this respect, after due warning, is
quickly shown to the border. Such offenders Khama
never forgets. They may present themselves at his
town years afterwards, but the chief has a wonderful
memory for faces, and they are soon known. When
one sees the shocking demoralisation among Cape
Kaffirs and other native races in territories where
liquor has been freely introduced, and compares the
wonderful method, peace, content, and order now
obtaining throughout Khama's country, one can
realise the inestimable benefits that his restrictions
in this respect have wrought among his people. It
is to be noted that the chief makes no objection to
Englishmen taking in their waggons liquor for their
private use, but it is assumed, as a point of honour,
that they will not offer drink to his subjects.

For years Khama had been longing to move his
chief place to some more desirable and better watered
locality than the old town of Shoshong; for years
his wishful thoughts had wandered to the fair streams,
the wooded flats, and encircling hills of Palachwe;
but Palachwe lay scarce seventy miles from the
Matabele border, and the Matabele had been always
dangerous foes to the Bamangwato.

At last, when British interests became stronger and
more defined in these regions, and when two years
before a force of the Bechuanaland Border Police was
stationed at Elebe on his frontier, near the debatable
ground between the Matabele and Bamangwato, a
move was decided on. But the Bamangwato were
extremely loth to leave their old town, and the
exodus of 20,000 souls with all their worldly gear
was no easy matter to arrange. Khama went among
his people telling them they must pack up and trek,
and still they dallied and stirred not. At last the
chief saw nothing for it but to transport himself and
his chattels to Palachwe, and leave the tribe to follow
him. The device proved successful, and then for
many days was to be witnessed an extraordinary
flitting. Waggons, Scotch carts, and old tumble-
down vehicles of all kinds were pressed into service.
Many carried their gear about them, and tramped it ;
many others used the old Bechuana sled, formed of
branches of trees and drawn by an ox or two : others
again resorted to that yet more ancient Bechuana
conveyance, the pack-ox. Within a wonderfully
short space Shoshong was deserted, and Palachwe
had sprung, as if by a stroke of magic, into a great
town. When I was first there in June of 1890, less
than twelve months had elapsed since the flitting,
and yet the new town seemed complete and settled,
the huts were well built, roofed and thatched against
the summer rains, crops had been sown and gathered,
all was flourishing. Only the genius and the incessant toil of Khama could have made these things
possible.

The moving from Shoshong of so large a population, and the building and settlement of Palachwe

in so short a period, are things unique in South African history.

The year 1890 was a profitable one for the Bamangwato. The sale of corn and cattle to the Chartered Company's expeditionary forces, as well as to the Border Police, and the hire of waggons (numbers of which are now owned by natives), brought quite a sudden accession of wealth. Prices rose rapidly, and at the end of May it was hard to obtain Kaffir corn or mealies for love or money. It has been computed that Khama's people were paid in hard money £20,000 during the six months of traffic. This may be a slight over-estimate, but it is not far from the truth. As a consequence, the stores were crammed day after day with eager purchasers, and as fast as fresh stocks came in by waggon, they were sold out. I saw in the compound of the Bechuanaland Trading Association 300 American ploughs ready for sale. After Khama had chosen the two or three required for his own use, his tribesmen were allowed to buy, and in one day the whole stock was bought, paid for, and taken away. Not bad business this, when it is remembered that each plough sold for the price of £5 cash, or the up-country equivalent of a good ox.

The Bamangwato are now as a whole well armed ; many of them are fine shots and much attention has been paid to drill, and it is probable that their regiments would make a far better fight of it with the Matabele than many people suppose.

Khama's systems of police intelligence and education are for a native state wonderfully complete. Few are the incidents in the remotest corners of his vast domain that are not speedily reported to him.

At distant cattle-posts, far away on the edge of the desert, native scholars may be found teaching the people to read and write. The traveller and hunter will meet with nothing but civility throughout the land, whether he treks to the Victoria Falls to the north or in the direction of Lake Ngami to the west. And yet in the old days, in Gordon Cumming's time, and much later, the Bamangwato were a troublesome people to pass through. The wise, firm, yet kindly rule of one strong man has effected in less than twenty years this wonderful change.

Although Khama is now getting into years, his spirits are as keen, his habits as active as ever; and for the sake of his people, and of the English, and of civilisation generally, it is to be hoped sincerely that he may long reign and prosper.

No one can have come in contact with this remarkable man and great reformer, the staunchest friend and firmest admirer that England has ever yet had among native chiefs, without wishing him still many years of life. South Africa can ill spare him; and it is scarcely too much to say that, as in the past she has never yet produced his like, so in the future it will be long ere she may see his like again.

It is a pleasant sight to see Khama moving about among his people. He passes an aged woman—one of the old-fashioned sort of Mangwato—clad in the hanging leather skirt, the heavy bead and metal anklets, and hartebeest-skin cloak. She is old, so old that her face is nothing but a mass of wrinkles. "Dumela! Khama" (Greeting! Khama) she says, as she passes him. " Eh-heh-ra [1] dumela " (Thanks!

---

[1] It is a difficult matter to translate this expression. " Eh-heh " means with the Bechuana very much what "Aye" or "Yes" means

greeting) replies Khama, with a kindly smile. It is the same with the little brown smiling piccaninnies as they pass and salute the great chief.

The history of the Bamangwato has been an interesting one. In the earlier part of the last century the present Bangwaketse, Bakwèna, and Bamangwato tribes were one. Later on in the century the portion now called Bangwaketse seceded; and afterwards the remainder of the tribe broke into two segments, which became known as the Bakwèna and Bamangwato respectively. Still later, during the chieftainship of Matipi, the great-great-grandfather of the present Khama, another portion of the original tribe fell away from the Mangwato, and, settling themselves at Lake Ngami, became known as the Batauana, or "people of the little Lion." Matipi aforesaid had two sons, Tauane (the little Lion), whom he loved, and Khama[1] (another Khama), whom he hated. The sons fell out, and Matipi and Tauane, taking half the tribe, moved to the lake, leaving Khama, the elder son, to rule in Bamangwato proper. But presently Tauane in his turn broke with his father and drove him forth. Matipi betook himself to the once despised Khama, and, being repulsed by him, slew himself in despair, somewhere in the Bamangwato Hills. Quite a touching piece of historical romance this!

In the first quarter of the present century there reigned a chief named Khari (grandfather of the present Khama), who seems by all accounts to have

with us. "Ra" is a sort of affectionate diminutive signifying little father. "Eh-heh-ra," freely translated, answers very much to our affirmative, with a dash of thanks thrown in.

[1] Khama is a well-known Bechuana name signifying Hartebeest, one of the fleetest of all the large antelopes.

been greatly loved and revered by the Bamangwato. Khari, however, was slain in battle, and the tribe fell upon evil days. Khari left two sons, Sekhome and Macheng. Sekhome was captured as a boy by Sebituane, the Makololo chief, as he passed through towards the Zambesi; and was kept some time in exile in the Lake and Chobe River country. At length, being suffered to return, he set to work to reorganise the broken tribe, a task in which he seems to have fairly succeeded. Meanwhile, the boy brother, Macheng, finding himself in a position of danger and difficulty, fled away and took refuge with Sechele, chief of the Bakwèna.

From this time—probably about 1840 till 1870—succeeded a period of incessant intrigue between the brothers, Sechele always acting as king-maker, and, curiously enough, affording comfort and aid to the deposed king between times. For a long while —until after Gordon Cumming's last visit, 1848— Sekhome ruled; then Macheng had an inning; then Sekhome wriggled back to power, to be again deposed. Petty skirmishes and a constant state of unrest characterised this long period.

Meanwhile the young Khama—son of Sekhome —although his life was often threatened and even attempted by his unnatural father and uncle, played a wise part and remained in the background. In 1870, however, during the lifetime of Sekhome and Macheng, he was chosen chief for a short period, only to retire, in consequence of incessant intrigues, to the Botletli River country two years later. In 1875 Khama was again called by the unanimous voice of the tribe to the head of affairs, since which time the Bamangwato have enjoyed perfect internal peace, and have progressed materially and morally in an astonishing degree. Khama himself has not always had a thornless pillow during his long and memorable reign. His late uncle, Macheng, his brother, Khamane, and other relatives, have plotted against his power. Khamane, who lives at the present time under Boer protection on Transvaal soil, not far from Pallah Camp on the Limpopo, still makes what mischief he can. Khama, who hates shedding blood, has a successful method of dealing with traitors and disturbers. Instead of putting them to death, as in the old days, he fines them of their cattle, puts them across his border, and resolutely declines to allow them to enter his country again. Cases of murder are, however, punished by the death penalty. And, in the rare instances of insurrection and civil war, very short and summary measures are taken. Selika, a chief sitting under Khama on his eastern border, beneath the furthest range of the Chapong mountains, repeatedly and with insults defied his over-lord. There was a short battle, Selika and his recalcitrant tribe were exterminated or driven from the locality, and the bones of the offenders lie to this day, speaking monuments of Khama's righteous wrath and power.

Roughly speaking Khama's country, which is an enormous one, extends from the junction of the Notwani and Limpopo rivers in the south to the Zambesi in the north, and includes the great Victoria Falls. His eastern border is formed by the Matabele country, while the Limpopo girds him in on his south-east flank, and separates him from the Transvaal Republic. Between the Shashi and Macloutsi rivers there is a patch of debatable country, separating the Bamangwato and Matabele, the title to which lies in abeyance. Why the title to this debatable land—which has been referred to in Blue Books for years past—has not been settled by agreement between the British authorities, Khama, and Lobengula, it is difficult to say. Probably the Colonial Office has had the fear of Matabele troubles before its ken, in case of the award going against Lobengula. And so the matter drifts on from year to year. The south and south-west portion of Khama's country runs far into the Kalahari close to the tropic of Capricorn, and includes the shallow temporary waters known as Andersson Vlei, and Makapolo Vlei. Thence the line of western boundary runs northward, cutting the Botletli River nearly in twain at the Letter Boom (letter tree) near Sebituane's Drift, which, by the way, on nearly all modern maps is wrongly marked as upon the Okavango instead of the Botletli River. North of the Botletli Khama's western boundary seems to run with the Tamalakan and Mababē rivers; thence, going due north, it ends at a point on the Chobe River not very far west of its junction with the Zambesi.

Much of this great domain is undoubtedly at the present day—whatever it may be in the future—sheer desert, rendered almost useless by scarcity of water. Along the spreading flats of the Botletli River there is of course much rich alluvial land, upon which fine crops are raised, while there is good grazing, and cattle-posts are fairly numerous.

Here, too, tobacco has long been grown by the river tribes for the purposes of snuff-making. And over much of the whole country—even at places in the desert, where waterpits will allow of it—cattle-posts are to be found. Along the Zambesi also there are rich lands, which some day, when the fever is conquered, will yield great results. Cotton, tobacco, grapes, and other fruit might be raised freely in many places. But unquestionably the best and richest portion of Khama's land lies in the south-east corner, in the neighbourhood of Palachwe and Shoshong, and along the northern banks of the Limpopo. Here are splendid grazing districts and broad corn lands, and water is upon the whole plenti-ful. Over much of Bamangwato large areas of timber, giraffe acacia, mopani, and upon the rivers, great forest trees, such as the motjeerie and others, are to be found. Khama has done much to extend the area of cultivation, and his tribe now raises sufficient Kaffir corn and mealies to be able to sell largely, as in 1890, to strangers.

In the future, it cannot be doubted that in addition to the natural occupations of the Bamangwato—cattle raising, corn growing, transport riding, kaross making, and the export of skins—fruit growing, the production of tobacco, cotton, indigo (which already grows wild throughout Bechuanaland), coffee, sugar, and other crops will add largely to the wealth of the state. As a cattle country Bamangwato, in common with the other parts of Bechuanaland, cannot be surpassed. Some mineral wealth will, too, undoubtedly be found in the little-explored hills of the country. In and about the Chapong range for generations there has flourished an ancient aborig-inal tribe known as the Bachapong, who were expert workers in iron, and sold axes, knives, and assegais to surrounding and even far distant tribes. A few years since Khama granted certain concessions (now held by the Bechuanaland Exploration Company) to exploit minerals in his country. I believe that valuable gold reefs, continuations to the westward of the well-known Tati fields, have been already discovered ; and it seems more than probable that paying minerals will be found in the broken, rocky country near the Zambesi.

When the railway is continued from Vryburg and Mafeking—as undoubtedly it is to be—the country will become better known and explored, trade will be greatly augmented, and distant tribes, which now have little intercourse with the white man, will be supplied, and valuable sources of wealth will be opened up even among the teeming population north of the Zambesi.

There is still much game left in the western and northern portions of Khama's country, and it is to the chief's credit that he has set limits upon the wanton destruction which for fifty years has been going forward. Boer hunters are not permitted ; even Englishmen, visiting the veldt, have to obtain permission ; and the hunting parties of the tribe, which annually go forth to collect skins, are regulated by the chief himself. Of late years, owing to fear of Matabele disturbance, the tribal hunting expeditions to the Botletli, Mababē, and Chobe districts have been few, and the game has consequently increased. Elephants have almost vanished, and the rhinoceros has gone, or all but gone, even in Khama's vast hunting veldt ; but all the other game is there— lions, leopards, giraffes, hippopotami, Burchell zebra, ostrich, eland, roan and sable antelope, koodoo, wildebeest, lechwē, waterbuck, and almost all the rest of the great South African antelope tribe are to be found.

The Bamangwato are great hunters, and many of them fine shots. It is the ambition of all to possess a gun, and Khama is well pleased, having in view his dangerous proximity to the Matabele, that this should be the case.

I have no doubt that Khama could muster in time of war without difficulty from 8000 to 10,000 fighting men, mostly armed with guns. Of these, probably some 2000 to 3000 would be found to be good shots armed with Martini, Snider, or Westley Richards rifles (mostly Martinis); the rest would be indifferently provided with muzzle-loading smooth-bores carrying spherical bullets, Enfields, old Tower muskets, and suchlike weapons. It is to be remembered, however, that poorly armed as are the bulk of these men, they can, even with their old muskets, manage to knock over a buck now and again, and are therefore as shots not wholly despicable. But it is also to be borne in mind that the Bamangwato are by far the bravest, most united, and most intelligent of the Bechuanas; that they have successfully repelled the Matabele in pitched battles; and that they are led by perhaps the most heroic and high-minded chief South Africa has ever seen.

Among his forces Khama can reckon some 400 mounted men, all good rough-riders and accustomed to the chase of big game. These hunters would give a very good account of themselves if required. It is a misfortune that horse-sickness is very severe in Bamangwato, and that each season a great drain upon horseflesh has to be made good.

A good deal of drilling was going on while we were at Palachwe. There are regular native regiments who are accustomed to exercise together.

Since the advent of the Border Police the bugle has become an institution, and the familiar calls were to be heard at morning and night. The little brown piccannins were delighted with these martial sounds, and might be heard at all hours of the day imitating very successfully, with their tiny fists to their mouths, the shrill and inspiring notes of the various bugle calls.

In 1885, when Sir Charles Warren drove out the filibusters and settled Bechuanaland, he travelled to Khama's country, and was cordially received by the chief, who expressed himself ready in every possible way to welcome and assist British interests throughout the country. In the same year a Protectorate was declared as far north as parallel 22 of south latitude, a halting measure, which included only the half of Khama's country, and to a native chief must have seemed an incomprehensible piece of statesmanship.

Khama's letter written to the authorities at this time is clear, generous, and well reasoned ; I have thought it well to reproduce a portion of it :—

"I Khama, Chief of the Bamangwato, with my younger brothers and heads of my town, express my gratitude at the coming of the messengers of the Queen of England, and for the announcement to me of the Protectorate which has been established by the desire of the Queen, and which has come to help the law of the Bamangwato also. I give thanks for the words of the Queen which I have heard, and I accept of (receive) the friendship and protection of the Government of England within the Bamangwato country. Further, I give to the Queen to make laws and to change them in the country of the Bamangwato, with reference to both black and white. Nevertheless I am not baffled in the government of my own town, or in deciding cases among my own people according to custom; but again I do not refuse help in these offices. Although this is so, I have to say that there are certain laws of my country which the Queen of England finds in operation, and which are advantageous to my people, and I wish that these laws should be established and not taken away by the Government of England. I refer to our law concerning intoxicating drinks, that they should not enter the country of the Bamangwato, whether among black people or white people. I refer further to our law, which declares that the lands of the Bamangwato are not saleable. I say this law also is good; let it be upheld and continue to be law among black people and white people."

Khama then proceeds to point out his boundaries, and referring to the absurd Protectorate line, cutting in half his country, he says :—

"The word which I hear speaks about 22° as shown in maps ought to be taken away. I do not express thanks for it. It speaks of nothing which has existence. Boundary line there is none at 22°. It is to cut my country into two. But I say, is not this a word spoken before my boundaries were known? On account of matters of this description, and to make known to the Queen the largeness of the country which is under her protection, I put in a map in which it is tried to show with correctness the boundaries of the Bamangwato. My people enjoy three things in our country; they enjoy their cultivated lands, and their cattle stations, and their hunting grounds. We have lived through these three things. Certainly the game will come to an end in the future, but at present it is in my country, and while it is still there I hold that it ought to be hunted by my people. I know that the help and protection of the Queen requires money, and I agree that that money should be paid by the country protected. I have thought how this can be done; I mean plans which can be thought out at the beginning so that the Queen's people may all be pleased—the black people and the white people. I propose that a certain country of known dimension should be mine and my people's for our cultivated fields and our cattle stations, as I have shown in the map. Then I say with reference to all the country that remains, I wish that the English people should come and live in it, that they should turn it into their cultivated fields and cattle stations. What I wish to explain is, that my people must not be prevented from hunting in all the country, except where the English shall have come to dwell. My people shall be stopped by cultivated lands and the cattle stations of the English inhabitants of the country. I speak this in effect inviting the English because it is a nation with which we have become acquainted, and with whose ways we have had pleasure. Then I request that the Queen's Government appoint a man to take charge of this matter, and let the protection of this country come from the English who will settle in it. I am of opinion that the country which I give over will exceed in value the cost of the Protectorate among the Bamangwato. But I feel that I am speaking to the gentlemen of the Government of England. Shall I be afraid that they will requite me with witchcraft (deception leading to ruin)? Rather may I not hope that they may see both sides of the question of to-day, that they will regard the protection, and then regard also the country which I now say is theirs? That which I am also willing to contribute is to make due arrangements for the country of the lands and cattle stations of the Bamangwato, whether as to roads, or bridges, or schools, or other suitable objects. And further, I shall be ready along with my people to go out, all of us, to fight for the country alongside the English; to stop those who attack, or to go after them on the spoor of stolen stock. Further, I expect that the English people who come into the country shall protect it and fight for it, having provided themselves with horse and gun for this purpose. Having done this, without doubt, if there came a great difficulty, we would appeal for the help of our Queen in England. The right kind of English settler in the country will be seen by his doings on his place. Some may make themselves out to be settlers for a time only, while they are killing game, after which they would take their departure with what they had collected, having done nothing with their place. Therefore, I propose that it be enacted that the English settler who newly arrives should build his house and cultivate his lands, and show himself to be a true settler and worker, and not a travelling trader. Those who shall be received in the country, to become settlers in it, ought to be approved by the officer of the Queen appointed to this work; and I add, let us work together, let me also approve of those who are received."

It is to be remembered that the ideas and diction

s

are those of Khama, who is very careful that no
letters shall be written in his name except from his
own dictation.

At this time, although Khama thus offered the
British Government a great portion of his country,
the colonial authorities declined the offer, and were
content to let matters rest without seeking to throw
open the country to European settlers. Khama was
undoubtedly disappointed at this decision, the more
so that the formation of the new Protectorate was
manifestly an act of diplomacy at once inchoate and
unsatisfactory. For seven years matters in the Protectorate have drifted—there is no other expression
for it—and now quite recently, Khama is startled
to find an Assistant-Commissioner (Mr. J. S. Moffat)
settled at his town with power to levy taxes, issue
licenses, hold courts, and perform other formal acts
of government. As Khama feels and complains, this
is hardly the right way of doing things. He says,
and very forcibly, " Years ago I offered to the British
Government much of my country ; I offered to throw
it open to the English on certain conditions ; in fact,
I gave them a free hand. I believed in the English
and their justice and good government. They declined my offer, and I heard no more of the matter.
And now without formal conclave and agreement,
when I should have the opportunity of consulting my
headmen, and putting all important matters fairly
before my people, they proceed to place a ruler in
my town, so that I myself, before I can buy a bag of
gunpowder, have to go and obtain a permit. This
is not fair or openhanded ; it puts me in the wrong
with my tribe, who say, ' How then, is Khama no
longer chief in his own country ? ' and I feel deeply

that I am slighted and made small. All my life I
have striven for the English, been the friend of the
English, have even offered to fight for the English,
and I am at last to be treated thus!"

This is what Khama feels and says, and it certainly
appears that he has been hardly used; that he—of all
native South African chiefs!—has been treated with
scant courtesy; and it is scarcely surprising that his
sentiments towards the British Government are not
(and cannot be expected to be) quite what they were.

I do not for one moment suppose that Khama could
even now ever be induced to take a part against the
English or do them an unfriendly act; but I believe
that in future he will not be found so staunch or
so keen an ally as of yore. It is a thousand pities;
it would have been a small, a very small matter to
have so conducted this affair as to have soothed
Khama's susceptibilities, and kept him right with his
people. The relations of a native chief with his
tribesmen are of a peculiarly close and delicate nature,
their interests are so very closely knit, and they
surely ought to have been considered in this case.

It ought not to be forgotten that our position in
South Central Africa is not by any means too strong
or too well assured at present. The Matabele are
still unconquered, and the Protectorate chiefs are
disaffected and unfriendly. Khama's influence and
aid in time of disturbance would be immense; and
it seems unwise to jeopardise them. It is, too, to
be remembered that Khama recently married as his
second wife a sister of Batoen,[1] chief of the Bangwaketse, and that he and his tribe are nearly akin
to the Bangwaketse and Bakwèna, their nearest

[1] Khama has since lost this second wife.

neighbours, and live on terms of peace and friendliness
with them. Khama's influence in this quarter alone
is worth paying a good deal for.

It is sincerely to be hoped that, before it be too
late, this matter may be adjusted, that Khama's
wounded feelings may be soothed, himself set right
in the eyes of his tribe, and the strong and enduring
friendship of this great and influential chieftain thus
retained to us.

CHAPTER XII.

ACROSS THE KALAHARI DESERT TO THE BOTLETLI RIVER, NGAMILAND

Troubles of equipment—Photograph Khama—Our outfit—Servants—"Piccanin"—My waggon home—Its comforts and appurtenances—A dry trek—Bird shooting—Beautiful country—Koodoo—Mackay ill—He leaves us—Moqui River—A break-down—Double-banded sandgrouse —Reach Mesa—Zambesi wayfarers—Hartebeests—A Bushman's oracle —Sandgrouse at Maqua Pool—Masarwa Bushmen—Mode of life— Rollers and butterflies—First giraffe—T'lala Mabeli—Kalahari hardships—Routes through the Thirstland—T'Klakane Pits—Ride for the Lake River—Great saltpans—Mirage—Reach the Botletli—Its sights and scenes.

IT is no light matter to equip and start upon a shooting and exploring expedition into the wilderness, and it was not till June 19, after lingering for the best part of a week at Palachwe, that we were ready to trek.

In waggon-travel there are so many things to be done at the last moment—servants to be collected ; corn procured for the horses ; oxen, slaughter-goats, and sheep got together, and such like. The Pioneer Column for Mashonaland had just preceded us, creating a dearth quite unexampled in these regions, and we had the greatest difficulty to obtain sufficient Kaffir corn and mealies to feed our nags to the Lake River. Khama, as usual, came to the rescue, and exerted himself in every possible way to assist us, helping us in innumerable ways. Every morning early his pleasant kindly face appeared at our camp,

and the last thing in the evening he usually rode
up to see how matters were progressing. The chief
took the greatest interest in our expedition, sending
us to his best hunting veldt, which, owing to the
fear óf Matabele troubles, had been little disturbed
by his people for two years. Mr. Hepburn, the
resident missionary, Mr. T. Fry, Mr. Gifford, and
Mr. C. Clark, also rendered us much assistance.
Before leaving, we photographed Khama, as well- as
several places of interest about his town. The chief
is a bad sitter, and has a habit (as may be seen by
his pícture) of casting down his eyes just at the
critical moment.

Our outfit consisted of two waggons, drawn
respectively by eighteen and sixteen oxen, nine
hunting-ponies, including one knowing old veteran
belonging to Khama, used by our principal hunter,
two pointers, a greyhound and some useful waggon-
dogs, and a couple of goats and a sheep to be used
for slaughter purposes till the game was reached.
Of these last, the sheep refused to trek, and, being
carried on Dove's waggon, broke its leg the first
night and had to be forthwith devoured. Thanks
to the supply of game, one of the goats was never
eaten, and found his way back with us to Khama's,
trekking merrily with the waggons, and often amusing us with his absurd ways and antics.

For servants we had two of Khama's best hunters
—David, a Batlaping, and Patshalaan, a Bamangwato
—who also acted as drivers, two leaders, two horse-
boys, a cook and hunter named Joseph, who spoke
English, Dutch, and Sechuana, and acted as interpreter, and a small fat Makalaka named Meti. This
last, a boy of ten or eleven, interviewed Mackay and

insisted upon accompanying us, and, having obtained
Khama's consent, we took him. "Piccanin," as he
was always called, acted as cook's help and bottle-
washer, and being a ready, active little chap, became
a most popular member of the trek. It was Piccanin's black, good-humoured face that appeared to
us at dawn, as he drew aside the canvas "foreclap"
of the waggon and handed us our early morning
coffee, and it was Piccanin who always picked out
a hot ember from the fire for our pipe-lights, and
performed innumerable acts of service for us.

In a subsequent chapter—"Waggon life and camp
requisites"—I have dealt pretty fully with the
matter of stores and provisions; so that a fair idea
of what is required on an expedition of this kind
may be formed by intending travellers.

It was not till we had been on the road for a day
or two that we had shaken down and got things
ship-shape in the waggons. Let me picture the
interior of these desert-ships. At the bottom are
disposed all the heavy goods—cases of ammunition,
tinned vegetables, fruits, jams, baking-powder, and
other necessary stores, as well as trading articles
for barter, bags of meal, corn, coffee, sugar, &c. As
these things disappear their places are taken by
hides, horns, heads, and other trophies of the chase.
Above these stores is slung the kartel, a wooden
framework laced crosswise with strips of hide so as
to form a most comfortable bed. A mattress or
blankets placed on the kartel and another blanket
and sheepskin kaross as coverlet, provide one with
as roomy and comfortable a bed as the traveller can
desire. Round the sides of the waggon interior are
nailed ample canvas-pockets, which contain field-

glasses, pipes, tobacco, cigarettes, knives, sewing materials, matches, curios, books, candles, and innumerable other odds and ends. Above the kartel is suspended from the waggon-roof a lantern, so that, if so minded, one may read in bed at night, when the waggons are outspanned. At one side rest in their skin or canvas cases, on carefully padded hooks, a rifle and shot-gun ; on the other side are other rifles, fastened to the framework of the waggon tilt by riems of hide. The skin gun-covers made by the natives are the best for waggon use. They are dust-proof, the gun slips easily in and out, and their wear is everlasting. The Bechuanas usually make these cases of leopard, lion, or otter skin ; a lion-skin cover, one of which I possess, is considered *the* thing. Cartridge-belts, a long stalking-glass, and other adjuncts hang here and there. Dove occupied the smaller half-tent waggon ; Mackay and I had two kartels fixed in the big hunting-waggon ; but as Mac had, most unfortunately, to leave us a few days later on account of illness, I had any quantity of room and could dispose of my camera-case, portmanteau, and books close to my head. Beyond, on the other kartel, are saddlery, cartridges and other personal effects, rolls of tobacco for the men ; and, later on, heads and horns of game, bird-skins, and other specimens reposed there. Comfortably ensconced thus in a good roomy waggon, one cannot wish to be better housed, and with the foreclap (or curtain) fastened down on cold nights, or raised in warm weather, one is perfectly independent of the elements. A silk or woollen nightcap is a useful accessory, and renders one still further oblivious of draughts. Under the waggon, in a kind of hanging box, are our small Boer waggon-chairs, a tiny folding-table, pots, pans, and other cooking implements. In boxes at the side near the buck-rail are plates, knives, forks, and so on. Along one of the buck-rails was lashed our small tent, which, however, we never once required to use.

There is a wonderful charm about waggon-life far away on the veldt, and at early morn as you wake and hear the horses (always fastened to the wheels at night) contentedly crunching their mealies, and look out upon the dawn just paling the eastern sky, and hear the soft whistle of the pelicans and the *honk* of wild geese from the river, or the sharp call of the African partridge from the veldt ; or doze off at night with the loom of the dark blue, starry sky filling up the open front of the waggon—you realise that such a home has its pleasures, and very deep ones too.

We had expected to find the remains of waterpools in the bed of the Lotsani River, but were disappointed, and after the first outspan, where we filled the barrels from some very indifferent mud and water, we met with no water for two days—a long dry trek for the oxen and horses. On the 21st we passed the Manatookoo range, and the Chapong Hills above Khama's Town began to fade behind us. On the 22nd we reached water and a cattle-post, and here discovered, for the first time, that we were now beyond the region of money and of clothes, the Bamangwato hereabouts being innocent of the use of either. From this point milk, corn, and other articles had to be bartered for in kind— percussion-caps, powder, knives, and gaudy handkerchiefs always serving as current coin. This morning

early we passed through some picturesque grassy
kopjes (small hills), where pheasants abounded in great
plenty. We had some very pretty shooting before
breakfast, and got several brace of these and a small
partridge. Except near the Lake river and Crocodile
I never saw francolins more numerous. The pheasants
shot on this occasion, and, indeed, commonly found
near water throughout North Bechuanaland and the
Lake Ngami country, are of a mottled, dark brownish
drab colour, having red legs and bills. They are
identical with the *Francolinus adspersus* of Water-
house, first discovered in Sir James Alexander's
Expedition to Great Namaqualand in 1836. They
lie extremely close, and are hard even to kick up,
and, when flushed, will usually shelter in dense bush
or fly into trees. The "partridge" shot this day,
Francolinus subtorquatus, or Coqui francolin, is, in
my judgment, one of the most elegant little game
birds in the world. The brilliant golden tan of its
head and neck, the curious hawk-like markings of its
creamy breast, the black gorget upon the hen-bird's
throat, and its diminutive size, serve to distinguish
it readily from all other South African francolins.
This bird we first found in the northern part of British
Bechuanaland, and its range extends certainly as far
as Lake Ngami, probably much beyond. A pretty
little slender-legged courser (*Cursorius Burchellii*)
was also shot during the day. Passing the rough and
very precipitous bed of a dry, stony watercourse in
the evening, we entered a beautiful park-like stretch
of most game-like country towards sunset—a broad,
open valley, well clothed with timber, and long,
yellow grass reaching up to one's shoulders, the
whole enclosed in a setting of picturesque mountains.

At night we outspanned under a big, flat-topped, rocky hill, near which was a small pool of water, the place being known as Seleba Samoutchana.

Here Mackay, who had been suffering from fever, seemed much worse, and we decided to rest a day or so to give him a chance of recovery, as he seemed too ill to proceed. Next morning, Dove and I rode out with Patshalaan to look for koodoo, word having come that these fine antelopes were to be found in the neighbourhood. Dove got away from us, and, shortly after, my hunter having hit upon the spoor, a grand bull, carrying his fine spiral horns with majestic grace, and three cows, cantered across a glade to our right. We were quickly after them. The bull was too smart for us, however, and the bush too thick, and I only had a shot at the cows, one of which I hit hard, but rather too far back from the shoulder. We followed her blood-spoor all the afternoon into and through dense mopani forest, and then reluctantly had to give her up. Patshalaan's spooring in the forest was a treat to watch ; no European and few natives could have followed the intricacies and windings of the track, in difficult country, in so steady and persistent a manner. Some natives at a kraal near were told of the wounded koodoo, and I have no doubt afterwards secured her. Dove, whom I found at the waggons, had had no luck, although he had seen on a far-off kopje two or three of those graceful little mountain-antelopes, the klipspringer, the chamois of South Africa.

Next morning Mackay, to our great dismay, was worse, and had made up his mind to turn back for Palachwe. This was a most unfortunate break in our expedition, and was keenly felt by all of us. However, there was no help for it; we were going into a country where the chances of a successful cure diminished daily; and so, taking with him two horses, and a boy to assist him, he bid a sorrowful farewell and left us. We took photographs of the camp and of our parting with Mackay, which resulted afterwards pretty successfully. It was a severe wrench parting thus with an old and tried comrade. We had now been together uninterruptedly since the 3rd January. Many a good day had we enjoyed together, many a mellow evening outside our huts, many a yarn and song by the camp fire's cheery blaze. " *Comes jucundus in via pro vehiculo est* " [1] we might well say of our departing friend. Mackay subsequently got well at Khama's, and afterwards joined the Pioneers in their eventful march to Mashonaland.

Trekking on, we came towards evening to a most beautiful stream of clear water—the Moqui River—running over a clean, rocky bed, a most unusual thing in this part of South Africa. Here we had our last bathe for some time to come, and in the morning obtained some capital shooting among the Coqui francolins. Among the thorn trees at this place, and, indeed, in most parts of North Bechuanaland where water is to be found, numbers of Rüppell's parrots (*Psittacus Rüppellii*), pretty little fellows clad in brilliant plumage of blue, green, and yellow, were to be seen, their shrill, squeaking cry and rapid flight instantly marking them out. These parrots are easily tamed and make gentle and affectionate pets.

[1] Freely translated—" A merry comrade upon the road is as good as a waggon."

GOOD-BYE TO MACKAY

(From Photo. by W. Dove)

Moving on through a fine, grassy, well-wooded country, among picturesque, broken, flat-topped hills, we came upon our second trouble on the 25th, when the after-axle of the light waggon broke down. This necessitated a day's delay, during which David, our head-driver—the best native workman I ever saw, and a wonderful man with the adze—fashioned and fitted a false axle out of the hard wood of the camel-thorn tree. This operation had to be repeated several times during the expedition, and our false axle was a constant fear and anxiety to us, especially in crossing the thirstland. After a frightfully rough trek over stony declivities, we came at sundown of the 26th to a small stream, where we had some very pretty flight-shooting at double-banded sandgrouse (*Pterocles Bicinctus*) as they came down to water. The flight of these beautiful birds is extremely swift, and after a few shots they become exceedingly dodgy, unless in large numbers. Even Dove, who is an exceptionally fine shot, found himself firing behind his bird every now and again. Unless one could get them against the light of the fading sunset, it was a case of hearing their curious whistle and then snapping at a dark form as it flashed by.

On the evening of the 27th June we reached Mesa, the last of Khama's cattle-posts on this side of the thirstland lying between here and the Botletli. At Mesa there is a sharp descent, and thereafter, right away to Lake Ngami and beyond, the country is perfectly flat. After some weeks of travel through this everlasting plain, our delight, on returning, at seeing the blue hills of Khama's more immediate country may be well imagined. For the first time since leaving Ramathlabama, fifteen miles north of Mafeking, we heard to-day the well-remembered harsh, grating call of the black-and-white bustard (*Eupodotis afroides*). After so long a silence, it was quite refreshing to hear the "craak-craak" of this old friend. At Mesa we met, as we often did till we quitted the Zambesi road, a band of natives from beyond the Zambesi, on their way down country to seek work at Kimberley or Johannesburg. These poor people make the long and fatiguing journey on foot, with but scanty preparation. They carry, as a rule, a calabash or two of water, a piece or two of rough salt, a few handfuls of grain, their assegais and short skin-cloaks, and trust to luck and pluck to pull them through. It argues well indeed for their faith in the British paymaster, distant so many a weary hundred leagues from their homes, that they will thus tempt fortune. As a rule they carried with them beautiful samples of native ironwork, in the shape of battle-axes and assegais, the latter very curiously barbed; and, by giving them meat and meal in exchange, we purchased some very good specimens in this way. Strange, wild-looking fellows they are mostly, with skins of an intense black, and long-woolled hair, often fantastically decorated with feathers, heads of birds, and other strange fancies. These people differ greatly from the races south of the Zambesi. I noticed one boy among the pilgrims at Mesa with beautiful, almond-shaped eyes and even eyebrows—quite Egyptian in his type. His long, straight hair, each kink of wool twisted, oiled, and pulled down, added greatly to the resemblance. While outspanned this afternoon we shot, in some thick trees and shrubbery near the water, one of the curious lemur-like animals known to naturalists as the galago. This particular species (*Galago Maholi*), which belongs to the order *Lemures*, is well known to the Transvaal Boers, by whom it is called the night-ape. They are occasionally captured, and their soft furry skins and large brilliant eyes make them rather pleasing pets. They are, however, delicate and difficult to rear.

At Mesa, Khama's hills end, and the true water-less Kalahari country stretches away westward to the Botletli River. This evening, after some more flight-shooting, we met with four Masarwa Bushmen, who informed us that a day or two further on we should find giraffe. We arranged for three of these men to spoor for us on the following day, and, having trekked beyond Mesa during the night, we rode on with Joseph, leaving the waggons to follow us to Maqua (or Makwe), a pool in the desert a little to the left hand of the Zambesi road. Our Masarwa friends took us left-handed until, after an hour through thin bush, we emerged upon a huge open plain, yellow with long winter grass. We had been following the spoor of hartebeests for some time, and surely enough, some way out on the flat, we could discern a good troop; and, further on, yet another. We now spread out in line and walked quietly towards the nearest, which presently began to be disturbed, and, an old bull sentinel having given the alarm, the game moved slowly off. I succeeded eventually, by riding hard on the extreme right, in driving the troop left-handed. Dove's horse, however, put his foot in a hole while galloping hard, and, throwing his rider heavily, bolted; while the after-rider, who had a good chance at some of the buck as they passed him, missed clean and let them go unscathed. The rest of the far-distant hartebeests at the sound of firing took to their heels, and, lopping away with that wonderful untiring pace of theirs, soon left the plain tenantless. The Bushmen presently came up, and, I having caught Dove's horse, we off-saddled for a few minutes.

While we sat down, one of the Masarwas took from his neck four curious-looking pieces of ivory, three triangular in shape, the fourth longer and rather pointed at either end. All four pieces were flat and had a sort of pattern rudely worked upon them. Shaking the ivory pieces in the hollow of his hands, the Masarwa cast them on the ground, and, after gazing intently for a moment, all three burst into a torrent of their extraordinary clicking language, pointing at the same time earnestly at the dice, for such I may call them.

Our after-rider, who partly understood the Bushmen, now explained to us that they were throwing their dice to ascertain what sport was in store for us. As the pieces of ivory fell, so should fortune favour one or other of us. After several castings, much gesticulation, and a perfect ocean of their singular speech, we were informed that Dove was shortly to kill two giraffe and I one. This prophecy was partially fulfilled within two days. The whole of the performance was conducted with the most perfect seriousness and intent, and the manifest scepticism of Dove and myself had no effect upon our prophets, although in their good-humoured way they laughed with us.

Proceeding across another typical South African plain, and through fine open camel-thorn forests, we saw little or no game during the rest of that day, although we came across spoor of blue wildebeest. We met a miserable-looking Bushman during the afternoon collecting a meal of ground-nuts or small bulbs in a tortoise-shell. We tasted these bulbs; they were sweet and nutty, but not much of a stand-by for a hungry man. In the evening, the waggons having come on, we outspanned at Maqua Pool, a miserable water of most foul smell and consistency, now rapidly disappearing under a too ardent sun. Here enormous flights of doves (*Turtur Senega-lensis*) came down at sunset, and one of our boys, taking a shot-gun, secured sixteen in two shots, thus providing a good banquet for his fellows and the Bushmen. Curiously enough, no sand-grouse came to this pool at evening, although we had seen them at other waters at about sundown; but on the two following mornings, while we lay there, many hundreds came down.

The lame waggon had again broken down this afternoon, and, the next day being Sunday, we arranged to stand at this water until repairs were completed. We were awake next morning early, and after coffee, as I was writing up my diary on the kartel, Dove called out from his waggon that the sand-grouse were coming to water. During the next two hours, that is, from 8 to 10 A.M., enormous numbers of two species — the common Namaqua sand-grouse (*Pterocles Namaqua*), always called in South Africa the Namaqua partridge, and the largest and rarest of this family, the yellow-throated sand-grouse (*Pterocles gutturalis*), came sweeping and whirling round the pool, every now and again settling down in a pack with a swift rush to drink

T

at the water's edge. It was the prettiest sight in the world. Our numbers had been recruited by the wives and children of our Masarwa hunters, who had arrived over-night. These poor people, who had been living on nothing but bulbs and ground-nuts for some time, were in the most miserable condition, and Dove and I felt, therefore, small compunction in shooting them a number of sand-grouse, as they came whirring, with shrill whistle, over our waggons. During the two hours of flight we shot eighteen brace —often getting two at a shot—and could have killed with ease twice that number, and our Bushman friends were soon at work enjoying a solid breakfast. The yellow-throated sand-grouse, although not more beautiful than the exquisite double-banded variety, is in some ways more remarkable. We found it and the variegated sand-grouse rarer and more local, and it is considerably the largest of the four species in South Africa. It is, too, by far the most grouse-like of its genus, and approaches more nearly, in the deep chocolate-red colouring of the under part of the body, and in its cry, to the red grouse of Scotland. Dove, who is a Lowland Scot, compared its cry to that of the grouse as they fly among the corn-stooks in autumn, and his simile is apt enough. In the male bird the colouring of the breast and upper part of the body is in life of a peculiar sulphur-green, the back and tail are greyish buff, the sides of the head and chin pale yellow, while a dark brown, crescent-like band crosses the breast. The hen is less remarkable, her upper colouring being buff-yellow thickly sprinkled with brown and black, while the under part is of a rich chestnut and black. We had our guns beside us as we sat at breakfast, every now and then jumping up at a tempting shot.

I took some interesting photographs of the Masarwas at this place, and of their wives as they filled their ostrich eggs, calabashes, and miserable clay vessels at the water. These people are pure and simple aboriginal hunters ; they build no houses, a mere screen of bushes serving them for shelter, and wear but the scantiest suspicion of clothing, and apparently nothing will tempt them to give up their wild roving life and take to the more civilised habits of the Bechuanas. These latter call them dogs, and treat them very much as slaves.

Their skin-cloaks are small and barely reach to their middles, and from lying close to the fire at night they burn their legs in a dreadful manner. I have seen a great many Masarwas, but I never yet saw one who had not his or her legs either scarred with sores or burnt perfectly raw from this cause. The old men and women are even more dreadful objects, their chests and stomachs being usually shockingly burnt.

As a rule we found these people thin and poorly nourished, and their legs and arms were often mere sticks, and yet they will keep in front of a horse, walking fast or trotting all day under a hot sun. The three men who first showed us giraffe, and whose photographs may be seen in the illustration, were, however, very well-nourished examples of their race. They had recently been feeding on flesh, and were in excellent condition. I took down their names, which were, Sinikwe, Ganakhow, and Siklish —phonetically rendered. It is one of the strictest axioms of South African hunting etiquette that, although you are mounted, your Bushman shall carry your rifle ; and thus encumbered with rifles, their rude choppers, assegais, skin-cloaks, and often a calabash of water, all day—day after day—they will toil manfully in front of you in the hope of finding and seeing game killed. True sportsmen are they, indeed, and the most wonderful trackers, perhaps, in the world. It is a fact that a Masarwa can, from the appearance of the spoor, tell you to within a few minutes how long it is since game has passed. Their instinct in this respect, and the faculty of finding their way in the wildest veldt, is quite unerring.

These Bushmen bear no sort of resemblance to the small Chinese-like Hottentot Bushmen of the old Cape Colony. As a rule they stand from 5 feet 4 inches to 5 feet 6 inches in height, and their skins are of a deep red-brown. Their language is an extraordinary succession of clicks, often sounding like a high, querulous grumble, and is apparently of a very primitive order. Their weapons are assegais, and small bows shooting tiny poisoned arrows. With these light reed arrows, tipped with bone and smeared with the poison of the Ngwa caterpillar, or of snakes and euphorbia, they will bring down even the tall giraffe. To do this, however, they have to steal up and pierce this animal beneath the legs in the thinnest part of its tough hide, and even then they often have to follow their quarry four or five days before the poison completes its work upon so huge a frame. Other animals die more speedily. These wild hunters are in no way akin to the Bechuanas, or apparently any other tribe of Central South Africa. Of their own origin they are

MASARWA BUSHMEN—MAQUA POOL, NORTH KALAHARI

perfectly ignorant. Probably the truth is they are aboriginal hunters settled in these regions during untold centuries. Unlike the fierce Bushmen of the Cape Colony, they are peaceable and harmless, and almost invariably friendly to the white man.

The rest of the day was spent quietly cleaning guns and rifles, skinning birds, and helping to fit a new axle to the crippled waggon. News came in during the evening that nine giraffe had been seen not far away.

The next morning at grey dawn we were up, and had breakfasted and saddled up by sunrise—about 6.15 at this time of year, June. After riding three hours steadily in a north-westerly direction, during which time we only saw small buck and some enormous troops of guinea-fowl—sixty and eighty in a band—we came up to the scherm of a Masarwa living with his wife and child far out in the bush. This man, for a wonder, appeared or pretended to know little about the game we were after ; but his wife, a most voluble lady, volunteered all necessary information, and, with an astounding profusion of clicks, pointed out the direction in which we should find the giraffe. Her husband, before we came up, had been setting fire to the long, over-ripe grass, and the wind shifting suddenly, the flames came our way, and we had to move further into the bush. My companions and I were intensely amused at the woman's desperate anxiety to save her household effects. These consisted literally of half-a-dozen dried guinea-fowls' crops, neatly skewered on a stick, and containing the bulbs or ground-nuts on which guinea-fowls and Masarwas alike feed, the feet of a dead eagle, a calabash or two, and a small and very dirty skin-cloak or kaross. Two stein-bok skins completed the outfit, and yet this lady displayed as much anxiety over the safety of her *lares* and *penates* as would have done any English housewife over the contents of a well-furnished mansion. This particular family were better-looking than the average run of Masarwas, and were all singularly alike.

We noticed a most curious spectacle as the flames sped, with a low crackling roar, through the long dry grass. Numbers of butterflies and insects, driven out by the fire and smoke, were flying aloft, and some scores of brilliant rollers were darting hither and thither, eagerly hawking at them. These rollers, erroneously called blue-jays throughout Bechuana-land, are marvels of an almost impossible colouring. Nature has painted them with a bewildering blending of dark greens, light greens, purples, light and dark blues, purplish-pink, and pale reddish-brown. And yet, as one handles this bird, one cannot quarrel with any part of its wonderful scheme of colour. It is in every respect perfect and beautiful. Naturalists know this particular roller as *Coracias caudata*. Up-country it is familiar as Moselikatse's bird, for the reason that this renowned Matabele chief con-stantly wore the two long tail-feathers in his hair and allowed no one else to do so.

Within another hour from leaving these Masarwas, our hunters had taken us up to a troop of five camelopards, out of which Dove secured the first giraffe scored during our trip. Details of this and other days among these animals will be found in the following chapter. There was great rejoicing at the camp that night, and for the next few days much feasting and a great making of sjamboks out of the thick hide.

From Maqua we trekked for two days across hot, open grassy plains, and through dreary mopani forests, all alike waterless, until, on the evening of July 2, we reached T'lala Mabeli, a small limestone pit, which, however, held but a bucket or two of water. There was nothing for it, therefore, but to outspan and send the oxen on early next morning to Dinokani, another water some miles further. The horses were sent on a little later, and were glad enough, poor brutes, to get a drink after forty-eight hours' thirst.

At this place I lost my pointer Don, who had been run over by the waggon some days before, and had, poor beast, to be finally destroyed. These accidents are a constant source of anxiety to the traveller. Dogs, to escape the heat, will get under the waggon, and are run over, or injured, usually just as the waggon starts. I missed Don one morning, rode back three miles, and found him lying helpless by the road. I then put him in front of my saddle, and carried him to the waggon—no slight undertaking with a big pointer. We did all we could for him, but he was injured internally, and daily became worse. I was sorry to lose the poor old dog, although he was by no means perfect. But he had a good nose, and up-country in South Africa a pointer, however indifferent, is priceless. Without one, bird-shooting is impossible. We had now only Dove's pointer, "Scotty" (who, poor old lady, was still half-lame from a crushed foot), to work for us when after game birds.

At T'lala Mabeli we quitted the Zambesi road and struck in a south-westerly direction for T'Klakane, a

water on the old trek-Boer route to Lake Ngami.
We had hoped to find a little water for the oxen at
the limestone pits of Maruti, Tauane, or Soronyan
between these points, but were disappointed. It was
now getting well on into the season of drought, and
the scant waters were drying up everywhere in the
desert.   At Maruti there were a few bucketsful of
the vilest and foulest water imaginable, and among
two spans of thirsty oxen a mere drop in the ocean.
Few people, until they have witnessed it, can appreciate the enormous drinking capacity of a thirsty
trek-ox, and even a good-sized pool diminishes very
alarmingly when many oxen are watered there.
Barring, therefore, the few mouthfuls of bad water
our oxen and horses got at Maruti, they had no real
drink from the afternoon of Thursday, July 3, until
about the same hour on Sunday the 6th, practically
three days and nights of thirst.   Mr. John Strombom, the Lake Ngami trader, who followed us later
upon this route with a large expedition, suffered more
severely.   The water at Maqua had given out, and
between Mesa and T'Klakane he lost many oxen from
thirst and exhaustion.

There are two ways of crossing the thirstland
lying between Khama's and the Lake River—one
by the waters of Kannē, Inkouane, and T'Klakane,
along the old road whereon the trek Boers suffered so
frightfully in 1877–78, on their memorable Promised-
land Expedition ; the other and more northerly by
the route we were now taking.   By the old road
the " thirsts " are longer, especially in winter, and the
sand more severe ; yet if your cattle are stout and
in good heart, I think this road, being the shorter,
is the preferable of two evils.

MARUTI PITS, NORTH KALAHARI

We took this route on the way home, and although from the Botletli to T'Klakane we had two days and nights without water, from T'Klakane to Inkouane (the middle of the desert) two days and three nights, and from Inkouane to Kanne three days and four nights without a drop of water for the cattle, we only lost one ox. Our oxen were, however, terribly enfeebled, and looked mere wrecks of their former stout selves, although many of them were notoriously the best cattle in Khama's country. The route we were now travelling is a long roundabout trek, and although, nominally, there are more waters along its course, they are not to be depended upon in the dry season, and are as likely to play you false as not.

Between Maqua and T'Klakane we were too much engaged in pushing on to water, and in husbanding our nags, to look for game ; we occasionally saw small troops of ostriches in the hot distance, and the spoor of blue wildebeest (brindled gnu), but shot nothing larger than sand-grouse and a pheasant or two, until we reached the real hunting veldt at the Lake River. From T'lala Mabeli to T'Klakane we followed an old waggon-spoor of some two years before. How our foreloupers held the spoor through bush and long grass, trekking as we were night and day, was one of those things no Englishman can understand. It is very hard on these boys, leading the lagging oxen through the thirsty sands ; trying work, too, for the drivers, who have to be hard at it with whip and voice, half their time running alongside the span, to keep their teams in motion. At the end of these "thirsts" the drivers are nearly voiceless, and the foreloupers, who guide the leading oxen, worn-out and footsore. A day's rest, however, soon pulls them together again. During these hot, weary days, when the sun seemed to beat down with tenfold intensity, we sometimes moved across mighty open plains which, stretching, apparently illimitable, to the vast horizon, almost persuade one that all the world is flat; sometimes we moved slowly through forests of the pleasant giraffe acacia, amid tall yellow grass and thorny bush; anon through dreary wastes of mopani forest, whose scorched and shrivelled leafage told eloquently enough the tale of the long months of drought of African winter. Yet almost everywhere, even in these wastes, grass is good, and capable of supporting cattle, if only water could be found.

All the game of this region thrive, even to fatness; elands, gemsbok and giraffe, the duyker and the tiny steinbok, all flourish. The giraffe shot near Maqua, in quite waterless country, was fat; and elands shot by us on the return journey in the very heart of the thirstland, between Inkouane and Kannē, were all in magnificent condition, quite equal, indeed, to well-fed cattle, which, in bulk and appearance, they somewhat resemble, true antelopes though they are.

This portion of the Kalahari, known to Boer hunters as the " Doorst Land," is the most unpromising and forbidding of the so-called desert, and here, from the apparent scarcity of water, it may reasonably be doubted whether, even in the distant future, any use can ever be made of it, even as a ranching country. Lower down, however, the Kalahari, as it becomes opened up, is proving itself a really good cattle country. In places where water exists, scattered here and there in many parts of this little-known

land, septs or clans of Bakalahari, or Vaalpense, as
they are colonially called, Bastards and other natives,
make their homes and run large numbers of stock.
Moreover, the Bechuana tribes periodically make
use of much of the Kalahari near their borders as a
grazing ground for their store cattle.

At T'Klakane there are some good pits of water,
but they are carelessly tended, and much fouled by
cattle ; and, as noticed by Livingstone in his journey
of discovery to Lake Ngami in 1849, the water has
a peculiar purging action, especially upon horses.

It should be mentioned that through the thirsts
we carried just sufficient water for ourselves and
servants, in barrels and vatjes, but it had to be
very carefully husbanded, vile stuff though it was,
and washing was quite out of the question. For
three or four days at a time one small beaker of hot
water between us was as much as my companion
and I could spare ourselves for ablutions—a painful
but necessary privation.

We rested at this place for a day and a half before
setting out to accomplish the further three days' and
nights' thirst to the Botletli. Here we first saw
tall Palmyra palm-trees, and the graceful fan-palm,
and here, too, we witnessed immense flights of sand-
grouse. At the waterpits we also secured a few of
our best specimens of butterflies.

The altitude at T'Klakane is 2700 feet; at Chukutsa,
between here and the Botletli, 2600 feet ; and, at
the outspan, where one first strikes the Lake River,
2640 feet. Having tested these altitudes with my
own aneroid, I found them substantially correct.
From T'Klakane, in order to save our horses the
long dragging trek at the pace of the waggons, we

prepared to ride on for the sixty odd miles to the Botletli; and on the afternoon of the 7th, each riding one horse and leading another, on which were strapped a kaross, food, water, kettle, &c., Dove and I set off, accompanied by Joseph, also riding, and leading two horses.

We had ridden, perhaps, ten or fifteen miles, when we could see in the far-away distance dense columns of smoke rising far into the sky. Our boy Joseph, who had been this way several times before, assured us that the smoke rose from the reed-fires, burning on the banks of the Botletli. At this season of the year the natives are busily engaged in burning the dense reed-beds, and the smoke may be seen in this flat country for immense distances. We rode on through most of the night and all next day, occasionally off-saddling to rest the nags, until, after passing the huge saltpans of Chukutsa and Machanning, we reached the Botletli River just at sundown. These saltpans ("karri-karri" of the natives) are a feature of this country; some of them, such as Chukutsa, are of vast extent, and it is weary, suffocating work cantering tired horses across the miles of their heated expanse. During the rains these pans are covered with water, in the dry season with an efflorescence of lime. The mirage to be witnessed on these salt-pans is something wonderful. I have seen good, dishonest, deceptive mirages on the Great Karroo, in Cape Colony, and in many parts of Bechuanaland but these were as nothing to the extraordinary illusions presented at Chukutsa and other pans. The water looked so limpid, the trees so natural, the islands so real, that one might swear there was no deception.

We saw springbok and the spoor of a good deal of game hereabouts, and, late in the afternoon, Dove had a gallop after some blue wildebeest, but to no purpose. As we approached the river, the smoke-clouds grew to gigantic size, and after sunset, as we led our spent horses through the reeds to drink, the frightful roar and crackle of the reeds blazing around us, the heat and the smell of burning, and the vast sheets of flame formed a scene almost appalling, and never likely to be effaced from memory. The reed-beds at this end of the river stretch for miles over a kind of swamp, in which the Botletli loses itself, and as each reed stands some twelve or fifteen feet in height, and is highly inflammable, some idea of the sight of acres upon acres in conflagration may be imagined.

Some Makalakas at a kraal near informed us as we passed that a lion was prowling about, troubling their flocks. We could find no wood that night, and only sufficient dung to make a small fire and cook some coffee. Fastening our horses close to our heads, we covered ourselves in our karosses and slept till dawn, too tired to trouble ourselves about lions or other disturbers. Very early we were awake to hear the mournful whistle of many hundreds of pelicans, which, rising from the reed-beds, were stringing themselves in wavy lines of flight against the red sky. These great birds are a peculiar feature of Botletli scenery, and the recollection of their strange soft whistle, prolonged into five notes, never fails to remind one of dawn and sunset upon this noble river. As we breakfasted, numbers of women, Makalakas, Moteti, and others appeared up the little rise on which we had camped, each one bearing on her head an enormous pumpkin or a basket of mealies or Kaffir corn.   As they arrived they squatted themselves at a little distance, waiting for their lords and masters to open negotiations.   Very little clothing seemed to be in vogue among the men and women here.

The people at the kraal, hearing that our waggons were coming on (a great event in this region) were willing enough to supply us on credit with milk, corn for our horses, and other things.   After breakfast, leaving Joseph to look after the camp and horses, Dove and I strolled down to the river.   At this time of year the Botletli, which rises so mysteriously in the middle of the dry season, was low at this end, and showed but a comparatively small channel of water.   As we trekked with the waggons up the river, however, we found the water rising, and a great stream overflowing its banks, flooding the country round, and forming vast lakes, channels, and lagoons in every direction.

On this morning, though the water was low, we found a superabundance of aquatic life.   Ducks and wigeon of many kinds, great gaudy geese, coots, kingfishers, pelicans, ibises, and fishing-eagles were everywhere to be seen.   The curious Senegal spur-heeled cuckoo, which at first we mistook for a hawk, fluttered heavily from one reed-bed to another, and that rare and beautiful waterfowl, the African jacana, ran with slender elongated feet in troops over the thinnest film of weed covering the water. It was a charmingly characteristic scene, and a welcome introduction after the weary waterless wastes we had recently traversed.   At last, then, the game country was reached, and the dream of many years accomplished.   During the next few weeks we were to enjoy an abundance of sport, as we moved slowly up the river, among giraffe, Burchell's zebra, blue wildebeest, lechwē (a rare local waterbuck), springbok, and other game, in addition to quite a plethora of wild-fowl shooting. But I must fain leave the Botletli and its fauna and avi-fauna to subsequent chapters.

W. MACKAY.

CHAPTER XIII.

GIRAFFE HUNTING

Giraffes and their haunts—Our first troop—Bushman spooring—Sight a
gemsbok—A noble picture—Chase five giraffe—Lose my horse—
Dove shoots a cow—Rifles for giraffe shooting—Notes on the chase
—Marrow bones—Lake River flats—Camp near bush—In the forest—
Dove slays a big bull—Immense measurement—A thorny gallop—
Wild hunting dogs—Kalahari solitudes—Again cross the plains—Nine-
teen giraffe—A wonderful spectacle—A glorious hunt—Four bagged
in fifteen minutes—Taste giraffe milk—Weary ride to camp.

GIRAFFES, which in the old days were to be found
and hunted just across the Orange River, upon its
northern banks, have, decade after decade, been
decimated or driven Zambesi-wards, until at the
present time the hunter must penetrate into the
remote thirstlands of the North Kalahari, or the
most distant portions of Khama's country, before he
may come up with them. And, even in their present
habitats, these animals are so shy and so little
dependent during a great portion of the year upon
water, that their downfall demands from the hunter
and his horse an immense amount of patience and
endurance. Yet, once to set eyes upon these beautiful and extraordinary creatures in their natural
haunts, and to follow them when found in the headlong chase which their speed and staying powers
require, will, in the opinion of all who have hunted
them, repay a hundredfold many a blank day of
toil, many an exhausting ride in the heated and

desolate forests in which they love to seclude themselves. The best giraffe country to be found south
of the Zambesi at the present day is that portion of
the North Kalahari abutting on the Botletli River,
and on the Mababē flats north of that river ; and
to hunt in most of this territory Khama's permission
has to be obtained, for the reason that he reserves
it as the peculiar hunting veldt of himself and his
people.

As I have said, we first heard of giraffes, after
leaving Khama's, in the true Kalahari country between Mesa and the Botletli, most of it sheer, waterless desert. On the 29th June, near Maqua, a desert
pool just west of the Zambesi road, a troop of the
great game we sought was reported to be in the
bush not far away.

We were up at early dawn of next morning,
prepared, with the help of three Masarwa Bushmen
who had come in, to hunt "camel." Dove rode his
white pony called Witbooi, I the bay rejoicing in
the euphonious name of Buggins. Neither of these
horses had ever hunted giraffe before, and their
behaviour on this their *début* was not quite all that
could be desired. David, our head hunter, rode an old
horse well known at Palachwe, and a first-rate hunting
pony. Patrick, as the old "schimmel" (roan) was
called, had, with his rider, been captured by the
Matabele in a raid on Lake Ngami a few years before;
and had afterwards run the gauntlet and escaped,
and, I suppose, knew as much about the hunting
veldt as any nag in South Africa. The Bushmen,
as is their invariable practice, shouldered our rifles,
besides carrying each an assegai and small rude chop-
per, and we started away at a brisk pace. For three

hours we rode at a smart walk, silently following our
spoorers until we came to the Bushman's scherm
I have mentioned, where we off-saddled for a short
time while our guides obtained intelligence of the
giraffe.

Saddling up again, we rode on through thin bush
and forest for another three-quarters of an hour, and
then, taking a sweep towards camp, our Bushmen
suddenly came on the fresh spoor of one giraffe, and
the newly broken leaves of the camel-thorn tree upon
which it had been feeding that morning. Quartering
the ground, and casting about like hounds at a check,
they soon came on more spoor, and, very shortly,
quite fresh indications of the whole troop, and then
trotted forward on the spoor at a brisk pace. We
had been following for about five minutes, when
David, who was on the right, stopped and held up
his hand. Dove and I joined him, and, looking
through the bush, saw in an open glade, about
seventy yards away, a magnificent old bull gemsbok
(*Oryx Capensis*) standing staring at us. He was a
heavy, portly beast of most noble aspect, carrying
long, straight, sharp horns which glinted in the sunlight, and was in wonderful condition. It was a
most tempting sight, but we were close on the heels
of the giraffe, and dared not fire. After staring at us
for nearly half a minute, the old fellow trotted very
quietly away, and was lost to sight. I do not know
that I ever saw a more beautiful picture of animal
life than this unique and singularly marked antelope,
fat as a good ox, standing swishing his long black
tail, and staring coolly at us that hot African morning.

We quickly rejoined the Masarwas, who were now
trotting eagerly upon the spoor of the giraffe, reminding

one still more of hounds running mute on a good scent at home. They ran rather apart, and each man followed the footprints of one or more giraffe, the troop having evidently moved on together. Five minutes later Dove first saw, above some low trees and bush on which they were browsing, the tall heads of five giraffe. David and I saw them almost immediately, the Bushmen not quite so soon, probably for the reason that they were on foot. There was some slight delay in getting our rifles from the Masarwas, and then the giraffe, catching sight of us, began to set themselves in motion, apparently not at all in a hurry. There was a singular waving to and fro of the tall heads and necks, and then the troop moved away, with a strange limping shuffle, at what seemed merely a fast walk. The pace of giraffe when first encountered is extraordinarily deceptive, and for some minutes, so leisurely appeared their movements, we could not at all realise how fast they were going. We set our horses quickly into a fast canter, and dashed after them through some thickish bush, and then, emerging into more open ground, we could see the game very plainly 200 yards in front of us. The troop consisted of a dark chestnut bull, a young one; a tall, fat cow; two rather smaller cows, and a young half-grown calf. The first sight of any big game in South Africa is exciting enough, but to have at length in front of one such rare and singular game as these beautiful giants—creatures which in these modern days seem almost to belong to another age—was enough to send the blood thrilling through one's veins.

Finding we were not gaining, we now stuck in spurs and galloped as hard as we could go and the bush would allow us, and still the giraffe, now thoroughly roused, kept their lead. Dove, who was on the right, got a heavy fall in the first hundred yards, but was quickly remounted, and, driving his horse at his hardest gallop, turned the troop, which were sheering to the right, so that they shifted their course and came my way. Buggins, my horse, hitherto the steadiest shooting pony in the world, had, early in the run, got wind of the strong musky odour which all giraffes possess, and bored to the left hand, and I had a good deal of trouble to persuade him to keep straight. Poor Buggins! he soon after died of horse-sickness at the Lake River, and his shortcomings on this occasion were easily forgiven. The troop now came obliquely across my front, their long necks sawing up and down, and their tails whirling vigorously as they ran. With their rich colouring (for giraffes in the wild state are, as a rule, much darker and more vivid in their colouring than those one sees in the Zoological Gardens), immense height, and their long and singularly ungainly strides, they formed, as they swung past, a pageant not easily to be effaced from memory. They were now less than 150 yards from me. I jumped off, took aim at the biggest cow, running second in the troop, and heard the bullet clap; and, as David, who was close to me, said, she "kicked" to the shot. She went on, however, at a great pace, and, turning for my horse, I found, to my intense disgust, that he had bolted. Without a horse, one might as well chase the wind as a giraffe, and there was nothing for it but to follow and secure my errant nag. The last I saw of the chase was Dove on his white pony riding close at the heels of the troop, which he had overhauled by dint of downright hard riding and a brilliant spurt. It took me half-an-hour to find and catch my horse, during which time I heard several shots in the distance, and imagined, with a curse on my own ill-luck, that Dove, and probably David, were busily engaged with the game. Guided by the firing, I galloped on in search of the rest, and, presently emerging into more open veldt, saw Dove and our hunter standing over something, with their horses knee-haltered and grazing. On riding up, I found a grand cow giraffe, full-grown, but young and fresh, lying almost hidden by the long yellow grass, hereabouts exceedingly tall. The rest of the troop had long since gone right away, with my wounded cow among them, but apparently tailing off, and we determined, if time allowed, to set the Masarwas afterwards on her spoor.

Dove now gave me the history of his run. He was shooting with a very good .450 express rifle, but, with such thickskinned game, found the bullets expanded too quickly, and did not give sufficient penetration. He had broken the cow's leg, and hit her in the hip, back, and shoulder, but it was not until he got pretty close, and gave her a shot in the back of the head, that he brought her down. We found, on examination, that the bullets in the back and shoulder had barely penetrated beyond the skin. Always after this we hunted giraffe with " Afrikander " double barrel sporting rifles, carrying the ordinary Government ammunition, and we found that the solid bullets did their work far more effectually.[1] It must be remembered that the giraffe is

[1] These rifles, which have been recently introduced, and, I believe, are now well known in the trade as the " Afrikander," are excellent

encased in a tough and very thick skin, which on the back and shoulders grows, in the adult animal, to a thickness of an inch to an inch and a quarter.

We now took a pull at our water-bottles, and set to work to skin and cut up the quarry, and the Masarwas, who soon came upon our spoor, were, not unnaturally—for the death of a giraffe is an event for them—more than pleased to relieve us of the hard work. In a couple of hours' time we had loaded our horses with as much meat and skin as they could carry, besides the feet and tail, which we invariably kept as trophies, the skin of the head, and the tongue, the latter a preternaturally long one. Leaving the Masarwas to bring in as much more flesh as they could carry and the marrow bones, we rode for camp, which we reached at about seven o'clock, tired but happy. Although this had been our first experience with " camel "—as the giraffe is invariably called by all hunters and traders of the South African interior—we had learnt the lesson that it is useless to try a steady stern chase with these animals. With " camel " there are no tactics like cutting-down tactics, and afterwards, riding our hardest, we invariably drove our horses with spur and whip right up to the heels of our quarry in the first mile of chase, and, shooting from horseback, in that way bagged our game. Of course, to attain this end one must have good ponies and be prepared to ride desperately, heedless of holes and obstacles,

and most serviceable weapons and of very moderate price—£14 or thereabouts. They are plain, strong rifles, made expressly to carry Government cartridges ; and as Martini-Henry ammunition can be obtained all over South Africa, and as far north as Palachwe, one is never likely to run short. I wonder that such a rifle has not been made for the South African market long since.

during the brief period of the chase ; but in the opinion of Dove and myself, and I believe of all who have shot giraffe, you must bustle them at first if you wish to secure them. In a long tail-on-end chase they will as often as not wear you out and get away from you.

On the following day, leaving our Masarwa spoorers and their families to finish off the remainder of the dead giraffe, the skin and flesh of which must have been a perfect godsend to them, we trekked away from Maqua. That night my companion and I for the first time tasted that acme of South African luxuries—giraffe marrow-bone. The ordinary English beef marrow is excellent in its way, but giraffe marrow is undoubtedly a dish fit for a king. One of the huge marrow bones (nearly four feet in length) was roasted over the camp fire and sawn in half, and the contents furnished us with a memorable repast.

On July 23, by which time we had crossed the thirstland and were trekking up the Botletli River towards Lake Ngami, having sent our light waggon across the flats bordering the river to the edge of the forest, where the giraffe were to be found, Dove and I rode in the afternoon quietly on the waggon spoor, and at night outspanned just on the edge of the bush, where we proposed to hunt next day. At this time of year the nights in the Ngami-land and neighbouring country are perfection. The low and extremely keen temperature experienced lower down in Bechuanaland has been left behind, and supper by the camp fire, and a smoke and chat afterwards in the balmy night air, under a brilliant starlit sky, are thoroughly enjoyable.

Very early next morning we were up, and after a

hasty breakfast, the horses having been fed, we made our way at once to the forest. We were not long in finding giraffe spoor, but it was not too fresh, and after two and a half hours' search my companion and I got separated, my hunters taking me to another part of the forest—hereabouts very thick, and with vast expanses of horribly dense haakdoorn, the toughest and most dangerous of all the thorny acacia family. At eleven o'clock, having found no game, I off-saddled for a short while, having ridden nearly five hours, and almost instantly heard two shots, then another. Cursing my luck, for I at once guessed that Dove had found "camel," I hastily saddled up again, and with my hunters made off in the direction of the shots. After a period of dead silence I fired a signal shot, and presently, hearing a reply, made my way with some difficulty to Dove, whom I found kneeling by an enormous old bull giraffe, busily engaged cutting off and skinning the feet. It was a typical hunting scene ; the giraffe had fallen dead in a small clearing, crashing down a good big sapling in his last struggle, and his mighty bulk and magnificent hide, almost black with age upon the back, could not fail to excite admiration. This was the biggest giraffe shot during the trip ; we took his height as he lay, and from his hoof to the tip of his false horns he measured within less than half-an-inch of nineteen feet. His feet, which we carried away with us, were enormous, and gave a proportionately mighty spoor, as I had observed before reaching the fallen giant.

Dove's narrative was a short one, and as follows : Soon after we separated, his men, in searching for fresh spoor, got away from him, and almost immediately he spied, about a hundred yards in front of him, two old bulls, who at the same moment sighted him, and made off through the dense bush at a tremendous pace. As a rule we always, when hunting giraffe in this terribly thorny forest, wore thick cord coats; but thinking the chance of coming on "camel" nearly over, and the day being very hot, Dove had doffed his coat and fastened it in front of the saddle. Pressing his pony to his top speed, he flew along after the bulls, gaining rapidly, thick though the bush was. The way in which giraffes dodge bushes, and duck their long necks under trees which almost touch their withers, is wonderful, and on this occasion the quarry led my friend a headlong and extremely thorny dance through the very thickest of the forest. In ten minutes, however, Dunboy had taken him right up to the heels of the game; and when within twenty yards he fired, hitting one giraffe, but not stopping him. This bull quickened and passed his fellow, to which Dove now directed his attentions, giving it first one shot and then another in the stern, at very close quarters. These bullets, as we afterwards found, had traversed the body and penetrated into the heart and lungs, and the bull, suddenly staggering, crashed through a small tree and fell dead. So sudden was the fall, and so close was the pony on the heels of the game, that horse and man all but fell on top of the giraffe. I found my friend's flannel shirt torn almost to ribbons, and his chest and arms very considerably excoriated by the thorns he had gone through in the gallop, and our united advice to hunters may be summed up in the words, "Don't follow giraffe without a stout coat in bush country."

We assisted in the skinning operations for some time—it took the united efforts of four of us to turn over the dead giraffe from one side to the other—and then, leaving two of the Bakurutse to finish the operation and get the skin off complete, we made our way back to the waggon, where again we passed the night at the edge of the forest. On the following morning, just as day broke, as we were preparing for breakfast, a troop of wild hunting dogs (*Lycaon pictus*) came tearing full cry along the edge of the bush in hot pursuit of some antelope or other—probably koodoo, whose spoor I had seen abundantly the day before. They halted at sight of our waggon, within 150 yards, and in the coolest manner had a good stare at us; then, flinging off, they resumed their chase. Few wild animals have less respect for man than these fierce creatures; and it was an unexpected pleasure to have had so good a look at them in their native hunting grounds.

Breakfast concluded, we again rode into the bush for giraffe. After a couple of hours, Dove turned home for the main camp in order to send back the oxen, which all this time had been waiting by the river. Later in the day, the Bushman hunting with me found fresh spoor of seven giraffe. We followed them steadily hour after hour into the recesses of the forest, but could never come up with them, and reluctantly returned to the waggon, where there was still a little water left, and I passed another night. To-day I realised to the full the intense solitude of these waterless North Kalahari forests. The utter loneliness, the silence, the complete isolation—for no human beings, and only a few kinds of game independent of water, can sustain life here—cannot fail to strike upon the imagination. And yet the giraffe acacia trees are plentiful, and the grass abounds and is good. Next morning early two of the oxen (pack animals) were despatched for the skin and meat of the dead giraffe. After much trouble, the skin was finally got to camp in two pieces, and there pegged out.

On August 3rd, having had good sport with Burchell's zebra, blue wildebeest, and lechwē for the last few days, I again crossed the plain from Masinya's kraal to hunt giraffe. The Bakurutse were very anxious to obtain the meat and skin of some heavy game—giraffe if possible—and I had with me Joseph, two Bakurutse hunters to spoor, and a pack-horse to carry our karosses, kettle, water, spare cartridges, &c. Dove was unfortunately laid up with a broken rib, and remained behind to trek on with the waggons.

After a long, heated, and fruitless run after zebra, we reached a patch of thorn trees a little before sundown, and, although still some way from the forest, camped there. After supper and a pipe, we wrapped ourselves in our karosses and turned in for the night; my after-rider and I on one side of the fire, the Bakurutse on the other: the horses fastened up to a tree close to our heads.

We were up at earliest dawn, and in two hours were well on our way into the forest. Just outside the bush we noticed a gemsbok feeding. He soon took himself off, and we reserved our powers for the heavier game we sought. After four hours' tracking upon the spoor of a troop of six giraffe, we found they had got our wind and run. It was now after eleven o'clock, and, shut up as we were in dense bush, it was extremely hot. However, we at once made off for another part of the forest, in hopes, now rather

faint, of finding fresh spoor elsewhere. For another
hour and a half we pushed on without result, and
then decided to off-saddle and give the horses, which
had been without water for twenty-four hours, a rest
and a pull at the grass. We waited nearly an hour
under the shade of a big camel-thorn tree, and then,
having finished the water and the remains of the
food, set off somewhat discontentedly, for we were
all disappointed, on the long journey homewards.
In half-an-hour we had cleared the forest and reached
the open flats. In ten minutes more, as we were
moving silently along, my boy Joseph, who had been
staring hard at some scattered trees a good way to
the right, suddenly exclaimed, in his broken English,
" I tink, sieur, dere are two camels." I looked hard,
and at first saw nothing but what appeared to be
trees; then I made out two long necks, and then,
pulling out my glasses and taking a long steady gaze,
I saw at once there were giraffe, and a number of
them. Mindful of the thorny forest into which we
expected the game to run, we hastily put on our
coats, and then, leaving the Bakurutse behind with
the led horse, we turned sharp right-handed and
walked our nags quietly along, so as to place ourselves
between the forest and the isolated patch of bush
and timber where the giraffe were evidently feeding.
As we stole quietly nearer and nearer to the game,
which we now saw consisted of a very large troop,
the suppressed excitement of the situation became
intense. I know that my after-rider's usually im-
passive face was a pretty plain index to his feelings;
and I know that long before the time arrived when
we gave our nags the spur, and rushed forward at
the game, my own throat and tongue were parched

and dry with intense anxiety lest the " camel " should escape us, for every instant we expected to be discovered. I suppose we were nearly fifteen minutes making our approach, but the quarry fed on unsuspectingly, without noticing our advent, until at length we had got within 300 yards of them, and could see plainly every member of the troop. Never, if I live to a hundred, shall I forget that amazing and most beautiful sight.

We were now right between the giraffe and the forest, and had turned our horses' heads to the game. In front of us there rose a slight swelling of the plain, and upon this stood perhaps half-a-dozen trees —giraffe acacias—all of them just bursting into the tender greenery which, after the long dry winter, they begin to assume at this the African spring of year. The nearest to us of these trees was a very large one, even and umbrella-like in its spread, and verdant with its new leafage. Round this one tree were fifteen tall giraffes, most of them full-grown, all feeding busily, with their long necks upstretched, and never suspecting for one moment the presence of a dangerous foe ; four more were feeding a little to the right at two more trees. Probably the whole troop had come up fresh from the Kalahari ; certainly they had never been hunted before. I do not think a more beautiful picture of wild animal life could well be conceived than this bevy of gigantic game, all gathered round the green camel-thorn. Even now, as we rode straight for them, they never looked our way until we were within 200 yards, and could scarcely contain ourselves. Then a tall head swung round, and indulged in a long stare, followed by one or two others, and then the owner, a huge, dark old bull, began to shuffle off. Immediately there was a commotion, the fifteen beautiful giants were all in motion, and, joined by the other four, and headed by the old bull, they started off at a good pace right across our front, evidently making for the forest. Our tactics were, of course, to drive them into the open, and run them down there; and we now rammed the spurs into our horses, which, willingly enough, galloped obliquely to the right also, with the object of cutting off the troop. As we neared them yet closer, the sight was even more wonderful. Stringing along in a line came the giraffe, still sticking to their point, their long necks swinging backwards and forwards, and their extraordinary gait reminding one somehow of tall ships rising and falling upon an uneasy sea. When within less than 150 yards most of the troop halted, feeling, I suppose, that they could not pass us; we jumped off, fired hastily at the nearest, heard the bullets clap loudly, and then, the greater part of the troop swinging off and bearing for the open plain, we jumped up again, and galloped after them at our very best pace. Seven more, including the old bull, succeeded in making their point and reaching the forest, leaving us with twelve in front of us.

We had now to cross some troublesome, low, haakdoorn bush, through and over which our nags raced and jumped without much thought for the cruel thorns they bore. Here I lost my left stirrup leather, clean torn away from the saddle; and carrying, as I was, a heavy double rifle, and hampered by bush and uneven ground, I had my work cut out for me. A few moments, however, saw us clear of the haakdoorn, and then, on fairly open ground, I raced up to a young bull which I had before hit, gave him a shot in the stern, and had the satisfaction of seeing him break sharp off to the right towards Joseph, run another fifty yards, and fall. I now picked out the biggest of the troop—a very large dark cow, so dark that at first I took her for an old bull—and made after her. She was running on the extreme left hand, and going a tremendous pace about 200 yards ahead. I knew what a good game pony I was on, and, calling upon Dunboy with knee and spur, he answered gallantly with a wonderful and prolonged spurt, so that in a few minutes he had taken me right up to the tail of the big cow. Within ten yards of her I fired twice from the saddle, first hitting her in the stern, and then breaking her off fore-leg close up to the shoulder. Now she reeled perceptibly, as we raced up a slight incline, and fell behind the rest, and I saw with a feeling of indescribable exultation that, barring accidents, she was mine. She ran but another hundred yards, staggering as she went; faltered, tottered on again, and then, trying hard to save herself, toppled over and fell with a crash on to her left side. Jumping off, I went up to finish her, and twice she raised her beautiful head and tried to rise. Another bullet at the back of the head quickly put an end to her sufferings, and then, before remounting, I hastily looked round for my after-rider. I had heard his rifle going during the chase, and I now saw him not very far away, having killed his own giraffe, putting the finishing touch, as it lay prone, to the bull I had first shot.

Hastily remounting, we rode after the rest of the troop, now sailing away a good distance in front,

and bearing right-handed as if towards the forest.
Joseph, who was nearer their line, forged ahead,
and, after a longish chase, he got within 150 yards,
jumped off, and by a lucky shot hit a young cow,
the bullet breaking her leg, and bringing her down
at once. Galloping up, he quickly finished her. In
fifteen minutes we had thus bagged four giraffe—
three cows and a bull; a sufficiency of sport to
satisfy the most ambitious hunter. It is difficult
to say which was the most exciting part of the
business—the wonderful and prolonged view we had
of these rare and extraordinary creatures as they fed
together at their favourite acacia, or the short but
intensely thrilling minutes of the actual chase. The
remainder of the troop gradually disappeared from
view, half hidden by bush, and the last time I saw
their long necks they were nearing the forest from
which they had so relentlessly been driven.

It is seldom nowadays, even far up in the hunting
veldt, that one happens upon so large a troop of
" camel," and we had been fortunate indeed to have
surprised them on fairly open ground. In their own
much-loved bush they would have given us far more
trouble. Right in the Kalahari, some days south
from the Botletli, in country perfectly waterless
except during the summer rains, large troops yet
wander; the almost insuperable difficulty is to provide water for a week's hunting in such a veldt. I
have heard of seventy and eighty giraffe being seen
at one time in that country even within the last
few years; but such sights are, I imagine, of rare
occurrence.

Taking the tail and feet of the last-killed giraffe,
Joseph and I now rode slowly back to where we had

Joseph

H. A. Bryden

AFTER THE GIRAFFE HUNT
(From Photo. by W. Dove)

shot the first three. It was now desperately hot, our horses were beginning to feel the effects of their hard work, and we were as dry as limekilns. We found the Bakurutse, in a state of immense delight, hard at work skinning the big cow I had shot. She proved to be in milk, and they had taken it from her yet warm body into a beaker. This I tasted, and, thirsty as I was, found it excellent drinking, rich and well-flavoured. Her calf, which must have been a big one (for we saw no very small calves in the troop), had got safely away. This cow—which was one of the largest size, and must have been, from her bulk, height, and dark colour, at fullest maturity—measured close on seventeen feet, that is, to the tip of the false horns. Taking some huge pieces of the hide, the feet of the two largest cows, some meat, and the tails of all—the latter being trophies which no South African hunter would ever think of omitting—after resting our horses we started home for camp. Leaving one Bakurutse with the dead game, we took the other with the pack-horse, so as to send him early in the morning to acquaint his friends of the abundant supply of flesh and hide that was in store for them. We had a long, weary ride of more than five hours before reaching camp, and, after getting lost in the darkness, finally struck the waggons at 8.30, guided by the stars, and latterly by the far distant camp fire.

Next day the Bakurutse villagers turned out with pack-oxen and on foot, and set off for the dead game, no part of which was wasted.

x

CHAPTER XIV.

THE GIRAFFE AT HOME

OF all that wonderful profusion of game with which the continent of Africa has been so richly endowed, the giraffe is perhaps the most singular, certainly one of the most beautiful. Sharing with the zebra, and its extinct cousin the true quagga, the gnu, and the hippopotamus, the distinction of being peculiar to Africa, and to no other country, its towering form, extraordinary shape, and rich colouring, point to it, even among the zoological marvels of the Dark Continent, as one of Nature's rarest and most singular efforts. Even in the days, now becoming remote, when this great game was to be found close to the Orange River, its shy habits, and the parched nature of the country inhabited, rendered it always a prime reward for the hunter's skill and labour. At the present time, the giraffe-hunter must wander, far afield indeed before he may hope to set eyes upon this stately quarry. Ever since youth, one of my most cherished ambitions had been to see the tall giraffe in its native wilds. To have witnessed these beautiful quadrupeds browsing quietly in their desert haunts; to have watched their swift and extraordinary paces when pursued; to have ridden close beneath the towering bulk of such gigantic game; and, after the fastest gallop that an African hunting-horse can compass, to have at length laid low that colossal form—these were rewards surely sweet and ample enough to repay the many weeks of toil and trouble that had been expended in reaching those remote hunting grounds.

It has been asserted by naturalists, with some show of reason, that the giraffe was never to be found south of the Orange River. There is certainly no actual and direct evidence that even in ages past it browsed within the confines of the present Cape Colony; but this may probably be put down as a moot if interesting point, never now likely to be decided.

In the quaint old-fashioned travels of Paterson, Le Vaillant, and Campbell—*circa* 1777, 1784, and 1813 respectively—it is undoubtedly shown that giraffes were shot very close to the north bank of the Orange; and there seems no real reason, other than the known peculiarities of geographical distribution, why this animal should not have wandered farther southward. In support of this latter hypothesis may be adduced an old Hottentot tradition to the effect that the giraffe was anciently found in the Amaebi thorn-country, in the present Queen's Town district of Cape Colony. There are, too, to be seen to this day in the Bushman caves near Graaff Reinet, and in other portions of the Eastern Province of the Cape, rude but unmistakable likenesses of this animal, which may or may not be considered evidence in favour of the contention that the giraffe did once make its habitat south of the Orange River.

Five or six decades since, the giraffe might have

HEAD OF GIRAFFE COW SHOT NEAR MAQUA, NORTH KALAHARI.
Drawn by G. E. Lodge.

been found in many parts of Great Namaqualand, and throughout the country of the southern Bechuanas. In the Kalahari Desert, between these countries, it was extremely plentiful. In 1836, Captain Cornwallis Harris met with it in the present Trans-

vaal territory ; and in considerable abundance near
the junction of the Marico and Limpopo rivers.
Even till within the last few years it has lingered
in the unhealthy low country lying upon the eastern
border of the Transvaal. A few still remain to that
region. But year by year it has been hunted from
one sanctuary to another, until now the giraffe must
be sought in the far corners of Khama's country,
or in the waterless recesses of the North Kalahari,
before it can be found in any numbers. Even
then, its habits are so shy, and its love of extreme
solitude is so constant, that great precautions have
to be taken, and the most skilful of Bushmen hunters
employed to track the beautiful giant to its forest
fastnesses.

The giraffe, for at least three parts of the year—
that is, during the spring and winter months in
Africa—seems to be perfectly independent of water.
I have taken great pains to get at the truth of this
matter ; and all hunters, native and European—including, of course, Boer hunters—that I have met
confirm this fact. It is certain that the only giraffes
found by myself and my hunting companion were
standing in perfectly waterless bush, far remote from
water ; and it is equally certain that during that
season (the winter) they never attempted to drink
in the Botletli River, their only possible source of
supply. This faculty of going for months without
water the giraffe seems to share in common with
certain of the South African antelopes, notably the
eland, gemsbok, and hartebeest among the larger
antelopes ; and the steinbok, duyker, and springbok
among the smaller. The food of the giraffe consists
almost exclusively of the leaves of the giraffe acacia

(*Acacia giraffæ*), known throughout the interior as
the "kameel-doorn" or "camel-thorn." The Boers
know the giraffe only by their Dutch name of
"kameel;" and English hunters and traders invariably term it "camel"—a sufficient explanation of
the name of its favourite tree. There are few more
beautiful sights in nature than the spectacle of the
giraffe, its tall neck upstretched, plucking with long
prehensile tongue at the sweet young leafage of the
acacia.

Although familiar to the Romans in the days of
the Empire, when camelopards—doubtless from North
Africa—were exhibited in the arena, this animal
seems in later times to have become completely
unknown to Europe. There is indeed mention of
one solitary giraffe shown at Florence by Lorenzo
de Medici some four hundred years back; but, until
the close of the last century, the animal seems usually
to have been classed more among the creatures of
chimera or fable than as anything belonging to earth.
Colonel Gordon, an officer serving under the Batavian Government at the Cape, appears to have been
the first to dispel this illusion, and in about the
year 1777, in company with Lieutenant Paterson, a
British officer, he shot a giraffe just across the Orange
River. A quaint portrait of this specimen is given
in Paterson's book of Travels, published a little
later. Le Vaillant, the French naturalist, to his own
incredible joy slew another giraffe about the year
1784; and some of the most ecstatic portions of his
amusing if highly-coloured narrative are devoted to
the chase and death of this specimen, as well as to an
analysis of the traveller's own over-wrought feelings
upon such an unparalleled event. In Le Vaillant's

Travels also, a figure of the giraffe is given. Even at the present day it is difficult to convey an adequate idea of this quadruped. From the scarcity of its occurrence and the singularity of its gait when roused, no animal in the wild state is so difficult to depict. A dead specimen is not easy to draw, even if the hunter—as very seldom happens—is a draughtsman; while the skin is so thick and of such enormous weight as to require cutting in half and disposing on two pack-oxen to be brought into camp.

On three succeeding occasions during our expedition, as I had a camera with me, I employed Masarwa Bushmen to carry my photographic implements in hopes of "taking" a dead specimen. On these occasions, after long hot days of severe toil, no giraffes were sighted. Needless to say, during the next hunt, when the camera was left behind, the big troop was found, of which four mighty camelopards were laid low.

It is true there were till lately specimens of the giraffe in the gardens of the Zoological Society in Regent's Park, but these pallid and undeveloped captives do not fairly represent the mature specimens of wild Africa. The colour of an old bull giraffe is of the richest dark orange-chestnut, deepening almost to black upon the back. Old cows in the same way darken very much with age. The younger and mature members of the troop present the most beautiful array of colouring, varying from a rich ruddy chestnut to a bright lemon-fawn.

It is a thousand pities that the authorities at the Natural History Museum do not procure good representative specimens of the giraffe while yet they can be obtained. Within the last few years, wonderful strides have been made in the stuffing and setting-up of skins ; and the specimens of rare game sent home recently by the great hunter Mr. F. C. Selous now afford faithful representations of the living animals, instead of, as in the case of many of the older specimens, absurd and hideous caricatures. The only stuffed giraffe in the collection of the Natural History Museum is certainly of great size ; but it is wretchedly set up, and gives no sort of idea of the animal in its natural state. This specimen is very old and worn, and was shot, I believe, during the expedition of Dr. Andrew Smith about the year 1835. Similarly, at the Cape Town Museum the solitary example is little better than a misshapen monstrosity, and the skin is in a wretched condition. When it is remembered that this very skin lay for three years upon the open beach at Walfisch Bay before it was sent to Cape Town and set up, some idea may be formed of its miserable plight. But the Cape Government is not renowned for its anxiety to further the interests of science and natural history, and hard-working and zealous as are the Museum authorities, the establishment is in a pecuniary sense very ill supported.

The most beautiful point about the giraffe is the eye, which is large, dark, full, and of the most melting tenderness, and shaded by long lashes. The eyes of the most beautiful gazelle cannot hope to surpass the bewitching softness of the timid giraffe's. Dependent as this animal is, from its sheer defencelessness, for its safety upon its scent and vision, those senses are extraordinarily acute ; and the eye is so formed and set in the head that the animal has, without moving, a wide field of vision both in front and rear.

The pace of this animal is singularly deceptive. When the hunter first sets eyes on it as it moves away, he thinks it is merely going slowly, at a curious gliding walk, and can be quickly overtaken. He canters slowly, and is surprised to find he is still losing ground. Even at a hard gallop it takes a good South African horse to run up to a giraffe; and unless a tremendous dash is made during the first mile of chase, forcing your horse at top speed with spur and sjambok, the tall quarry is as likely as not to get clean away from you. When pressed, the gait is most extraordinary. The giraffe progresses by moving two legs on one side simultaneously, and, when forced to its greatest speed, its action resembles a series of striding leaps in which the hind-legs are kept very wide apart. As it runs thus, the great neck swings up and down, and the long black tail switches, with the regularity of clock-work. Nothing can be more wonderful or more exciting than to have a large troop of this most beautiful and stupendous game thus rocking and swaying in front of one.

As a rule, the giraffe is found in open bushy forest, and when pursued, it invariably runs for the most thorny and entangling portion. Its own thick hide and great weight enables it easily to force a way through the densest obstacles, which tear the rider and his horse terribly. Nothing is more remarkable than the way in which these tall creatures duck and evade the branches of trees. The long neck is bent and the beautiful head lowered, so that branches which all but graze the withers are passed; and the operation is performed with great rapidity. In the same manner trees and bushes are avoided with sudden and astounding ease, the great creatures sheering and tacking in thick forest in a perfectly bewildering way. Curious though it may seem, the giraffe is extremely hard to find in forest-country, even although a troop may be feeding with their heads above bushes and low trees within the vision of the hunter. The long neck has a strange resemblance to the trunks and limbs of dead trees, and the colouring of the animal assimilates very wonderfully, especially in winter, with the sun-scorched vegetation, the yellow glare around, and the play of light and shade through foliage. Every distant tree or limb is therefore most anxiously scanned when giraffes are known to be in the neighbourhood.

The flesh of young giraffes and of fat cows especially is excellent; there is the least musky flavour perhaps, but it is not unpleasant. The tongue and marrow-bones are great delicacies, the latter, particularly, furnishing the rarest and most delicious banquet of the African hunter. Old bulls, on the contrary, are rank and excessively strong in scent and flavour, and their flesh is only eatable by half-starved Bushmen.

Few beasts of the chase are more poorly endowed with means of defence; but even the mild giraffe when wounded and brought to a stand, will, if the hunter approaches from the front, chop at him with its fore-feet, and a blow from such a limb is an exceedingly dangerous one. I have questioned many hunters on this point, and cannot ascertain that the giraffe uses its legs in any other system of defence. The keepers at the Zoological Society's Gardens tell me, however, that the animals will strike with their heads; and, undoubtedly, a blow delivered with the full swing of that long neck would be a very serious one.

At the present time, the giraffe is mainly sought after for the value of its hide, which, even so far up country as Khama's Town (Palachwe), now commands a value of from two pounds ten shillings to four pounds ten shillings a skin, varying according to age and sex. The hide of a tough thick-skinned old bull, from an inch to an inch and a quarter in thickness, is of course the most sought after. When one of these great creatures lies prone upon the veldt, it seems as if enveloped in a mantle of brass, and the fingers can make no impression whatever upon the carcase. Not many years since, the hides of the rhinoceros and hippopotamus furnished ox-whips and riding-whips—colonially known as *sjamboks*—all over South Africa. But the rhinoceros is all but exterminated south of the Zambesi; the hippopotamus becomes scarcer year by year; and the hide of the giraffe is consequently in greatly increased demand. A few years back, there happened a dearth of sjambok hide, the price of whips rose immensely, and a giraffe skin sold readily for five pounds and more. Forthwith, parties of Dutch and native hunters flocked into the Kalahari, and scores upon scores of giraffe were slaughtered. On coming out with their loads, the hunters discovered that they had overstocked the market, and that prices had rapidly fallen again. Most up-country natives, especially the Bechuanas, use the hide of the giraffe for making the neat sandals they habitually wear, preferring it for its strength and toughness to any other. It seems a pity that for the sake only of whips and sandals, and to furnish the hunter with meat and an exciting form of sport, this stately creature should be exterminated from South Central Africa, as it bids fair soon to be.

It is a difficult matter to restrain one's sporting instincts, and to content one's self with merely *looking* on at such extraordinary creations of animal life. Upon a first and even second occasion, it is, I will admit, from personal experience, a physical impossibility to repress one's natural hunting instincts —instincts deeply implanted during long ages— in a moment of such supreme excitement. But having fairly tasted the delights of giraffe-hunting, and they are very keen, I would never again, if I could help it, lay low another of these creatures, except to furnish a supply of absolutely necessary meat.

Its speed and staying powers, and the nature of its habitat, will always render the giraffe well worthy of the sportsman's skill; but in these days, when game is vanishing, almost as if by magic, from the face of the earth, unless its flesh is actually and imperatively needed, this, the most rare and characteristic of the African fauna, should, in my judgment, be suffered to go unmolested.

The North Kalahari will not for long retain its waterless renown; already concession - hunters are everywhere securing "veldt;" water will sooner or later be found in places hitherto considered to be lacking; and one of the last southern strongholds of the giraffe will then be gone.

Khama, who owns or controls a very large proportion of the best giraffe country now left to South Africa, might be induced to protect these rare and

harmless animals. Already he only allows his own
people or his own friends to shoot them, and a chief
of such intelligence and such power could do very
much towards staying extermination in his vast
territory. But, on the other hand, after Khama, the
deluge—otherwise extermination—is, I am afraid,
pretty sure to come. The British South Africa
Company, which it is said intends to preserve game,
may, however, do something in the countries under
its control.

The recent lamentable decease of the two last
giraffes left to the collection of the Zoological Society
is one of the heaviest losses sustained of late years
by that excellent body. Camelopards are always
"kittle cattle" to deal with, even when captured;
and, by reason of their shy and timid dispositions,
and the extreme remoteness of their habitats, they
have ever been among the most difficult of all fauna
to procure. The Soudan troubles have for years
hindered their collection and exportation from North
Africa by way of the Red Sea. East Africa, it is
true, still holds giraffes in moderate plenty; but
there, too, the tribes are disturbed and troublesome,
and little assistance in the way of capturing the
young of these towering quadrupeds can be looked
for among the Masai and other East African races.
If giraffes are to be exported from Southern Africa
—and there is no reason other than a tedious land
journey, the difficulties of a parched habitat and a
heavy incidental outlay, why this should not be done
—they will be found most plentifully in Khama's
country, in the direction of Lake Ngami. But
even from there, and with the assistance of Khama
and his hunters, which could without difficulty be

arranged—the capture of a single young giraffe and its transport to England would probably cost, at a low estimate, £400 or £500. Only the young of this extraordinary animal could be taken alive and rendered amenable to a state of captivity. An old bull of nineteen or twenty feet high, with a hide of brass, the speed of a stout horse, a proportionate amount of strength, and a kick capable at a stroke of slaying a man—or even a cow a foot or so less in stature—can hardly be expected to offer itself meekly to the ropes of the hunters. It is true that in the hunting veldt a mature giraffe is often run to a state of collapse, and thereafter driven slowly by the hunter right up to his waggon ; but even in such a case the hunted beast has to be slain out of hand, else, having recovered its wind, it would be off again. Probably the Zoological Society will, by hook or by crook, again display these beautiful and interesting creatures in their collection ; but it may be many months, perhaps even years, before we shall gaze again upon the towering, painted form so long familiar.

Roughly speaking, the present geographical distribution of the giraffe may be said to extend from Khama's country—Bamangwato, North Bechuanaland—in the south, to the southern Soudan in the north ; and in dry, suitable localities, where the giraffe acacia is to be found, its range extends all over Africa between these limits. Utter extinction is for the present, therefore, happily not immediately assured. But as Africa becomes opened up year by year—almost month by month—these beautiful and defenceless animals must surely pass away. At the end of another century, our successors will probably, as they gaze at pictures of the extinct camelopard, marvel that so extraordinary a creature could have lingered so late into the world's history. Yet another hundred years and their successors will be inclined to rank the giraffe among dragons, unicorns, and other creations of fable.

CHAPTER XV.

MOONLIGHT TREKKING ; MY HUNTER'S YARN

Pleasures of moonlight trekking—My span of oxen—Dutch names—Good
  qualities of the African ox—Bechuanaland cattle—Breaking in—Pack
  oxen—Excellent conveyances—A chat with David—His adventure
  with the Matabele—Captured in Mababē veldt—Evil treatment—
  Attempt to escape—Subsequently successful—A ride for life.

THERE is, I think, no keener pleasure in the ups
and downs of South African waggon travel than a
steady trek on a clear moonlight night. The oxen,
refreshed by the rest they have enjoyed during the
fierce heat of mid-day, and invigorated by the cool
night air, pull themselves together and press gallantly to their yokes ; the echoing crack of the great
waggon whip is not so often needed ; and the voice
of the driver calling occasionally upon the names of
his span—for every one of the eighteen oxen knows
and answers to his name ; the deep breathing of the
cattle, and the wail of a kiewitje plover or a far-off
jackal are almost the only sounds that break upon
the still, sweet, night air of the desert. The un-
speakable majesty of the moon, the shining army of
the stars, the dim mysterious vault that cradles the
constellations within its deep ineffable blue ; all
these things contrive to cast a strange peace and
yet withal an undefinable longing upon the mind.
Seated upon the waggon box on such a night, puffing
contentedly at one's favourite pipe, and lulled by

the repose and the glamour of the moon-drenched veldt, one feels, even after long days of stress and toil, at rest with all mankind—almost as if no such things as the troubles, calamities, and passions of the outer world could exist.

On the 27th of June (I am harking back a little), after a good afternoon's rest at Mesa—the last decent and reliable water before crossing the desert between Khama's and the Lake River—we inspanned and trekked from 7 P.M. till 9.15, when we outspanned for an hour for supper. The day had been fine, warm and balmy, with light clouds flecking the hard, pale turquoise of the sky; and the night was, for the time of year (winter), warm, and as usual marvellously clear. A wonderful African moon illumined the flat open country through which we were moving, casting its silvery spell upon bushes, tall grass, and other objects near at hand, and leaving the dim distance shrouded in mystery. It was an absolutely perfect night, and, during the earlier part of the evening, Dove and I had walked together ahead of the waggons discussing future sport.

After supper, the oxen, which had been resting in their yokes, were set in motion. The span attached to my waggon consisted of eighteen picked cattle supplied by Khama. They were all magnificent, evenly matched fellows, of a deep red Devon colour, level and symmetrical; all carried the great horns dear to the Bechuana, and were in splendid condition. Indeed, as David my driver said, "Khama has given you the best span in his country," and verily I believe he had.

David, best and most careful of native drivers, loved these oxen and knew them intimately well.

Y

He had their little idiosyncrasies by heart, knew to an ounce what each one should pull, and had them in the most perfect control. When they had to be inspanned they came up to their ranks for yoking, knew their proper places, and there was little of the turmoil and fighting so often seen when oxen have to be inspanned.

David seldom used his whip, except in the worst bits of the " Thirst," where no water was, and where the waggons had to be got through and dire disaster averted by trekking day and night. The team knew and responded cheerfully to his voice, and the after oxen (wheelers) in particular (Kapje and Ringhals) answered to him as a well-trained dog answers to his master's voice. It is seldom in South Africa that one comes across a humane and at the same time a capable driver, and I gladly bear my testimony here to the cleverest and kindest native driver I have ever encountered—David of Khama's Town. Of course, even in this model span, there were lazy ones—there always are ; but David with a minimum of punishment extracted a maximum of work out of his horned charges ; and although this span suffered terribly on the return journey, and one of them actually died of thirst, I doubt if any other man in the country could at that time of the year have got our heavy waggon through so ably—most drivers would, I firmly believe, have left the bones of a third of their team to bleach in that terrible desert.

By this time I was beginning to understand something of the new span, to admire their merits, and to be amused at their respective idiosyncrasies and habits. I had got their names by heart, Kapje and Ringhals, Zeeman and Snijman, Witfoot and Donker,

Blessman and Blauwberg, Donkerman and Roman, and the rest of the great phlegmatic fellows. It is a signal proof, by the way, of the amazing grip which the Dutch language has laid upon South Africa, that here in a Bechuana and decidedly anti-Boer state, the very cattle of the chief himself are all known by Dutch and not Sechuana names.

In another book (" Kloof and Karroo ") I have borne testimony on behalf of the much-enduring, much-maligned ox of South Africa. How, indeed, could the country have been opened up without him? For 240 years he has toiled, and struggled, and died for the explorer, the hunter, the farmer, the miner, and the missionary ; he has helped in no small degree to make a great and interesting history ; and his bones, littering the veldt and forming the silent dust in every nook and corner of this vast land, bear dumb yet eloquent testimony to his strength, patience, and endurance.

The Bechuana cattle, whether as slaughter or trek oxen, can hold their own with any in South Africa ; and, especially in the countries bordering on the Kalahari, they are—no doubt from centuries of natural selection—peculiarly fitted to combat the long "Thirsts" and distressing sands of much of the south-western part of the continent. Most Bechuana cattle are distinguished by the immense spread of their horns. Those reared in the vicinity of Lake Ngami are still more redoubtable in this respect, and measurements that would astound the European grazier are to be met with. A measurement from tip to tip of 8½ feet has been authenticated, whilst a single horn has been known to accommodate as much as twenty-one pints of water.

Probably, as ranching under European management comes into vogue, this excess of horn will disappear —fashionable breeders don't delight in such a point —but it may be doubted whether the admixture of European blood will be of any advantage for trekking purposes in the interior. On the contrary, I believe that for travelling in a dry desert country the present stamp of ox is unsurpassable. There is often to be seen in Bechuanaland a breed of cattle whose horns are short and have the peculiarity of hanging loosely in front of their heads. The horn itself is hard with the exception of the part close to the skull, where it seems to be replaced by a strong membrane or skin formation. When the beast owning these curious appendages is in active motion the horns waggle about in what to the unaccustomed eye seems a very ludicrous fashion.

To the westward, in Ovampoland, the cattle are much smaller, as too they are in Mashonaland and the countries about the Zambesi. But these Ovampo cattle, which periodically are brought across the desert with Damara and Namaqua oxen, are capital little beasts, and have the faculty of putting on flesh very quickly.

We in this country seldom see a bullock of much over four years of age, and English people, unless they have set eyes on that rare spectacle nowadays, even in Sussex or Oxfordshire, a team of plough oxen, can have faint idea of the size to which an old trek ox can attain. Some of the Bechuana spans are enormous, and many of the Transvaal Boers can show oxen of tremendous size and strength. In the indigenous African ox the withers are high, and the tendency to hump is very pronounced. This hump formation is, by the way, a very useful one in trek oxen, where the yoke presses against the high withers. During the short period of breaking the young cattle are subject to very severe usage, but then they are very obstreperous. I have assisted at some of the wildest scenes in spanning in cattle. I shall never forget seeing the feats of some Namaqua Hottentots, who were breaking in fresh teams, from a troop of cattle brought across the Kalahari. Some of the beasts seemed half-mad, and time after time we had to scamper for our lives, amid yells and shrieks of laughter. If an ox is more than usually troublesome he is summarily cast, his legs are fastened tightly together, and his head is firmly roped with hide riems close up to the hub of the waggon wheel, when he can stir neither head nor foot even for an inch. In such a position he lies, after a sound thrashing, for hours, sometimes for a day; after which his spirit is considerably quelled, and he rises, like Uriah Heep, "very 'umble."

Trek oxen are always managed by strong raw hide riems noosed round the horns; these riems are immensely strong, and it is not uncommon to see a refractory ox dragging after him three or four perspiring natives, all pulling and straining in a thorough tug-of-war fashion. Occasionally the maddened beast will charge at his taskmasters, when ensues a *sauve qui peut*.

How many years the native ox has been a denizen of Southern Africa we shall never know. When Van Riebeek landed in Table Bay the Hottentots possessed great herds, and no doubt the Bechuanas and Hottentots have raised cattle south of the Zambesi for many centuries—the Hottentots, who are the more ancient inhabitants, probably for at least a thousand years. The Bechuanas are very expert at cattle management; they remember every individual ox by heart, and will without hesitation pick out a beast which they have once seen, after years of absence; and they have probably more affection for their cattle than for anything else on earth. In the remoter parts of Bechuanaland the ox is constantly used as a pack and riding animal. The natives make long and rapid journeys in this manner; and for a rapid march there is, I think, no better way of crossing the Kalahari than according to the old Bechuana method. A stick is passed through the animal's nose; to this is fastened a rough bridle of raw hide; a sheep-skin forms the saddle, and the nag is ready. I have seen natives crossing and recrossing the Kalahari in this way, and making comparatively light work of journeys that were pain and vexation to waggon wayfarers. I do not say the ox is a comfortable conveyance to the horse-riding European, he is anything but that; but he is steady, and a safe and strong traveller in parched desert country.

But all this is, I fear, a long digression. After supper on the evening I speak of, we moved off in the usual procession—Dove and the light waggon going first, " Piccanin," our waggon boy, being already fast asleep in front of Dove's kartel; myself in the big waggon following; our one solitary goat march-ing independently, as he always did, between the waggons, occasionally plucking a mouthful as he went; the dogs rambling hither and thither not far away; the horses, who had had their evening feed of mealies, just behind, with Seleti, their guardian, bringing up the rear. The evening, as I have said, was without flaw, and the radiant moon threw the inky shadows of our long caravan in strong relief upon the right hand, as we moved steadily and silently through the yielding sand. I sat on the waggon box beside David, and having given him a fill of fragrant Transvaal tobacco, we puffed away

"PICCANIN," OUR WAGGON-BOY.

full of contentment, and chatted on various subjects in a patois of Dutch and broken English.

David, an old hunter and interior man, knew every yard of the country to the Zambesi and the Chobe River, and being an acute, thoughtful fellow, was a valuable mine of information. He was, as I have

said, a Batlaping by birth, and at Kuruman in his
younger days, in the time of the veteran missionary
Moffat, had picked up a good knowledge of carpentering, at which he was singularly expert.   During the
week I stayed at Palachwe on our return, he made
me a most excellent chair, which he insisted on presenting me with, and which I still possess and value.
David remembered as a youth most of the interior
explorers and hunters—Moffat, Livingstone, Gordon
Cumming, Baldwin, and the rest ; and, in the days
when elephants were yet plentiful, he had hunted far
and wide.   As one of his most trusted pioneers and
hunters, Khama had picked David for our expedition,
and he could not have rendered us a better service.

Well ! we talked upon a variety of topics, all
interesting to me—the habits of game, native races,
far-off hunting districts, and so on ; and at last
David, speaking of that famous hunting ground of
Khama's, the Mababē veldt—north of the Botletli—
was regretting that time would not permit of our
shooting in that direction.   " Dar is de veldt, Baas,"
said he, " kameel, buffel, quacha (Burchell zebra),
wildebeest, gemsbok, bastard-gemsbok (roan antelope) zwart-wit-pens (sable antelope), leeuw (lion).
Banje ! (plenty)—sometimes oliphants, even now."
Then continuing, amid long-drawn puffs at his pipe,
he said : " Once not long ago I had to find my way
through Mababē stark naked, and with nothing to
eat but roots and herbs."   I should here interpolate
the remark that I am giving but a bald translation of
David's very vivid patois.

" It happened in this way," he went on.   " Khama
sent me to Mababē to hunt and bring in giraffe and
other skins.   I had heard that the Matabele were

threatening a raid on Moremi's people (the Lake tribe) that year (1884), but I thought it might be only Lobengula's talk, and troubled my head not at all about it. Well! one day, I had been out in the veldt all morning with Patrick there (jerking his thumb back towards the old roan horse still used by him, and now with our waggons), and was resting by the waggon, when a band of men armed with assegais and shields and a few guns came up. They were in their war dress, and were part of the great Matabele impi. It was too late to attempt to escape. They took possession of the waggon, stripped me of every atom of clothing, and tied me up. My men, who had less clothing, they served in the same manner; and having robbed us of all our little possessions, and insulted us in every possible way, they fastened us up securely, threatening instant death if we attempted to escape. The Matabele are as you know kaal (naked) Kaffirs, but they now put on what clothes they had found—the headmen I mean—and paraded about, amid roars of laughter, in their fine new feathers. After that they speared one of the best of the trek cattle—for they had little food with them —and had a tremendous night of feeding; and moreover,. having discovered my coffee and sugar, which some of them understood and could appreciate, they boiled and drank potful after potful of it. Next day the Induna gave me to understand that they would require me to drive the waggon, and so, naked as I was and half-starved, I was compelled to do their bidding.

"Now I had always kept my eye on Patrick, and as we were outspanned on the third day I thought I would try and escape with him. I was now allowed

to move about, and seeing Patrick feeding, knee-haltered, some way from the waggon, I walked towards
him slowly as if to drive him in. At last I got
pretty close to him, and then to my dismay I found
that, naked as I was and without my usual clothes,
the old schimmel didn't recognise me, but shuffled
away each time I approached him. At last, after
repeated efforts to catch hold of him, I became aware
(for I kept my eyes pretty wide open all this time, I
can tell you) that the suspicious Matabele scouts
had encircled me, and that escape was out of my
power. I made therefore as if I was driving Patrick
to the waggon, and, having got him there, was about
to give him a feed of mealies to disarm suspicion
still further, when the Induna angrily snatched the
bucket from my hand, telling me that he required
the food for his warriors and not for horses. All
this time I was leading the life of a Kaffir dog, with
scarcely anything to eat and plenty of blows and
curses ; still I looked for my opportunity. Two days
after most of the Matabele were away scouting, and
there were about forty men only in camp. Again
I watched my opportunity, and with the greatest
caution made after Patrick, now quietly feeding on
the veldt. This time he knew my voice, and let me
get hold of him ; I instantly unfastened his knee-
halter, jumped on his back, and digging my heels
into his ribs, set off. I knew all the time that the
Matabele scouts were round about watching me,
but they were not so numerous as before, and were
further apart. As soon as I was mounted there was
a yell, the men at the waggons ran out with their
assegais, and those in the bush closed in to cut me
off. It was life or death now ; I picked out the

weakest point in the ring of men, put Patrick to his top speed, and just managed to run the gauntlet although several spears flew about me. Once beyond the Matabele I was pretty safe, but all the rest of that day, and well into the night, when I rested in thick bush for an hour or two, I pushed my flight. Well! to cut a long story short, I kept Patrick moving day and night as much as he could travel, until we were far from the Matabele. I lived for some weeks naked in the veldt, picking up what roots, fruits, and bulbs I could find, and often suffering much from want of water, until I struck the trade road, and presently came on Mr. John Strombom, the Lake trader, who was then in the country. From him I received some clothes and provisions, and presently I got safely back to Shoshong. I was weak and starved, and very sore from riding my horse barebacked so long and so much, and I had worn clothes so long—all my life almost—that the sun burnt me a good deal. As for the Matabele, they had my waggon and oxen and guns, and other things, which I never saw again; and they looted Mr. Strombom's stores when they reached the Lake; but I am heartily glad to think that Moremi and his people, who had lots of guns, gave them a good beating, and killed numbers of them, and very few of the bloodthirsty, bragging impi ever saw Matabeleland again.

"And so, Baas, you can understand why I am still fond of my old horse Patrick. He did me a good turn in his younger days, and by his speed saved my life; and so now, although he is getting old and stiff, I treat the old fellow well and look after him."

The moon was still shining brightly as David

finished his yarn, the night was as magnificent, as full of glamour as ever, the air as still and sweet, though now a thought chillier.

Loth though I was to quit the waggon-box on such a night, I now grew sleepy; Dove was already abed in his waggon; and so, having finished my pipe, I got into my pyjamas, and then, leaving David outside on the "voer-kist" (waggon-box), I crept into my kartel, pulled down the fore-clap, nestled beneath my big sheepskin kaross, and slept the refreshing sleep of the veldt. Meanwhile the waggons slowly moved on for an hour or two more, till morning broke and we were outspanned again.

CHAPTER XVI.

SPORT AND NATURAL HISTORY ON THE BOTLETLI

Among the waterfowl—The African jacana—Fish and fishing—Scenery —Trading corn—Native snuff—Death of a horse—Bee-eaters—First wildebeest shot—Lechwē waterbuck—Camp-fire scenes—Masinya's kraal—The Bakurutse—Curious granaries—Egyptian geese—Lechwe hunting—Bird life—Black and white kingfishers—Spur-winged plover —Burchell zebra shot—Sebituane's Drift—Brilliant sunsets—A wilde-beest hunt—Dove breaks a rib—The blue wildebeest—Scene on the Botletli—Makoba fishermen—Our bag.

OUR first care on the morning of July 9,[1] after our overnight arrival at the Botletli, was to shoot some ducks for dinner. The waggons toiling laboriously in our rear would not strike the river for a couple of days, and we had ridden on with scant sup-plies—some coffee, meal, and sugar comprising our outfit. Arrived at the river-bank, we had small diffi-culty in securing two couples of the yellow-billed duck (geelbec of the colonists, *Anas flavirostris* of scientists) which we found here, of great size, fat, and in splendid condition. We noticed also numbers of that showy bird the Egyptian goose, and of the Cape wigeon (*Mareca Capensis*) and crested coot (*Fulica cristata*). We had little difficulty in getting to the water's edge, as the reeds had been burnt down to stumps. Proceeding a little further up stream, along the now dry mud-banks, we presently noted a knot of that most singular and beautiful

---

[1] I resume our journey from the end of Chapter XII.

bird, the African jacana (*Parra Africana*). These
birds are usually placed by naturalists in the family
of *Palemedeidæ*, or screamers, between the snipes
and rails, but as a fact they partake more of the
nature of the latter than the former, the head in
particular being distinctly rail-like. Their general
colouring is of a brilliant shining chestnut; the
throat and front of the neck are spotless white,
which is separated from the stomach by a shining
golden-yellow gorget, which imparts a remarkable
effect; below that being a darkish streak. There
is a curious bare patch of bright blue skin between
the base of the bill and the top of the head, which,
however, fades greatly after death. The body is
lightly framed, and the dark green legs are long and
stilty. The average length of the bird is from nine
to eleven inches, the females being larger than the
males. Viewed at a distance, these light-framed
birds appear to be actually running upon the surface
of the water; a closer approach shows that they are
merely perambulating the thin film of weed and
vegetation which often lies upon the river. Their
feet, the most singular part about them, are manifestly designed exactly for this dainty method of
progression, the toes being slender, spreading, and
extraordinarily elongate. I shot a pair of these
beautiful waterfowl this morning, and afterwards
brought home the skins of two or three good
specimens. The river was low, and I waded waist-
deep to recover my birds; if I had then known more
of the fierceness and voracity of the Botletli crocodiles, I should have hesitated a good many times
before doing so. As we sauntered along the banks
we came upon numerous heads of a species of barbel

(*Glanis silurus*, mosala of the natives) which swarms in the Botletli. These fish grow to large size, and are prized by natives and raptorial birds alike. So thick were the fish in some places, that when we fired a gun the whole pool appeared to be a mass of them; they leaped desperately over one another in their anxiety to escape, reminding one much of a school of porpoises. I watched one day a number of natives spearing barbel. Having first made sure of the absence of crocodiles, they entered the pool in a line, and feeling their way delicately with arms uplifted, thrust as often as they moved a fish. Every now and again an arm would suddenly descend and a fish would be struck, and then would occur a scrimmage till it was secured and brought to bank. Oftener than not the fish would be missed. Among the men were some boys, and it was intensely amusing to see little fellows with tiny assegais entering fully into the sport, although sometimes almost up to their necks in water. At this end of the river we noticed some well-constructed fishing weirs, in which the natives capture quantities of fish.

Having secured enough ducks for the day, we strolled back to the camp. From the rising ground on which we stood we had a fine prospect of the country round. Looking across the river, the view was a typical one. To the right the dense reed-beds extended apparently for miles upon miles, covering the vast tract of marsh called Lake Komadau, in which the Botletli loses itself. In front the reeds had been partially cleared by burning, but upon the further bank they were thick again; beyond stretched a flat plain in apparently limitless expanse.

Here and there along the river, marking its course

very plainly upon the opposite bank, grew tall palm trees. These, and the hot expanse of yellow plain running into the far-off distance, brought irresistibly to mind one's childhood impressions of a flat and burning Africa—impressions which are completely dispelled among the rugged mountains and stern magnificence of much of the southern part of the continent.

Behind us, not very far off, lay one of the huge saltpans of this region; beyond that again open plains extended until checked by the waterless bush and forest of the North Kalahari, about half a day's ride to the southward. We shot two pelicans during the day—one with a charge of No. 5. shot, a lucky chance, the other with the rifle. When brought down they are enormous. One which I afterwards shot and photographed measured from wing to wing nine feet eight inches. A wild goose when shot comes to earth with a good solid clump; a pelican falls with far greater effect.

The waggons did not appear until the night of July 10. The oxen had had nearly three days and nights' severe trek without water, and needed rest. We therefore devoted the 11th to a day's barter with the natives. We had by this time exhausted the supply of corn for our horses and required more. The large waggon was unpacked, therefore, and trading goods were got out. At first my companion and I thought the whole business immensely amusing. We had round us a dense throng of men, women, and children, Makalakas, Motetis, and others, all provided with mealies and Kaffir corn in every conceivable receptacle—skin-bags, calabashes, baskets, skin-cloaks, &c. We exhibited our wares—such as

To face page 352

BAKURUTSE PEOPLE—MASINYA'S KRAAL, NGAMILAND

gaudy cotton handkerchiefs, clasp knives, percussion caps, powder, lead, blankets, and so on, and then began a regular scrimmage of competition. After much gesticulation, laughter, and bawling, we established, by the aid of Joseph our interpreter, a standard of value—so much corn for a *teepa* (knife), so much for a *toqui* (handkerchief), and so on, and our empty sacks soon began to fill. It was a most entertaining spectacle, and Dove and I laughed till we cried again over the financial squabbles and misunderstandings with our black friends.

After two hours of this sort of traffic, under a hot sun, and amid a throng of excited and perspiring natives, the thing began to pall a little. We therefore deputed David to continue the trade; and by two o'clock, when we had filled four or five sacks, the price of corn had risen, and trade was practically at an end.

Owing, I suppose, to the strong female influence, *toquis* went off decidedly the best, *teepas* next; then came copper caps, powder and lead. We only sold one Kaffir blanket, which was bought by a native gentleman for half-a-sovereign, the only piece of money in all this country, with which he was ludicrously anxious to part.

Dove and I had our midday meal, sitting, as we always did, at our little table under shadow of the big waggon, surrounded by a dense throng of admiring natives. We dispensed bread and jam to the piccaninnies amid much applause. The old headman here—a Makalaka—turned up during the morning with a lion skin, which he wanted to trade. Eventually we secured it for about the value of 12s. 6d., and having regaled the old fellow with coffee, and

z

made him presents of powder, lead, and coffee, in
return for a goat which he had sent us, we separated.
Tobacco, of which we had brought a large supply, we
found of no value here. All the natives along the
Botletli grow tobacco, which they cure in a rude way
—for snuffing purposes only—and manufacture when
wet into small pyramidal lumps. The way these
people snuff is amazing. They take it, till the tears
stream down their cheeks, with manifest enjoyment;
and they employ a flat piece of polished iron, turned
up at the end and embossed with neat patterns, as
a means of clearing away superfluous tears. In the
same manner this flat kind of spoon, which always
hangs upon the breast, takes the place of a pocket-
handkerchief and scratcher.

This day died " Buggins," an excellent shooting
pony left to me by Mackay on his departure. He
died very suddenly and incomprehensibly of horse-
sickness, and was the last case we had of that terrible
disease this season. Buggins's untimely decease was
a great loss. My stud was now reduced to two,
Giltboy and a bay called Captain; while Dove still
possessed three—Witbooi, Bluebuck (the grey), and
Dunboy. David's old nag " Patrick " brought up the
entire stud to half-a-dozen. Luckily we now had
plenty of corn to stuff into them, and they were
daily picking up condition after the desert journey.

The horses and oxen were disturbed this night,
and we found spoor of a lion within 100 yards of our
waggons in the morning. We broke camp next day
and trekked away up the southern bank of the river,
reaching T'Kom, a small Makalaka village of a dozen
huts, on the 15th. At a reedy pan of water near
T'Kom, I shot a pair of tiny bee-eaters (*Merops*

erythropterus), whose diminutive size and lively colouring render them notable even among this beautiful family. These birds are fairly plentiful in reedy places along the Botletli and round Lake Ngami, but I have never seen them in South Bechuanaland, the Transvaal, or Cape Colony. The hue of the back and upper parts is green; the throat and chin are a full rich yellow; to this succeed, before the breast is reached, a narrow band of bright blue, a tiny line of white, another of black, and a patch of chestnut, the whole forming a most perfect bit of colouring. When I had them both in my hand, I could not sufficiently admire the gem-like beauty of these birds. We skinned these diminutive creatures next evening by the lantern, after a long day's hunting; they were a difficult task, but their skins well repaid the trouble we were put to.

On the 14th, having seen spoor of wildebeest, Burchell's zebra, gemsbok, springbok, and koodoo, mostly trekking across the flats to the river, we were up very early and in the saddle. Dove shot a heavy springbok ram just after daybreak; I saw shortly after an old solitary blue wildebeest in thick bush, but only got a snap-shot and missed him. Afterwards we rode across another saltpan, on the spoor of roan antelope, but failed to come up with them. It was the prettiest sight in the world to witness the "pronken" (pranks) of the springbok on the dazzling expanse of pan. They frolicked, cantered, trotted with heads low and a peculiar mincing gait, then leapt high in air, displaying the snowy blaze of hair upon their croups, and altogether made charming pictures of themselves.

On the 16th we rode out from our outspan near

T'Kom, and, guided by some Bushmen, sighted a troop of blue wildebeest about three-quarters of an hour after sunrise. They were mostly cows and three-quarter-grown calves, and, going straight away, ran at a tremendous pace, pointing for the bush on the far side of the plain. The veldt was villainous hereabouts, soft and full of holes, and I got two falls to start with. Dove, after a long stern chase, broke the leg of a cow at two or three hundred yards, and after a long gallop—for these beasts go almost as well on three legs as four—secured her. For a cow she had a good head. Rejoining him later on, we left the Bushmen to skin and cut her up, and pushed on after the troop. We sighted them again, but they were extremely wild, and, led by a small troop of zebras which had meanwhile joined them, they went right away and made good their sanctuary in the bush. We reached camp at four, loaded up with meat, after being ten hours in the saddle, and after supper and oceans of tea, turned into our waggons at 7 o'clock P.M.

The plain here is immense. It extends along the river bank for four or five days' journey, and is fringed to the south and west by the North Kalahari bush, in which much of the game finds shelter. Wildebeest and zebra cannot exist without water for months together, as can giraffe, gemsbok, and eland. They cross the flats after dark and drink at the river most nights. At early morning they are to be found feeding on the plain, and, when chased, invariably betake themselves to the bush and forest. The plain is crescent-shaped, and at its broadest point takes the best part of a day to cross on horseback at walking pace. In the waterless forest of which I have spoken numbers of giraffe wander comparatively undisturbed. To get near them, we had either to cross the flat, sleep at the edge of the bush and hunt next day, our horses thus being the best part of two days without water, or send the light waggon across loaded up with water, by which means we could hunt two days consecutively. To do this, however, the oxen had to return to the river and thence be driven back to take the waggon to camp. All this created no small amount of hard work— indeed, to hunt successfully nowadays in South Africa, hard work and hard condition are essential. Still, the reward was well worthy of the toil, and the downfall of a tall giraffe, or an old blue wildebeest bull with a good head, or a handsome zebra, or still handsomer lechwē ram, well repaid one for long fatiguing rides under a burning sun and over scorching, shadeless plains. It was near the bush, on the far side of the flats from T'Kom, that our best day with giraffe was scored on the return journey.

Next day, our waggons still standing near T'Kom, my companion and I sallied out on foot for a long tramp by the river. We sighted some lechwē (*Cobus leché*), a rare kind of waterbuck, only found on the river systems of South Central Africa, and, after wading middle deep through a lagoon, concealed ourselves on a sort of island on which grew palm trees, expecting the Bushmen to drive the buck towards us. The lechwē, however, declined to be driven, and escaped. In the afternoon Dove shot two springbok on the way home, I some duck at the lagoon, having exchanged my rifle for a fowling-piece which my Bakurutse carried. The river was rising rapidly up here, flooding the country round, and forming great lagoons upon which thousands of wildfowl disported themselves.   The quantity of bird-life gathered on these lagoons was astounding ; they literally covered the water in places, and the babel of chattering, quacking, and gobbling was almost ludicrous.

We reached camp after a long hot day of seven and a half hours on foot and without water.   There was water in plenty, it is true, but so full of decayed vegetable matter that we preferred to do without it.   David had also been down to the river, and had stalked and bagged a lechwē ewe ; the females of this species unfortunately are hornless, and are of little use except for the skin, the flesh of this, and indeed all water-loving antelopes, being as a rule very unpalatable.   A springbok, wounded by one of us this day also, was secured by the Bushmen and brought in next morning.

Having fairly reached the game country, we had now and for long after any quantity of meat for ourselves, our men and dogs, not omitting Bushmen and other hangers-on.

It is very amusing as well as interesting to watch the men at night gathered round the camp fire, discussing their food, exchanging witticisms, and relating tales and adventures to one another.   Dove and I sat apart at our own fire a little way off, where, however, we could observe all that was passing.   Whoever had accompanied us hunting during the day would relate faithfully every particle of sport.   How the Baas (master) did this, shot that, galloped this way or that way, or was thrown or missed his shot ; the whole accompanied by a running

fire of commentary from his companions. If anything out of the way had been accomplished the
listener would sometimes cover the mouth with the
hand in the old Bechuana manner, expressive of
astonishment and admiration. Then they would
begin to yarn themselves. Patshalaan, our second
driver and hunter, was great at narrative. He spoke
very rapidly, and usually had thrilling tales of adventure and of terror to unfold. He accompanied
his tales with copious action, his eyes rolled, his
naturally high voice rose to a shrill scream at exciting points, and the perspiration poured from his
face. Every now and again Dove or I would call
out to Joseph to interpret the choicest bits for us.
I usually took my chair later on and sat by the
big fire, entering into the men's talk, and obtaining in this way very interesting information. I,
in my turn, was frequently catechised, and had
to endeavour to explain such mysteries as Cape
Town, the ocean, steamship life, and England. It
was far more difficult than it sounds to impart
any adequate idea of these things to men, shrewd
indeed after their lights, but most of whom
had never been further south than the Limpopo
River.

Our next halting-place, reached July 18, was at
Masinya's Kraal, the village of a tribe of Bakurutse
people, tributary to Khama. As we intended hunting for a week here, we formed a capital outspan,
having both waggons drawn up under the shade of
a big camel-thorn tree on rising ground about half-
a-mile from the village. Masinya's itself is a poor
collection of reed huts, surrounded by the usual tall
fences, also of reeds. I suppose the population barely

exceeds 200. Here, as we wished to fill the rest
of our corn-sacks, we had another half-day's barter,
and the scenes I have before described were repeated.
I took several photographs at this place, some of
which turned out fairly well. The Bakurutse corn-
bins were full to overflowing, and we had small
trouble in getting what we required at very moderate
rates. We obtained also in the way of trade some
good curios, handsome skins of the river otter (*Lutra
inunguis*), hippopotami teeth, strips of hippo skin
nearly two inches thick, for whips, and other odds and
ends. It is not often that a waggon passes up the
Botletli, and the anxiety of these poor people to
acquire the most elementary articles of trade was
really touching. I had some trouble to get one of
the girls to stand to be photographed ; eventually a
bright-coloured cotton handkerchief worked the oracle
for me. The lady who thus honoured me with
a sitting from among a score of giggling damsels
was quite overcome by the magnificence of the
handkerchief (price, in Mafeking, 4d.). Next morning she sent me a bowl of Kaffir corn as a present,
to which I replied by a quantity of bread and jam
as she sat near me at dinner-time. Another morning she brought me a bowl of Kaffir-corn porridge.
I had to be very diplomatic over this. I tasted a
mouthful, and then, as I had springbok for breakfast—a far preferable dish—I watched my opportunity, and, when the lady's back was turned, gave
the stuff to my boys to eat, a plan I had to adopt
on other occasions. When we left this outspan I
presented the fair creature with some needles, cotton,
and a thimble, the whole of which, I grieve to say,
were annexed instantly by her very disreputable-

looking father. Dove and I used to hold levées from our waggon-boxes, exhibiting looking-glasses and other amusing trifles to never-wearying eyes. The odd grimaces and remarks made by these girls and children, on seeing their own astonished images in the glass, made us roar with laughter. An exhibition of photographs of my wife and children never failed to bring down the house.

All the Bakurutse women have a very unpleasant habit of shaving the head, leaving only a small circular patch of wool upon the crown. This they oil and pull out in kinks, so that it lies in a kind of circular fringe upon the top of the head. They are not, with some few exceptions, a good-looking race ; but many of them are tall and well set-up. In fact, we noticed all along the Botletli that the people as a whole, whether Makalaka, Moteti, Bakurutse, Makoba, or Batauana, were strong, hardy, and well-developed. It is possible that fever, which kills a good many, takes off the weakly and leaves the strong. It must be remembered, too, that all these people are well nurtured ; they grow excellent crops of mealies and Kaffir corn, as well as pumpkins, melons, and tobacco ; they have plenty of milk, and the river and the veldt supply them with fish and game. The lot of these Lake River people in truth is a far happier one than that of the teeming thousands of poor in our own great cities. They have perennial sunshine, a fire when they need it, and plenty to eat and drink. Of late years they have been little vexed by war. Small wonder, then, that these Africans are merry and light-hearted. I gathered from Masinya that his sept, the Bakurutse, were in old days a not unimportant branch of the Bechuana people, allied, if I remember rightly, to the Bamangwato. Many years ago, however, they became broken by wars, and have since sunk to a mere clan or sept, tributary to Khama. So sunken are they, indeed, in the tribal scale that the Bamangwato appear to rank them very much with the Vaal-pense or Bakalahari, who exist throughout the desert. The granaries of these people are worthy of note. They consist of huge urn-shaped receptacles made of strong and beautifully plaited grass, standing about four feet high, and are perfectly weather-proof. When filled with grain the top is fastened up with clay, and collections of several of these curious granaries are enclosed in thorn fences close to the village.

As usual, we were awake at early dawn on the morning of July 19, and hearing the "honk, honk" of geese among the trees close by, we soon bundled into our clothes and sallied out. Close to this outspan, lying among a grove of giraffe acacia trees, was a fine vlei or lagoon, fed by the river, and now rapidly rising. From this some Egyptian geese had paid us a visit. We had no trouble in securing a brace between us, and then, Dove having also shot a couple of duck, we breakfasted. These geese rather astonished us by settling in trees, a fact in natural history we were not prepared for.

We rode down to the river—about a mile away—after breakfast, to try for a lechwē. We had a day of exciting sport, but of rather unlucky incident. The result was one ram; as a matter of right we should have had two at least, the crocodiles robbing us of another.

HOME LIFE AT MASINYA'S KRAAL—NGAMILAND

We had with us two Bakurutse, who led us straight down to an angle of the river, where we could see a small troop of lechwē feeding not far from the reeds. Spreading out a little, we gradually closed up, and galloping on hard, flat, alluvial ground, got right among them. Jumping off, we fired at about fifty yards, and each hit a buck hard. Dove's, a fine ram, fell to the shot, but was quickly up and tearing away for the river about two hundred yards distant. Following up quickly with the hunters, they saw the ram stagger and fall again at the water's edge, and felt sure of their quarry. The lechwē, however, struggled to his feet again and plunged into the river, where he stood, evidently very sick, up to his neck in water. The Bakurutse ran in to finish him, and were just in the act of thrusting their assegais into him, when with a mighty swirl of the water a crocodile snapped away the buck from under their very noses, and dragged him below the surface. As Dove said, the two hunters came flying from the river in a very panic of fright, and their danger had no doubt been very great. They saw neither crocodile nor lechwē again. While this scene was enacting, I was following the other wounded buck, which, however, swam a lagoon and escaped into the reed beds.

We hit off a troop of fine rams a little later near a chain of lagoons, and, driving them in front of us towards the mainland, forced them across some shallows, through which they plunged amid showers of spray, diamond-tinted by the strong sunlight. After much manœuvring and several shots, by one of which a buck was hit, we forced two old rams on to a tongue of open flat, and tried our hardest to

drive them right away from the river towards our
camp and run them down. We raced them for two
miles on end, and found them possessed of extraordinary speed and bottom. One of these rams had
had its left horn shot clean off by a bullet from
Dove's rifle. They ran and carried themselves much
like red-deer, occasionally bounding into the air in
gallant fashion. We did our best to prevent them
gaining their point—another patch of reedy marsh—
but just failed. One of the two rams left wounded
this morning was secured later on, and the head
brought into camp by the Bakurutse.

The lechwē (*Cobus lechē*) is a stout handsome
antelope, half as big and heavy again as a good
fallow buck, carrying a handsome, well-rounded head,
and having a very thick coat of bright yellowish-
brown hair. All the waterbucks are distinguished
by this thickness of coat, but the lechwē and its first
cousin, the still rarer situtunga, or nakong (Speke's
antelope), are further distinguished by the elongated
feet and the bare patch of dark, smooth skin (not
covered with hair as in other antelopes), lying between the hoof and the dew-claws. The horns, borne
only by the male, are stout, strongly annulated
almost to the tips, and incline first backward then
forward to the points. When first surprised, they
will trot slowly, carrying the head very low down
in a most uncouth manner, but when in full gallop,
the horns are laid back and the head is carried very
gallantly. At present, I believe only one specimen
of the lechwē has been brought alive to Europe.
They are the most tenacious of life of all the antelopes ; they carry away wounds that would ensure
collapse to much larger game, and when seized

bellow like a lusty calf. Although they always be-take themselves to water and reeds when pursued, they rarely face the open river, and the ram first wounded by Dove in the morning must have been sore put to it to have tempted fate and the croco-diles.

Next morning we strolled about the vlei near camp, shooting ducks and geese, and admiring the many beautiful forms of bird life. Close to our camp were to be found, among the trees or by the water, rollers of two kinds (*Coracias nævia* and *Coracias caudata*), hornbills, Rüppell's parrots, wood-peckers, shrikes, kingfishers, francolins, many kinds of finches, and innumerable waterfowl. There were many black and white kingfishers (*Ceryle rudis*) about our lagoon. This neatly-plumaged bird, with its black and white body, silvery breast and stomach—the breast marked by two jetty bands—and crested head, is, I think, quite the boldest fisherman I have seen. He will hover hawk like a good height in air, and then fall like a stone into the water, raising quite a splash about him. This dive he will repeat time after time. I note that when two of these birds meet they have a sweet interchange of voice, not unlike the chippering of a small songster. Another inter-esting but extremely tiresome bird, also black and white as to its plumage, is the spur-winged plover (*Hoplopterus albiceps*). Very frequently as one shoots by the water-side this bird will follow; some-times there are three or four at a time wheeling above one's head, and pestering one with the most worrying, unpleasant, metallic voices. It seems that they do this out of pure spite and annoy-ance, and with the direct object of spoiling sport.

Occasionally I have become so enraged that I have shot a peculiarly gross offender, for peace and quiet's sake. The sharp horny spur upon the point of the wing is a curious survival, shared also by the great spur-winged goose (*Plectropterus gambensis*). The Bechuanas have a very appropriate name for this plover—" Setula tsipi," or " iron hammer "—from the peculiar resemblance its cry bears to the clink of the blacksmith's hammer.

On the afternoon of this day, July 20, we rode across the flats, slept in our karosses, and tried the bush next morning for giraffe. In this we were unsuccessful, although we found spoor, and so rode back again across the hot weary plain for camp. We had not long quitted the forest before we sighted a good troop of Burchell's zebra, feeding quietly. We spread out in line and rode up to them. The troop, which consisted mostly of mares, with a yearling foal or two, was guarded by an old stallion, who stood sentinel nearest to us with his head up. Presently, turning half round, he gave some sort of signal, and the rest of the band galloped briskly off, curvetting and capering as they ran. After moving a few hundred yards the troop suddenly wheeled round in line to have a good look at us again. With their showy action, beautiful forms, and rich colouring, they presented a very noble appearance. Indeed, of the three kinds of zebra [1] now found in Africa, this zebra of the plains is by far the handsomest. Its perfect form, short ears, shapely head, and full black and white

---

[1] *Equus zebra* (the mountain zebra) ; *Equus Grévyii*, an Abyssinian variety of the mountain zebra ; and *Equus Burchellii*, of which I now speak. *Equus Chapmanii*, a so-called variety of Burchell's zebra, is identically the same animal with a few more stripings upon the legs.

mane—(hogged by nature just as are hogged the manes of horses in the old Greek bas-reliefs)— distinctly entitle it to this position.

These tactics of the zebras were displayed in a retreat of some miles, the old stallion always covering the rear, until the troop, outflanked by Dove, shot off to the right, and my chance came. I galloped hard to intercept them ; and, as they stood for a minute on seeing me in the line of flight, got a steady shot at two hundred yards. The bullet clapped as if on a barn door, and as the troop continued their flight, I saw one zebra turn away alone. Presently she stood again. I was soon within sixty yards, and with another bullet finished her. She proved to be a fine mare in beautiful coat, and her head and skin now decorate a room at home.

I quickly lighted a grass fire to attract the Bushmen, and, Joseph having cantered up, we set to work to skin the prize. Dove, who was thrown out, made for camp alone, securing on his way a springbok.

On the following day we were down at the lagoons after duck and geese, and after wading about for half the day nearly up to our armpits, came home with a huge bag. Having had good sport till July 28, we left Masinya's Kraal, and trekked for Sebituane's Drift, higher up the river.

After crossing the usual heated yellow plains, looking for all the world like an expanse of over-parched hayfields, and pied here and there with droves of springbok, we outspanned three miles off the river at some waterpits in the middle of open veldt. There were springbok grazing quietly around us as the sun set, and a big belt of tall leafy motjeerie trees, with their oak-like growth, standing on the further side of the river, gave welcome relief to the eye in that direction. The sunsets on the plains were very gorgeous; a vast amber vault of sky after the sun dipped; then a wonderful after-glow of still more brilliant yet translucent yellow. Below the light stretched the sea of grassy plain, now toned to a greyish-yellow, with the cattle, horses, and here and there a springbok, standing in sharp relief. Anon the yellow glow changes to a narrow arc of ruddy orange below a pale blue-green sky, and then darkness falls upon the solemn veldt, and the night plovers, jackals, and hyænas begin their cries. At this outspan, where we remained some time, we often heard the cry of zebras as they trekked to the river under cover of night. A good many wildebeest also came past not far from the waggons.

We were up very early on the morning of the 29th, prepared for another campaign against giraffe. After breakfast, just as the sun rose, Dove, standing on my waggon-box, looked out to the south-east for game, using a very powerful stalking-glass, which he rested on the waggon tilt. Half a mile away he saw, stringing across the veldt, a dark line of blue wilde-beest, evidently trekking from the river back to the flats. It was a most inspiring sight. There were about thirty-five of them, mostly full-grown bulls, many of them very heavy ones, as their massive shaggy fronts plainly indicated. Having enjoyed a prolonged inspection, we saddled-up hastily, buckled on spurs, got out our rifles, and went after them, the Bushmen following.

We rode quietly until within three hundred yards, when the herd became disturbed, and, tossing their heads and whisking their long tails, they lumbered off at a heavy gallop, which, however, is much faster than it looks. The heavy Roman-nosed, buffalo-like head, and the quantity of mane and hair about the neck, throat, and face all tend to create the wild and cumbrous aspect which the bulls of this singular antelope wear.

Dove and I were mounted to-day on our best nags, he on his favourite Dunboy—the mouse-coloured pony with black points—I on my good Marico chestnut, Giltboy ; and the ponies presently catching sight of the game, we touched them lightly with the spur and raced our hardest, hoping to get within hail of the gnu in one sharp spurt. As we ran side by side at full gallop, my comrade's nag unexpectedly put his foot in a hole, and, with his rider, came down a most imperial crowner. I pulled up for a second, but Dove, although half-stunned, motioned me to go on, and, as the Bushmen were running behind, I set my horse going again. After a long and most exciting chase, in which I only prevented the wildebeest from entering the bush by sending a bullet or two in front of them, thus turning them, I got within 250 yards as they stood, and hit a good bull, which, after myself sustaining a heavy fall, I secured at short range. I found him a fine full-grown bull, with a good head. Meanwhile Dove and the Bushmen had come up, and, having cut off the head for preservation, I left the boys to bring in the meat. Dove was in great pain from an injury to his side, and although we rode on and picked up the troop again with the idea of turning the wildebeest to my comrade, we had no more luck that day.

The brindled gnu or blue wildebeest is assuredly one

of the most eccentric of nature's creations, even in Africa. Some naturalists have catalogued its points in this wise—the head of a buffalo, body and tail of a horse, with the legs of an antelope. This is not accurate, for the blue wildebeest and its grotesque cousin, the white-tailed gnu, although standing alone in the animal kingdom, are true antelopes. This animal (*Catoblepas gorgon*, kokoon of the Bechuanas) is in colour of a bluish-drab, having brindles or stripes of a darker shade upon the neck and fore-quarters. It can hardly be classed as dangerous game; yet a wounded bull is not to be approached carelessly on foot, his sharp hook-like horns rendering him an awkward customer, as many a slain dog has testified. The range of this antelope extends widely over Central South Africa, but is, curiously enough, not prolonged north of the Equator. The white-tailed gnu (*Catoblepas gnu*, black wildebeest of the Dutch), now approaching extinction, was much more circumscribed in its habitat. It was formerly inordinately plentiful on the karroos of Cape Colony and the plains of the Orange Free State, but seldom ranged north of the Vaal River. On the other hand, the brindled gnu was rarely found south of the Orange River, even in the good old days when game swarmed in countless thousands.

Gnu or gnoo is merely the old Hottentot name of the white-tailed species, which subsequently clung to both animals. The Hottentot designation for the brindled gnu was *Kaop*, signifying Baas or master. The blue wildebeest has plenty of pace and great staying power, and it takes a good horse indeed to run into a troop.

From this point in the trek Dove was confined by

his injuries (a broken rib) to the waggon for some days, and could not bear to sit a horse for a fortnight. Our journey to Lake Ngami was therefore abandoned, and I contented myself with making expeditions with Joseph and the Bushmen in various directions, in which we had excellent sport with giraffe, wildebeest, zebra, and springbok. It was a keen disappointment not to be able to set eyes upon the lake itself, after coming so far. By riding hard for four days, I might have reached it on horseback (it would have taken nearly a fortnight by the waggon), but my friend was seriously ill, and hardly in a position to be thus left.

I walked from this outspan to the river on the day following Dove's injury, and striking it not far from Sebituane's Drift, came to a high bank, below which a broad and stately stream, three hundred yards in breadth (a stream surpassing every other waterway south of the Zambesi) flowed in deep majestic volume slowly to the south-east. Here and there a crocodile might be discerned floating log-like on the surface. Some Makoba fishermen put across in a dug-out canoe from the reeds on the further side, and, having my camera with me, I seized the opportunity to take some photographs of these singular people, and of this beautiful reach on the Botletli, hitherto virgin to the camera. These Makobas (sometimes also called Bayeiye, especially near the Zambesi) are here tributary to Khama and the Lake Chief, and are essentially a race of fishermen and boatmen. They live in small reed villages upon the banks of the river, and are most expert fishers, whether with net or with hook and line. I found them baiting their hooks with mice and a kind of

small rat—a novel kind of lure to me.   Here they
catch principally the barbel I have mentioned, mullet,
and a kind of bream.

Near Sebituane's Drift—where Livingstone's favourite chief, Sebituane, crossed the river in his
conquering career northward—Khama's country ends
upon the south bank of the river, and the territory
of the Lake Chief, Moremi, begins.   Moremi died
soon after our sojourn on the Botletli, and Sekhome,
his young son, now reigns in his stead.

As to the mysterious overflow of the Botletli in
midwinter—the dry season in Africa—the capabili-
ties and prospects of its immense and undoubtedly
rich alluvial lands, and the various tribes upon its
course, they are vast subjects, and require space
whereon to enlarge.   It is certain that the Botletli
and Ngami country have a great future in the production of grain, tobacco, cotton, rice, coffee, sugar,
and other crops.   The people are friendly, peaceable,
and fairly industrious after their lights.   Sooner or
later it must fall to the lot of Ngamiland to be exploited by Europeans; but in this exploitation the
hard fact has to be faced that, for at least four
months in the year, fever of a nature very deadly
to the white man prevails.   It is true that malaria
yields to the advances of civilisation; but the fever-
stricken districts of Ngamiland and the Zambesi
Valley are hardly likely, I fear, to become portions
of a habitable South Africa within the lifetime of
living people.

We had, on the whole, fair sport (thirty-eight head
of game in a month's shooting, besides a great variety
of feathered game), but it must be remembered that
the nobler animals, even in these remote regions, are

THE BOTLETLI RIVER — NGAMILAND
(*Taken near Sebituane's Drift*)

fast disappearing, and can only now be obtained by long days of severe toil under a burning sun, and by downright hard work. South Africa is no longer the undisturbed playground of a superabundant fauna, and each year sees the gallant game more and more difficult of access.

CHAPTER XVII.

NOTES ON THE PURSUIT OF GAME

Brindled gnu and Burchell's zebra—Habits modified by persecution—
Blue wildebeest hunting—Perplexed game—Extraordinary vitality—
Burchell's zebras—A hot chase—Touching episode—A hunting fall—
Pace of zebras—Scorching ride—Welcome water—Quagga quite
extinct—Remarks on zebras—The lechwē—Hartebeest—Koodoo—
Eland—Giraffe—Springbok—Science of spooring—Remarks on spoor
of various game animals.

HUNTERS' luck, which, of course, rests mainly upon
a man's own powers, is at the same time dependent
to some extent on the nature of the country in
which he is shooting, and of the game themselves.
For instance, if brindled gnu and Burchell's zebras
are found upon broad open plains, at some distance
from the bush in which they shelter themselves,
they will nowadays make straight away in a tail-on-
end gallop for the bush, without affording the hunter
much chance of getting near. In such a case long
shots, after the Boer manner, fired so as to strike
somewhere about the middle of the troop as it gallops
away from you, are all that can be employed to secure
a head of game. The hunter jumps off his horse
quickly, judges his distance as well as may be—
he will get the elevation with very little practice—
and puts in shot after shot. The usual result is that
some one of the quarry is "winged" and drops
behind, after which, with care and judgment, it may
be secured.

Brindled gnu (blue wildebeest), like most other South African antelopes, take an infinity of killing, and, with a broken leg or a bullet through the middle of the barrel, will run on for miles before they are brought to bag, sometimes, even, getting away altogether. Burchell's zebra, on the other hand, seem to be with the eland the softest and most easily disabled of the larger game. A broken leg will usually bring one of these handsome creatures very quickly to a standstill; and to body shots also they are far more vulnerable than members of the tough and tenacious antelope family. I have found that if either of these animals (gnu and zebra) are met with grazing near the edge of the bush and forest to which they fly for sanctuary, they are far less timid, and can be easily approached. I am speaking more particularly of the habits of game near the Botletli River, Ngamiland, where immense grassy plains bordering upon the river are, at a distance of some miles, fringed by the bush and forest of the North Kalahari region. It is, I think, an undoubted fact that in recent years the habits of plain-frequenting game, such as the brindled gnu and Burchell's zebra, have been much modified by contact with firearms. In old books of travel these animals are constantly spoken of as denizens, pure and simple, of broad and open plains, such as the flats of the Orange Free State and the high veldt of the Transvaal. I am inclined to think that a plethora of firearms and much persecution have changed the habits of these animals, and that they are nowadays much more frequenters of bushy and semi-bushy country than they used to be.

Some notes from my diary of August will perhaps

give a fair idea of the habits and paces of these
animals.   On August 1 we were outspanned at some
waterpits in the middle of the plains south of the
Botletli.   Dove being kept to his waggon, I rode with

HEAD OF BRINDLED GNU (BLUE WILDEBEEST) BULL, BOTLETLI
RIVER PLAINS, 1890.

Joseph (whom I mounted for the day) across the plains
in a westerly direction.   We saw plenty of springbok,
but fired no shot, expecting to find heavier quarry.
A Bakurutse native went with us to spoor and find
game.   After an hour's steady march we came to

a swelling in the plain, from whence we were in sight of the bush and forest. Away between us and the dusky line of bush we instantly noticed some dark forms, which, after a steady inspection through my field-glasses, I at once recognised as " kokoon "—blue wildebeest. There was only a small troop of them—about a dozen all told—and a heavy-fronted old bull was keeping guard at the end of the line. We now took a big circuit, and finally got between the game and the bush — from which they were grazing about half-a-mile away—and then walked our horses quietly towards them. The old bull put up his head once or twice, but seemed little disturbed until we were within 500 yards, when, at a signal from him, the troop broke away at a heavy lumbering gallop, upon which we put in spurs and raced after them. The veldt just at this place was splendid galloping, and, for a wonder, free from holes, and Dunboy—entering, as he always did, heartily into the chase—carried me at such a pace that I was enabled to head the game, now boring to the right hand, and prevent them from making their point in the bush. Seeing this, the gnu pulled up, perplexed, at 300 yards, when I jumped off, fired a shot, and missed. As the bullet whizzed by them, the game broke round to the left, and shortly turned again for the bush, right across Joseph's front. The native, who had been following me in an oblique direction, now rode hard at them, and as they swept by him, within sixty yards, jumped off and fired. As the report of his Martini rattled out I was de-lighted to see a young bull, about the middle of the troop, turn a complete somersault and lie prone. It turned out that the bullet had smashed both his forelegs below the knee, completely disabling him. Meanwhile, I was tearing along after the game, and, getting within hail, jumped off, fired, and heard the tell-tale thud of a very palpable hit. Again, as I pressed my pony to his hardest gallop, the troop broke off from their point and swung round to the open veldt, giving Joseph another long shot or two, which he failed to make use of. Once more the now distracted yet obstinate wildebeests swerved round for the bush, galloping at their best pace. Again I was enabled to cut them off, and my pony, flying along over the hard even ground, took me rapidly alongside the troop as they passed me in an oblique line. The grand old man bull was leading, four fine cows followed, and the rest—yearling calves—swept at their heels. I jumped off, fired at the best cow, and struck her well behind the shoulder; she staggered, but went on. I fired another shot, but my pony, happening to tug at the cord by which his bridle was fastened to my belt, spoilt my aim, and the bullet went wide. By the time I had mounted again the gnu were 300 yards away, and were entering the bush. Joseph coming up, we took up the blood spoor, and tracked it for some three miles into the forest. The bullet had evidently raked the lungs; occasionally the wildebeest had stood under a thorn tree and coughed up pieces of bright red lung, which lay among the dark patches of blood beneath. Yet, such is the vitality of these animals, the poor beast had gone on and even regained its comrades, who had now, as was apparent by the spoor, fallen to a fast walking pace. As the spooring process seemed likely to be long and tedious, we now returned to the plain, with the object of setting a Bushman to follow up and secure the wounded buck, and bring in the head and meat. On reaching the young bull shot by Joseph, we found one of our Bakurutse men busily employed in skinning it and cutting up the meat. The sun was broiling, and, having taken the head, skin, and as much meat as we could carry, we rode off leisurely for the waggons, which were reached at 1.30 P.M. On this occasion the foolish persistency of the wildebeest, in pushing always directly for the forest after we had circumvented them, had delivered them into our hands. If they had straightway raced off for a distant point, as I have seen them do from the river side of the flats, they would have had a good start, would possibly have lost not a single member of their troop, and would assuredly have got clean away from us. As it was, by cutting them off here and there, we had them thoroughly bewildered and perplexed, and were enabled to chase and turn them repeatedly within a radius of two miles. No doubt the hard, level veldt assisted us, and we were mounted on excellent ponies.

On the next morning, August 2, I was off again early, attended, as usual, by Joseph. My chestnut, Giltboy, carried me; Joseph was mounted on a bay pony, while a Bakurutse undertook the duties of spooring. We rode off for the same point as on the previous day, intending to look for giraffe or koodoo, whose spoor we had seen abundantly in the forest. But, curiously enough, on reaching the point where yesterday we had seen the brindled gnu, our eyes at once fell again on the dark forms of "poloholo" (game). Looking intently through my glass, I saw they were Burchell's zebra. Repeating our tactics of yesterday, we cautiously swept round, and presently, having put ourselves between them and the forest, we slanted our nags quietly in their direction. The zebras stood on the side of a gentle wave in the

HEAD OF BURCHELL'S ZEBRA (MARE), BOTLETLI RIVER PLAINS, 1890.

grassy plain. Between us and them some hundreds of springbok were feeding, and, as we approached, these dainty creatures began to trot in their elegant way towards the larger game. The zebras, fourteen in number, looked puzzled, and stared with their heads up, and a big old stallion on the right was manifestly somewhat uneasy. At length the spring- boks started at a canter, occasionally bounding high in air from all four legs, after their marvellous fashion, and displaying the white blaze on their rumps ; and the zebras, whisking their tails and tossing their handsome heads, setting off at the same time, the intermingled game bounded away before us in a charming confusion. It was a pretty sight indeed. The springboks swept away for the open plain, and were soon far out of reach. The zebras —as had done the wildebeest—bore right-handed, trying for the bush. Joseph and I now raced after them with the object of preventing this manœuvre, and, after a few minutes, the handsome animals, seeing themselves cut off, wheeled sharp round, paused a second, and then at their fastest gallop made to run the gauntlet between Joseph and myself, heading straight for the bush. My hunter and I were separated by some 250 yards, and as the game swept past we fired almost together. Two loud claps proclaimed that the bullets had found a mark ; yet nothing fell, and the striped beauties swept on. I was immediately in the saddle again, and by dint of hard riding managed to turn the troop, which now ran parallel with the bush, all going great guns. We now entered upon a long tail-on-end chase, and, getting into soft veldt much riddled with holes, the zebras, which hitherto we had gained upon when riding hard, gradually edged further from us. After running a couple of miles or so, a young stallion, that had been hit by one of us—which, it is impos- sible to say—turned out from the troop. I saw he was bleeding from the shoulder and done for, and, telling Joseph to secure him, pressed steadily on after the main troop. It is a curious fact that, after Joseph had forced this young zebra from its fellows, it suddenly seemed to make up its mind that his horse must be one of its own species, and, turning round, trotted up in the most confiding manner possible. It was too severely wounded to be driven to the waggons with any prospect of saving its life, and this touching little episode had, perforce, to be concluded by Joseph's inexorable rifle, which finished the poor colt as it stood.

I rode on at a gallop for another two miles, some 300 yards in rear of the main troop, hoping to see another wounded one drop behind, or, as sometimes happens, that the zebras might perchance wheel round to reconnoitre; until, presently, Giltboy put his foot in a hole, and we came crash down together. Giltboy, who was beginning to feel the long gallop, fell on his head, and was up less quickly than myself; I therefore picked up my rifle, put up the sights for 400 yards, and fired two or three unavailing shots at the retreating game. Then, remounting the chestnut, I set him going again, and followed on. The chase was now hopeless; I rode for another mile, and then, seeing the zebras make their point in some dense bush fringing the plain, I turned and rode back along the spoor. It was easy to see from the blood marks that another wounded one had got away; and shortly afterwards, meeting a Makalaka who was returning from the bush with a snared steinbok, I set him and his friends on the blood spoor, which they confidently looked to make good; but I never heard the result of their efforts, as the waggons had meanwhile trekked on.

During the early part of this hunt, on sound veldt, we galloped at least as fast as the zebras, and turned and drove them from their points, much as we had driven the wildebeests on the day previously. On softer ground, however, and with a fair start and a straight-away course, the zebras had the best of us ; and on their own ground, and under such conditions, they will, no doubt, more often than not beat the average hunting pony, handicapped, as it usually is, by a heavy man and his accoutrements. Pitted at level weights—or rather with the horse carrying no weights at all—there can, I think, be no shadow of doubt that a decent South African hunting pony would run down over and over again the best Burchell's zebra that ever scoured the plains. It is no light matter to carry, and carry successfully, day after day, a man of twelve stone, a heavy double rifle, bandolier filled with Martini cartridges, saddle, bridle, head-stall and knee-halter, water-bottle, and etceteras. And yet, under a burning sun, sometimes without drinking water for two days, our 14-hand hunting ponies did this service gallantly, and with never-failing pluck and zest. One cannot sufficiently admire the hardy and most useful breed of South African horseflesh.

Having taken the skin and some of the meat of the dead zebra, we set off on our march for the waggons, which were now trekking back for Masinya's kraal. From 11 o'clock A.M. until 3 we rode steadily over the parched, yellow, shadeless plains. The heat was intense ; we had emptied my water-bottle in the morning, and we were thoroughly grilled that afternoon. At last we approached the river, and presently coming to a place where the rising flood was pouring a cool rivulet down a shallow channel, we whipped off our clothes and lay down with our heads to the softly flowing stream, so that the rivulet just covered us. Never shall I forget that most luxurious sensation; and the spreading Botletli will by me ever be gratefully remembered, if only for the relief it gave on that burning African afternoon. The ponies drank as I never saw horses drink before or since. Riding on, we picked up the waggons at Masinya's just at sundown.

Before I finish with this subject of Burchell's zebras, let me again say a word against the misleading practice, in vogue among so many travellers, of calling them quaggas. The true quagga is, as I have shown, now quite extinct. I will grant that up-country hunters more often than not refer to Burchell's zebras as quaggas. But this is a familiar and well-known mistake, or rather piece of carelessness, made in a country where the real distinction between the animals is known and recognised. When, however, distinguished travellers, such as Lord Randolph Churchill, relate in page after page of their books that they have been hunting or shooting quaggas, it gives rise to misapprehension, and even English naturalists are led to doubt whether the real quagga may not after all yet be in the life. Mr. Selous, of course, never makes this mistake; and his book will be found to contain frequent references to the Burchell's zebra, never to the quagga.

It is quite time that naturalists once for all realised the hard fact that the Equus quagga—a beast striped only upon the head, neck, and shoulders—is now as extinct as the dodo. Burchell's zebra (*Equus burchellii*) is still fairly plentiful in South Africa, north of the tropic of Capricorn ; and, beyond the Zambesi, immense herds are still found in places where the game has not been disturbed. The mountain-abiding zebra (*Equus zebra*) still lingers on the sierras of Cape Colony and along the Drakensberg, but year by year waxes scarcer, and bids fair to become extinct, even in its northern stronghold, mountainous Abyssinia, long before its congener, Burchell's zebra.

With the latter quadruped English people are very familiar in the gardens of the Zoological Society ; and it is a pleasure to find, during the last year or two, the rarer mountain zebra in the adjacent boxes, so that the two species may be compared.

On the South African veldt there is no more beautiful or characteristic form than Burchell's zebra, and, except for the purposes of procuring specimens and killing meat for the camp, it seems a pity to slay such peculiarly equine beasts. The condition in which these animals are usually found is very remarkable. Their coats are clean, shining, and, as it were, well groomed. The feet (of which I brought home specimens) are perfectly formed, small, elegant, and hard as flint ; the legs invariably clean, wiry, and free from blemish. If these zebras were not so often found in high condition, they would, no doubt, prove much tougher opponents in the chase than they do. In the wild state, when untroubled by hunters, they may be usually seen feeding or pacing quietly about, or, in the heat of afternoon, lying down. They often, however, have to make long nocturnal journeys to water, which, as a rule, they drink once in twenty-four hours.

After reading the books of Baldwin, Selous, and

2 B

others, we had scarcely expected to find the lechwē
waterbuck far from water and reed beds. As a
matter of fact, we saw them often feeding on the

HEAD OF LECHWĒ WATERBUCK (RAM), BOTLETLI RIVER, 1890.

alluvial flats, a mile and a half from water. Although
they will always fly to water when hunted, they
can gallop a tremendous pace ; and it takes a very

good horse to run them down, even if, as sometimes happens, they can be circumvented, and driven across the hard, sun-baked flats. Splashing through the shallow lagoons in a series of bounds, as they will do when pursued, driving about them showers of spray and broken water, they offer a most pleasing picture to the hunter's eye. Although seldom, from fear of crocodiles, venturing into the deep river, they are excellent swimmers, as I have found to my cost.

Hartebeest (*Alcelaphus caama*), the most difficult —almost impossible—of South African game to run down in fair chase, will often offer a shot by their habit of wheeling round suddenly in a body to survey their pursuers. This I take to be a mere effort of curiosity ; but, in the case of such fleet and untiring game, it is a singularly providential one— for the hunter. On bare open plains these fine antelopes are difficult of approach ; but in the grassy woodlands of Bechuanaland, among the kameeldoorn trees amid which they are often found, they can be approached and shot much more easily. The smooth machine-like gallop of these antelopes when really extended—so different to the high lopping canter of their slower paces—is, to my mind, the perfection of ferine motion. I am told, however, that the tsesseby (*Alcelaphus lunatus*), a near kinsman of the hartebeest, often called by Boer hunters the Zulu hartebeest, which I have not seen, is an even finer mover. The hartebeest, too, is marvellously tough and tenacious of life. The flesh is palatable, and in much request for bültong. Like the gemsbok and eland, the hartebeest seems to be independent of water for much of the year.

The koodoo (*Strepsiceros kudu*), perhaps the handsomest and most characteristic of all South African antelopes, is, in its own peculiar domain of mountain and forest, a difficult beast to account for. Despite its bulk, its speed and activity give it great advantages, especially to the stalker on foot, encumbered with a rifle, and under a hot sun. But when found in fairly open country, the koodoo can be run down on horseback with no great difficulty. This antelope also seems able to exist for long periods without water.

The eland (*Oreas Canna*), from its immense bulk and weight, and the fatness it usually attains, falls a ready victim to the hunter; and from this reason, and the extraordinary zest with which it has been pursued these two hundred years, is now becoming very scarce, and is not to be found until the recesses of the North Kalahari are reached. Unless a troop of lean, light cows is happened upon, the eland can be usually run into, on a fair horse, within a mile or two. After the first canter they break into a slinging trot, and the hunter finds no difficulty in picking out his quarry, riding up to it, and shooting it from the saddle. Light cows, however, especially in mountainous country, are capable of giving considerable trouble. Considering their immense bulk, the activity of elands is wonderful. I have seen heavy cows, when chased, buck lightly over bushes and timber as high as a good-sized gate. In my judgment, the eland is by far the most vulnerable and most easily bagged (once found) of the African fauna. It is soon exhausted, and falls readily to the bullet. Plethoric old bulls—which, by the way, have been known to attain as much as a height of nineteen hands at the withers, and a weight of 2000 lbs.—are most easily ridden into, and will even fall dead from heart disease without a shot. When found near the waggons, they can be driven right into camp before being shot.

With giraffe the wisest course is to race at them, when seen, at top speed; force your pony close up to their tails in the first mile or two of chase, and put in your shots, firing from the saddle. Solid Martini-Henry bullets are desirable for this thick-skinned game, and with the short bodies of these gigantic quadrupeds the bullet, if planted somewhere in the region of the tail or rump, penetrates readily to a vital part. If a leg is broken, the giraffe, as I have found by experience, is quite disabled, and can be easily finished off. In open country, where, however, nowadays the camelopard is not often found, it is not a difficult matter to run up to a giraffe if your nag is good, and you are willing to ride hammer and tongs; but in the dense, thorny bush country where they love to roam, it requires some determination, a strong cord coat, and no little steering, to follow this tall game amid trees and the frightful thorns and jungles through which they crash so easily. Nothing in nature can, in my judg-ment, equal the first sight of giraffes in the wild state; and the rare spectacle of these beautiful giants feeding busily and undisturbed in their remote native haunts is unsurpassable. A giraffe can sometimes be singled out from the troop and driven right up to the waggon and there shot. For this masterly opera-tion the wind must be in the right place, and the game has to be humoured; and the novice will pro-bably find that he requires some considerable veldt experience before he can successfully accomplish the feat.

The springbok—of old so abundant that the Hottentots often spoke of them as "their sheep"—is still moderately plentiful in Cape Colony. In South Bechuanaland and the Transvaal they have been pretty well exterminated, along with other game; but towards the Kalahari and northwards they are again numerous. On the Botletli flats we always had some hundreds within view of our waggons, and one or two were brought into camp on most days for our special food supply. Springbok venison cannot, I think, be beaten.

Instead of galloping them on horseback, we found it a far more efficacious plan to get off our horses as we approached a knot of these antelopes, walk very quietly towards them, leading the horse, and manoeuvre a little until one or two or more were got together—into a "klompje," as a Boer would say—when at 200 to 300 yards a buck could usually be secured. If the distance was too great, and the bullet missed, the springbok would usually run a short distance and stand again, when, with care and deliberation, the same tactics could be repeated. My companion, Dove, using a .450 Henry Express rifle, was extraordinarily successful at this shooting.

Although the old days, when millions of these most elegant and characteristic antelopes covered the plains and karroos from beneath the Zwartbergen of Cape Colony to Lake Ngami and beyond, are past, it will be many a long year before the last of them is seen. In Cape Colony, and parts of the Orange Free State, timely preservation is doing much to restore the sadly thinned ranks of the springbok.

On the great saltpans round about the Lake River we always found these graceful creatures in some numbers. They appeared to have a great liking for these smooth and dazzling expanses ; and their dainty forms could not be better displayed than in such a region. No horse, and not many greyhounds, can run into a springbok in fair chase ; and, when hunting on horseback, they are only secured by driving, and then cutting across the unerring line which they usually take.

The science of spooring or tracking is extremely interesting. All South African natives have this art in a high degree ; but the Bushmen and inhabitants of the game countries to the north, who still live much by the chase, bring it to perfection. The Boers, from an intimate knowledge of game extending over more than two centuries, are also very expert. The average European eye at first finds much difficulty in distinguishing even between the varieties of antelope. A little practice, of course, overcomes this ; the difficulty then arises of detecting new from old spoor. This difficulty the white man can never hope to completely overcome, unless he is content to live for years in the wilds and study closely the habits of game.

The imprint of the giraffe is immense, and, when first seen, rather puzzling. Dove and I first met with the spoor of this gigantic game crossing the waggon road between Mesa and Maqua. It was hard ground, and the spoor was not very distinct. At that time we were not thinking of giraffe, and the immense footprints—something like those of an elongated and colossal cow's foot—quite puzzled us.

All the antelopes, even the large ones, have extremely elegant spoors. Perhaps the most beautiful is that of the koodoo, which resembles very much the shape of the heart in a pack of cards. The harte-beest's foot is sharper at the point; the blue wilde-beest's larger and easily recognised. And, considering its size and bulk, the spoor of the magnificent gems-bok is singularly neat and dainty.

The eland's spoor, as I have said, is not unlike that of small cattle—the neat Alderney for instance. The lechwē, especially in the soft muddy ground in which it loves to stand, is instantly recognisable by the imprint of the singularly elongated foot, so dif-ferent from all other antelopes except the situtunga. The mountain-loving klipspringer has very rigid pasterns and very hollow feet, and always moves upon the *points* instead of the flat of its hoofs. Its spoor, therefore, whenever it comes off the rocky places it usually frequents, is easily "spotted." The klipspringer's hollow foot and habit of moving on the tips of its toes are manifestly developments due to its rock-leaping proclivities. This little beauty springs about the giddiest cliffs and precipices in the most daring manner, and will leap through mid-air on to some tiny, isolated pinnacle in a way calculated to make even a wild goat shudder.

The springbok's spoor is neat and beautiful, but of all the smaller antelopes the tiny steinbok's is, I think, the most perfect. The dainty impressions left by this diminutive creature in the clear sands by some desert pool are absolutely perfect; they might well be those of a fairy fauna.

The soft round pads of the lion and leopard are always interesting; the jackal's and hyæna's are somewhat doglike. The spoor of the porcupine is at first puzzling to the uninitiated, especially when found among the tracks of hyænas and jackals. I saved specimens of the feet of nearly all the game we shot—from the giraffe to the steinbok—and they are by no means among the least interesting of our trophies.

CHAPTER XVIII.

THE WATERWAY AND WATERFOWL OF THE BOTLETLI RIVER

QUITE one of our pleasantest outspans on the Botletli River was Masinya's Kraal, which we reached, as I have said, on the 18th July. The native name of this Bakurutse village, which lies about a mile from the river, is actually Sangeleko ; but to most travellers passing up the river it is familiar as Masinya's, from the name of its headman.

The spot where we elected to pitch our camp for a week was in its way perfect. It lay amid a charming grove, on a little rise a few feet above the naked plains, which stretched, a blinding expanse of pale yellow, far as the eye could reach to the south and west. Our waggons were drawn up on either side of a spreading camel-thorn tree, which afforded a scant yet grateful shade from the blazing tropical sun. Hard by was the great lagoon, now being rapidly filled by a deep channel connected with the

OUR OUTSPAN AT MASINYA'S KRAAL—NGAMILAND

rising river. Duck, geese, wigeon, and teal of many
kinds resorted thither, and if we required a change
of scene and sport, there were other and larger lakes
and rivulets a little farther away by the Botletli,
where the rising waters were to be seen black with
fowl.

Our outspan lay nearer to the river than Masinya's
by half-a-mile. It is not advisable, for more reasons
than one, to be in too close proximity to a native
village ; and, even as it was, we had usually a fair
number of visitors squatted about our camp, all
eager to hear news of the dim outer world and to
feast their eyes on the abounding treasures and
curiosities contained in the white men's waggons.

The Bakurutse behaved extremely well, however,
and during the whole of this and a subsequent
sojourn on the return trek, we missed not a single
article from our equipment. No doubt the fact that
Masinya and his people are tributaries of the great
chief Khama, and that some of Khama's chief hunters
accompanied us, had something to do with this exceptional behaviour.

After the parched and trying trek across the
thirstland, this outspan, with its pleasant shade and
the abundance of water and of game, was a very
Capua to our men. The belles of the kraal at once
set their caps (figuratively, of course) at our younger
boys—the leaders, cooks, and horse-boy ; in the
evenings native dances, got up for their especial
benefit, were almost nightly held, and the still air
resounded until early morning with the monotonous
chants sung on these occasions. For ourselves, each
morning we rose and breakfasted before dawn, and,
after a long hot day in the saddle, we were not sorry,

having dined or supped usually at five or six o'clock, to turn into our waggons at an early hour. Unless I had to change and put away my photographic plates and negatives, for which purpose I made a dark room of my waggon, I was usually asleep by nine o'clock. Sometimes we had turned in by seven or eight o'clock —once, after an unusually hard day after giraffe, by 5.30—for Europeans an unconscionably early hour.

Usually, if we were back in camp early enough, we had a turn at the duck in our lagoon 200 yards away, and invariably returned with a few couple of fowl (just now in magnificent condition) as a valuable aid to our flesh-pots. Round the shores of the lagoon were always to be found numbers of that water-loving game bird, *Francolinus adspersus*, of which we generally shot a brace or two. But the duck, and especially the yellow-billed duck, were at this time so fat and so delicious, that our breakfasts and dinners usually alternated between them and springbok chops and fry—the latter the most tender and well-flavoured game meat to be found in all Southern Africa.

The springbok, which grazed in hundreds on the plains around, were at this time in higher condition than I ever remember them. Our hunter-cook Joseph was a capital *chef*, and his particular *morceaux*—double chops cut right through the loins— cooked in the frying-pan with tinned tomatoes, afforded the best tasted venison I think I have ever enjoyed. Our men and dogs revelled and waxed fat on a variety of fare; and in addition to giraffe meat and marrow-bones, which we ourselves enjoyed, they disposed with an equal relish of wildebeest, zebra, lechwē (none of which we cared for), and as many wildfowl as we chose to supply them with. The villagers from Masinya's, and the Masarwa Bushmen who spoored for us, also came in for their share of meat.

After the dry plains of Bechuanaland and the still more trying wastes of the Kalahari, the change to the vast water-system of the Botletli is great and welcome. The transformation is yet more enhanced by the sight of this great river rising so mysteriously in mid-winter—months after the rains have ceased —flooding the surrounding alluvial flats, filling up great lagoons and lakes, forming deep rivulets— almost rivers—and silently spreading its majestic way to the drier and lower reaches, until the vast reed swamps of the so-called Lake Komadau are attained, and the river course is ended. In extraordinary seasons the waters penetrate even beyond Lake Komadau, and the ancient and now practically disused bed of the Botletli, which may be traced until lost in the wastes of the Great Makarrikarri Saltpans, is to a slight extent again filled.

Ever since Livingstone first penetrated hither in 1849, this wonderful inundation of the Botletli has puzzled the few travellers and explorers who have made their way to Lake Ngami.[1] I believe there can be no other explanation of this rise and overflow than the flooding during the rainy season of the immense marsh systems of the lower Okavango and the Tso, Mababē, and Tamalakan (sometimes called Tamunakle) rivers, the slow but steady flow (slow

---

[1] The Lake, or Lake Ngami, has no meaning for the natives of this region. They have only one name, 'Nghabe, for the great water, and we had some difficulty to make them comprehend our inquiries for "Lake Ngami."

manifestly from the excessive flatness of all this country) thence, from the slight tilt of the land, south-eastward, and the subsequent discharge early in winter—long after the rains have ceased—of the surplus waters of these systems, by means of the Tamalakan River, into the upper Botletli. Thence, still slowly yet unceasingly, the lower reaches of the river are filled up, and the surrounding country in many places—as near as Masinya's and T'Kom—is flooded for miles. The distance from the point where the Tamalakan discharges into the Botletli down to Lake Komadau is some 200 miles; but the actual course of the river along its windings is probably another thirty or forty more. From the mouth of the Tamalakan westward to Lake Ngami is about forty miles.

It is probable that subterraneous percolation from the marshes of the Chobe and Sunta rivers, as well as from the Okavango marshes, aids also in the volume of the Tamalakan's discharge. This subterraneous percolation plays, I have reason to think, a more considerable part in the country of the North Kalahari than many people imagine. As I have shown in a subsequent chapter, some of the waters of the " thirst-land "—notably the pits of Inkouane a hundred miles away in the desert—have been strengthened and recruited within recent years coincidently with an extraordinary rising of the Botletli.

It is worthy of remark that Lake Ngami itself, although connected with the Botletli by a sort of arm densely overgrown with tall reeds, has no part or share in this annual overflow, for which the Tamalakan and its upper systems are solely responsible. I often asked the natives along the river how they accounted for the inundation. They had only one reply — that a man under ground was responsible for it and sent the waters forth. At certain periods, when I suppose the flow of the Tamalakan is at its highest, the Botletli appears to run both ways, west towards Lake Ngami and east down its proper course. Livingstone long ago pointed out that this might possibly happen, and the phenomenon, if phenomenon it may be called, has, since his early discoveries, been witnessed, and is well known to the natives.

Mr. H. H. Johnston, in his excellent monograph on Livingstone, appears to be under the impression that the Botletli has since Livingstone's discoveries been gradually drying up and losing its volume. This is not the case. The yearly inundation seems to be as copious as ever, and the mass of water has suffered no diminution for fifty years past. In some seasons, indeed, it would appear to have exceeded its modern limits. Beginning in the month of April, the inundation slowly proceeds until, late in the month of August or early in September, the highest point is attained, the lower reaches are flooded, and the subsidence begins. But even before the Tamalakan begins its discharge, there is in the upper reaches a considerable body of water in the Botletli. Lower down, near Lake Komadau, the channel is at this time narrow and shrunken ; yet there is always water— occasionally deep pools—between the flat, dry mudbanks even here.

From my own observations, and from the information I collected among the river natives, I am satisfied that the Botletli has, since the year 1849, when Livingstone, Oswell, and Murray first struggled

across the Kalahari, and in their search for Ngami
fell upon the adjacent Botletli (then more often
than not called Zouga), this curious river-system has
suffered no diminution, whether in time of inundation
or otherwise.

Considering that the neighbouring Lake Ngami has
undoubtedly receded since Livingstone's discovery,
it is singular that the Botletli should thus have been
able to retain its volume. During and after the
period of subsidence the flats and shores of the river
reek with fever of a malignant kind, and it is extremely unadvisable for Europeans to travel along
its banks from November till May, by which time
the exhalations have ceased and the country is dry
and safe enough. Even the natives, who might be
expected to be " salted," suffer a good deal and occasionally die in large numbers.

All along the river crocodiles and hippopotami
are to be met with ; but the latter have been so
hunted for the sake of their hides and teeth, that
they are now scarce and exceedingly shy. Crocodiles
are numerous, fierce, and daring. Otters of a species
not unlike the European kind are very numerous,
notwithstanding that they are a good deal hunted
by the Makobas and Makalakas for the sake of their
handsome skins, which are readily marketable.

Naturally enough the majestic inundation of the
Botletli, occurring in the midst of an otherwise
parched country, and spreading far and wide in the
flatter places along its course into a bountiful system
of water spaces, is the means of congregating vast
quantities of bird life. All the feathered fowl of
Africa—and they are many—that are attracted by
water, fish, weeds, and soft soil, are to be found here.

Ibises, cranes, storks, pelicans, flamingoes, cormo-
rants, rails, egrets, herons, coots, snipe, and of course
geese, duck, wigeon, and teal, are to be seen in
astounding plenty. Eagles and hawks of many
kinds are also plentiful, as is to be expected where
fish and fowl alike abound. We had seen a goodly
number of waterfowl upon first striking the river
at its lower and at that time (July) shallower end,

PELICAN OF THE WILDERNESS, BOTLETLI RIVER, 1890.
Drawn by G. E. Lodge, from a Photograph by the Author.

but I shall never forget the first revelation my
companion and I had of a real African display of
aquatic life.

On one of our earliest days by the river, although
we got no shot at lechwē, we were able to feast
our eyes on a scene of incredible charm—acres upon
acres of water all black with waterfowl. There
must have been thousands of them. At this point
the river was in flood, and its waters were in process

of being spread, at first in a network, afterwards in one vast sheet, over the adjacent flats. Here and there islands dotted with graceful palm-trees were already girt about with water ; and to approach them we had to wade armpit-deep through the flood.

Even from a distance the noise and clangour of all this bird life was very wonderful ; as we approached the clatter, the babel and the uproar— well ! whether from a gunner's or a naturalist's point of view, it was nothing less than enchanting.

The river, as it spread this way and that, was not muddy. The water itself was clear, yet charged with decayed vegetable matter, so much so that we neither of us cared to risk drinking it unboiled, hot though we were ; and no doubt the quantity of feeding stuff, whether vegetable, insectile, or piscine, was immense, and well calculated to satisfy the appetites of every kind of water-loving fowl. The alluvial flats, too—long sun-baked though they had been—doubtless yielded, under the softening influence of the inundation, great store of dainties loved by the long-billed birds.

Well, on this occasion we did no execution ; we carried only our rifles, and we simply walked among and admired these galaxies of fowl. If we approached too near, up got the swarms of geese, duck, wigeon, and teal, which, after wheeling round our heads two or three times, either settled at the far end of the lagoon, or upon some neighbouring water. The roar of their uprising and the whistle of their pinions, as they flew about us, were things to remember.

Far beyond the further banks of the river stretched

the plains, in a monotonous expanse, to the pale blue horizon; around us were the vast alluvial flats, with an over-shy lechwē or two standing here and there beyond shot; massy banks of tall reeds masking the river itself. A few palm trees upon the islands and along the river margin; sheets of water shining beneath the sun glare; vast flocks of fowl on the water or in the air; a fishing eagle or two soaring in the background;—such was the scene.

One morning, after two days and a night spent away from the waggons in the pursuit of large game, I took a shot-gun and strolled down to the lagoons for a quiet turn at the waterfowl. Here I had some excellent and most enjoyable sport. After a little manœuvring I waded middle-deep into a shallow lagoon, and sent my boy, Seleti, to the far end. The duck and geese soon rose and flew several times past me, and I had no difficulty, during a couple of hours of this sort of thing, in bagging six couple of duck and wigeon, and two knob-billed geese—as much as my boy and I could carry comfortably. The duck, as I shot them, fell into the water round about me, and gave me some little retrieving. Although there were large numbers of fowl, utterly unused to guns and gunners—for the natives never use shot-guns—they by no means gave themselves away, but afforded good fair shooting. Occasionally, of course, there were easy shots, and, after a few flights up and down, the birds would betake themselves to some other water, when I too had to shift my ground.

One of the geese, an enormous fellow, I dropped on the hard, sun-dried flats; he hit the earth with almost as mighty a thud as a stricken pelican. Speaking of shot-guns reminds me of the intense surprise manifested by some Makobas higher up the river on first seeing me knock over flying duck. They knew only of bullets, and imagined I was shooting the fowls with single balls. Their "ous" of surprise, on being shown the mysteries of a shot-gun and shot-cartridges, were most ludicrous.

Wading through a pool on my way home to gather a wounded duck, I kicked up a huge crocodile skull, from which I extracted most of the teeth as curios. A crocodile's tooth is well worth looking into. The edges are rough and sharp (almost imperceptibly serrated), and aid not a little towards the severe flesh-wounds which these hideous reptiles are observed to inflict on those who are lucky enough to escape from their jaws alive. The fangs are long and hollow, and are found to contain, exquisitely bestowed one within the other, a batch of incipient teeth—often two or three—each ready to replace the outer one as it is periodically cast off.

Of the duck shot this day (I might easily have doubled or trebled the bag), there were three kinds, yellow-billed duck, the South African pochard, and red-billed teal. The first, the *Anas flavirostris* of Smith, is the commonest and biggest duck in South Africa, averaging 22 inches in length. Those shot on the Botletli were of unusual size and fatness, and delicious eating. This is a light-brown duck, and is easily identified by the bright yellow bill from which it takes its Boer name—"geelbec." The South African pochard (*Nyroca brunnea*) is a handsome, dark-brown duck—rather smaller than the last-named —mottled with grey, and having a ruddy tint underneath and at the sides. The neck and breast are nearly black, while the cheeks and upper sides of the neck are deep chestnut. The bill, legs, and feet are lead-coloured. The female is of a lighter colour. This duck always appeared to me to be of a wilder and more wary nature than many of its fellows, and its flight is very rapid. The red-billed teal (*Anas erythrorhyncha*, smee eendtje of the Boers) is well known all over South Africa. Its general colour is brown, faintly variegated, on a closer inspection, with pink, green, and white. The head and neck are of a darker brown, the latter mottled with white, while the chin and cheeks are pure white. The wing-bar is very noticeable—pink with a thin green streak across the upper portion. In length this fine teal runs from eighteen to nineteen inches, and it weighs well up to its size. The bill is more pink than red.

A very near relative of the red-billed teal, also found on the Botletli, is the Cape wigeon (*Mareca Capensis*). This fowl, also pink-coloured as to its bill, is almost identical in size with the last-named, and, although varying somewhat in colouring, is, to the unfamiliar eye, difficult to distinguish.

These ducks, however, should be easily identified. The wigeon's bill is reddish pink, that of the teal bluish pink; the legs and feet of the wigeon are reddish brown, those of the teal purplish black; moreover, the white mottling and white chin and cheeks, and pink wing-bar of the teal, further serve to distinguish it from the wigeon. The knob-billed goose (*Sarkidornis melanotus*) shot this day, is, with its cousin the Western spur-winged goose (*Plectropterus gambensis*), and the beautiful Egyptian goose (*Chenalopex Ægyptiacus*), common along the Botletli.

The black knob or comb, which extends down the upper mandible, is worn only by the male, and is only assumed during the breeding season. The general colouring of this goose is a dark metallic brown; the wings are remarkable for the wonderful sheen of their green plumage; the under parts are whitish or grey; the head and neck white, having a line of dark spots running down to the back of the neck. This goose averages a length of two feet or more, but in this respect cannot compare with the spur-wing, which attains to a good foot longer. Of these three African geese, the spur-wing is by far the best table-bird; the knob-billed comes next; while Ægyptiacus, quite the pick of the three in beauty of form and colour, furnishes very poor eating. This last bird is better known in Cape Colony by its Dutch cognomen of "berg gans"— mountain goose.

There is yet another goose found on the water systems of Ngamiland, and that I suppose the tiniest and most dainty in the world. The Madagascar goose, or African dwarf-goose (*Nettapus Madagascariensis*), notable for its diminutive size (it is little more than a foot in length, rather more than half the size of a lusty duck), its perfect form, and brilliant painting, is of a very dark shining green as to its upper plumage, with a white stripe along the wing. The chest—marked with black crossbars—and sides are ruddy; the under parts, throat, cheeks, and front of head pure white. The top of the head is of the same swarthy green as the back, while on either side of the neck is a remarkable patch of dull

green, showing distinctively from the dark green
of the head. The bill is orange in the male,
olive in the female ; the legs and feet are black.
I first saw a flock of this very curious dwarf-goose
near Sebituane's Drift. I fancy they are extremely
partial to dense reeds and plenty of water space.
They are unknown in Cape Colony, and I never
heard of them in Bechuanaland or on the Limpopo
River.

It would be impossible here to describe at length
all the other members of the bands of waterfowl
found on the Botletli. I can only briefly indicate
some of them. The curious widow tree-duck (*Den-
drocygna viduata*), with its white face, ruddy chest,
and dark brown body-colouring, is common, and
sometimes found its way to our cooking-pots. The
Hottentot teal (*Querquedula Hottentotta*), a handsome
bird rather larger than the Madagascar dwarf-goose,
was shot occasionally here as well as lower down-
country, but was not as common as many other
duck. The Cape shoveller (*Rhynchapsis Capensis*),
the dark brown "black duck" (*Anas sparsa*), and a
diving duck, which I took to be *Thalassornis leuco-
nota*, were also noted.

A very common acquaintance was the crested coot,
to be seen in numbers at every point of the river,
usually swimming in large flocks or flapping along
the top of the water when disturbed. This member
of the interesting rail family (*Fulica cristata*), with
its dark grey-blue body-colouring and black head
and neck, is distinguished by its curious double-
knobbed red crest and green legs. It is by no means
bad eating. We were short of food on reaching
the Botletli, two days in front of our waggons, and

our boy Joseph, being sent to the river to shoot a
few duck, brought back instead, rather to our disgust,
a batch of these coots. We ate them and found them
not unpalatable. The beautiful blue gallinule (*Por-
phyrio smaragnotus*), was also found, but not so
abundantly. The combination of shining violets,
blues, greens, and violet-blues of this exquisite fowl,
sharply contrasted with the fine crimson of the legs
and bill, cannot be sufficiently admired. Other rails
and waterhens, redshanks, greenshanks, stints, the
avocet, painted snipe, stilt-plover, and indeed innumerable other interesting birds are to be seen on the
Botletli.

A keen naturalist might spend easily (if the fever
would allow him) a couple of years—aye ! half-a-dozen
years—on this river, and yet not complete the catalogue of its avi-fauna. Andersson and Chapman have
done a good deal in this direction, but even their
work is necessarily incomplete. The sacred ibis (*Ibis
religiosa*)—sacred in Egypt thousands of years ago
—was common, the roseate ibis (*Tantalus ibis*) and
hagedash ibis—or hadadah—fairly so. The ibis is
easily told by its curved sickle-like bill. The modern
Egyptian name, Abou Mengel (father of the sickle),
is very descriptive. A glance at the Egyptian monuments in the British Museum will demonstrate to the
inquirer how excellent as draughtsmen the ancient
Egyptians were. Even after these thousands of years,
the ibis, and the Egyptian goose, and the hawk are
instantly recognisable, carven though they are on
intensely hard stone.

A familiar figure wherever tall reeds were handy
was the great Senegal spur-heeled cuckoo (*Centropus
Senegalensis*), identical, undoubtedly, with Burchell's

lark-heeled cuckoo (*Centropus Burchellii*). The first morning that Dove and I strolled down to the river, after our weary seventy-mile ride, we noticed numbers of these birds fluttering with short, laboured, lazy flight from point to point of the reeds. Their flight was never more than a hundred yards or so at the outside. They hung in a curious clinging manner to the stems of the great reeds, hereabouts twelve or fifteen feet tall, and seemed to be doing nothing in particular, although, I have no doubt, they were hunting insects after their manner. At first they bothered us ; they looked not unlike hawks in the distance, and yet the flight was not that of a hawk. Afterwards we shot one or two, held a *post-mortem* at our waggon, and the mystery was solved. In colour this bird, which attains a length of seventeen inches or more, is reddish chestnut upon the wings, ashy upon the back ; the head is black and crow-like ; the tail a metallic greenish black, tipped with white ; the breast and stomach are of a dirty cream colour. It has a peculiar plaintive scream in two notes, thus : " hoo-hoo ; " a name by which the natives appear to recognise it. Altogether, a very singular bird. I do not think it is found south of Ngamiland. I brought two skins of this cuckoo home in good condition amongst other treasures of the feathered sort.

On the 26th July, Dove and I had two of our ponies saddled up and rode for a quiet afternoon at the lagoons. I had ridden in from the bush (where we had been hunting two days) after superintending the despatch of two pack oxen for the skin, meat, and marrow-bones of a giraffe ; Dove had stalked and shot a lechwē in the morning ; and we were glad of a quiet afternoon with the shot-guns. Following the channel between our nearest lake and the river, and occasionally stopping for a shot by the way, we reached the riparian network of waters and had a most enjoyable afternoon. The river was rising so fast that our horses were up to their throats, and sometimes even had to swim a few strokes, in places where a day or two before we had crossed without wetting our girths. We saw an immense lot of mullet —" springers," the Boers well call them—leaping merrily out of the water as they swam in on the rising flood. Rambling, wading, splashing hither and thither, we secured as many duck as we could carry and returned contentedly to camp. It was only occasionally that we indulged ourselves in these off days, and they were a delightful change, full of a quiet charm, when we took them. It was so pleasant in a dry and thirsty land to feast one's eyes on a water-scape, and to ride or wade about in cool depths that spread and quickened actually before one's gaze.

Neither I nor my hunting comrade are ever likely to forget the sights and scenes so peculiar to the Lake River. The vast illimitable flats—at times almost terrible in their monotony; the gorgeous sunrises and sunsets; the spreading waters; the multitudes of fowl; the skeins of pelicans outlined against the morning and the evening skies; the drear desert champaigns (tolerable only for the game they held) skirting upon the river, and beyond them the silent waterless forests of the North Kalahari—fitting sanctuary for the tall giraffe; the naked primitive races in their poor reed kraals; the black-skinned Makoba fishermen; the wild, houseless Bushman hunters, living, as they have lived for ages, by their tiny bows and poisoned arrows : these are pictures and memories never likely to be effaced. Here, indeed, we had found a place of nature as remote, as wild, almost as undisturbed, as in the long past centuries, before the dawn of Africa had come.

CHAPTER XIX.

OUR RETURN THROUGH THE THIRSTLAND; ELAND HUNTING

Start across the desert—Heavy trekking—T'Klakane—Mr. Sichel, a German trader—My library—Reach Inkouane—Trek-Boer relics—Inkouane pits: how recruited—Eland spoor—A big troop—Four elands bagged —Hot work—Set off for waggons—Lost in the bush—A desperate thirst—Find the waggons—Dove lost—A trying trek—Dove turns up —Pits of Kannē—Foundered oxen—Three days and four nights without water.

AFTER some weeks of hunting and exploring on the Botletli, my companion and I quitted the river on August 7, and started upon the harassing return trek across the desert.

At this season of the year, when the few limestone pits in the Kalahari region are getting low, and all other waters have long since failed, this journey across the thirstland is the most trying and dreaded in all South Africa. We had sent on our horses, and now, travelling steadily day and night, through a dreary, monotonous region, alternating in heated saltpans, parched mopani forests, and flat plains covered with long grass, now scorched to a pale yellow by the fierce sun, we reached the pits of T'Klakane soon after sunrise on the morning of the 9th. The trek of two days and nights had been entirely waterless, under intense heat, and through heavy sand, and the oxen had suffered proportionately. One of them—old Roman, belonging to the lighter waggon (we had a Roman in each span)—had lain down, and utterly refused to move. It is painful on these occasions to observe the tactics of the drivers. The oxen must be got up, or left to die, and some cruel remedies are brought into play. First, flogging with the great whip having failed, the after ox sjambok, a tapering whip of hippopotamus hide, is employed. This failing, a severe tail-twisting follows. If the ox is very exhausted or very obstinate, even this painful remedy is useless. A handful of sand blown into the poor beast's eyes will often make it struggle to its feet, after which it will follow the waggon unyoked. If not, a combination of the last three punishments usually proves too intolerable, and, unless completely foundered, the ox will rise.

At T'Klakane, not far from the palm trees noticed by Livingstone on his journey to Lake Ngami, we rested until the afternoon of the following day, and then inspanned again. Although no rain had fallen for six months, the thorn veldt hereabouts was putting on green leafage against the approach of African summer, and the rich yellow balls of flower of the thorny acacia (exactly resembling round yellow plush pon-pons), everywhere perfumed the air and adorned the scene. Even the three other varieties of acacia found in the vicinity, the haak-doorn, haak-en-steek-doorn (hook and stick thorn), and the wacht-een-bitje (wait a bit), masked their thorny terrors with a bravery of verdure and sweet scented blossom.

At T'Klakane a German gentleman, trading from Damaraland with nearly a thousand head of cattle, whom we had fallen in with on the Botletli, rejoined us, and we had pleasant little banquets together.

He had to leave his cattle behind at the river till rain had fallen in the desert, and was now going on to see Khama. He had quitted Damaraland with 1200 head of stock, mostly taken in barter; there now remained only a trifle over 800; pitfalls, lions, and the food-supply of his retainers having accounted for the balance. This gentleman had seen no white face for seven months, during his journey across Damaraland and down the Okavango and Botletli rivers, and had completely exhausted his stores. We were fortunately able to assist him with baking powder, tea, coffee, sugar, and other luxuries. During his last month's travel he had made the useful discovery that Eno's fruit salt is a capital substitute for baking powder, and makes excellent bread. This is a wrinkle worth noting by sojourners on African veldt.

We, on the other hand, were greatly indebted to Mr. Sichel for a supply of books; and during these long hot days through the " thirst," we greedily de- voured novels by George Meredith, George Moore, and others. Even that old favourite, Mark Twain's " Innocents Abroad," contributed again to our amuse- ment. We had come up-country very ill supplied; my library, which served my hunting companion also, comprising only Baldwin's " South African Hunting," Selous' " Hunter's Wanderings," Layard's " Birds of South Africa," and Andersson's " Birds of Damaraland" for reference; Burrough's " Winter Sunshine," a charming little American book; and a sixpenny pocket encyclopædia—a wofully short supply. Having exhausted the other books, we had perforce to fall back upon the encyclopædia, and cram ourselves temporarily with all manner of odd

BERG DAMARA AND BUSH BOYS
(*With Mr. Sichel's outfit from Damaraland*)

facts and information. Indeed, in our spare time, there was quite a rivalry for this humble little volume.

We met at T'Klakane some Barolong, who were taking horses to trade at Lake Ngami. These people told us we should find elands and giraffe near Inkouane, the next water, news which proved true enough.

From the afternoon of August 10 we trekked steadily night and day without water until the same hour on the 12th, when we reached a curiously deep pit, called Bachukuru (place of the white rhinoceros), in the usual limestone formation. This pit held some ten buckets of water, which we distributed among the after-oxen of each waggon. Trekking on again through the night, we reached Inkouane at eight o'clock next morning. There is a shallow circular pan or vlei here, which holds a little water during the rains, but which was now dry and sunparched. In one corner are some deep limestone pits, which we found to contain plenty of good clear water—a blessed relief to our poor overwrought cattle. The horses had again been sent on, and we found them safely here.

It was at this place that the trek-Boers suffered so terribly during the famous Promised Land expedition of 1877-8. They had been warned by Khama not to cross the thirstland in large numbers, but to travel in groups of two and three waggons at a time. Foolishly suspecting treachery, they chose rather to attempt the journey in one band, and as they had seventy or eighty waggons, each one drawn by from fourteen to eighteen oxen, and each one carrying a whole family, the consequences were disastrous. The pits soon ran dry; the oxen, mad with thirst, fell in, died, and choked them up, and had to be cut out piecemeal; and the foul remnant of blood and water was then doled out as far as it would go. Women kept their children alive with vinegar and brandy, the blood of oxen and goats, and other dreadful substitutes for that most precious of all elements, pure water. Household goods and farming gear were cast away, whole waggons were left behind, and the veldt was littered for years with the impedimenta of this ill-starred expedition. After incredible sufferings from thirst and fever, the survivors of the trek reached Ovampoland years after, and a remnant yet lingers at Humpata, in Portuguese territory.

Even after this lapse of years we found lying about the pan at Inkouane a ploughshare or two, the iron tyres of waggon wheels, and other odds and ends, touching mementoes of that disastrous time.

A native runner, carrying letters to Mr. Strombom, the Lake Ngami trader, stopped at our waggons this morning. On unwrapping his skin parcel we found it to contain a batch of letters and papers for ourselves, and here in the middle of the desert we eagerly devoured home news, and first read of Bismarck's fall and of Mr. Rhodes' elevation to the Cape Premiership. To our German friend the news was even more interesting than to ourselves. We got out the indiarubber bath, and had a most luxurious tub before starting upon the three days and four nights of waterless desert that lay before us. We also cleaned up heads, horns, and trophies, including a number of giraffes' feet, which gave us no end of trouble. It is a most difficult matter in Africa to keep away the living organisms which are engendered in such specimens and trophies, from the tiniest bird skin to the largest head of game.

There is a curious fact in connection with the water supply at Inkouane. When the trek-Boers came through they attempted to enlarge the wells, and, as a result, greatly lessened the volume of water. For some years these pits were much less reliable than they had been. Then came a season, a few years ago, when the distant Botletli, in its mysterious annual overflow, far outran its banks, and flooded the country with much more water than usual. Since then the supply at Inkouane has been greatly enhanced. From the Botletli River to Inkouane the distance cannot be less than 100 miles, and how the pits of the latter place have been affected by the overflow of the river is a mystery passing my comprehension. That there must be some subterraneous communication between the two places is, I think, unquestionable.

Between Inkouane and Kannē, where the worst of the "thirst" is ended, lies a bushy country, much of it well timbered with giraffe acacia, mopani, mohorohoran (Kaffir orange), and other growth; and in this stretch of veldt a great number of elands, giraffe, gemsbok, and other game that are independent of water are often found. But, except for the Masarwa Bushman, who seems quite unable to lose himself, this is a most dangerous bit of country, pathless and utterly waterless as it is, especially just before the rains fall, when the heat is appalling, and even natives have been known to die of thirst within twenty-four hours.

On August 14, having well rested and refreshed our oxen, we trekked at 4.30 P.M., and just at sundown came to a single well about 12 feet deep, known as Nahahane, containing a little water. Here we watered the horses only from buckets, the oxen having drunk at Inkouane before leaving. We found at this place a solitary Masarwa, who had hunted with us near Maqua Pool on our way to the Botletli. Maqua had since run dry, and the Bushman had, therefore, transferred his quarters to Nahahane. This man told us there were elands in front, and volunteered to spoor for us next day. On the following morning, therefore, after breakfast at dawn, we rode out into the veldt, leaving the waggons to move steadily on for Kannē. Dove had now been laid up three weeks with his broken rib, and this was the first time he had been able to sit his horse. We rode steadily all day in search of eland, but although we came upon quantities of fresh spoor in the afternoon, could never get on terms with the troop. We sighted and had some long shots at ostriches, which, however, were very wild, and we saw further a quantity of hartebeest spoor; but, saving a silver jackal which Dove shot magnificently at 150 yards with a Martini bullet, we bagged no game before reaching the waggons one hour before sundown. Much of the veldt hereabouts had been set fire to by Bushmen, and our march during the whole day lay through blackened and dreary wastes. Unluckily for us and himself, the Masarwa left us after supper and returned to Nahahane without much meat, poor fellow; if he had waited till morning he could have had the flesh of a whole eland, or even more. Water was precious, however, and we had barely sufficient in our barrels to last ourselves and our followers to Kannē. All this night the waggons trekked on through deep sand, and we outspanned just before morning broke in dense forest country.

David, usually most reliable of drivers and hunters, had decided to quit the usual waggon road from Inkouane to Kannē, and trek along an old spoor of his own, more to the eastward. This turned out to be a mistake. The track was overgrown, nearly imperceptible, and exceedingly difficult to follow, and we lost much precious time in cutting away trees and clearing a path.

We were at breakfast at dawn of the 16th, when Ditsamico, one of the boys tending the oxen, brought word that a troop of eland had been feeding close to the waggons. Hastily swallowing our coffee, my comrade and I got out our rifles, saddled up our nags, and taking Joseph, who rode and shot well, to spoor for us, at once followed after the game. "Wait while I fill a water-bottle, Dove," I called out. "Oh, we shan't be more than an hour gone," was the reply; "the buck are close at hand. Come on!"

We went waterless, for the first time during the expedition, and never did unfortunates rue a mistake more bitterly. Before nightfall we would have readily given £5 for a good pull at that same water-bottle.

The spoor we found to be perfectly fresh, the elands had evidently been disturbed less than an hour before, and we had no difficulty in following rapidly on the trail. For an hour we rode silently on, during which time, unknown to Joseph and myself, we crossed the track—hereabouts all but

obliterated—along which the waggons were to pass.
This, as it afterwards turned out, was a great misfortune, and helped to throw us much more out of
our reckoning.   Dove, who was riding a little apart,
noticed the path, and thought we had done the
same.   After an hour in thick forest and bush the
spoor led us into an open glade, beyond which was
more bush.   Just as we were entering a belt of
timber, I, who was riding last, saw half-a-dozen
great fawn-coloured antelopes, as big as large cows,
trot out from the forest a little lower down.   I
called to my comrades, "Here they are," wheeled
short round, and galloped for the elands, which,
however, immediately betook themselves to the bush
again.   With the view of intercepting them on the
other side of the belt, we again turned our horses'
heads, and flew round thither.   Here, as we expected, the game were emerging in a state of dire
alarm.   There was a noble troop of them, more than
thirty all told.   They were mostly great, full-grown
cows, in high condition; there were besides one or
two young bulls, and a few yearling calves, but no
heavy old bulls, as we had hoped.

We now set our willing nags going in earnest,
and galloped hard at the elands, which had obtained
a slight start.   Finding themselves pressed, the
troop broke up.   Dove, who was on the left, followed
the main body; Joseph and I fixed our attention
on those bearing right-handed.   I soon singled out
a fine cow, carrying a remarkable pair of horns;
Joseph stuck to a young bull more to the right.
Considering the great size of these antelopes and
the faculty they have of putting on flesh, their
activity is remarkable.   The eland I was chasing,

although surpassing in bulk an average cow at home,
jumped over good-sized bushes and fallen timber
that fell in her path with a quite extraordinary
agility.   At the first onset the troop had started
at a sharp canter.   My cow was now going at a
slinging trot (their favourite pace), so that although
my horse, normally a very good one, was now in
low condition, I had no difficulty, aften ten minutes'
sharp run, in pushing him up to within a few yards
of the tail of my quarry.   I now fired three shots
from the saddle.   With the first barrel I missed
clean, my aim being disturbed by the rapid motion.
It is not so easy as it sounds to hit at even a short
distance, when using a heavy double rifle and firing
from a galloping horse in broken country.   The
second and third bullets both struck the eland,
however, the first high up in the thigh, the second
breaking her off foreleg just below the shoulder.
To this last shot she fell so suddenly, that my
horse and I all but came on top of her, the nag
just escaping a fall by leaping over her rump.
Jumping off, I finished her troubles.   She was a
magnificent fat cow, weighing, I suppose, 1000 lbs.,
or slightly over, and carrying a long pair of horns,
curving very singularly to the right.   As a rule,
the horns of this antelope grow straight and very
evenly from the head, spreading between the points.
The horns of a good cow rarely extend to more than
2 feet 9 inches ; those of this specimen measured
2 feet 8 inches.

The eland, I may here remark, is the largest and
heaviest antelope in the world, and attains to an
extraordinary fatness.   A heavy old bull will scale
from 1500 lbs. to 2000 lbs., and stand nineteen hands

high at the withers. The cows do not attain quite
so enormous a bulk, but even they outstrip in size
and weight every other antelope in Africa.

The usual colour is a bright rich fawn ; the hair
is short and smooth, and as the bulls get older they
lose much of their hair, and assume a greyish-blue
tint from the colour of the skin beneath. The horns
of the bull are much stouter and more massive than
the cows, but do not attain so great a length. In
some parts of Africa, and notably in Mashonaland
and beyond and near the Zambesi, elands are found
thinly striped with white ; but those of the Kalahari
are never known to share this peculiarity. Formerly
abundant all over South Africa, the eland has been
so relentlessly pursued as to be now exceedingly
scarce, save in remote and inaccessible regions.

Fastening up my horse, I set to work at once
to cut off the head of my prize and skin her. As
I stripped away her sleek, smooth coat, a strong
sweet perfume, redolent of pleasant herbs, came
warm into my nostrils. Meanwhile I had heard
Dove's rifle speaking far to the left, and, just as I
brought down my cow, Joseph's to the right. Dove,
as it afterwards turned out, had shot two fine cows,
from the best of which he had taken the head and
some of the meat, and failing to find us, and not
hearing our signal shots, had struck for the road.
When I had partly skinned my game, I fired a
couple of signal shots, and soon after Joseph arrived
on the scene, looking very hot. He informed me
that he had run into and slain his young bull, and
then fell to work with me to complete the skinning
of my eland and secure the best of the meat. It
sounds an easy matter to skin and cut up an eland.

I can assure the reader that on a blazing hot African morning in August, shut up in dense Kalahari bush, and without a breath of air, it is no light matter. By the time we had finished I was streaming with perspiration, and already had acquired a highly respectable thirst. Having loaded up my nag with the skin and meat, and taking the huge head on the pommel, we went on to Joseph's bull, where also we secured the head and took more meat. We then fired a number of signal shots to attract Dove.

By this time it was nearing twelve o'clock, and the heat was terrific; nevertheless, thinking that a ride of another hour or so would land us at the waggons, we set off contentedly enough. As a rule Joseph, my after-rider, was a capital hand at finding his way in the bush. On this occasion, however, although we steered, as we judged by the sun, correctly enough, we were in dire ignorance that, during the run up, we had crossed the track along which the waggons were to pass, and in the excitement and meanderings of the chase, we had no doubt still further lost our reckoning. However, we marched away in a southerly direction boldly enough. We travelled steadily on for three hours through thick bush and forest of camel-thorn. The veldt seemed to grow wilder and wilder; there was a good deal of giraffe spoor about, besides that of eland and gemsbok, and I never saw anything like the quantity of steinbok and duykers we put up during the afternoon. But, although we saw small buck and giraffe, the desert was perfectly devoid of bird life; we saw not even a sandgrouse, far though these birds wander from water during the day; the bush was birdless, silent as the grave. After three hours, as it began to dawn on Joseph that we were lost, or losing ourselves, he looked a little more serious, and proposed striking more to the westward. I did not exactly agree with him; indeed, in my own mind, I still stuck to a southerly course, believing that in the end we should strike the old Inkouane-Kannē road at any rate; but, trusting in the native's usually unerring instincts far more than in my own poor woodcraft, I gave way, and we turned our now jaded nags to the south-west.

For another hour we marched steadily on, silent and serious; then, in very thick forest, we espied, less than 100 yards away, a huge old giraffe bull, very dark as to his colouring, moving slowly off with the shuffling gait peculiar to the camelopard. It was very tempting, but we had plenty of meat and our horses were tired, and the situation was becoming serious, so the old bull got off for a wonder unmolested. At four o'clock we halted for a few minutes, and, in this silent, sepulchral forest, held consultation. First I relieved my horse of the weight of the eland skin—no light matter. The poor nag had been very hard worked giraffe-hunting on the Lake River a week or so before, and had not yet recovered from the effects. He was nearing the end of his tether; he had been already close upon forty-eight hours without water, and certainly would not stand up for another day. Horses cannot battle with thirst as oxen can. If we were really lost, as now seemed the case, the white horse on which Joseph was riding might hold out for another twenty-four hours, but not more, and he would probably have to carry the two of us alternately. We

were already suffering badly from thirst ourselves,
but we might struggle on, even if we lost our horses,
for another forty-eight hours. We knew that the
pits of Inkouane on the one hand, and those of
Kannē on the other, lay within a radius of forty or
fifty miles. But when one has lost one's reckoning,
it is, as every person who has been "bushed" knows,
almost an impossibility to find a given point in so
enormous an expanse, much of which is monotonous
veldt without a distinguishing feature. On the other
hand, it was open to us to take our own spoor back
again to the spot where we had slain the elands; but
it was a long ride, the sand was light and shifting
with the slightest breath of air, and a troop of game
might easily obliterate our track. Our position,
therefore, was a grave one. The waggons had to be
constantly moving on for Kannē to save the lives
of the oxen, and if we were lost it would be impossible to obtain a fresh supply of water and to come
in search of us for two days at least, when it
would be quite a hopeless chance. "Joseph," I said,
"there's only one thing to be done; you can track
well, you must take our spoor back to where we
skinned the elands, and we must try again from
there." Joseph concurred, and off we started again,
this time on our back trail.

At this point the native did a very risky thing.
He realised that if we slowly followed our own spoor
back, round the wide semicircle on which we had
ridden, we could barely reach the remains of the dead
elands before nightfall. He therefore took a cut
across country, in the confident hope of striking our
spoor some miles nearer to our point of object, the
scene of slaughter of the morning. As I thought it

then, and as I think now, it was a horrible risk.
If Joseph's unerring eye and instinct had failed him
for a yard or two, and we had missed the spoor; if
the trail had been obliterated by the passage of game,
as it might easily have been where he expected to
cut it, I am firmly of opinion that we should have
been lying in that awful desert now. I do not think
I ever spent a more anxious two hours than those
that followed. Moreover, all this time I felt that
Dove was lost also; he had scarcely recovered from
a severe wound (his broken rib), and had no guide,
so that, if lost, no water could reach him for at least
two days and nights. What would his friends at
home say if we regained the waggons and yet lost
him? My thoughts became almost intolerable at
times.

On the other hand, I knew that my friend had a
wonderful eye and a real faculty for grasping the
characteristic features of a country; I knew he would
never lose his head, and had plenty of pluck. So I
hoped for the best. As the afternoon wore on my
thirst became intense. What with the blazing heat,
the exertions of the morning and the worry of afternoon, my throat and tongue were becoming like pieces
of parched and extremely painful leather. It was
curious afterwards to remember how one's thoughts
ran upon visions of cool and soothing scenes at
home. I thought of friends gathered under the
cool shade of great English trees, drinking their
afternoon tea, and watching the lawn tennis; of
the thirsty players (thirsty for a few brief minutes
only) quaffing down icy claret-cup or foaming
draughts of ale.

I am not a greedy or a particularly thirsty man

naturally; I only record these memories as peculiar to the condition of mind and body I was then in.

At length we cut our spoor again, and hunted it along carefully and slowly, until, to our intense relief, about half-an-hour before dark we found ourselves by the carcase of the bull eland shot by Joseph in the morning. I say carcase; I should say rather, bones. The vultures had been busy since we left the spot. The eland was picked nearly clean, and the hideous birds sat, drunk and gorged with flesh, helpless and stupid upon the trees around. With my rifle I could have picked off a score, one after another, within twenty or thirty paces. There were two or three species, one of which—a very dark bird, smaller than its fellows, and remarkable for its bright red head and neck—I had not before noticed in South Africa. Two or three stumbled from the eland's remains and fluttered heavily up to the thorn trees close at hand. Passing on, we soon reached the cow eland I had shot, where the same scene was repeated. After this the eland spoor (of which there were quantities) and our own became so intermingled, that Joseph had great difficulty in keeping the right direction. However, every now and again hitting off our horses' tracks, we moved steadily on. The sun sank and went down, we were still in thick forest, and, as darkness fell, I said to my after-rider, "We shan't hit the road to-night, Joseph; we may as well off-saddle and camp till daylight." Two minutes after I had spoken, the native suddenly half-turned in his saddle and said, "There's the road, sieur," and there indeed it was. I cannot express in words our thankfulness at this discovery. We immediately off-saddled, and gave the poor jaded nags nearly half-an-hour's rest ; they were too thirsty and too exhausted to feed much, but they plucked a few mouthfuls of the sun-dried grass, and had a roll.

The last streak of ruddy sunset had faded as we saddled up again in the glooming dusk, and rode painfully and steadily on through the darkness. Hour after hour went by under the warm starlight, and the horses became slower and feebler ; I had the greatest difficulty to keep mine moving at all, and I am afraid my spurs bore painful testimony next morning to the poor brute's evil plight. At last we passed a smouldering fire, and within an hour after overtook the waggons. It was now between 11 and 12 o'clock P.M. That five hours' ride through the dark seemed a perfect nightmare. What with kicking and spurring along a half-foundered horse, aching all over from the long day spent incessantly in the saddle, and supporting with difficulty the huge eland head in front and a heavy double rifle, and that ghastly eighteen hours' thirst burning in one's throat, it was an unpleasant experience, as I think of it even now. The instant we reached the waggons I inquired of David if Dove had arrived. " No," was the answer. He was lost, undoubtedly, and the situation demanded no half measures. The spare horses had gone on to the next waterpits at Kannē. I determined to send on Joseph, after an hour or two's rest, to bring out natives with calabashes of water, wait myself for the refreshed horses, and take up the search next day. It seemed a horribly hopeless business to track a lost man far into the wilderness with the scant supply of water we could carry, but it had to be faced.

There was still some water left in one barrel. We

gave our poor spent nags half-a-bucket apiece—all
we could spare—had a tremendous drink ourselves,
then some coffee and meat, and trekked on again.
The oxen were still standing up fairly well, on this
the second day and third night of the " thirst," but
we were travelling through dense forest, winding
about among the trees, and progress was terribly
slow. That was a wretched night. I stretched
myself for awhile on my kartel, but not to sleep ;
my mind was too full of worry for that. What
was to befall my comrade in this frightful, waterless
desert—that was the rub. I could see that David,
a cool-headed, resourceful native, was extremely
anxious also. To a certain extent he was answerable
to his chief, Khama, for our safety, and I could
see he keenly felt the responsibility of the situation. Slowly, slowly we trekked through the hot
weary night, the waggons ploughing heavily through
the deep sand, and occasionally halting while we
cut away a tree or sapling. I sat on the waggon
box, or walked alongside for a spell now and again
until morning broke. The oxen I could see by daylight were getting weaker and slower, and required
much punishment from the long whips and constant
scolding to get them along. The drivers were nearly
voiceless from incessant rating and calling on their
long-horned charges by name ; still, we pushed on.
Joseph had ridden on long since to fetch the fresh
horses.

The morning wore on, and I fretted and fidgeted
within myself at the horrible yet unavoidable delay,
and pictured Dove in all sorts of straits. David
and I argued the matter out together some fifty
times. At length, at eleven o'clock, as I sat on

the waggon box in bitter rumination, David uttered an exclamation. I looked up, and there was Dove riding towards us on the grey pony. I can safely say that never in the whole course of my existence did I set eyes on a man with half so keen a pleasure. What a load was lifted from my mind! I jumped down, ran up to him, and we shook hands warmly. The trouble was over in an instant, and the remainder of the trek, even with sinking oxen, a mere bagatelle. My comrade now related his adventures. After killing his second eland and taking her head, he rode straight away in the direction of the road, as he imagined it. After riding for hours, he realised that the faint track he had crossed during the hunt must have been the road the waggons were taking. It was too late to turn back, and he pushed on, therefore, hoping to strike the old trek-Boer road. He had long realised that he was lost, and felt, as well he might, extremely uneasy, and suffered, as we did, much from thirst; but still he rode straight on. Just at sun-down, as he prepared to off-saddle for the night, he providentially cut the old waggon track, and was safe. He then off-saddled, as we had done, for a spell, and cantered on seven hours through the night, and reached Kannē. Here the supply of water was so scant, that natives were sleeping in the open by the pits, with fires around them, to guard the water. Only by payment of 2s. 6d. could he obtain enough water for himself and his nag, both half dead with thirst. He lay by the fires for the rest of the night, occasionally rising to quench his thirst; and, knowing my probable anxiety, rode back to meet the waggons in the morning.

AFTER THE TREK THROUGH THE THIRSTLAND: A JADED SPAN

Soon after one o'clock we emerged from the forest, and then saw, with a delight I cannot express, the bold blue hills of Khama's more easterly country filling the horizon, in the neighbourhood of Letloche and Shoshong. We had not seen anything approaching an altitude of 100 feet for many weeks, and, after the monotonous plains of the Botletli River country and the interminable flats of the Kalahari bush, our joy was very keen at setting eyes again on noble mountains. Descending presently from the plateau, we reached Kannē (sometimes marked on the maps Klaballa, from the name of its old chief), where we found half-a-dozen sandpits, with water just oozing through the bottom, which as fast as it came was "skepped" up in gourd spoons, and thence transferred to clay vessels. Here was no chance of watering the oxen, which were now frantic with thirst. They ran this way and that, came round the waggons, licked at the barrels, and even cooled their poor parched tongues by licking at the iron tyres of the wheels, and their bellowing was distressing to hear. We kept them away from the pits with the greatest difficulty, and, after a rest, sent them on to Seruë, which they reached towards early morning. Poor beasts, they had trekked almost incessantly for three days and four nights without a drop of water, and must have been tough cattle indeed to have stood up so long. Three of them, which had lain down and utterly refused to move during the last twelve hours of the journey, came on in the night; of these, one was found dead in one of the pits next morning, the other two survived. So ended our trek through the thirstland —a sufficiently trying experience.

We stood at Kannē part of the next day, during which the oxen rested and recruited, while we skinned and prepared our three precious eland heads, took some photographs, and put the waggons straight before proceeding to Palachwe.

The three heads, for which we underwent so much toil and trouble, reached England safely with the rest of our trophies, and now look down, placidly as in the life, from walls at home.

CHAPTER XX.

DOWN COUNTRY

Billy the goat—Eland meat—Picturesque hills—Athletics in the wilderness—Reach Palachwe—Selling the outfit—Start down country—Trotting oxen—Molepolole—Kanya—Tame klipspringers—Rain attractors—Vryburg foxhounds—The Junction again—A model farm—Life in Vryburg—A murder trial—Illness at Kimberley—Reach Cape Town—A glorious view—Kamps Bay—Sea-fishing in Kalk Bay—Good sport—Stellenbosch—Old Cape houses—Cape wine—Fruit—Victoria road—Meet Mackay—Cricket—Up-country again—Crossing the Vaal—General Joubert—Vryburg once more—Homeward bound.

QUITE the freshest individual of our entire outfit was Billy the goat, who had marched steadily through the "thirst," picking his sustenance wherever he had a mind, and getting a scant drink of water from our vatjes twice—once he declined—during the last three days and four nights. The dogs had suffered greatly and were now as lean as crows, the horses were terribly run down, and the oxen mere gaunt frameworks of skin and bone. Yet Billy the goat came up to time on the morning of the 18th August at Kannē as fresh as paint, and apparently quite prepared, if necessary, to turn his face again for the Lake River, and march stoutly across the dreary wastes through which we had won our way.

There was practically no water to be got at Kannē —except a few pints for ourselves—so after noon we pushed on for Masookoo, a pit in the sandbed of a periodical stream which held fair water.   Mr. Sichel, our German friend, had meanwhile picked us up again at Kannē, and finding no water there, trekked on with us to Masookoo.   We had a final and very cheery supper together, at which pea-soup, eland steak and tomatoes, and Bartlett pears, were the main attractions.   Eland, by the way, is of all African game-meat—excepting only the venison of the dainty springbok—by far the best.   It is fat, tender, and extremely well tasted ; not unlike young beef, but paler and with a game-like flavour.   Giraffe meat, as distinguished from the marrow-bones of that tall quadruped, which are *the* luxury of South African hunters, I consider distinctly inferior to eland.

This night we had an addition to our party, or rather several—Molly, our greyhound, having taken the liberty of bringing forth an interesting family of seven pups on Dove's waggon.   The proceedings actually began upon Dove's kartel ; this was thought, however, to be pushing hospitality too far, and the party were shifted to the body of the waggon.   We fitted up a large box for her under the waggon, and the old lady, with the five puppies which were spared to her, made the rest of the journey comfortably enough.

Next morning, 19th of August, after Mr. Sichel had breakfasted with us, we moved off across the hills. Mr. Sichel meanwhile was staying at Masookoo until his second waggon, which was following him through the "thirst," should catch up to him.   The season was now very dry, and as there was little or no water on the circuitous route between Kaleekie, the next water, and Palachwe, there was nothing for it but to trek boldly across the hills.   The travelling, as it turned out, was rough and very precipitous for the

next few days, until we fetched Khama's Town
again ; but the hill scenery through which we passed
was so magnificent, so full of wild charm and
picturesqueness, and the atmosphere so brisk and
invigorating, that we would not willingly have missed
this portion of the journey. It was amid all this
fine hill country that Gordon Cumming had found
elephants in such profusion less than five-and-forty
years before. To-day, as we rode over hill and
through valley, we saw only spoor of the koodoo,
and a few active klipspringers, which, however, never
gave us the chance of a shot. Nowadays there
are too many guns and cattle-posts in this locality.
This evening we outspanned at the small pool called
Kaleekie, which is fed by a tiny spring.

20th August.—Joseph stupidly not having made
bread last night, we had an idle morning at Kaleekie while this operation proceeded. I took some
photographs, and then Seleti, our comic horse-boy,
with whom there had been a good deal of chaff
during the journey, inveigled me into a foot race.
Now, years before, when I could run, at half-a-mile
or a mile I would have backed myself cheerfully
against any man in Khama's country. It was now
a dozen years since I had run a race in earnest, and
my day was long past. However, I humoured Seleti,
ran him a hundred yards on a smooth flat piece of turf
towards the fountain, and beat him easily enough.
Alas ! Moara Kotla, one of the leaders, a smart, well-
built youth, and reputed to be the best runner in
Palachwe, now wanted to take me on. It was too
bad. A hundred yards never was my distance ; my
knees were horribly stiff from riding day after day
for long months ; and I still had a reminder in the

right knee of the fall I had sustained in our steeplechases at the Junction ; and here was this athletic
young 'Mangwato burning to take my number down.
However, I could hardly back out with credit, and
we ran. We ran neck and neck for seventy yards,
and then Moara Kotla, who moved in beautiful form,
had me beaten, and won by several yards. Dove,
who sat on his waggon and acted as judge, was
highly amused and not sympathetic. As I said to old
David, the driver, " It is a mistake for a man to take
up running again in his old age." " But," said David
with a grin, " the Baas is not so old." " Anyhow,
David," I replied, " I was running races when Moara
Kotla and Seleti were piccanins tied to their mothers'
backs, and I was rash to begin again."

All through the afternoon we toiled up hill and
down dale through a most beautiful country, curiously
dotted with stony kopjes, which lay here and there
upon the hill sides and tops as if pitched from the
clouds. These kopjes are mere huddles of enormous
detached rocks, heaped together and intergrown with
trees and bushes. The largest stones are frequently at
the top, and in several instances there occur immense
rocks, balanced like Logan stones one upon another
in picturesque confusion, which would go far to make
the fortune of an English health resort.

We toiled steadily through the hills as fast as our
now weak oxen would allow us, until the night of the
21st, when we struck the road again and outspanned
in a most beautiful valley thickly set with fine trees.
This place is called Makwarrie, and the hills through
which we had been stumbling for the last two days
are known as Qualeepi : they lie between Shoshong
and Palachwe, rather to the westward. We had

several " sticks "—often nearly upsets—in the spruits and watercourses between the hills, in one of which the dissel-boom of the big waggon was smashed, and had to be mended with chains and riems. The light waggon broke down after we left her next day, and caused another delay.

Early on the morning of the 22nd, Dove and I rode off for Palachwe, expecting to get in about noon. We rode on and on without an off-saddle until two o'clock, and then, after a short halt, found the town not far away and got in about four. We saw much spoor of koodoo and rooibok in the wild, bushy, and apparently uninhabited country through which we came in the earlier part of the day. The down-country post cart happened to be leaving that night, and my companion was in a hurry to get home ; and so, after dinner at the hospitable mess of the Bechuanaland Trading Company's officials, the cart came round, I bade a regretful good-bye to Dove, and our trek was over.

And so this long-hoped-for, long-talked-of expedition of ours was past and finished. The free roving life of the wilderness, the cool of the morning in the desert, the glare of the plains, the dark lines of game trekking from the river, the good nag between one's knees, the lone parched forests, the first thrilling sight of giraffe, the stir, the splendid freedom, the pure sense of living, and the blessed evenings by the camp fire, as we sat drinking bowls of tea after the burning day of chase ; the myriad stars burning overhead, the milky nebulæ defining still more sharply the strange black patches to be seen here and there in the deep night-blue of the southern heavens ; the taste of good Transvaal tobacco, the chatter of the men, and finally the deep refreshing slumber in the snug waggon—most of these things, as I say, were past and done with for the time; but the memories of them will remain written in scarlet letters in the pages of one's existence.

After my friend's departure I stayed a week at Palachwe, during which I disposed of our outfit—horses, oxen, waggon, and all—at good prices. I saw much of Khama, and had many long chats with him by the help of my interpreter, Joseph; and the more I saw of the chief and his government, the more there seemed to admire. Sekhome, his son and heir, a tall stripling of one or two and twenty, seems a fine amiable youth; though it is early to judge if he possess the strength of character of his father. Palachwe was now excessively hot, and there was a good deal of dysentery about the town. The situation, picturesque though it is, is not altogether a good one. The place is too much shut in by the hills; in the wet season it is in parts swampy and unhealthy; and the Bamangwato have suffered heavily from fever and dysentery since they have settled there. This last season (1892) 2000 deaths are said to have occurred in the town, and the mortality included, unhappily, Khama's newly married second wife, the sister of the Bangwaketse chief Batoen. Water is more plentiful than at Shoshong, it is true; but, from a sanitary point of view, the people are worse off than in the old town, and it is quite on the cards that another exodus may take place and a fresh town be formed. During my week at Palachwe I received much kindness and hospitality from Messrs. W. Mosenthal and M. Gifford of the Bechuanaland Trading Association, as well as from

Mr. Moffatt, Mr. Clarke, and others. I had my tent up, and on my part was able to entertain on a humble scale; and some very cheery dinner-parties we enjoyed together. The tinned plum puddings, which Dove and I never had been able to unearth from among our voluminous stores, now came to hand, and excited the warm admiration of my Palachwe guests.

At last the day came when I had cleared off the kit, packed all the trophies, paid and said good-bye to the men—including the Piccanin, who went off with a golden sovereign or two in immense glee—and on the 29th of August I started down country by post cart.

The only other occupant was Lieutenant Ricketts of the Bechuanaland Border Police; so that we had plenty of room and made ourselves as comfortable as possible for our four days and nights of jolting. We had a kettle with us, and made some coffee, and ate some tinned food now and again. For the first two days, until well down the Crocodile (Limpopo), the cart was drawn by four oxen, which were exchanged for fresh ones every fifteen miles or so; these animals had been trained to trot, and did their work exceedingly well. At the head of the fore oxen, leading them by the usual hide riem, ran a naked boy, who trotted briskly through the heavy sand, with occasional rests, for the whole of his stage of twelve or fifteen miles—no slight performance. On the Crocodile we changed the teams for mules and horses. From Lentswe's Town (Mochudi) we turned off right-handed through a grand hill country, which brought us to Molepolole, Sechele's town, where we halted for an hour or two. The town lies hidden away on the summit of a rocky hill, and it is a tough scramble, as one threads one's way amid rocks and boulders, to attain it. Sechele lives in a good, square, well-furnished cottage, but, as the old chief was having his afternoon siesta, we did not disturb him. Molepolole, one of Livingstone's earliest mission stations, takes its name from a great cavern high up in the mountain wall, which we noticed as we drove past, and is perhaps one of the strongest and most inaccessible native towns in South Africa. It would be an extremely nasty place to carry by assault. At Molepolole resides Mr. Harry Boyne, a well-known trader, who knows the Kalahari well, and can fit out hunting parties and give excellent advice.

Pursuing our journey in the evening, we passed during the night Pilans', a small native town, and came next morning a little before dawn to the principal store at Kanya, chief town of the Bangwaketse. One gets little sound sleep on these journeys, and so Ricketts and I spread our blankets under the outspanned post cart, and enjoyed a sound sleep for an hour or two. I was awakened by something or other touching me, and opening my eyes found a beautiful tame klipspringer busily engaged in licking my face. Its fellow was doing the same by my companion. These beautiful little antelopes were excessively tame and in perfect condition. They made free of every part of Mr. Williams's store, and might often be seen upon the topmost shelf, as if perched in imagination upon their native hill-sides. They are playful as kittens, gentle as lambs, and are well known to all travellers coming down country. The Bechuanas have a curious tradition that the klipspringer can attract rain. Even so late as last year, during the dry season, the Bangwaketse organised hunts for the purpose of capturing these mountain antelopes. They take them alive and carry them about in their arms, pinching the poor little creatures to make them squeal; their plaintive cries being popularly supposed to attract the much-needed rain.

Kanya, which also lies upon a fine bold hill amid rolling country, enjoys an excellent situation, and in my opinion, when the Protectorate is opened up, offers one of the best sites for a township in all Bechuanaland.

At Kanya the post cart was joined by Mr. W. H. Surmon, the newly appointed Resident Commissioner for the Protectorate, and, after compassing the seventy-five miles to Mafeking in eleven hours, once more I was within the outer limits of civilisation. For the next three months, owing to matters of business, my time was chiefly passed at Vryburg, varied by occasional journeys to Kimberley, Mafeking, and our old camp at the Setlagoli and Maritsani Junction.

With the arrival of the railway at Vryburg and the consequent incursion of loafers, thieves, and habitual criminals, hotel life became for a while almost unbearable. Thanks, however, to the kindness and hospitality of several friends, these unpleasant weeks gradually wore along. Occasionally a day's fishing, or a run with the foxhounds came in to vary the monotony of hot winds, dust storms, and a general existence of discomfort, passed amid a population largely composed (for the moment) of Transvaal scum, gamblers, and drunkards. Mr. Newton, the Colonial Secretary, had at this time obtained from Sir Frederick Carrington the loan of a few couples of foxhounds from the pack kept by Sir Frederick for some years past at Mafeking. With these hounds we had some capital spins after steinbok, duyker, and jackal, in the country round Vryburg. Occasionally there was a kill to enliven proceedings and hearten up the hounds. In this dry climate, and particularly at this season, scenting was extremely bad and catchy—especially so when duyker or steinbok were afoot. Jackals—near relatives as they are to the fox—give a much better scent, and I remember one run, in particular, after a jackal, which gave us as fast and merry a twenty minutes' gallop as one could wish for.

At the end of September I rode up to the Junction, where I found the Gethins almost at their wits' end for water, and the veldt terribly parched from drought. Their only supply now came from a sandpit in the Setlagoli, five miles off, and the water was foul and unpleasant. Gethin had a touch of fever (no doubt from bad water) which I was able to alleviate by aid of Warburg's tincture, a bottle of which I had by me. One day at the Junction at this time was, I think, the hottest and most uncomfortable I ever experienced in Africa. The wind came from the heated north-west, and was inexpressibly withering and oppressive. Happily there are few such days in Bechuanaland, except just at this season, before the rains fall. It was curious to notice the acacia trees and bushes putting forth their greenery and fresh leafage at this season of drought—African springtime—before the falling of the summer rains.

A few days after, on my return to Vryburg, I drove out with a friend to New Grennan, a farm some fifteen miles east of Vryburg, where the skill and energy of the Messrs. Hannay (farmers from the Eastern Province of Cape Colony) had created in three short years a very charming place. Here in limestone formation they had, even in time of drought, a good water supply, which, by opening up fresh veins ("aars," the Boers call them), they had largely augmented. In front of the neat, comfortable farmhouse a small lake of water stood. The house was approached by a short trellised walk, over which luxuriant vines were just beginning to put forth fruit. Roses, syringas, and other familiar flowers (tended by the ladies of the family) were about the garden. A little way off was a large fruit orchard irrigated from the water pool, wherein peaches, apricots, apples, pears, quinces, and strawberries (the last of which we tasted) were all flourishing to perfection. Several kinds of vegetables were also thriving here.

Round about the neighbouring veldt roamed herds of cattle, for which an ample water supply was always at hand. Mealie-ground was ready for its crop as soon as the rain should fall. New Grennan is, indeed, a picture of what Bechuanaland farming, conducted under proper workmanlike conditions, and with the vigorous energy of Scottish blood, may attain to in three or four years.

This day, for a change, the wind blew from the Southern Ocean, and the morning was quite cold. From such a scene, one returned to the squalid life of a Vryburg hotel with a good many regrets. At dinner in the public room navvies and gangers, flush of money from rapid railway work, came in and sat down in their shirts unrebuked. Robberies were daily and nightly perpetrated. My portmanteau was stolen from under my bed, taken on to the veldt outside the town, ripped open with a knife; the contents—new clothes and all—were pillaged; and the papers, many of them of extreme importance to me, scattered on the hillside. I luckily recovered most of these latter, thanks to the kindness of a friend, who had discovered my forlorn papers and portmanteau next morning. A faro table, at which many of the more unwary Vryburgers lost most of their loose cash, was at this time almost nightly held either in the public room of the hotel I speak of, or in one of the bedrooms. The holders, strangers in the town, did well until a well-known Jewish gentleman, from the Transvaal, came in and in turn proceeded to spoil the Egyptians. He succeeded so well, in fact, that he had to be admitted to partnership; after which things went swimmingly again for the bankers. This is the gentleman about whom a well-known Transvaal story is related. In the early days of Barberton the diggers' oxen were occasionally troubled by lions. Ikey was asked one day to join a hunt and go out and look for a lion which had been more than usually daring. "No, thanks," said Ikey, "it's not in my line, I ain't lost a lion." Ikey's is strictly a business nature, and his dry humour, flavoured with a slight American nasal twang, made the retort additionally amusing.

On the 10th of October a Cape (coloured) boy was stabbed by another half-caste on the railway works close to the town. A Hottentot woman, wife of the murdered man, and, of course, Cape brandy appeared to have been the predisposing causes. I went into court next morning to hear the case. It was a curious scene. The dingy little court-house; the crowd of white and coloured onlookers—representing every race almost in South Africa; the stalwart Basuto policemen; the miserable criminal; Catherine, the Hottentot woman, who, despite her grief, had meanwhile obtained possession of her dead husband's stock of money and arrayed herself in some brand-new, gaudy clothing, all contrasted sharply with the quiet, self-contained English Resident Magistrate, the Crown Prosecutor, and the defending counsel, and the matter-of-fact Anglo-Saxon way in which the charge was put forward and defended. Through the window one looked out upon the courtyard, a straggle of gaunt blue gum-trees, groups of Boers and natives; beyond, a corrugated iron house or two; then the bare yellow veldt. Over all blazed the strong African sunlight. Two sunburnt, decent Afrikander women, who had witnessed the murder, were giving evidence. The criminal, by the way, escaped the death penalty.

On the 16th of October slight rain fell, the first I had seen since April. The following day the hounds were out; we found a duyker, and had a capital run of forty-five minutes, but without a kill, unfortunately.

In November, the railway, meanwhile, having been formally opened for traffic, business took me to Kimberley. The weather was again terrifically hot there, and I was unlucky enough to be laid up with a severe attack of dysentery, just then rather prevalent. From this I recovered, but a long hot ride from Vryburg to Mafeking and back (200 miles), towards the end of the month, and the extreme heat, retarded complete convalescence; and I therefore, towards the end of December, ran down to Cape Town for change and sea air.

After all but a year passed in the dry interior, where great waters are scarce, and a swim is almost an unattainable luxury, it is, for an Englishman, a glorious thing to set eyes once more upon the measureless blue of the ocean; and it was no bad thing either, after the dreary experiences of the life of a frontier town, to move once more among tolerable houses, and the comforts and refinements of cultured people. Cape Town, since I first knew it years before, has vastly improved, and, with its new drainage scheme, will improve yet more; and it is not, I think, too much to say that in the future this southern city, with its magnificent situation, its surrounding wealth of scenery, its noble bay, and its pleasant society, will attract crowds of English folk anxious to escape the fogs and rigours of a northern winter. Nowadays, it should be remembered, Cape Town lies but a short fourteen days' run by the *Scot* or *Dunnottar Castle* from English shores; and the voyage is the smoothest and the easiest in the world.

I was staying at the International Hotel on the slopes beneath Table Mountain, in an airy situation well removed from the heat of the town. From my bedroom window was a view of which I never tired. The white town below, the bay of turquoise blue, dotted near to the town with shipping; far across lay shores of glittering, snowy sand, backed by the bold range of Blaauwberg; while beyond rose chain upon chain of rocky sierras in dim blues and soft purples upon the horizon. To the left Robben Island swam in flat outline upon the entrance to Table Bay; beyond it the South Atlantic bounded all. More to the left lay the villas of Green and Sea Points, and above them the smooth, bold outlines of the mountain, modelled by Nature to resemble a couchant lion, the extremities of which are known to Cape people as the Lion's Head and Rump. No prospect in the world could be well fairer.

The day after my arrival I was taken to a charming bungalow on the shores of Kamps Bay, a breezy and most picturesque spot, lying beneath the series of rocky headlands known as the Twelve Apostles. Here, between sea-fishing and bathing,[1] we thoroughly enjoyed ourselves. This bungalow, a summer residence of my entertainer, is a sort of wing to the fine old thatched residence built by Lord Charles Somerset, an old-time Governor of Cape Colony. The fish we caught here were principally kreef (crayfish), hottentots, and klipfish. We angled with rod and line off the rocks.

A few days later I spent Christmas (1890) at Muizenberg, a seaside resort just across the Cape Peninsula, on the shores of False Bay. The weather here, tempered by the fresh sea-breeze, was perfect, and I rapidly recovered strength again. All round the Cape Peninsula the sea-fishing is excellent ; the waters swarm with many kinds of fish ; and the visitor to Muizenberg, Kalk Bay, and Simon's Town can always reckon upon good catches. On the 28th December, accompanied by two friends, I went to Kalk Bay —another Cape watering-place adjoining Muizen-

---

[1] It may be well to mention that the bathing in Kamps Bay, except in Bachelor's Cove and one or two other spots, is exceedingly dangerous, owing to the strong currents and the rocky nature of the coast.

berg—where we chartered a whale-boat, manned by Malays, and started for a day's fishing. The Malays are the chief fishermen at the Cape, and are very expert boatmen. We were soon pulled out into the bay, and began operations with long hand-lines, to which were attached two or three hooks and a weight. We were not long engaged before the fish began to pay us attentions. First we had a succession of "Romans" (*Chrysophrys cristiceps*), one of the most striking and delicious sea fish of the Cape, which we caught freely for a time. These fish, when taken out of the water, are of the most brilliant vermilion possible to imagine. They are perch-like in shape, and have sharp, white teeth; those we took ran from about two to four pounds. Presently some bigger fish made themselves felt; these were the rooi stompneus (red stump-nose), a big, heavy-shouldered fish, vividly striped in red and silver. Some of these fellows gave us excellent sport, and required humouring. We took some from eight to ten pounds in weight. Among these I hooked a tremendous fish (steenbras), which, how-ever, broke me and got clean away. These steenbras run to a great size (seventy or eighty pounds, I believe); the fellow that broke me must, from his strong, unyielding pull, have weighed between thirty and forty, I imagine. We caught also at this time hottentots, a small brown fish (*Sargus Capensis*), steenje, another small fish, which we cut up princi-pally for bait, and klipfish (*Blennius versicolor*), the latter a very well-tasted table fish.

Sport now tailing off a little, we hoisted sail and moved on towards Simon's Bay. Here we fell among numbers of silver-fish (*Dentex argyrozona*), a clean, silvery, rather whiting-like fish, which swims in immense numbers round the Cape and is largely eaten. We pulled up these fish by dozens, the luck being occasionally varied by a Roman or stompneus. The day was perfect, the blue sea smooth, and the heat relieved by a soft and pleasant breeze. Far away to the east, across the bay, loomed the mainland, the far Stellenbosch sierras, and the Hottentot's Holland Mountains, terminating in the bold rugged outline of Cape Hangklip, which projected far into the Indian Ocean. Behind us rose the rocky backbone of hills which runs down the Cape Peninsula, the heights of Muizenberg, and beyond them again the pleasant slopes of Wynberg. It was a goodly scene. But then the whole of the Cape Peninsula teems with scapes of the most varied and romantic beauty, as the visitor may quickly discover for himself.

We moved about from one ground to another during the day, almost always getting good sport; so that by the time we had finally weighed anchor, and (after winding up by a pleasant sail about Simon's Bay) reached Kalk Bay, we had a goodly show of fish on board. Many of the Cape fish are endowed with the quaintest Dutch names. Here are a few of them : Kabeljouw, Baardmannatje, Poempelmoesje, Katunka, Elftvisch, Stinkvisch, Poeskop, Dageraad, and others. For a hot climate, many of the fish in Cape waters furnish excellent eating ; the Roman, kingklipvisch, stomncus, steenbras, and klipvisch being among the choicest. We landed, well satisfied with our day, and a good quantity of the catch was sent to the cosy little hotel—" Farmer Peck's "—at which I was staying at Muizenberg, where Cape fish are to be tasted in the highest culinary perfection.

I made with a former fellow-passenger a pleasant trip to Stellenbosch. I had a letter of introduction to a large wine-farmer there, Mr. Marais of Mosterd's Drift, the possessor of one of the roomy old Dutch houses to be seen at Paarl and Stellenbosch. Stellenbosch is an educational centre, and with its great oak avenues, planted by the early settlers, fine old houses, and general air of old-time seclusion, is well worth a visit. In the gardens of another Dutch house here (also belonging to some Messrs. Marais) is to be found the finest collection of native flowers and plants in Cape Colony. Here were · flowers gathered with infinite care and trouble from every quarter of Southern Africa ; the collection was unique and very beautiful, and would have gladdened the eye of the late Miss Marianne North.

The old eighteenth-century mansion-houses of the Cape Dutch aristocracy, in the vicinity of Cape Town—at Wynberg and elsewhere—are many of them very fine. Notably the houses of Groote Constantia and Alphen. The former of these, for many generations in the Cloete family, is now the headquarters of the Government wine farm, where instruction in the latest systems of viticulture is given. I had the pleasure of attending a picnic, or rather a garden party, at one of these old places. We lunched at long tables spread under one of the ancient avenues of the estate. The oaks grew thickly overhead, so that the sun was excluded, and we were as cool as in the depths of an English forest. The master of the house, a fine old white-haired gentleman, was at the top of the long line of tables, at the other end of which sat his wife. Besides all manner of cold refections, the most beautiful fruits and excellent wines—all produced from the estate—loaded the board. The hock and other wines grown upon this estate, produced under very different conditions from the average run of Cape wines, and cool from the cellars of the old house, were fit to put upon any European table. I tasted claret, made from French vines grown upon this same estate, which had all the best qualities in taste and bouquet of French *grands vins*. But then, unfortunately, such wines are not at present to be procured in the Cape markets. Cape wines, however, have during the last few years immensely improved all round. Here, too, that fine old Cape liqueur, "Vanderhum," was to be tasted in perfection. The grapes from which Cape wines are made are, unlike those in Continental vineyards, fine table fruit also. We wandered afterwards through the vineyards of which I speak and gathered the luxuriant fruit, now just attaining perfection. Large and delicious grapes at a penny a huge bunch, and peaches equal to English hothouse fruit, were at this time— January—very abundant in Cape Town. Figs, apricots, apples, and pears were also plentiful. In the way of fruit—and by this I mean really fine fruit—few places are more favoured than the Cape Peninsula.

I had some pleasant mornings at the Cape Town Museum, and, thanks to the kindness of Mr. Roland Trimen, the Curator, was enabled, with Mr. J. E. Yale, to photograph various interesting specimens of natural history. Mr. Trimen's collection of

South African butterflies is very large and quite unique.

Thanks to the plentiful employment of convict labour, there are some magnificent roads now round the Cape Peninsula. The Victoria Drive, which has been mainly scarped from the steep mountain-sides, and runs far down the Peninsula to Houts Bay and thence round to Wynberg—whence one drives right round again to Cape Town by the other side of Table Mountain—is in its way perfect. For miles one drives along a fine smooth road, cut from the side of a precipitous mountain, far above the intense blue of the South Atlantic, and, after quitting the sea, the way passes through most lovely scenery at the back of Table Mountain.

On the 14th January (1891) I was overjoyed to meet quite unexpectedly in Adderley Street (the Bond Street of Cape Town) Mackay, who had just got down from Mashonaland. We had not seen or heard from each other since parting in the wilds of Khama's Country, and, during the week before he sailed, had much to talk of and many pleasant days together.

I saw some good cricket during this stay at Cape Town. The great tournament of the year was on ; teams from all quarters of Cape Colony were contesting ; and it was a pleasure to watch the game again at the beautiful Newlands ground, with the magnificent Devil's Peak towering over all. Here, instead of the usual up-country ground of naked and sunburnt earth, the greenest of turf covered all the vast enclosure. As, however, most of the other teams had been used to playing on cocoanut matting, the Western Province men courteously agreed to play, upon this occasion, on matting also. Although thus handicapped, they managed to win the tournament.

After four or five weeks' stay in Cape Town and its suburbs, and my health being again restored to its normal fitness, I proceeded once more by rail to Bechuanaland, before finally leaving for England. Tremendous rains had been falling for some weeks up-country, and, after waiting for several days in the hope of hearing that the Vaal River temporary bridge, which had become flooded, was passable by rail, and that the Harts River bridge, which had been swept away, was again repaired, I set off on the 26th January for Vryburg. The Orange River, as we crossed it, was swollen and muddy, but after passing Kimberley and reaching the Vaal we found the temporary bridge still twelve feet under water, and of course impassable. We had now to adopt the method of crossing, which obtained for some weeks at this time. We bundled out of the train and got into carts and waggons which carried us and our luggage down to the Vaal, now tearing and foaming along a terrific mass of yellowish water, a good half-mile between bank and bank. Here whale-boats, which had been got up from Port Elizabeth with special crews, were waiting for us. As soon as a boatload was complete we were towed up under the lee of the bank for a quarter of a mile, and then, turning the boat's head for the further shore, the sinewy rowers pulled with might and main across the raving mass of water. It was a magnificent sight. Just as it struck the full force of the current, the great boat was tossed and shaken very much as if it were a cork. Presently the worst was

mastered, and we slipped gradually down to the
northern landing-place, whence we were conducted
to a train waiting for us.

I crossed with General Joubert and his family,
who were just returning from England to the Transvaal, *via* Fourteen Streams. The General, whatever
his pluck may have been in Boer warfare, appeared
to be very far from happy on the flood, and was
infinitely relieved when it was over. I had a chat
with this celebrity at Fourteen Streams. He was
manifestly extremely vexed at the Mashonaland
expedition ; which, considering the fact that for years
he had been endeavouring to persuade Lobengula
that he, the Transvaal Codlin, was his friend, and
not the English Short, was not surprising. However,
he was civil enough, and we chatted on many topics.
It was amusing, indeed, to watch this Boer Command-
ant-General, who a few years before was to be seen
in his native veldt, clad in broad-brimmed hat,
moleskin trousers and jacket, and home-made velschoens, a typical Boer of Boers, now, fresh from
Europe, attired in broadcloth of shining black, frock-
coat, *silk top-hat*, and *patent leather boots*. Upon
the Vaal River too! It was enough to make his
stout Dutch Afrikander ancestors turn in their quiet
graves.

The General had with him a presentation sword,
carefully enveloped in a waterproof case, which he
was evidently vastly proud of and never suffered
out of the hollow of his arm. Joubert is a fine,
strongly-built man, tough as an oak. He has a
remarkably keen, if small eye, and looks all over,
what I believe him to be, a first-class rifle shot.
Since the Witwatersrand goldfields have brought

such wealth and opportunities to the Transvaal, he has, I believe, made his hay while the sun shone, and is now, like Oom Paul Kruger, a very rich man.

From the Vaal River I reached Vryburg without further trouble ; and, after completing what business I had to do there, I again left it on the 3rd of February, and, with no great reluctance, started for Cape Town. Vryburg had not yet recovered from the effects of its railway opening, and was still a place much given over to loafers and drunkenness. It is only fair to say that the town has long since thrown off the results of its temporary debauch, and is now a quiet, decent place again. Just now, in the midst of the torrential rains, it was a sea of mud, and locomotion was a matter of extreme difficulty. A new and better hotel had been opened, at which I put up ; but the preparations for visitors had barely been completed, and the way to one's bedroom, across the yard, lay over a frightful quagmire, through which one ploughed blindly and miserably in the dark.

As I passed down country the veldt was everywhere magnificent, the Batlaping cornlands down the Harts Valley were perfect pictures, and among the green grass great pink lilies were, in the moister situations, growing luxuriantly. Again the Vaal River had to be crossed in whale-boats ; but this time the flood had somewhat abated, and the stream ran less fiercely. Near the banks of the Orange River I noticed the country clothed in a charming array of primrose-coloured flowers. After passing the Orange, curiously enough, the immense rainfall had disappeared ; and the karroo, as we crossed it, was looking as parched and dreary as it was possible to imagine.

Cape Town was reached in good time, and a few days later I was on board the *Roslin Castle* steaming rapidly for the old country.

CHAPTER XXI.

FISHING IN BECHUANALAND

South African streams—Sand rivers—Siluroid fish—Common species of fish—Barbel on the Botletli—Brussels Farm—Our tackle—Among the karpers—Free biters—Silver-fish—A good bag—The "Wonder-gat"—Fishing at Mahura's—Barbel—Total bag.

SOUTH AFRICA in general, and Bechuanaland in particular, can hardly be cited as great fishing countries, and yet at intervals, in nearly all the vast territories that go to form Southern Africa, fair sport can be obtained. There are few rivers between the Cape and the Zambesi that run perennially; those that do, such as the Orange, the Vaal, the Crocodile (or Limpopo), the Botletli, and a few others, may almost be counted upon the fingers of one's hands. The average South African river is, indeed, a matter of keen disappointment to the new-comer, consisting, as it does usually, either of a dry watercourse dotted here and there with standing pools, or of a stony, sandy bed, innocent, save for a month or two during the rains, of any sign of water throughout its course. One often wonders why such shams should have been dignified, as they invariably are, with the name of rivers at all.

Here and there the "sand-rivers," characteristic of this strange land, are to be found. In these the stream flows under the sand, and can usually be found, even during the dry winter season, at a little

distance beneath the surface. This is so well understood that zebras and other water-loving game in the
old days came and pawed themselves their water
supply in these rivers. Occasionally this underground flow emerges from its sand bed and forms a
large pool, or chain of pools, at which flocks and
herds may be watered throughout the year. Such a
river is the Setlagoli. During the summer months,
when the rains fall, all rivers, from the lordly, ever-
flowing Limpopo, margined with great forest trees,
to the merest parched "spruit" that here counts as
river, race, foam, and roar along in dense masses of
yellow, turbid water, most of them, unfortunately,
to disappear almost as quickly as they sprang into
being. But in all these streams, even at the driest
period of the year, wherever the semblance of water
is to be found—nay, even where a deep mud-hole
represents what was once a pool—fish are to be met
with all over Southern Africa. Naturally siluroid
fish occur most frequently, capable as they are of
supporting life even when nothing but a half-dry
mud-hole remains to them. The fish I have most
often found, from the Cape to the Ngamiland
region, may be ranked as follows : Barbel, karper
(carp), yellow fish, silver-fish, mullet, a kind of
bream-like fish found abundantly in the Botletli, and
a sort of perch, common to the same river. Other
fish no doubt exist, but the piscatorial treasures of
Africa are at present very ill-explored, and most
people, like myself, are far more often and more
profitably employed with the gun than with rod
and line.

Barbel, for some odd reason always called "bar-
bers" by the colonists, are, on the whole, the most

numerous and commonest fish. On the Botletli, we found them in extraordinary profusion; pools were thick with them, and at the lower end of the river, as we walked along the shores, we often came on large fish, just abandoned by the numerous fishing eagles that here preyed on them. We were too much engaged in hunting to trouble much about fishing on this expedition; but, curiously enough, the first time my shooting companion put a line into the river he only had one bite, and, although there were swarms of barbel to be seen, he came back to the waggon without having landed a single fish. The natives along the Botletli River, and notably the Makoba, capture large quantities of fish with primitive hooks and lines, which are often set very much as night-lines for eels are set at home, as well as by spearing, netting, and by means of weirs.

On returning to Vryburg, the tiny capital of British Bechuanaland, from the interior, I had one or two excellent days' fishing in the vicinity. On Oct. 12, I drove out with two friends to Brussels Farm, where is a capital little "spruit" or watercourse standing between some low hills or undulations in the veldt. Brussels was a well-known post during Sir Charles Warren's expedition; and the remains of two rude stone forts, which command the water beneath, testify yet to the preparations made to guard the principal water supplies on the line of march. After two hours' rather windy drive, we reached the farmhouse, and were hospitably welcomed by the occupier, Mr. Steyn. Brussels, I believe, now belongs to the Southern Land Company, and in the hands of the present tenant is assuming a charming aspect. Water has been led out in various directions. Fruit trees—apricots, peaches, apples, and pears—were flourishing, and lettuce, radishes, and other vegetables [1] (rare luxuries in Bechuanaland) gladdened the eye and refreshed the palate. A large piece of good alluvial bottom land had been ploughed and sown with oats, and a grand crop of oat-hay, or, as it is locally called, "forage"—some 20,000 bundles in all—was standing all but ready for the sickle. Forage is one of the best-paying crops in South Africa, and 20,000 bundles at from 3d. to 6d. per bundle, wholesale price, represented a by no means bad result of a few months' farming operations. So at least we thought.

We now proceeded to put our extremely primitive tackle together. Our rods consisted of light bamboo whip-sticks about twelve feet long ; to these were attached common lines, ending in about two feet of gut. We used the most ordinary painted cork floats, such as are bought in English toy shops for 1d. or 2d. apiece. We had plenty of worms, dug for us by a sharp little Bechuana boy, who kept us well supplied in this respect during the whole of the day. We started angling about 200 yards from the farmhouse, at a point where the spruit broadens out into a respectable pool about thirty yards in width, and where the water was fairly deep. We had no sooner put our lines in than the fish began to bite freely ; and then for an hour we had capital sport with " karpers," pulling them out almost as fast as we could take off the captured fish and rebait our

---

[1] Although vegetables are at present scarce in Bechuanaland, there is no reason why, with a little care and irrigation, they should be. The soil will produce amazingly. A cauliflower weighing twenty-seven pounds, grown near Vryburg, was brought into the town when I was there in 1890.

hooks. These fish ran from a quarter to half-a-pound in weight, and averaged probably about a quarter of a pound each. The whole business, the primitive tackle, the plucky free-biting fish, and the bright hot day, reminded me irresistibly of early essays with the perch in my youthful days in summer holidays in Northamptonshire. There, in my juvenile explorations, I discovered that the old field bridges over a certain " feeder " or stream harboured in the heat of summer shoals of gallant perch, which in those days must have been utterly innocent of the mysteries of hooks and floats. Save that these perch were much heavier—they ran mainly from half-a-pound to a pound and a quarter — they and their eager, free-biting, unsophisticated ways were at once brought back to mind as I pulled out, in distant Bechuanaland, these plucky " karpers." The karper or carp (Rooivlerk karper, red-finned carp, of the Dutch colonists ; *Barbus* (*Pseudobarbatus*) *Burchellii* of Dr. Andrew Smith, first identified, as its name implies, by the traveller Burchell, *circa* 1812) is a handsome little fish, not unlike a perch in shape. Its colour is of a warm olive-bronze, its fins are red, and its flesh is white. Although small, it is a capital table fish, sweet as the English perch, and our friends at Vryburg were not a little glad, on our return from the day's fishing, to have fresh fish wherewith to vary the dreadful monotony of Bechuanaland dietary. Every now and again we drew out, glittering gaily beneath the strong sun, shining silver-fish ; a small delicate fish, very much resembling in size, colouring, and the tenderness of its scales, our gudgeon at home. We landed only one or two barbel on this occasion, and those but small ones—a couple of pounds or so apiece in weight—but the karpers kept us very fully employed. In about three and a half hours' fishing we captured (four rods) 160 of these fish, of which I, who had had the most luck, contributed fifty-four. Our hooks were too large and clumsy ; if we had had smaller hooks we could probably have nearly doubled our score without great difficulty. We lunched in the middle of the day at the pleasant hospitable board of Mr. Steyn, and towards evening set off on the two hours' drive to Vryburg, very well contented with our day's sport.

Speaking of the silver-fish, as they are called, there are numbers of them to be found, curiously enough, in a huge, rock-encircled tarn of very deep water about fifteen miles from Mafeking. This tarn lies just over the Transvaal border in Marico, and is well known in the neighbourhood by its Boer name of " Wonder-gat " (Wonder-hole). This singular square hole, clean rent in the encircling rock by some mighty convulsion of nature, is about 200 yards by 150, and is evidently of volcanic origin. It lies among pleasant groves of thorn trees, and is one of the chosen picnic spots for the people of the rising town of Mafeking. Numbers of silver-fish can be seen playing in the clear blue depths of this cool and shady tarn, which hitherto has borne the reputation of being unfathomable. It is certainly of great depth. I believe a year or two since Sir Charles Metcalfe swam into the middle, and attempted to touch the bottom with a long line ; and I believe I am right in saying he was unsuccessful. It is said that the Molopo River partially owes its source to the Wonder-gat, by means of some subterraneous communication.

A week after our expedition to Brussels Farm we went out in another direction to Mahura's, a native location under the headman of that name, a brother of Mankoroane, chief of the Batlapins. This place lies some two and a half hours—or fifteen miles—from Vryburg. A pleasant stream flows quietly between low hills, upon the further of which is planted the native " stadt," a clean, orderly Bechuana village. Mahura's, or Takwaning, was formerly one of the early missionary settlements, and amid the corn lands that bespread the valley, fruit trees, planted by the loving hands of Moffat and of Livingstone, stand silent yet eloquent witnesses of their untiring efforts to help and improve the Bechuanas. We were in greater force on this occasion ; there were ladies of the party ; the day was a blazing hot one ; and the fish were not quite so eager. On the whole, however, we did fairly well, and we were particularly successful among the barbel. This fish (*Glanis silurus*) grows to enormous weight and size in the larger African rivers. In the Crocodile, Botletli, and others they are captured up to twenty pounds in weight, and are strong, vigorous fish, requiring, of course, stout running tackle. In the small stream at Mahura's the heaviest we took was about four pounds only. Our bag this day amounted to thirty karpers, twenty fair barbel, and a quantity of silver-fish, most of which latter were thrown back as soon as captured. We reached Vryburg at 7.30 (after dark in this region), after an enjoyable day in Mahura's pleasant valley. South African fishing cannot, of course, compare with European sport. Still, to the disciple of Walton, angling, however humble, is angling, all the world over ; it comes occasionally as a pleasant diversion in the monotony of up-country life, and for such reasons these notes on Bechuana-land fishing are, perhaps, worth recording.

CHAPTER XXII.

THE GAME-BIRDS OF BECHUANALAND

BECHUANALAND is a great territory, extending as it does from Griqualand in the south to the Zambesi in the north; and as much of it, especially in Khama's northern country and towards the Kalahari region, is, even to this day, quite unexplored by the naturalist, it will probably be many years before any systematic codification of its prolific bird-life may be looked for. Traveller-naturalists, from the time of Dr. Andrew Smith's expedition in 1835, have, however, been quietly pushing their way northward, each adding his mite of discovery ; and although nothing at all approaching a representative avi-fauna of the country is yet obtainable, a goodly number of birds have been identified from the land of the Bechuana.

Nowadays, as the nobler game disappears, the average up-country traveller finds himself more and

2 G

more dependent upon feathered life for his daily
supply of meat ; and, naturally enough, his attention at once fixes itself upon the game-birds as a
food product.   Running down the gamut of selection,
he will probably choose in the following order of
merit : First, the guinea-fowls ; second, the francolins
(partridges and pheasants, as they are called all over
South Africa) ; third, the bustards other than the
paauw—which is, of course, *the* table bird of South
Africa, but which is not always to be obtained ;
fourth, the sandgrouse.   Next to that king of sporting birds the paauw or kori bustard (*Otis kori*),
the guinea-fowls are by far the most desirable for
the pot ; and a stew of these birds, seasoned with
onions, potatoes, pepper, salt, and, if you have it in
your waggon, a wineglass or two of Cape Pontac (red
wine), will furnish forth a dish fit for an alderman,
and soup worthy the praise of Lucullus.

But all this, the reader will say, is treating of the
game-bird from an extremely sordid point of view.
My reply is, that the traveller bound on a long
waggon journey, say to Mashonaland or the Zambesi,
has scant opportunity of getting far from the road
in search of heavy game, frequently very little
chance of buying a goat or a sheep from natives
who hate breaking into their flocks, and he is therefore ofttimes absolutely dependent for his modest
meal on the game-bird, which may be shot wherever
he passes along the road.

Wild duck, wigeon, and teal are, of course, always
welcome ; but, except on large rivers, such as the
Limpopo, Marico, Botletli, Zambesi, and others, or
upon the pans and pools of water after the summer
rains, they are not always obtainable in Bechuana-

land. The African wild goose is, as a rule, not
highly delectable as a table bird, being often tough
and ill-flavoured ; for choice—when choice can be had
—the spur-winged goose (*Plectropterus gambensis*)
is the best of a poor lot.

Following the classification of Gray in his " Genera
of Birds," I will begin these notes on Bechuanaland
sporting birds with the guinea-fowl. Of this genus
the only member found throughout the country is
Numida Mitrata, the Cape guinea-fowl. No single
example, that I am aware, of *Numida Cristata*, the
variety common to Eastern Africa, has ever been
found in Bechuanaland or the Kalahari. This handsome and prolific game-bird (*Numida Mitrata*),
known also to naturalists as *Numida Cornuta* (Finsch
and Hartlaub), distinguished by its crimson head
and wattles, and pale blue neck—the space round
the eye being of like colour—is common, wherever
water and bush are to be found, all over Bechuanaland. Beyond the Kalahari I have met with them
along the Botletli River up to within a few days
of Lake Ngami. They extend right through to
Damaraland on the west coast, and indeed are found
almost everywhere south of the Zambesi. In the dry
season they collect in immense troops—Andersson
speaks of having seen over a thousand gathered in
one spot. At ordinary times they are to be found
in bands of from twenty to a hundred, but often
in the interior more may be seen together. In the
forest country fringing the Botletli River we put
up troops of between two and three hundred. It
is a wonderful thing towards evening to see and
hear these birds preparing for their night's roost.
A large troop will fill two or three good-sized trees,

and the noisy clamour of their metallic notes, once
heard, is never forgotten.   These birds are such
swift and determined runners that they often give
a good deal of trouble to circumvent.   Frequently
an old dog accustomed to their habits is employed,
his tactics being to gallop them hard till they take
to the trees, as they always will do ; they are then
easily secured.   In shooting for the pot they are
often marked into their roosting trees and approached
at night, when good bags are readily obtained.   This
mode of shooting will not sound very reputable to
the English gunner, but in a rough, wild country
necessity knows or recognises little of sporting
morality.   From their running habits these birds
are terribly apt to spoil sporting dogs, and even
old seasoned pointers find them very trying.

Of the francolins there are at least six species to
be found in Bechuanaland.   By far the most widely
distributed and in some respects the handsomest
of this family is the Orange River francolin (*Francolinus Gariepensis*).   This bird, as I have elsewhere remarked, bears a strong resemblance to the
" red-wing " partridge of Cape Colony (*Francolinus
Levaillantii*), and is indeed always referred to by
sportsmen in Bechuanaland as the " red-wing."   A
comparison of the plumage of these two birds,
however, clearly establishes considerable difference ;
the colouring of the Cape red-wing is darker than
and the size slightly inferior to the Orange River
francolin.   The general colouring of this extremely
handsome bird is reddish brown upon the back ; the
feathers are barred crosswise with a darker brown,
and marked lengthwise down the shafts with
creamy white.   The under parts are reddish yellow,

blotched and marked with ferruginous brown, and upon the stomach with dark chocolate colour. There are, as in the Cape red-wing, peculiar distinguishing bands of brown, mottled with white, running from the eye and mouth, and separated by an orange and brown stripe, the upper band continuing to the base of the neck, the lower one forming a half moon in front of the neck. The chin and throat are white, and the head and neck ferruginous brown.

I found these birds plentiful in nearly every part of Bechuanaland, in the Kalahari, and north westward along the Botletli River, where, however, they seemed less plentiful. They are found as far eastward as Mashonaland. They are by far the best sporting birds in the country, lie well, and have a strong, well-sustained flight. Of all the South African francolins they approach, I think, most nearly to the English partridge ; but, as with nearly all African game - birds, they are somewhat dry eating, and are not to be compared to their English brethren as table birds. They average about thirteen inches in length, and are heavier than the English partridge. They are extremely partial to the slopes of low grassy hills, and, during the heat of the day, to adjacent bushy cover. Along the banks of the Maritsani River in British Bechuanaland we found them extremely abundant. Whenever we shot in the vicinity of this river we had capital sport, and, with two or three guns, usually accounted for ten or eleven brace in a day's shooting, besides guinea-fowl, koorhaans, hares, dikkop (a kind of plover), small buck, and other game. To shoot these, or indeed any other game-birds in South Africa, a decent pointer is a *sine qua non,* and, even with tough, South African bred dogs, it is a hard matter to keep them at work in the heat of midday, even during winter time.   If water can be found once or twice during the day, the dogs will of course stand the work better.   The sharp call of these birds, which usually run in coveys of from five to eight or ten, is one of the best-remembered sounds at dawn and towards sundown on the up-country veldt.   Round Vryburg and Mafeking these birds afford the principal shooting to the inhabitants, and are to be found just outside the towns ; indeed, there was at least one covey in Vryburg itself in 1890. The true red-wing partridge of the Cape (Le Vaillant's francolin) I have never encountered in Bechuanaland, nor do I think it is often found north of the Orange River.

Next to the Orange River francolin, the red-billed francolin (*Francolinus adspersus*) is one of the commonest game-birds, especially after the Molopo River is crossed and the Protectorate is reached. Wherever water and bush are to be found, these "pheasants," as they are called, are not far distant. They are, I think, the most water-loving of all the francolins, and their presence is an infallible token that a stream or fountain is not far distant.   Along the Limpopo River they are plentiful, and round the lagoons and rivulets formed by the rising of the Botletli they are found in great profusion.   Trekking in 1890 down the Crocodile (Limpopo) River, it was a wonderful sight to see these francolins running along the road in front of the waggons at early morning and during the hour before sundown. They are rather smaller than the *Francolinus Gariepensis*, averaging about a foot in length.   The colouring is of a much more sober hue—a brownish drab in general effect ; the bill and legs are red, the space round the eye is yellow. They are great runners, and will either seek the thickest bush or, if pushed from thence, will fly up into trees, where they sit motionless and often evade the gunner's eye. The flesh is slightly inferior to that of the Orange River francolin. Along the Botletli River I found these francolins the most common, and their harsh successive screams, rising in gradation, were very noticeable.

Another "pheasant" encountered, but not nearly so commonly, was Swainson's francolin (*Francolinus Swainsonii*), a great coarse bird of drab brown colouring, yellowish underneath, chiefly distinguishable by the bare skin of the throat and chin, which is of a brilliant crimson colour, as is the space round the eyes. I do not think this bird can be at all common. During a year's residence in all parts of Bechuanaland from north to south, I saw it only on the banks of the Setlagoli and Maritsani rivers. It is no doubt to be found elsewhere, but is distinctly scarce. Andersson mentions having found it sparingly in North Damaraland and plentifully upon the Okavango River. Like the last-mentioned francolin, it will take refuge in trees, but is not quite so inseparably wedded to the vicinity of water. It is fond of dense bushy cover by the banks of dry watercourses. Like all the "pheasants," it has an unpleasant, harsh cry, and it is, I think, the poorest eating of its family. In length it attains to fourteen inches and even more, and is the largest francolin in Bechuanaland.

The Coqui francolin (*Francolinus Subtorquatus*)

is the most diminutive and by far the most beautiful of the African francolins. When our first specimens were shot near Mosita in British Bechuanaland, we were enraptured with the appearance of this most dainty, vividly painted game-bird. The rich chestnut brown of the head, the brilliant orange of the neck, eyebrows, and ear coverts, and above all the singular hawk - like markings of the breast and stomach—brown-black crossbars, on a creamy ground, extending even to the leg feathers—all serve to distinguish this little beauty instantly from its fellows. The back is of a dark brown colour, paler towards the tail, with transverse markings in white and chocolate. In the female there are slight, black, chain-like markings which form a gorget upon the throat. The legs are deep yellow, and, for the size of the bird, armed with very formidable spurs. We found this bird widely distributed throughout Bechuanaland and the Kalahari. Its range extends beyond Lake Ngami, and it has been found on the Okavango River by the late C. J. Andersson. It is also commonly met with in Matabeleland. This francolin is extremely partial to bushy, forest country alternating with open grassy spaces; it lies extremely close, closer I think than any other francolin, requiring a steady, careful pointer ; and, after being once flushed, it is often very difficult to put up, lying as it does in the most obstinate manner. As a rule these birds are found in coveys of from six to twelve, only rarely, however, exceeding eight or nine. They average about nine or ten inches in length, and are very good eating. Like the Orange River francolin, they rest for the night on the ground, not in trees as do the " pheasants " and guinea-fowls.   The Coqui and the Orange River francolins, from their wide distribution, may be said mainly to represent the "partridge" shooting of Bechuanaland and the interior.

The pileated francolin (*Francolinus pileatus*) is more local than some others of its genus.   Personally I only met with it along the Marico and Limpopo rivers, but it was nowhere common.   It is, I believe, found near rivercourses in other parts of Bechuanaland, and Andersson has recorded it in North Damaraland.   It frequents the grassy slopes near rivers. In colouring it is of a pale reddish brown, the breast and stomach are dusky yellow, the breast sprinkled with triangular red brown markings, the stomach barred with thin lines of the same colour.   The head is greyish brown, the chin and throat are white, while the neck is white, dotted with reddish brown. This is a handsome bird, very similar in size to the Orange River francolin, and almost equally good as a table bird.

Last on the list of the francolins known to have their habitat in Bechuanaland is the Natal francolin (*Francolinus Natalensis;* the *Francolinus Lechoho* of Dr. Andrew Smith).   Dr. Smith erred in taking the native name "Lechoho" to be the designation of a specific variety.   Lesogo, pronounced Lĕsōhō (the g in Sechuana being pronounced as h), is merely the name given by Bechuanas to all francolins ; Mosogo being the singular.   This is a species which may be referred to the so-called South African "pheasants" ; it roosts and takes refuge in trees, is fond of water and watercourses, and is a great runner.   Its general colour upon the top is of a lightish brown, variegated with dark brown and creamy white.   The neck, breast, and stomach are black and white, tinged with light brown at the lower part of the stomach and beneath the tail coverts. The legs and feet are orange. First discovered by Dr. Smith in his travels in Bechuanaland in 1835–6, it has been recorded by Frank Oates as far north as the Mahalapsi River (Khama's country), and probably ranges even further. It is found occasionally on the north-west portion of the Limpopo (of which the Mahalapsi is a tributary), but is nowhere so plentiful or so widely distributed as its cousin the red-billed francolin, which it resembles in size but not in colouring.

The common quail (*Coturnix Communis*) is distributed pretty generally over all Bechuanaland, but is, probably owing to drought and other migratory causes, much more numerous in some seasons than in others.

The harlequin quail (*Coturnix Delegorguei*), slightly larger than the common quail, with its brown head, drab upper colouring, singularly relieved with black and white, white and black spotted throat and neck, black chest, and ruddy stomach, is rare in Bechuanaland. Personally I do not remember to have seen a specimen, but 1890 was not a good quail year, at all events in the interior. It has been found by Chapman as far to the north-west as Lake Ngami, while Andersson makes mention of it at Ondonga in Ovampoland, north-west of the lake.

Of the bush quails (sub-family *Turnicinæ*), I am only aware of one referable to Bechuanaland, *Turnix Lepurana*, otherwise called the Kurichane hemipode. Dr. Smith first discovered this tiny game-bird (less than six inches in length) near Kurichane, north of Kuruman; but it is found sparingly in other open, grassy portions of the country. On our trek to Morokweng, South-East Kalahari (now part of British Bechuanaland), we shot some of these birds. We never, I think, found more than a pair at a time, and they are most difficult to flush, every foot of the ground having to be carefully worked before they can be put up. I well remember the extraordinary difficulty we had to flush some of these quail near Kudunque Laagte, on the road from Mosita to Morokweng. They are so small, and other birds so plentiful, that the gunner oftener than not lets them go unscathed; a small quail, or even half-a-dozen, being no great catch for a hungry man. Moreover, ordinary No. 5 or 6 shot make a sad mess of such diminutive game. Andersson records them in Great Namaqualand; and it is probable, therefore, that they extend sparingly throughout the Kalahari after the rains. We usually found them near water. The body-colouring above is a pale, reddish brown ; the head, neck, and back are barred with darker brown ; the chin and throat are creamy ; the hue of the breast is orange, marked with tiny brown spots, and the stomach is yellowish white. Altogether this is a very beautiful and remarkable little game-bird.

Of the sandgrouse there are four varieties found in Bechuanaland, viz., the Namaqua, the double-banded, the variegated, and the yellow-throated sandgrouse.

Of these the first, *Pterocles Tachypetes*, known all over South Africa as the Namaqua partridge, is found throughout the length and breadth of Bechuanaland, the Kalahari Desert, and even as far as Lake Ngami. Crossing the Kalahari, between Khama's new town Palachwe and the Botletli River, we found them at one or two pools in the desert, Maqua and T'Klakane, in astounding numbers, mingled with other varieties, and on the Botletli they were also frequently seen.

The double-banded sandgrouse (*Pterocles Bicinctus*)

YELLOW-THROATED SANDGROUSE, MAQUA POOL, NORTH KALAHARI, 1890.

the male of which is, I think, when freshly killed, distinctly the most beautiful of this family, we found very common after leaving Palachwe, trekking westward.   At desert waters it was very abundant, and

at Mesa, on the Zambesi road, and at a stream
shortly before reaching Mesa, we had some wonderful
flight shooting, just as they came down to the water
at sunset.

It is worthy of note that this species drink only in
the evening ; the Namaqua sandgrouse between eight
and ten in the morning, and sometimes in the afternoon ; while *Pterocles Gutturalis*, though sometimes
seen at water about the middle of the afternoon, also
drinks mainly between 8 and 10 A.M. The variegated sandgrouse came to the water quite early in
the morning, just after sunrise. Such at least were
the results of our observations.

Pterocles Variegatus we found the rarest species
in this country. *Pterocles Gutturalis* was plentiful
at pools in the North Kalahari, but it is, I think,
a more local bird than the double-banded and
Namaqua sandgrouse. It is, too, much the largest
and heaviest of all four species, and in the deep red-
brown colouring of the lower part of the body, and
in its cry, resembles most nearly of the family the
red grouse of Scotland. The peculiar sulphur-green
colouring of the neck and breast of the male,
and the dark-brown, gorget-like mark upon the
breast, serve still more to render it a notable bird.
The sandgrouse have, I think, the toughest skins of
any African birds, and we found the skinning of our
specimens uncommonly hard work.

In such numbers do these birds collect at desert
pools that almost any number can be shot. The very
rustle of their wings as they rise or settle down by
the water is a revelation. But although they collect
in such profusion at drinking time, they are scattered
during the day, usually in pairs, all over the veldt.

In a day's ride over the plains, no great numbers
seem to be encountered. Those vast armies that
sweep and circle about the fountains at morning and
evening must therefore be drawn from a very large
expanse of country. The wonderful flight of these
birds — swift and prolonged — takes them during
their daily search for food no doubt over immense
distances.

First of all the bustards in Bechuanaland, as in all
South Africa, stands, of course, the paauw or kori
bustard (gom paauw [1] of the Boers ; the *Otis Kori* of
its discoverer, Dr. Burchell). Kori, by the way, is
the Sechuana name for this noble bird. Pre-eminent
among all game-birds for its great size (a good male
will measure from 4 feet 7 inches to 4 feet 9 inches
in length, and weigh from 25 lbs. to 40 lbs. and even
50 lbs.) and extreme value as a table bird, the paauw
is eagerly sought by every gunner, white, black, or
off-coloured. We found it in every part of Bechuanaland, in the Kalahari, and as far north-west as the
Botletli River. Its range is, owing to its migratory
instincts, no doubt very wide ; Andersson has recorded it in Damaraland, Great Namaqualand, and
Ovampoland ; and, south of the Zambesi, it may be
said to occur in every portion of South Africa.

Probably for the reason that it is prized by every
sportsman, from the Masarwa Bushman with his tiny
bow and poisoned arrows to the Englishman with his
breechloader, the paauw is an excessively wary bird,
and requires a good deal of circumventing. It is
oftener shot with the rifle than with the " scatter-
gun." Very often, as one travels by post cart along
the up-country roads, a pair of these magnificent

[1] Literally, gum-peacock.

birds may be seen within thirty or forty yards of the
track. It usually happens, of course, that there is
no gun in the cart on these occasions, and I think
the paauw, from constant practice, is a pretty good
judge of post carts and the chances of the gun not
being on board. As a rule this bird is found in semi-
bushy country, varied by open flats. As its Dutch
name implies, it is extremely fond of the gum that
exudes from the mimosa thorns at certain seasons.
The general colouring is greyish brown strongly
mottled; the breast and stomach are white, and
there is a gorget or collar of black between the neck
and breast. The wing feathers are black, the top of
the head is black and strongly crested, and the legs
are yellow.

The lesser paauw (*Eupodotis Ludwigii*) is, I
believe, occasionally found in Bechuanaland, but
personally I have not met with a specimen during
some very extensive wanderings over that country.
This bird, large though it is, is considerably smaller
than the gom paauw; a cock measures about 3 feet
6 inches in length, the hen being smaller.

The rufous-crested bustard (*Eupodotis ruficrista*)
is one of the best sporting birds in Bechuanaland,
where it is always known as the bush koorhaan.
It has a singularly swift, dodging flight, gets up
suddenly and noiselessly, and wavers off among the
trees, when after a short flight it goes down again.
It is not so vexatious a runner as the black koorhaan, and can generally be marked and picked up
again pretty easily. Dr. Smith, who first discovered
this bird near Latakoo (Kuruman), says, singularly
enough, that it was restricted to grassy plains, and
" rarely occurred in districts supplied with brush-

wood." All I can say is that the exact reverse is
now the case, and the bush koorhaan is invariably
found throughout Bechuanaland in bushy country,
and more often still in forest or semi-forest country.
It is tender, and excellent eating. We found this
bird as far north as the Botletli River, and its range
extends to South Damaraland. In the giraffe acacia
forests round Setlagoli they are very common, and
were always a welcome addition to our bags. The
head and neck are bluish grey, the back is reddish
brown variegated in dark brown and black; the chin
and sides of head are dusky white, the breast and
stomach of an intense black; the legs are yellow, and
the head is crested in the male, the crest being of
a rufous pink. The most remarkable thing about
this bird is that the whole of the soft, fluffy, under
portion of the feathers is of a delicate rufous pink
tinge, the skin sharing the same hue. This beautiful
colouring fades a good deal after death. This elegant
game-bird averages in length about seventeen or
eighteen inches.

The Vaal koorhaan (*Otis scolopacea*) a handsome
bustard, slightly larger than *Otis Afroides*, is found
sparingly throughout Bechuanaland. It is distinguishable by its pale rufous and ashy general colouring, variegated with darker browns and black, and by
its black chin, throat, and quill-feathers. The head
is crested, and has a black lunate mark at the back.
The jet-black chin and throat are handsomely set off
by a border of pale yellow. Found in pairs. As
with the bush koorhaan, the under parts of the
feathers are suffused with a pinkish tinge, which
fades after death.

The blue-necked or Senegal bustard (*Eupodotis*

Senegalensis), a very handsome bird, distinguished by its bright rufous upper colouring, white chin and cheeks, black throat, and rufous neck and breast slightly tinted with blue, is found locally, but not very frequently, in Bechuanaland. Probably it is more plentiful in some years than others. To the best of my belief I saw a specimen shot on some flats at Woodhouse Kraal, near Setlagoli, in March 1890. The bird was, however, plucked and eaten, unfortunately, before I could identify it at camp in the evening. My friend Mr. H. Gethin, of Sligo Farm, near Setlagoli, who, so far as I could judge, identified this bird to me, shot a number towards the end of 1890 on the eastern frontier of British Bechuanaland, near the Transvaal border, between Vryburg and Mafeking.

The last on my list of the bustards known to Bechuanaland, the black-and-white koorhaan (*Eupodotis Afroides*), is the commonest. This bird is so exceedingly like the black koorhaan of Cape Colony (*Eupodotis Afra*) that it is always referred to by the same name in Bechuanaland. The two species, similar though they are, are easily identified ; the Bechuanaland bird having a broad band of white on the black wing-feathers, while the wings of the Cape Colony species are wholly black. This handsome and game-like bird renders himself so obnoxious to the gunner by reason of his terribly noisy habits, that he has actually been excluded from the close time granted to all other game-birds in British Bechuanaland, and may be slain whenever and wherever found, without benefit of clergy. Herein I think the authorities have gone too far.

True it is that whenever this bustard gets up he

utters the most harsh and noisy cackling, and continues it during his flight (usually a high but not a very prolonged one), until he drops again a few hundred yards away; and undeniably by this habit he often does spoil the chances of sport and disturb other game. Yet he has his good points. Many a time and oft he provides a dinner for the hungry wayfarer, travelling through a parched and desolate country; he is as handsome as a picture, as he stalks through the grass or dodges among the low brush, and he is after all a capital sporting bird. I trust, therefore, that in succeeding years *Eupodotis Afroides* may, in spite of his faults, have mercy extended to him by the Bechuanaland lawgivers.

The cock, with his notable jet-black breast and stomach, upper plumage handsomely variegated in black, brown, and white, white ear coverts, eye stripe and collar, black and white-blazed wings, and large size—he averages some nineteen inches in length—is always a satisfactory addition to the day's bag. He and his more sober-coloured hen are not bad eating, and the veldt would often be lonely enough without them. Curiously enough, although we had encountered this bird in every part of British Bechuanaland, we never set eyes on a single specimen after leaving Ramathlabama in the Protectorate, just north of Mafeking, until we had passed Khama's town, Palachwe, and half crossed the North Kalahari on our way to the Botletli River. This is a long trek, and the fact is remarkable. It may, however, have been sheer accident, and the character of the veldt (much of the Protectorate is mountainous and bushy) may have had something to do with it. All along the flats bordering the Botletli River this bustard was common. Andersson records it in Damaraland.

With the black-and-white koorhaan my list—which comprises one species of guinea-fowl, six francolins, three quails, four sandgrouse, and six bustards—is ended. It is much more than probable that other game-birds will in the future be remarked in Bechuanaland, as the country becomes opened up. I may claim only to have attempted a modest classification of such sporting birds as are at present identified in that vast and most interesting territory.[1]

It may be useful here to remark that, under a recent proclamation amending the game laws of British Bechuanaland, no paauw, koorhaan, dikkop, guinea-fowl, pheasant, partridge, grouse (by which, of course, sandgrouse are meant), hare and buck (including the whole antelope species) with the exception of springboks actually migrating, may be " pursued, hunted, or shot at," from the 1st September to the last day of February inclusive, in the divisions of Vryburg, Mafeking, Taungs, and Kuruman.

By the same proclamation wild duck, wild geese, and snipe are protected in the same districts from the 1st September to the 31st December inclusive.

---

[1] In those cases where I have not personally handled and noted the game-birds described I have taken my descriptions from Layard's "Birds of South Africa."

CHAPTER XXIII.

PRESENT DISTRIBUTION OF THE LARGE GAME OF BECHUANALAND, NGAMILAND, AND THE KALA-HARI

The good old days—Crowds of game—An ancient rubbing-post—Difficulty of checking slaughter—A picture of the past—Animals still to be found—The elephant and his strongholds—Black rhinoceros—White rhinoceros nearly extinct—Hippopotamus—Buffalo—Lion—Leopard —Cheetah—Giraffe—Burchell's zebra—Ostrich—Eland—Sable antelope—Roan antelope—Koodoo—Waterbuck—Gemsbok—Brindled gnu —Hartebeest—Tsesseby—Lechwē—Situtunga—Pookoo—Reedbuck — Blesbok — Pallah — Springbok — Bushbuck — Red rhebok — Vaal rhebok — Steinbok—Grysbok—Klipspringer—Duyker—Wart hog—Game laws.

WHEN the first English travellers crossed the Orange River at the beginning of this century and entered the country of the Bechuanas, what a wealth of animal life, much of it new and unknown, met their astonished gaze. In those glorious times, even in passing through the Cape Colony, they had trekked day after day across karroos teeming with an astonishing variety of game, which everywhere ranged in countless multitudes. But after passing the Orange River their delight became redoubled. New and interesting forms were constantly discovered. The giraffe, the Burchell zebra, the white rhinoceros, the brindled gnu, the waterbuck, the tsesseby, pallah, and other strange and beautiful species, were found ranging in an inordinate plenty through plains and forests, or by the rivers, their numbers little if at all checked

484

by the spear, the arrow, nay even by the hopos or gigantic pitfalls of the tribes that from them drew their sustenance.

Every explorer, every hunter from 1813 to 1860, expatiated on his return to civilisation with never-failing zest upon the wonderful natural game preserves of this favoured land. Nothing can well convey a sadder idea of the frightful waste of animal life that has taken place since the introduction of firearms into the interior, than a perusal of the travels of Burchell (1813), Andrew Smith (1835), Cornwallis Harris (1836), Livingstone (1840–56), Gordon Cumming (1843–49), and Baldwin (1851–60), and a comparison of the crowds of game then encountered with the present fauna. The game has not all gone, it is true, but the hunter nowadays, instead of having battalions of animal life blackening the plains around his waggons, has to trek very far and to work very hard to find sport. In another twenty years, unless preservation—a difficult matter in native territories —sets in strongly, African game in the countries between the Orange River and the Zambesi will be little else than a memory ; and in one short century the matchless fauna of Southern Africa, which countless ages have looked upon, will have been swept away.

Mr. Selous, the last of the great hunters, who has passed twenty years of a singularly stirring and active life in the distant wilds of the far interior, has himself seen and opened up almost virgin hunting grounds, especially in Mashonaland and the Chobe River country, nearly two decades since. But even these far-off preserves are being depleted ; the elephant and the rhinoceros have well-nigh gone, the buffalo is going, and the rest of the game will follow suit.

I cannot convey a better idea of the profusion of animal life which existed in South Africa for untold ages before the present century, than by a sight I saw in Griqualand West as I drove through to Bechuana-land. We outspanned one day at Thorngrove, the residence of a large farmer named Muller. Whilst we were speaking of game, Mr. Muller pointed out to me a large obelisk-shaped, upright stone, planted near his gate and used as a gate-post. The stone was black and of a very hard nature, and was smooth and shining as marble. That stone was taken by Mr. Muller from the middle of a large flat near his house, where it had evidently stood from a remote period. The game had used it as a rubbing-post ; every angle and inequality had been worn smooth as a mahogany table. It must have taken countless myriads of game during long æons of the past to have thus polished it, and it gave one instantly a wonderful idea of the wealth of life formerly found in that region.

The decadence of game is hardly to be wondered at. Modern science has placed in the explorer's hands weapons of deadly power and precision. Fond though he be of nature in the abstract, in the veldt, in pre-sence of great game, it is a hard matter indeed, even for the naturalist and lover of animals, to stay his hand. The unquenchable desire to pursue and slay leaps through his veins and will not be denied. I have known men, who in cool blood have held forth upon the sad and wanton destruction of game, quite unable to resist the attractions of the chase, when they have encountered the same animals in the

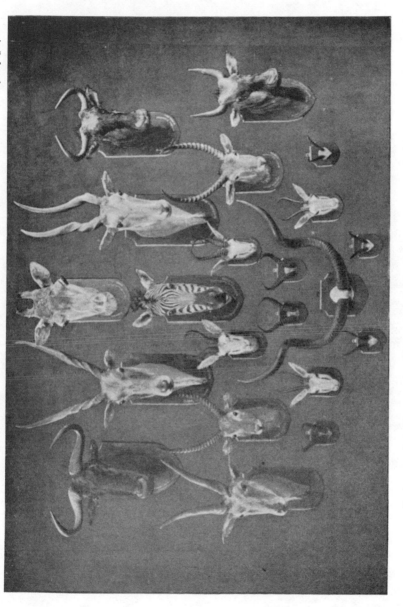

Blue Wildebeest (Bull)   Eland Cow   Giraffe Cow   Eland Cow   Blue Wildebeest (Cow)

Eland   Lechwē Ram   Springbok Ram   Burchell's Zebra   Springbok Ram   Lechwē Ram   Blue Wildebeest
(Young Bull—Horns immature)   Springbok Ewe   Horns of Koodoo Bull and Springbok   Springbok   (Young Bull—Horns immature)

SOME HEADS OF GAME SHOT ON BOTLETLI RIVER EXPEDITION, 1890

hunting veldt. The theory is so easy, the practice so very hard, as I can personally testify ; and so the work of destruction goes on.

What wonder, if the naturalist and the moderate hunter find it so hard to control their primeval instincts of the chase when in the presence of game, that the Boer, the skin-hunter, and the native sportsman, who have no æsthetic sentiments or compunctions to hinder them, set no limits upon their powers of destruction, but slaughter by scores, by hundreds, and by thousands, whenever and wherever they find opportunity. Yet such has been the wealth of life provided in these countries, that with all the slaughter, all the wanton destruction of animals in Bechuanaland, a good deal of game still remains, especially in the wilder and more waterless regions.

The inexpressible privilege and delight of travelling day after day through regions where the crack of the rifle never yet had been heard, and where the game approached and stared at the passing waggon, can never again be tasted. Never again will the traveller be able to stand upon his waggon box and, like Burchell, Andrew Smith, Cornwallis Harris, and Gordon Cumming, scan plains literally darkened by thousands upon thousands of wildebeests, quaggas, Burchell's zebras, blesboks, hartebeests, and spring-boks ; but, if he is of a mind to journey far and take pains, he may still set eyes upon many a rare species, many a gallant head of game.

At the present day there are to be found in Bechuanaland, Ngamiland, and the Kalahari country, the following species : Elephant, black rhinoceros, hippopotamus, buffalo, lion, leopard, cheetah, giraffe, Burchell's zebra, ostrich, eland, sable antelope, roan

antelope, koodoo, waterbuck, gemsbok, blue wildebeest, hartebeest, tsesseby, lechwē, nakong or situtunga (Speke's antelope), pookoo, rietbok, blesbok,
pallah, springbok, spotted bushbuck, rooi rhebok,
vaal rhebok, steinbok, grys steinbok, klipspringer,
duyker, and wart hog. Of these some are abundant, some moderately so, while others are very
scarce. As the range of many of these animals has
been much altered or circumscribed during the last
twenty years, I have here indicated briefly their
ancient habitats and the places where they may yet
be found.

The elephant (*Elephas Africanus*)—oliphant of
the Boers, tlou of the Bechuanas—whose range
formerly extended from South Bechuanaland to the
Zambesi, and of course beyond, is now very scarce.
At the beginning of this century one of the earliest
Dutch hunters stood at the Kuruman Fountain, and
there collected sufficient ivory to enrich himself very
speedily. Sechele's country, in Gordon Cumming's
time—1846–9—seems to have been well frequented,
but most of the great hunter's exploits were performed
in the hills round about Shoshong. Elephants were
found in extraordinary abundance along the Botletli
by Livingstone in 1849; and round Lake Ngami
not less than 900 are mentioned as having been shot
in a year or so after his first journey thither. Baldwin
had good sport with elephants on the Botletli in 1858,
but the trek-Boers in 1877–78 finished most of them
in that region.

Selous found the great pachyderms plentiful along
the Chobe River and the Zambesi in the early seven-
ties. Now, very few remain. A troop or two still
drink on the south bank of the Botletli (or did up till

1890), and range from there about the Queebe Hills, twenty-five miles south of the lake, where Messrs. Nicholls, Strombom, and Hicks followed them a year or two back. Along the Chobe River swamps, and occasionally in the Mababē veldt, an occasional troop yet wanders, as I hear. Elsewhere in Khama's country the only strong troop nowadays is to be found in some wild and almost impenetrable jungle country between the Zambesi and Linyanti roads. This troop is partially preserved, and the country where they have found shelter is so dense and thorny that they are now practically unmolested.

A strange event happened a few years since at Molepolole in the Protectorate (Sechele's Town). A troop of nine or ten elephants, presumably from the North Kalahari or Botletli River, had by some extraordinary accident lost their way, and were discovered in the hills near the town. The population of course all turned out, and the unfortunate beasts—mostly cows and calves—were quickly hunted and destroyed. One of the greatest and most wanton bags of modern times was made by some Dutch hunters—the Van Zyls's and others—in the country between the Lake and the upper Okavango about fifteen years back. A troop of 104 elephants was driven into a deep morass, where they were bogged and helpless. The Boers set to work, and before sundown had slain every member of the herd. There were few with good tusks, and the slaughter seems to have been as unprofitable as it was unpardonable. So vanishes the elephant from Africa.

The black rhinoceros (*Rhinoceros bicornis*)—rhenoster of the Boers, borele or keitloa of the Bechuanas—formerly found abundantly in every part of the country, and described by Harris and others as a positive nuisance to the gunner, is now seldom heard of. A few still linger in the swamps of the Chobe River, and near that portion of the Zambesi, but they are very scarce. Round about Lake Ngami they have quite disappeared. The rhinoceros is a water-loving, water-drinking beast, and in time of drought large numbers, gathered from a vast tract of country, were to be found at desert fountains and waterholes. Here the hunters of a generation since, such as Gordon Cumming, Baldwin, and Andersson, shot them at night by the half-dozen together. Oswell and Vardon in Livingstone's time slew eighty-nine rhinoceroses in one season; C. J. Andersson nearly sixty in a few months; and other hunters were constantly emulating these examples. As this sort of slaughter was practised by Dutch, Griqua, and native hunters also, it is not surprising that the rhinoceros, which even in daylight is not a difficult beast to bag, has all but vanished from the scene.

The white rhinoceros (*Rhinoceros simus*)—wit rhenoster of the Boers, chukuru or kuabaōba of the Bechuanas—once abounded in all the countries between the Orange and the Zambesi. This enormous rhinoceros, distinguished mainly from its black cousin of Africa by its vaster size, its more sluggish habits, its prolongate fore-horn, immense head, and blunt upper lip, adapted so evidently to its grass-eating habits, is now, I fear, from the reports of Mr. F. C. Selous and other hunters, on the very verge of extinction. The beautiful true quagga (*Equus Quagga*), another very interesting form, has been (as I pointed out two or three years back) the first to disappear from the once crowded natural game preserves of

Southern Africa. The monstrous white rhinoceros seems destined to stand second on the list of a lost fauna.[1]

After coming down-country at Christmas 1890, my friend Mr. J. E. Yale and I photographed several

[1] Since writing the above, an interesting letter from Mr. Selous has appeared in the *Field*, a copy of which I annex :—

" AFRICAN RHINOCEROSES.

" SIR,—It may interest some of your readers (especially my friend Mr. H. A. Bryden) to know that the great square-mouthed, grass-eating rhinoceros (*R. simus*) is not yet extinct. I have just heard from a reliable source that one of these animals (a female) has been killed lately about 100 miles N.W. of Salisbury, Mashunaland. This animal was one of six that were consorting together, and the two gentlemen who shot it—Messrs. Eyres and Coryndon—have, I believe, preserved the skin and skeleton. Whilst on this subject, I will take the opportunity of saying that I have never stated that the white rhinoceros was extinct, although I have often lately seen myself quoted as having done so. What I have said, and what I still say, is that this most interesting animal, the largest of terrestrial mammals after the elephant, is on the verge of extinction, its range being now confined to a very small tract of country in Northern Mashunaland.

" Had it not been for the occupation of this country by the British South Africa Company, I believe that the white rhinoceros would already be extinct ; but that occupation having kept all native hunters from Matabeleland to the west of the Umniati River, has happily preserved the few white rhinoceroses still left alive from the constant persecution which, in less than twenty years, has utterly exterminated them in every other portion of South Central Africa. There may yet be ten or even twenty of these animals left, but certainly not more, I think, than the latter number. I have some evidence that one or two have again crossed the Umfuli River to the west, and are now living in the Limuga, as the country is called between that river and the Umzweswe. They were very plentiful there in 1878 and 1880. I had always intended, after my term of service with the British South Africa Company was over, to make an attempt to secure a skin and skeleton of the white rhinoceros for our own magnificent national collection at Kensington, and left Salisbury last June for that purpose. Unfortunately a fall from my horse, whilst chasing an ostrich, bruised my leg, and laid me up for a time, and when I was all right again, my time was too short to allow of a journey into the rhinoceros country.

" Before closing this letter, I wish to call your attention to an article on African rhinoceroses, which appeared in the *Field* of July 2 last,

natural history specimens in the Cape Town Museum. Among these was the head of the last white rhinoceros brought down-country. This head belonged to an animal shot after much trouble and search by Mr. Selous in Mashonaland some ten years since; and

HEAD OF WHITE RHINOCEROS.
Shot by Mr. F. C. Selous in Mashonaland. From the Cape Town Museum.

it is undoubtedly the last (almost the only) specimen now left to us of an exceedingly rare and singular form. It is a thousand pities that no complete

from the pen of the eminent zoologist, Mr. R. Lydekker. In the course of his interesting and instructive letter, Mr. Lydekker says, *à propos* of the black rhinoceros (*R. bicornis*), 'Mr. Selous attributes to this species a gentle and unoffending disposition, but in this respect he is not in accord with Mr. Drummond and most other writers on African sport.' If Mr. Lydekker will refer to my book, he will find that he skin of the entire animal has ever been brought to Europe.

The fore-horn is not so straight or so prolonged as in some specimens obtained in bygone years, when this animal wandered over nearly all South Africa ; but on the whole the head is a good and typical one. Mr. Lydekker gives the extreme recorded length of such a horn as fifty-seven inches over the curve. This is an excellent record undoubtedly, and will now in all probability never be beaten. Yet in the old days when *Rhinoceros simus* abounded, and every chief's ambition was to possess a long kerrie or staff fashioned from the fore-horn of this beast, some horns of extraordinary measurement must have been in existence. There are still here and there in South Africa, in remote places, such kerries, but they are scarce, and the traders and hunters have had the pick of them. Probably at this day in England, in forgotten corners, some of these trophies are lying away in melancholy obscurity.

It has been the fashion to assume, since Cornwallis Harris's day, that the white rhinoceros was never found south of the Orange River. Undoubtedly in modern times (seventy or eighty years past) it was not ; but there has always been a tradition, supported by Barrow and other travellers, that the mighty quadruped once wandered and fed in the open wastes

has entirely failed to convey the sense of my remarks upon the general character of the black rhinoceros. The passage to which I presume Mr. Lydekker refers reads as follows : 'What I wish to argue is, not that the black rhinoceros is a sweet-tempered animal, but that, at any rate, in the great majority of cases, he is by no means the surly, morose, and dangerous beast that some travellers would have one believe.' And to this opinion I still adhere. F. C. SELOUS.

"CAPE TOWN, *November* 4." (1892.)

of Great Bushmanland, as well as in the country
north of the Orange River.

This tract is very similar in character to the open
plains of the South Kalahari and other adjacent
districts; the Orange River at certain seasons is
easily fordable, and there seems to be no sound
reason, other than a purely captious geographical distribution, why the white rhinoceros should not have
formerly grazed in this part of Cape Colony. Members of this species carrying the horn horizontally or a
little downwards (kuabaōba of the Bechuanas) appear
to have possessed a clearer vision than those carrying
the horn vertically (chukuru); in these latter the
sight seems to have been much obstructed, according
to Livingstone, by these enormously long horns.

The vast bulk and height of this animal may be
partly gauged if it be remembered that specimens
were formerly slain standing more than six and a
half feet high, measuring between sixteen and seventeen feet in length, and possessing a bulk in proportion to these measurements. Even the African
elephant is dwarfed by comparison, although, of
course, standing much higher at the shoulder.

Notwithstanding its size, the white rhinoceros
could display upon occasion immense activity and
speed, as the great hunter and companion of Livingstone, Mr. Oswell, and others can testify. In Ngamiland, and in the North Kalahari region, where formerly
it was plentiful, it has been, as I ascertained while
hunting in that direction in 1890, finished for some
years past. It seems to be quite clear that no
specimen has ever been known north of the Zambesi.

The white rhinoceros, from its sluggish habits and
poor vision, was even more easily killed than the

black, and the slaughter of these animals during the last forty years must have been enormous. Sir Andrew Smith, during his scientific expedition in 1835, saw in one day of travel in the Bechuana country, near the tropic of Capricorn, between one hundred and one hundred and fifty rhinoceroses; one hundred giraffe were seen upon the same day. Other large game was often found in a like abundance. Alas! for the vanished days!

The hippopotamus—zee koe (sea cow) of the Boers, kubu of the Bechuanas—formerly abundant throughout the country wherever rivers were to be found, is now much more restricted in its habitat. The Vaal, Molopo, and other northern streams all supported these unwieldy creatures in abundance; but for the sake of its flesh, and still more of its hide—from which the best sjamboks are made—the sea cow is becoming very scarce south of the Zambesi. The Botletli and Tamalakan not long since swarmed with these animals; now they are much less plentiful and very wary. Lake Ngami holds a good many still. In the Limpopo they are not now often found until some way past Selika's. In the Chobe and Zambesi they are still numerous.

When killed, the skin is cut into long strips, two or three inches wide, and having a thickness of about two inches; these strips dry out very much like the bark of a tree. When cut and polished they make tough, supple walking-sticks, and are semi-transparent, and of a deep yellow—much resembling fine clouded amber. For up-country use the strips are "brayed" to a softer consistency, and furnish ox-whips and riding sjamboks of terrible punishing power. The teeth, which provide ivory of extreme hardness and whiteness, are also articles of commerce, but nowadays fetch no great price.

The buffalo (*Bubalus Caffer*)—buffel of the Dutch, narē of the Bechuanas—was, seventy years ago, found right away down to the Orange River in suitable localities. Nowadays its range is much more circumscribed. The Botletli River was a great haunt of these fine animals; but the trek-Boers of 1878 seem to have hunted and driven them completely from the Lake Ngami region; and the Chobe and Sunta rivers must now be sought before the grim buffalo can be encountered in considerable numbers.[1] Along the Zambesi buffaloes are still to be met with, but, save in these localities, the hunter will not be able to find buffaloes in the Bechuana country. Directly the Zambesi is crossed, however, vast herds are to be seen by following the course of the river up the Barutse valley. To shoot in this region, the permission of Chief Lewanika has to be obtained. And it may be well to remark that this is a desperately feverish country to hunt in.

The lion (*Felis Leo*)—leeuw of the Boers, tau of the Bechuanas—is much scarcer than he used to be, and, save in new countries such as Mashonaland, where he has been little disturbed, far less inclined to risk his person than of yore. Here and there, however, his spoor lingers, even in British Bechuanaland, where, towards the Kalahari region, the country is quiet, and guns are few and far between. But not many lions are nowadays heard of until Khama's country is reached and Palachwe left behind. Along the Botletli they are still numerous, especially in the

---

[1] A few buffalo are still preserved in the dense bush of the Eastern Province of Cape Colony.

bushier parts nearing Lake Ngami. And round the lake, in the Mababē veldt, and about the Chobe and Zambesi, they are always to be found. In other places, too, between Palachwe and the Zambesi, lions' spoor is pretty sure to be seen in the vicinity of water. In the true Kalahari country there are few ; here water is scarce, and lions cannot exist without water. In the south-eastern part of Khama's country, along the Limpopo, and near the Shashi and Macloutsi rivers, they are still (or were till very lately) occasionally heard of.

In the virgin veldt, opened up in 1890 by the pioneers of the Chartered Company, lions, as Lord Randolph Churchill can testify, seem to have been extraordinarily plentiful and daring. Here, doubtless, they had had little experience of firearms, and many a pioneer and trooper during the last two years has some narrow escape to tell of. Despatch riders were followed at night along the waggon road by small troops ; and cattle and donkeys, over and over again, were taken. Men were actually chevied by them in broad daylight ; Mackay, after he left us, had such an experience in Mashonaland. He was riding home quietly to camp with a dead steinbok on his saddle. The lion ran him briskly for a time, forcing him to gallop hard to escape. Presently the beast stopped, when Mackay dismounted, fired and missed, after which the lion turned and made off.

In the Bechuana country, where guns are plentiful, a very different tale has to be told, and the lion now seldom shows himself. We saw their spoor round our camps a few times on the Botletli, but never had the luck to set eyes on *Felis Leo* in the flesh during the whole of our trip.

The leopard (*Felis pardus*)—tiger of the Boers—is, as I have mentioned in a former chapter, to be found all over Bechuanaland, where water is to be met with. He is, however, of even more secretive and nocturnal habit than the lion, and is very seldom seen. The Bechuanas, who prize the skins of these animals greatly for karosses, take them mainly by traps and spring guns. Mr. F. Lochner, whom I met with Mr. Broadwood (going and returning) on an expedition to the Zambesi in 1890, killed one very luckily during that trip. The brute came by night close to the camp fire, and was in the act of clawing down some meat. Mr. Lochner snatched up a shot-gun, took aim at the leopard's throat, and with a single charge of shot killed it dead as a door-nail.

The cheetah (*Felis jubata*)—luipaard of the Boers—is found also all over Bechuanaland, but more sparingly than the true leopard.

The giraffe (*Camelopardalis Giraffa*), kameel of the Boers, tutla or thutloa of the Bechuanas. At the present day the headquarters of the giraffe south of the Zambesi may be said to be in the parched desert country comprising the North Kalahari. A few years since they were to be found at no great distance from Khama's old capital, Shoshong; now they are first encountered in the bush and forest region beyond Kannē, or Klaballa, on the way from Shoshong to Lake Ngami. This waterless tract, well called Thirstland, serves them as a safe retreat. From Kannē to the Botletli River, and thence half-way to the lake, Khama reserves them for his own and his people's hunting, and Dutch hunters with their wasteful methods are not permitted, a very wise precaution.

In most of Khama's country, stretching north to the Victoria Falls and west to the Chobe and Mababē rivers and beyond, giraffes may yet be found, as well as in the Batauana country in the region of Lake Ngami.

Probably the pick of the giraffe country now left to South Africa is the desolate and quite waterless region lying south of the Botletli River. For eight months of the year most of this veldt is quite waterless, and cannot be thoroughly hunted unless water-carts are taken in; here very large troops of the giraffe roam free and undisturbed. I have been told by reliable witnesses of seventy or eighty being seen together at one time in quite recent years. Khama's hunters make an annual excursion to this veldt, and the average bag of each hunting outfit seems to be from twelve to sixteen or twenty giraffes. These are shot solely for the marketable value of their skins. All the natives in this part of Africa use the hide of the giraffe for making their sandals and whips.

From the Botletli, giraffes are found some way south into the Kalahari. In 1890 a troop or two must have wandered much farther down than usual, as, when near Honing Vley, in British Bechuanaland, I heard of Bareki's hunters suddenly flocking into the Central Kalahari, giraffes having penetrated nearly as far south as the Molopo River; this, however, is very unusual nowadays. Westward of Tunobis (Galton's farthest point in 1850) towards Damaraland, giraffes are not now found, the Namaqua hunters being too active in this region; but in parts of Ovampoland towards the Okavango River they are, I am informed, yet found in considerable numbers.

More to the eastward, on the south bank of the
Chobe, they are also numerous.

Mr. Selous tells us that in parts of the Matabele
country the giraffe was common ten years since;
and it is still to be found there, albeit in decreasing
numbers. In Mashonaland proper it is scarce, and
east of the Gwelo River, according to the same great
hunter, it scarcely ever wanders. This is a rather
singular fact, one of the often incomprehensible facts
of geographical distribution.

Burchell's zebra (*Equus Burchellii*)—bonte quagga
of the Boers, peetsi of the Bechuanas—formerly found
in immense troops from the banks of the Orange
River northwards, is not now to be met with until
some way beyond Palachwe. It is fairly plentiful
along the Botletli River, in the Mababē and Chobe
River country, and in other localities, where water
is to be found, between Palachwe and the Zambesi.

The ostrich (*Struthio Camelus*)—struis-vogel of
the Boers, nche of the Bechuanas—is to be found in
small bands all over the Kalahari, in the western
portions of British Bechuanaland and the Protectorate, and northwards throughout the whole country
as far as the Zambesi. It sticks mainly to the dry
open plains, where a good view is obtainable. Nowadays, in consequence of the poor price of feathers,
the ostrich is less hunted than formerly, and the
Kalahari people bring in far smaller quantities than
of old. We often sighted these great birds on the
hot plains of the North Kalahari, and along the
Botletli, but they are shy and wild, and require a
long and tedious process of circumvention. Ostriches
seem to be as partial to saltlicks as are the antelopes. We found their spoor about the bracks of

the western portions of Bechuanaland; and on the great saltpans of Ngamiland they were often noted in the same way.

The eland (*Oreas Canna*)—poofo of the Bechuanas, t'ganna of the Hottentots—formerly abounding in troops over the whole country, is not now found until the North Kalahari is penetrated; and, save in waterless and secluded deserts, it may be counted as a scarce antelope until the Zambesi is passed. The northern portions of the Kalahari hold large herds of this noblest of the antelope family. North-westward from Sechele's Town (Molepolole) the Bakwèna hunters annually slaughter a large number. I saw some magnificent heads just freshly brought in from the desert as I passed through Molepolole in September 1890; one of them, which I secured, carried the finest pair of bull horns I have ever seen.

This country is, however, exceedingly difficult to hunt from lack of water, and is practically known only to the natives. On the old road from Khama's to the Botletli, and especially round Inkouane, large numbers of elands are to be found; and, as few people pass that way, and those who do are mainly occupied in getting across the Thirst, these herds are not much molested. We saw great quantities of spoor south-eastward of Inkouane, not far from the road. Here and there in Khama's northern country towards the Zambesi elands are found, but only sparingly; westward of Lake Ngami, in portions of Ovampoland, they are, I am told, very plentiful. I had always looked upon the eland, which unites the finest points of the antelope and bovine races, and yet is a true antelope, as a beast unique in its way; but a re-perusal of

Wallace's delightful "Malay Archipelago" rather dispels that idea. At page 202 of that book Mr. Wallace describes the sapi-utan, an animal "entirely confined to the remote mountain forests of Celebes and one or two adjacent islands which form the same group." "I was surprised at their great resemblance to small cattle, or still more to the eland of South Africa. Their Malay name signifies forest-ox, and they differ from very small high-bred oxen principally by the low hanging dew-lap and straight, pointed horns, which slope back over the neck." And again he says, "In the adults the head is black with a white mark over each eye, one on each cheek, and another on the throat. The horns are very smooth and sharp when young, but become thicker and ridged at the bottom with age." "From the character of the horns, the fine coat of hair and the descending dew-lap, it seemed closely to approach the antelopes."

There is a strong likeness to the eland in this description, save that the head is black (resembling more the gaur and gayal of India), while in the eland it is pale buff in the cows and young bulls, and bluish grey in the old bulls. And again in size the sapi-utan seems to be inferior to the ox, while a full-grown bull eland often exceeds in weight and stature the largest ox. The foot and spoor of the eland, by the way, strangely resemble that of a small ox ; a European unused to spooring would scarcely distinguish between them.

The sable antelope (*Hippotragus niger*)—zwart-wit-pens (black with white belly) of the Boers, potoquane of the Bechuanas—was formerly abundant in much of the Bamangwato country eastward of the

Kalahari. It is still found in the northern portions of Khama's country and in the Mababē veldt. From old writers it would appear that this magnificent antelope was never encountered till about the tropic of Capricorn. It is still abundant in Mashonaland, where it seems to have been more plentiful than in any other part of Africa.

The roan antelope (*Hippotragus Leucophæus*), bastard gemsbok and bastard eland of the Boers, qualata or tai-hait-sa of the Bechuanas. Always scarce in its distribution (except towards the Mashona country), this great antelope is now decidedly rare in Bechuanaland. It is occasionally met with between Palachwe and the Zambesi. We found the spoor once or twice on the saltpans near the Botletli, but never came up with the animals themselves. Found forty years ago as far south as Griqualand West.

The koodoo (*Strepsiceros Kudu*)—tolo of the Bechuanas—is still plentiful in North Bechuanaland. In British Bechuanaland it is to be found not far westward of Mosita and thence towards the Molopo. It occurs here and there through the Protectorate on the eastern edge of the Kalahari, until Khama's country is reached, when it becomes more plentiful. In the bushy country west of the Limpopo, and round about Palachwe, there are still considerable numbers. Further northward and westward they are more abundant. We found them along the Zambesi road, and in some numbers in the dry forest country fringing the Botletli.

The koodoo seems able to exist for long periods without water. The fine spiral horns of the bull of this antelope are unique, and form one of the most coveted trophies of the up-country hunter.

The waterbuck (*Cobus Ellipsiprymnus*)—kringaat of the Boers, tumoga of the Bechuanas—was in the old days abundant along the Limpopo and its affluents, and over much of the Transvaal country. Now seldom met with near the Limpopo till past Selika's in Khama's country. Found along the Botletli, Okavango, Chobe, and Zambesi rivers. Not abundant.

The gemsbok (*Oryx Capensis*)—kukama of the Bechuanas—perhaps the most striking of the large antelopes, still abounds in small troops throughout the Kalahari region (of which it may be pronounced quite the most representative species), and over the more waterless and desert portions of Khama's country. We first met with this antelope between Mosita and Morokweng, British Bechuanaland; and throughout the whole Kalahari country, thence northward, they range freely to the wastes south of the Botletli River, where they are most abundant. About the great saltpans near the Botletli they are fairly plentiful. They extend westward into Damaraland. In the Ovampo country I believe they are seldom if ever found, and their range seems to be completely limited northwards by the Zambesi. The Bechuanas annually slay a large number of these most beautiful and characteristic desert antelopes for the sake of their horns and skins, the latter of which are in great demand for the making of riems or thongs.

The blue wildebeest or brindled gnu (*Catoblepas Gorgon*)—blaauw wildebeest of the Boers, kokoon of the Bechuanas—formerly swarmed in immense herds over all the country between the Orange and Zambesi rivers. Occasionally it was even found south of the Orange upon the northward plains of Cape Colony. Nowadays its range has become far more restricted.

The Transvaal and Free State practically know it no more. In South Bechuanaland they are first met with, towards the western portion of the Molopo River, where, however, they are few and far between. When Khama's country is reached they become more plentiful; they are still to be met with within thirty miles of Shoshong, Khama's old capital. On the plains of the Botletli and in the bush southward they are yet fairly abundant; and in the Mababē country, and thence to the Zambesi, they are also found in some plenty. Westward along the Okavango to Ovampoland they abound. It is not too much to say that within these forty years past thousands upon thousands of brindled and white-tailed gnu have been slain on the plains of the Transvaal and Free State. The blue wildebeest has always a strange predilection for the company of the Burchell zebra; they are still often found together—we saw them in close company several times on the Botletli—and have been well named the Damon and Pythias of the brute creation. Ostriches are often seen mingling with both.

The hartebeest (*Alcelaphus Caama*)—khama of the Bechuanas—is perhaps the most truly characteristic Bechuanaland antelope. The natives still prefer the skin of this animal to any other for their cloaks, and further north, where store-clothing has not penetrated, the graceful reddish skin cloak of the khama, with a bit of the black tail falling behind the wearer's neck, at once proclaims the true Bechuana or Bakalahari. This fine antelope, once widely spread over all Southern Africa, is still to be met with to the westward of British Bechuanaland within thirty miles of Vryburg, and thence northward nearly to the Zambesi. The Kalahari holds large numbers of them. North

of the Zambesi *Alcelaphus Caama* does not range ;
his place being taken, as Mr. Selous has shown, by
another nearly allied form, Lichtenstein's hartebeest.

The tsesseby or sassayby (*Alcelaphus Lunatus*)—
bastard hartebeest or Zulu hartebeest of the Boers
—a species nearly allied to the true hartebeest, was
formerly very abundant throughout Bechuanaland,
but is now seldom met with save in the remoter
regions.   During a year spent in various parts of the
country I never even saw the spoor of one.   I believe
that to the north-west of Lake Ngami, and in the
northern portion of Khama's country, and especially
towards the Mababē, they are fairly numerous.   Eastward in parts of Mashonaland they are still plentiful.

The lechwē (*Cobus Leché*), or lesser waterbuck,
as it is sometimes called, is, as I have shown, only
found in the river systems and reed swamps of South
Central Africa.   Along the Botletli and round Lake
Ngami they are still fairly numerous, though shy.
In the Chobe and Sunta swamps, and along the
Okavango, they are found in large troops.   This fine
antelope was first discovered by Livingstone in his
expedition to Lake Ngami in 1849.   Except by the
aid of a few stuffed specimens in museums, it is not
very familiar to Europeans.   The Bechuanas are very
fond of getting hold of the thickly-coated skins of
these animals, which they use for sleeping upon at
night ; they are, I fancy, very impervious to damp.
There was quite a competition in our camp for the
skins of lechwēs, collected along the Botletli.

The situtunga or Speke's antelope (*Tragelaphus
Spekii*)—the water koodoo of those trek-Boers who
have set eyes on it, nakong of the Lake Bechuanas
—is a still rarer form than the last, and from its

amphibious habits is most difficult to shoot or capture.   Mr. James Nicolls was lucky enough to
capture a young female in 1889 near Lake Ngami,
which may now be seen at the Zoological Society's
Gardens.   This water-loving antelope is, in Southern
Africa, only found in the swamps round Lake
Ngami, and along the Chobe and Okavango systems.
Beyond the Zambesi it has a wide range as far as
the regions of the Victoria Nyanza and Albert Nyanza
lakes.   Although named after Captain Speke, this
rare waterbuck was known and described by Livingstone in his earlier travels, and familiar to the late
C. J. Andersson as far back as 1853—some years
before Speke began his discoveries in Central Africa.

The nakong, notable for its dense coat and singularly elongated feet, seems to be never happy or at
ease unless plunged to its middle in water.   It is
most difficult of approach in its native swamps, and
has given endless trouble to Mr. Selous and other
hunters.   Mr. Nicolls was singularly fortunate in
procuring a live specimen on his first expedition.

The pookoo (*Cobus Vardoni*), named after Major
Vardon, a mighty hunter of Livingstone's early
period, is another rare, water-loving antelope, found
by one or two travellers near the Zambesi in the
direction of the Chobe River Junction.   Mr. Selous
has carefully described this animal and its habits
in his "Hunter's Wanderings."   The habitat of the
pookoo seems to be singularly circumscribed, and
its skin is not often brought down-country.

The reedbuck (*Eleotragus Arundinaceus*)—rietbok of the Dutch—was in the old days found throughout South Africa, wherever reeds and water abounded.
It is now becoming scarce.   A few still linger on

the Molopo, and they are found along the Crocodile, Botletli, Chobe, Lotsani, and other northern rivers. The reedbuck, however, is of an excessively shy habit, and from the nature of its sanctuary in dense reed beds, is not often seen unless in secluded districts.

The blesbok (*Alcelaphus Albifrons*)—nonē of the Bechuanas—which not long since scoured the plains of Lower Bechuanaland, the Transvaal, and Free State in countless thousands, is now seldom seen. A few are preserved on farms here and there, and from the Transvaal side they now and then cross into British Bechuanaland ; but they are rare, and, unless very carefully preserved, bid fair to become as nearly extinct as their old-fashioned-looking cousin the bontebok (*Alcelaphus Pygargus*), of Cape Colony and the Free State. Skin-hunting has wrought the downfall of these beautifully coloured buck in an incredibly short time, as it has largely destroyed the black and brindled gnus, the quagga, and Burchell's zebra. In 1860, when the Duke of Edinburgh (then Prince Alfred) was taken to the eastern part of the Orange Free State, a great hunt was got up in his honour. One thousand of Moroka's Barolong, then dwelling at Thaba Unchu, drove in the game from a large tract of country. It was computed that at least 25,000 head of game were in sight of the sportsmen ; black and blue wildebeest, Burchell's zebras, quaggas, ostriches, blesboks, hartebeests, and springboks were to be seen all charging hither and thither in affrighted squadrons, and rousing clouds of dust. The number of game slain that day ran into thousands—6000, some people say ; several natives were trampled or crushed to death by a charging herd of zebras; while others sustained broken limbs. Even at this distance of time, it is probable that the Duke of Edinburgh still remembers that wonderful spectacle on the Free State plains. Nowadays those plains stand bare and desolate. Even so late as 1882, when Vryburg was founded by the freebooters, and a few tents and huts represented the present capital of British Bechuanaland, hartebeests and blesboks were known to gallop right through the camp.

The rooibok (*Æpyceros Melampus*)—pallah of the Bechuanas—formerly abounded from South Bechuanaland northwards. Nowadays it is first seen or spoored in the bushy country bordering the Limpopo, beginning from near Pallah Camp. As one approaches Palachwe these antelopes become more abundant, and are pretty generally distributed over the interior, where streams or watercourses, in conjunction with shady bush, are met with. This is an elegant and beautifully coloured antelope, and its horns, which are of some length (averaging about seventeen or eighteen inches), form an outward angle at the centre, and differ in shape from every other species, and are well worth possessing.

The springbok (*Gazella Euchore*)—tsèpè of the Bechuanas—although now pretty well cleared from the plains of South Bechuanaland, in the vicinity of the Transvaal border, is still found in small herds towards the Kalahari. It is scarcely seen throughout the wooded and hilly Protectorate, except to the westward on the open plains. In the North Kalahari, and from thence in suitably open country nearly as far as the Zambesi, it is found abundantly. Along the Botletli flats it is plentiful; and as the waggon traverses the vast grassy plains, the grazing herds may be seen everywhere dotting the landscape. They are, like most game of that region, very partial to the saltpans, which are always a pretty sure find for those in search of these charming antelopes.

The spotted bushbuck (*Tragelaphus Sylvaticus*)— boschbok of the Dutch, serolomutuku of the Bechuanas—a very beautiful variety of the Cape bushbuck, or rather perhaps an intermediate form between that animal and the harnessed bushbuck of Western Africa, is found along the larger rivers of the interior in secluded localities. The northern parts of the Crocodile, the Botletli, Chobe, Mababē, Tamalakan, and others, all hold this beautiful creature. Its shy habits and extraordinary faculty of concealment render it, however, much more seldom seen than might be imagined.

The red rhebok (*Eleotragus Reduncus*) — rooi rhebok of the Boers—is met with in the hills of the Protectorate and the adjoining Transvaal border as far north as the south of Khama's country. I am not aware that this hill-loving antelope is found further north; I am inclined to doubt it. Messrs. Sefton, Whiteley, and other Englishmen living at Zeerust and Mafeking often have excellent sport with these antelopes among the Marico Hills.

The Vaal or grey rhebok (*Pelea Capreola*) is stated also, upon the authority of Mr. James Nicolls (joint-author of "The Sportsman in South Africa"), to be found in the hills of the Protectorate. As it is found on the Transvaal hills in the same latitude, this is probable.

The steinbok (*Nanotragus Tragulus*)—puruhuru of the Bechuanas—is found abundantly all over the

countries which are the subject of this chapter. In
open plains, bush, and forest—almost every variety
of veldt—and in the most waterless regions, this beautiful little creature is encountered. Small though it
is, and rather dry of flesh, its venison is nevertheless very good, and the traveller may often thank this
dainty and abundant antelope for a good dinner.
At the present day steinboks may be readily found
in the veldt within fifteen minutes of the town of
Vryburg.

The grysbuck (*Nanotragus Melanotis*) — grys
steinbok (grey steinbok—so called from its bright
bay coat being shot with white hairs) of the Boers—
is and always has been a scarce antelope in the regions
I write of. It is found very occasionally in pairs,
or singly, on the dry uplands of the far interior.
I only set eyes on this antelope once, on the rugged
table-land above Mesa. Dove also saw it on one
occasion.

The klipspringer (*Oreotragus Saltatrix*), kainsi
of the Hottentots. This active and handsome little
mountain antelope is abundant throughout the interior, wherever rocky hills are to be found.

The duyker (*Cephalopus Mergens*)—puti of the
Bechuanas—is as common and as widely distributed
as the steinbok. It is to be found in bushy or
semi-bushy country from the Cape to the Zambesi,
and, like the steinbok, shows little sign of extinction.

The wart-hog (*Phacochœrus Æthiopicus*)—vlakte
vark of the Boers—a wild hog, remarkable for the
curious fleshy warts or protuberances upon its face,
carries often very fine tusks, and is to be met with
very occasionally on the open plains, more usually in

semi-bushy localities. It is a shy, wary species, however, and is not so often seen as might be imagined.

So ends my catalogue, which, however imperfect, may perchance be found of use to travellers towards the Lake and Zambesi regions.   I have not attempted to deal with the Matabele and Mashona countries. Mr. Selous has long since made these, as well as the Chobe River region, his own, and his well-known book says all that may be said for the game of most of Central South Africa.   Since 1881, when that book was published, however, the game of Bechuanaland has receded and shifted very materially, and I have thought it worth while to put together these few notes on the fauna as at present to be found.

During the year 1892 the Government of British Bechuanaland has taken steps to enforce a more ample protection of game within its territory.   By Government notice No. 13, the public are informed that—

"No person shall, save as is hereinafter provided, kill, catch, capture, pursue, hunt, or shoot at, sell, hawk, or expose for sale game in any part of this colony, without having previously obtained a game licence, under a penalty of not exceeding thirty shillings sterling for the first offence, and not exceeding five pounds sterling for every subsequent offence, excepting herefrom any game found injuring crops in cultivated lands or gardens.   No person, however, shall be at liberty to pursue, shoot, kill, destroy, or capture any elephant, hippopotamus, buffalo, eland, koodoo, hartebeest, bontebok, blesbok, gemsbok, rietbok, zebra, quagga, Burchell zebra, or any gnu or wildebeest of either variety, without having obtained a special permission to that effect from the Governor, under a penalty of not exceeding ten pounds sterling for each offence, or, on failure of payment thereof, not exceeding one month imprisonment with or without hard labour :

" Provided, however, that landed proprietors and persons authorised by them shall, without having such special permission, be at liberty to shoot elephant upon the property of such landed proprietors."

A game licence costs ten shillings only, and is no great obstacle to the gunner. That part of the proclamation relating to large game seems to have been adapted mainly from an old Act of the Cape Colony ; and the elephant, hippopotamus, buffalo, eland, bontebok, zebra, and quagga (and probably also the Burchell zebra), unfortunately need no protective laws, for the simple reason that they are already exterminated within the colony. Such an Act, even with the best intentions on the part of the governing powers, is very difficult to enforce in so large and poorly policed a colony. Distant farmers and natives are, to my own knowledge, likely to pay small attention to such a proclamation. The veldt is vast, and they have none to say them nay.

The Chartered Company further north intend to protect game within their territories. All lovers of nature must wish them luck ; but they too have a vast and sparsely populated region to control, and the pioneer and the miner, if they see meat parading the veldt before their eyes, are scarcely likely to stay their hands.

CHAPTER XXIV.

WAGGON LIFE AND CAMP REQUISITES

I HAVE spoken of the keen pleasures attaching to waggon life in the South African veldt. For seven months in the year—that is, from the end of March to the beginning of November—almost no rain may be expected to fall; and, under cloudless skies and in a perfect climate, an absolutely ideal life may be counted upon; that is, for a reasonably strong and healthy man, who can content himself with the earliest of hours, simple fare, and an abundance of sport with fur or feather.

The very contact and communion with perennial sunlight and the sweet open air in a wild uncivilised country; the change and novelty of scene, the constant exercise, the reposeful sleep of the veldt; all these things tend wonderfully to renew the pleasures of existence, and to give tone and strength to the fibres. In ninety-nine cases out of a hundred, after six months of such a life, the wanderer will return to civilisation a stronger, better, and wholesomer man by fifty per cent. than when he started. There is an ancient and picturesque saying among the Arabs of the desert that Allah reckons not in the lives of men the hours spent in the chase; and so with the South African sojourner, the time will not have been time wasted. And in those unfading memories, those undying scenes of the African wilderness which he may recall with pleasure to the last day of his life, he will have, to boot, a treasure of which he never can be deprived.

But, even in the rainy season, a well-found waggon and a small waterproof tent will go far to protect the wayfarer, and, indeed, with such shelter he is at least as well off as he would be in the average up-country native hut. Waggon life, if the oxen are good, the servants well-chosen and willing, and the stores and provisions abundant and in good order, is an absolutely perfect one; and for the Englishman, jaded by contact with over-much civilisation (and in these times one can have far too much of that excellent good thing), I can think of no greater pleasure than the wandering, gipsy-like existence of a trek in the far interior.

Waggons are nowadays best purchased at Kimberley, where there is more choice than further up country, and good, sound, well-seasoned second-hand waggons can constantly be procured. A brand new waggon is of course best obtained in Cape Colony, and can be railed to Kimberley, but, all things considered, I should myself prefer to buy a waggon slightly seasoned by travel and yet fairly new. Such a waggon may be picked up for from £80 to £100. A still better plan is, I think, to hire. Waggons may be hired at Kimberley, Vryburg,

Mafeking, and even as far north as Palachwe. Oxen may be procured at the same time; and a good waggon with a full span of eighteen oxen may be hired for from £15 to £20 per month; prices varying, of course, with the state of transport, locality, and not a little with the bargaining capacities of the hirer himself. Most people in South Africa, and Afrikanders especially, are pretty good hands at a deal; and the motto *Caveat emptor* everywhere obtains. Good trek cattle may be bought outright for from £6 to £7, 10s. a head.

On the whole, I think, Mafeking is the best place to make a start from nowadays for a long journey into the interior. Waggons, oxen, and all kinds of stores can be procured there; and the waggons may be either sent on ahead (the owner proceeding a few days later by post cart and picking them up at Palachwe) or, as is, I think, the better plan, the whole outfit may set forth together from Mafeking.

If the traveller is going for a long trek into the waterless countries north and west of Khama's, the lighter the waggon the better, always providing that a sufficiency of stores can be carried. A full-tent waggon is of course preferable, but a half-tent one can be made comfortable enough. A mattress spread over the kartel is well worth remembering, as well as a large cushion to serve as pillow. Two or three good coloured blankets and a sheepskin kaross complete the bedding department. The kaross is best procured in Cape Town or Kimberley; Mr. Poole of the last-named town always has some on hand.

It should be seen that the canvas tent and fore and after claps are in good order, and that the trekking gear is sound and complete. Concerning

MY WAGGON—BOTLETLI RIVER PLAINS, NGAMILAND

(*From Photo. by W. Dove*)

the fitting of the waggon interior, I have offered some hints at the beginning of Chapter XII. which may be useful. Strong barrels and vatjes for carrying water must be taken; possibly they may be included in the waggon hire. Servants are, I think, best hired at Mafeking or Palachwe, and preferably at the latter place, where Khama's influence can be retained. Drivers' wages should not exceed £2, 10s. per month; native cooks' about £2 to £2, 10s.; leaders' from 10s. to £1; horse-boys' about the same. Of these servants, the drivers and cook are allowed coffee, sugar, meal, and meat daily; the inferior servants meal only, except in the game country, where meat for all is abundant. Milk when it can be procured is a treat for all hands, masters and men, and it is advisable, even if not amongst game, to give the under boys some coffee and meat as an occasional treat now and again. Boer roll tobacco is served out once a week to all, a strip of about eight or ten inches of the roll being a fair allowance per man. It is better for all parties that separate fires for masters and men be kept going.

If a prolonged trip is to be made and long halts are expected, a small waterproof oblong canvas tent is useful. This can be procured from Edgington's in London, and, if not too large, can be lashed with riems to the buck-board of the waggon. A small folding iron camp bedstead, having a piece of canvas for the bed, is very useful. Mackay and I procured one each at Kimberley. When folded, they measured about a yard in length, and weighed a mere trifle; they are worth noting.

Horses are an important item: good average ponies can best be procured at Kimberley for from £15 to

£20 a-piece. If, however, the sportsman is desirous of obtaining a first-rate salted hunting pony, with a character in the veldt, he must be prepared to pay a high figure—from £50 to £100. In such a case he gets a year's guarantee against horse-sickness, and in the event of the death of the nag within the year from that disease, the money is refunded. But again *caveat emptor*, and find out who you are buying from. On the whole, I should advise the average traveller to buy good useful riding-horses at about £20 a-piece at Kimberley, Vryburg, or Mafeking. They are pretty sure to understand the gun, and, once in the veldt, become very rapidly amenable. In the hunting veldt horses should be fastened at night to the waggon wheels. If there are two waggons, between the waggons and as near the light of the fire as possible, as a protection from lions.

Saddlery is best taken out from home. At Cape Town and Kimberley fair saddlery can be obtained at extremely moderate prices—at Kimberley especially so; but elsewhere it is doubtful if the traveller will be well suited. It is a mistake to use heavy saddles, as some men do. The horses have quite enough to carry. We ourselves used strong, plain, light saddles, with plenty of dees, and instead of a numnah or saddle-cloth we always used half a common cotton Kaffir blanket, folded small, and so placed as to keep the saddle well off the pony's back. With this simple precaution, we never gave our horses a sore back during the whole of our expeditions. Sore backs are the curse of South African travelling, and yet with a little care they can be very easily avoided. I saw the horses of a detachment of the 11th Hussars, who rode up to Palachwe and back from Vryburg

with Sir Henry Loch.   On their return the sore backs
of these unfortunate animals—they were all Cape
horses, too—were simply awful to behold.   Hardly
one had escaped.   And yet this ought to have been
avoided ; heavy military saddles, possibly, had something to do with it.

The up-country store bridle—made for the use
of the Boers—is a fearful instrument of torture.
It usually consists of a single rein and very severe
curb.   The Dutchman, who has no hands, has small
mercy for horseflesh, and these cruel bits save him
time and trouble, I suppose.   For cleaning saddles
and bridles, and indeed leather generally, soft soap
should not be forgotten.   Our boys always used a
little wood ash from the camp fire for brightening
spurs and bits.

When actually in the hunting veldt, where big
game abounds, it is, from my own experience and
that of many interior hunters, the safest and best
plan to have a piece of stout cord or raw hide riem
attached by one end to the bit, by the other to the
hunter's belt.   It is often a very serious business—
sometimes an absolute matter of life and death—when
man and horse get separated in the veldt.   With a
horse, the hunter, even if lost, can usually struggle
on to water somehow—the nag will probably find the
way for him.   Without a horse, in such a country as
the " thirstland," the chances of disaster are tenfold
increased.   Sometimes after a fall, or while the hunter
jumps off to shoot, the pony will decamp, and the
rider is left to curse his fate and find his way to the
waggon as best he can.   With the cord, one cannot
lose one's horse at any rate ; there is, of course,
the slight risk of being dragged after a fall ; but

horses almost invariably behave well in the hunting veldt, and the risk is not worth considering in comparison with the safety gained.

It often happens that upon a long journey one's pony becomes troubled with "scouring." The best remedy for this common equine complaint in hot climates is a dose of chloroform, or, if that cannot be obtained, a strong dram of chlorodyne. A simple and effectual Dutch remedy is to fasten a piece of common Boer roll tobacco round the bit, which prophylactic has the advantage of being always procurable. Upon long road journeys, where slow cantering is kept up during the whole of the day, the Afrikander practice of off-saddling every two and a half hours or so is a sound and proper one. Half-an-hour's rest is sufficient—perhaps an hour in the heat of midday—and the journey can be then resumed.

In the hunting veldt spooring is usually conducted at foot pace, and an hour's off-saddle towards noon under a shady tree (if it can be found) will be sufficient rest for the hardy South African horse. Whenever possible, it is advisable to release the willing nag of one's weight, loosen his girths, and shift or remove the saddle. Nose-bags save a deal of waste in feeding, and, as they occupy little space, may as well be taken in the waggon.

To hunt giraffe successfully in the waterless Kalahari bush south of the Botletli, water-carts [1] would be of great assistance. Even a Scotch cart, in which three barrels of water could be carried, would answer the purpose. Two or three horses could then be kept going for three or four days at a time, twenty

---

[1] A South African water-cart consists of a large barrel fitted upon wheels.

or twenty-five miles from the river, in the waterless country where the giraffe stand. We ourselves on one occasion took the light waggon over with as much water as we could load up, and sent the oxen back. By doing so we were able to be absent from the main camp three days. On other occasions we slept out in the bush and our horses had to go waterless for the best part of two days, besides undergoing the severe labours of finding and running the game.

In addition to the ordinary native servants, it is of the greatest importance to secure the services of Bushmen, or natives of the wild districts in which the hunting veldt lies, to act as spoorers and find game. These people know the haunts and runs of the quarry far better than natives from other localities, and are invaluable. They are usually only too glad to show sport and have meat shot for them; and if really good Bushmen are found, they are well worth retaining for a time. They only ask food, and perhaps some mere trifle of old clothing, and it is an act of charity to provide the poor creatures with meat. If strange to the veldt, and especially in the dangerous " thirstland," it is a good plan to attach a Bushman to oneself to hunt and spoor. He can be easily made to understand that he is to follow up his master's spoor, and will thus often save him a long and devious ride to camp, or even from getting completely lost.

Dogs.—Pointers are, as I have said, an absolute necessity for bird-shooting. A pack of mongrels and canine odds and ends is often taken with the waggon. They are principally useful for hunting lions, leopards (sometimes elephants), and other members of the feline race, as well as occasionally wild boars.

Clothing.—For veldt wear nothing is better than comfortable breeches or knickerbocker breeches, pig-skin gaiters, and strong but not too heavy buff-leather lace boots. For hunting in thorny country good velvet cord or moleskin is preferable to any other material. For ordinary light wear strong khaki, gabardine, or whipcord, or some tough material of that kind is useful. For wet weather a pair of field boots may be taken. A pair of moleskin trousers and South African velschoens for camp use are comfortable as changes. These last can be procured at any store up-country. Cheap cord suits are also always to be had up-country. I wore a 12s. 6d. "elephant-cord" store coat, which did me yeoman's service in the thorn veldt.

Flannel shirts cannot be beaten for South African wear. Pyjamas are of course necessary, and may be taken for waggon use. Coats, although little needed in the daytime, are often wanted in the evenings and at early morning; especially in winter time, when frosts are severe and winds piercingly keen. Strong tweed or whipcord, or better still, stout but not too heavy velvet cord or moleskin, are the best materials. A coat should invariably be carried strapped in front of the saddle when hunting. If the hunter is belated and has to lie out all night, or if he has to pursue game through the thorny African bush, he will find it an absolute necessity to carry his coat thus with him. A thick overcoat and stout mackintosh are prime necessaries. A soft broad-brimmed felt hat is the best headgear for South Africa; in the hunting veldt it should be fastened to the wearer by a piece of fine "riempje"—otherwise it is pretty sure to be swept from the head and lost, a rather serious calamity under a broiling sun.

Spurs should be taken, but should not be too long in the neck. The fashionable long-necked *fin de siècle* spurs that now obtain will be found out of place in the roughs and tumbles of South African hunting.

A good water-bottle—those of vulcanite, covered with felt, made by Silver & Co. are the best I know of—is a *sine qua non*. These bottles should be dipped in water before starting; the heat of the sun then sets up evaporation and the water within is kept cool for a long period. When water was bad we usually took cold tea or coffee in its place. The traveller of course must cater for his own palate; but spirits and water under an ardent sun are not the best of thirst assuagers. On a long hunting expedition beer cannot well be carried—it takes up too much room; and tea or coffee form the universal drink in the veldt. When decent water can be obtained, lime-juice and water makes a most refreshing beverage. A little brandy for medicinal purposes, and some whisky as a nightcap now and again, when the water will permit of it, are the only other alternatives; unless the traveller means to do his trek *en prince* and take a waggon load of wines and luxuries with him. After all, if a man cannot forswear these appurtenances of civilisation for a few months, he had far better leave the veldt alone.

We had with us two dozen bottles of dry Pontac (a low-priced red Cape wine); a glass with a pinch of quinine in it before the evening meal forms a capital pick-me-up, and if in a feverish country, such as the Lake region or Zambesi, a little quinine in one's system is by no means a bad preventive. Besides our Pontac, we had six bottles of three-star brandy and six of Scotch whisky, the greater part of which we brought back with us. At Mafeking the best brandy cost us 6s. 3d. per bottle, whisky 3s. 2d. per bottle, Pontac 20s. per dozen. The import duties, however, which were then, owing to a Bechuanaland rebate, very light, are now increased, and the liquor costs rather more.

Below I append a list of the stores carried in our waggons on our shooting trip to the Lake River: they will, perhaps, best give an idea of the articles likely to be useful on such an expedition. Most of these stores were taken on the advice of Messrs. Whiteley and Musson—old interior hunters and traders. The prices annexed are prices at Mafeking :—

		£	s.	d.
Sardines (large tins)	per doz.	o	8	6
Potted meats	„	o	8	6
Van Houten's cocoa	„	o	10	6
Marmalade (1 lb. tins)	„	o	12	0
Plum puddings (2 lb. tins) . . .	each	o	2	0
Canned fruits (pears, apricots, and peaches)	per doz.	1	4	0
Table salt	per pkt.	o	o	4
Danish butter (1 lb. tins) . . .	per doz.	1	4	0
Tomatoes (tins)	„	o	14	0
Carrots „	„	o	15	0
Barataria prawns (excellent fried with butter and curry powder)	per doz.	1	2	6
Worcester sauce	per doz.	o	16	6
Curry powder	„	o	15	0
Salad oil	per bot.	o	1	0
Vinegar	per doz.	o	18	0
Pears' soap	„	o	7	0
Oxford sausages (in tins) very useful .	„	1	4	0
Mustard	per tin	o	1	6
Elliman's embrocation . . .	per bot.	o	4	0

		£	s.	d.
Soft soap (tins) . . . . . per doz.		0	12	0
Tinned peas . . . . . . ,,		0	11	0
,, French beans . . . . ,,		0	11	0
Preserved ginger . . . . . ,,		0	12	0
Walnut pickle . . . . . . ,,		0	18	0
Mixed pickles . . . . . . ,,		0	18	0
Ground pepper (7 lb. tin) useful also for skinning birds		0	9	7
Oatmeal . . . . . . per 7 lb. tin		0	4	6
Baking powder (bot.) . . . . per doz.		0	7	6
Trade handkerchiefs . . . . ,,		0	4	0
,, knives . . . . . ,,		0	4	0
,, shirts . . . . . ,,		1	7	6
Sickles (for cutting grass) . . . ,,		0	9	0
Rangoon oil . . . . . . per bot.		0	1	0
Lime-juice cordial . . . . . per doz.		1	10	0
Large gridiron		0	3	6
Warburg's fever tincture . . . . per bot.		0	4	0
Thick twine . . . . . . per ball		0	2	6
Tin beakers . . . . . . each		0	0	4
Glue . . . . per bot.		0	0	6
Small axes . . . . . . each		0	3	6
Egyptian cigarettes . . . per doz. small boxes		0	12	6
Vaseline . . . . per doz.		0	12	0
Fine cabin biscuits . . . . . per box		0	3	0
Best tea . . . . per chest		1	5	0
Coffee . . . . . . per 50 lbs.		3	0	0
Java coffee . . . . . . per lb.		0	1	9
Transvaal tobacco . . . . . per roll		0	5	0
,, ,, cut . . . per lb.		0	2	0
White moist sugar . . . . . per lb.		0	0	6
Cotton blankets (for use and trading) . each		0	3	6
English smoked bacon (useful for cooking with game, fry, &c.) . . . . . per lb.		0	1	6
Pulp basins (papier-maché) excellent for making bread, washing, &c., unbreakable . each		0	4	0
Mixed biscuits . . . . . per box		0	3	3
White rice . . . . . per 50 lbs.		1	0	10
Sieve		0	5	0
Castor oil . . . . per bot.		0	1	0
American tobacco . . . . . per lb.		0	2	3
Dog's head cigarettes (American) . per 1000		1	15	0
Large iron buckets . . . . . each		0	4	0

				£	s.	d.
Matches .	. . . . .	per doz.		0	1	0
Screw wrench .	. . . . . .	.		0	10	0
Water barrels .	. . . . .	each		0	15	0
Riems (hide halters)	. . . . .	„		0	1	0
Lanterns .	. . . . . .	„		0	5	0
Kettles (8 pints)	. . . . .	„		0	5	0
„ (5 pints)	. . . . .	„		0	3	6
Rough salt (useful for preserving skins, and for						
natives)	. . . . .	per lb.		0	0	1½
Boer meal	. . .	per muid (180 lbs.)		3	0	0
Mealie meal	. . . . .	per muid		1	17	6
Yellow sugar .	. . . .	per 102 lbs.		2	6	0
Gossage's mottled soap (for washing clothes, trading,						
presents, &c.)	. . . .	per box		1	3	6
Candles (16 oz.)	. . . .	per box		1	5	0
Corned beef (2 lb. tins)	. . .	per doz.		1	4	0
Iron cooking pot	. . . . .	.		0	13	0
„ „	. . . . .	.		0	11	0
„ „	. . . . .	.		0	6	0
Baking pot	. . . . .	.		0	12	6
Waggon grease	. . .	per 14 lb. tin		0	8	0
Swiss milk	. . .	per doz. tins		0	10	6

Brandy, whisky, and pontac, as above mentioned.

In addition to these articles we had a bag of
potatoes, another of onions, as well as lead, powder,
and caps for trading. These figures will give an idea
of the moderate prices obtaining so far up-country
as Mafeking. As we took a large quantity, Messrs.
Whiteley, Walker & Co., who supplied us, charged
us somewhat less than the ordinary retail prices ;
but no doubt they and other traders would be ready
to do the same for other travellers. In packing for
the waggon, it saves endless trouble if each case is
numbered. The numbered lists of articles can be
then referred to, and an infinity of hauling and
opening up saved when the stores are required.
Packing and unpacking a waggon is no light
matter.

Than the above stores I do not think much more choice could be required for an expedition of six months or even a year. Many of the things we never touched; and, as Mackay had to leave us soon after starting, about a third was brought back to Palachwe and sold there.

Among the luxuries, perhaps the most useful in the veldt, where the soul is apt to become weary of a perpetual meat diet, are the canned fruits and vegetables. We found the pears, peaches, apricots,[1] and tomatoes excellent good things. One is apt to weary of the tinned jams and preserves, which usually supply the place of sweets and puddings in the wilderness. We carried usually some five or six sacks of mealies and Kaffir corn for the nags. Corn the horses must have, if they are expected to undergo the severe labour of finding and running game.

Besides all these things, our waggon contained a large supply of ammunition and our gunnery. As a general rule ammunition, I think, is better taken out from home. Martini-Henry Government cartridges can, of course, be got reasonably enough as far as Mafeking and even Palachwe; but all else is best procured and packed at a good gunmaker's in England.

The battery of the African sportsman can of course be made as varied as the taste and purses of individuals dictate. For up-country work, the fewer and plainer the weapons the better. One cannot go

---

[1] It may be useful to give the brands of some of these invaluable dainties. Bartlett pears; Hemskirk apricots, packed by the Pacific Orchard Canning Company, San José, California; and Richard's and Robin's peaches, Dover, Delaware—all American, of course!

wrong with a 12 bore, central-fire, top lever, shot-gun
(hammerless if you like), the left barrel choked.   For
the varied feathered game of South Africa, No. 12
is, I am convinced, the best bore.   Schultze powder,
(which we often used) is preferable to black.   In a
hot climate the gun fouls rapidly and requires frequent cleaning, and Schultze powder saved us infinite
trouble in this respect.   No doubt E. C. and other
wood powders would answer equally well.   I mention
Schultze cartridges for the reason that we were lucky
enough to pick up a supply at an up-country store,
after long using black powder.

2, 5, and 6 are, perhaps, the most useful sizes
in shot for all kinds of shooting.   Dust shot for
collecting small birds should not be forgotten.   A
No. 2 cartridge in the choke barrel is very deadly
in long shots at geese and guinea-fowl, as well as at
koorhaan and other large bustards.   The guinea-fowl,
by the way, is an immensely strong bird, and takes
a deal of stopping.   He is bigger than his English
domesticated relative, and weighs more.

In shooting larger game we found—as do so many
others in South Africa—that the Martini-Henry solid
bullet is very hard to beat.   The ordinary hollow
Express bullet, as at first used by Dove upon giraffe,
was not a success; although with smaller and
thinner-skinned game it did its work well enough.
Single Martini-Henry sporting rifles, which are light
and handy, are excellent weapons for shooting
with on horseback.   The " Afrikander " double rifles
shooting Martini-Henry ammunition (of which I have
spoken), did much of our work and did it well ;
I used nothing else.   They are, of course, heavier
than the single barrel, but then one fires two shots

for one without reloading—a clear advantage when running game on horseback. For myself, I confess to being a believer in the capacities of the solid bullet. The Martini-Henry lead bullet expands quite sufficiently for all purposes, and delivers a tremendous shock ; with hollow Express bullets the results are not always certain, and the immense expansion, amounting sometimes to a positive waste of shocking force, tends to defeat its object, at all events upon the bodies of heavy and thick-skinned game.

An accurately sighted single (or double) .450 Express, a double " Afrikander " (shooting Martini-Henry Government cartridges), a single Martini-Henry sporting rifle, as a spare weapon, in case of breakages, and a strong twelve bore double shot-gun, forms in my judgment a perfect battery for South Africa nowadays, for all game except elephant, rhinoceros, and buffalo, and perhaps hippopotami. If the first three of these animals are to be encountered (and it is a far cry to find them now anywhere south of the Zambesi), it would be advisable to take, in addition to or in place of one of the above, an eight or ten bore (rifled), single or double, according to the strength of the gunner. For the Express I would take solid but not hardened bullets, as well as hollow bullets. The sportsman can then judge for himself the merits and demerits of the two. Probably he will arrive at the conclusion that solid lead bullets are the superior.

There are various slings and buckets to be obtained for the purpose of carrying guns and rifles. As a matter of fact, we ourselves soon fell into the habit of always carrying our weapons in the right hand.

For the first few days even a shot-gun, when carried all day in the saddle, tires the arm not a little. This soon wears off; the muscles answer to their duty, and the weight ceases to fatigue. In the same way the rifle, especially a double one, tells for a day or two. Afterwards one carries the same weapon day after day without thinking of the matter at all. The forearm becomes strengthened very much as in the case of the blacksmith. In the hunting veldt the Bushman or Masarwa spoorer looks upon it as his right to carry the hunter's rifle, and hands it to him the instant the game is sighted.

A good pair of field-glasses—not too large—which can be carried slung over one's shoulder, are an absolute necessity for the open veldt. A good stalking-glass (Ross for choice), which can be kept ready slung in the waggon, is often of great assistance in scanning distant objects or sweeping the plains; but is not so invariably useful as the binoculars, for the reason that it cannot readily be carried about with one on horseback.

A pocket compass should always be carried in one's belt-pouch, and a box of matches; the latter have saved the lost wanderer many a night of misery. The habit of watching the sun soon grows upon one, and should be cultivated. The sun's position helps greatly to define one's course, and, as often becomes necessary when the watch is broken or disabled, the time of day can easily be guessed. An aneroid barometer for taking altitudes and a trochometer for recording distances are useful aids even to the unscientific traveller. A nautical almanac might also be packed.

A good leather belt with swivels attached, together with a leathern pouch and a sheath knife, is a necessary part of the outfit. A soft steel knife is by far the best for skinning purposes. The common American " Green River" knife, costing with sheath about 3s. 6d., I found as good as any.

Filters soon become fouled, and are of little use. If the water is very thick, a little alum (which is always useful) will precipitate much of the filth. Pour off the rest and then boil. Drink as little neat water as possible, unless palpably good. Again I repeat, tea and coffee are the safest drinks for the veldt.

Medicines.—If the traveller is bound for the river and lake systems of the interior, a few drugs should be taken in case of fever and dysentery. Chlorodyne is often useful. Quinine, calomel, and James's fever powders, for fevers ; ipecacuanha and Dover's powders for dysentery ; and strong ammonia or eau de luce for snake-bite, are drugs that may be useful in case of emergency. These should be obtained from a good chemist, with plain directions for doses. Savory and Moore, Corbyn and Co., and, I believe, other first-rate chemists now prepare these medicines in gelatine capsules, which occupy little space and are very handy. If hunting in the winter or dry season, however, it is improbable that any of these medicines will be needed. We never touched our drugs, except to take a pinch of quinine now and again. A bottle of loose quinine (Howard's) is always handy. Warburg's fever tincture is an excellent and well-tried remedy, and should be included. Antipyrine, which is largely used now for reducing temperature in African fevers, might also be taken. Eno's fruit salt, a box or two of ordinary pills, some oiled silk and bandages, complete the medicine-chest.

A mosquito net is useful near water. Dove extemporised one out of some muslin we had by us for butterfly nets. I myself am troubled little by these insects, and did without. Never sleep in old native huts if it can be avoided; the bite of the tampan, a tick-like insect haunting these dwellings, is most virulent, and troublesome sores often follow it. A folding indiarubber bath is an invaluable adjunct, and occupies little space.

A saw, axes, hammer, chisel, and a few other tools, and some nails, are of course always necessary about a waggon. An adze should never be left behind.

My camera was a half-plate one. On the whole this is, I think, the most useful size for a journey of this kind. My dry plates (Fry's) I kept in the waggon in the case in which they were packed. As I required them I got them out; and replaced them by the undeveloped negatives, which I had meanwhile been taking. I was of course extra careful about my packing and unpacking. I made a dark room of my waggon at night, carefully covering the tears and rents in the tilt with my blankets and kaross, and so excluding the fire and moon light. Moderate as are my sun pictures, they are to me well worth the trouble I took over them. At Palachwe, on my return, I carefully repacked my negatives in a tin-lined ammunition case, which I had soldered down. The plates were developed in Kimberley months afterwards, on getting down-country.

A small tin box (white-ant proof) containing plenty of sewing materials is indispensable. Besides one's own wants, the native servants, and even the native people through whose kraals one passes, are always begging for a needle and thread, which are to them luxuries indeed, and are greatly treasured.

In case the traveller should wish to amuse himself, if occasion should offer, for an hour on the bank of a river, a strong rod carrying running tackle, a good winch, and a line or two, and some strong hooks and floats suited to coarse-fish angling might be useful.

For bird-skinning a few simple knives and tools, which can be procured at Rowland Ward's, Silver's, or the Army and Navy Stores, are a great help. Of course, bird-skinning can be done with a simple penknife, and not very badly at that. But the neat implements now procurable are inexpensive and well repay the outlay. Preparations for dressing skins can be had at Gerrard's of 61 College Place, Camden Town, or Rowland Ward's of Piccadilly. We ourselves lost our only preparation—arsenical soap—and simply dressed our bird-skins with pepper and salt. We lost a good many skins from the ravages of that vile insect, *Dermestes Ladratus*, a kind of beetle; but a good many were got home in a fit condition for setting up.

It is a fact worth recording that, under the dry burning sun of South Africa, the skin of a bird dries up very rapidly, and in the case of some of the broad-headed hawks the beginner will find it a matter often of extreme difficulty (sometimes an impossibility) to get back the scalp over the skull after cleaning the brain-pan. For this and other difficulties, I cannot do better than refer the amateur bird-skinner to Rowland Ward's " Sportsman's Handbook to Practical Collecting and Preserving Trophies," which will teach many useful wrinkles to the ornithologist and naturalist.

All the heads of our large game we skinned ourselves—the average native will ruin a head by cutting the skin too close to the skull. In every case the skin was opened along the top of the neck and round the horns, so as to avoid the unsightly sewing beneath the neck usually to be found in old specimens in museums and elsewhere. The scalps were roughly prepared by being turned with the hair inside and then rubbed with salt and a little water, after which they were dried in the sun. At Palachwe they were put into cases with a quantity of camphor and a sprinkling of Keating's insect powder. Beyond an inspection at Kimberley on the way home, for the purpose of ridding the cases of parasites, nothing else was done for them. The heads, admirably set up by Mr. Gerrard many months after, turned out well, and now give every satisfaction to their owners. The skulls of all the animals except giraffe, which were too heavy, were of course saved, carefully cleaned of flesh, and brought home for the purpose of setting up with the scalps. The loss of our arsenical soap, therefore, was after all of small injury to us. It is to be borne in mind, however, that although our rough and ready treatment did well enough in the excessively dry atmosphere of South Africa, it might be disastrous in moister climates. Mr. Rowland Ward's instructions for the preservation of skins of heavy game are well worth taking note of.

These are some of the hints that have struck me as likely to be of service to the up-country traveller in South Africa. Many other camp notes might be included, until in fact the present chapter became swollen to the dimensions of a book.   One must stop somewhere, and I will end these notes by advising the sojourner, whoever he may be, who intends to exploit South Africa, to add two books to his modest waggon library—" Shifts and Expedients of Camp Life," by Baines and Lord, and "The Art of Travel," by Francis Galton ; both are invaluable.